THE GEOPOLITICS OF THE THIRD REICH

The spiritual roots of the conquest campaign to the east

Perry Pierik

THE GEOPOLITICS OF THE THIRD REICH

*The spiritual roots of the
conquest campaign to the east*

Aspekt Publishers

for my parents

THE GEOPOLITICS OF THE THIRD REICH
Original title: Hitler's Lebensraum. The spiritual roots of the conquest field trip to the east.
© 2023 Aspekt Publishers
Amersfoortsestraat 27
3769 AD Soesterberg, the Netherlands

Cover design: Anipa Baitakova
Layout: BeCo DTP-Productions, Epe
Tanslation: Isabel Oomen

ISBN: 9789463383172
NUR: 680

All rights reserved. No part of this publication may be reproduced, stored in a retrieval system or transmitted in any form or by any means, electronic, mechanical, photocopying, recording or otherwise, without the prior permission of the publisher.

Foreword to the second edition, autumn 2012

This book is a revised edition of the previously published book *Hitler's Lebensraum, the spiritual roots of the conquest of the East*, published in 1999. The new edition allows for some minor improvements. I would also like to point out some interesting studies that have appeared since its publication. On general geopolitics, the book by David Criekemans is not unimportant: *Geopolitiek, geografisch geweten van de buitenlandse politiek?* The book reflects on the influence of science on foreign policy. Uwe Mai, through publishing house Schöningh, brought the book *Rasse und Raum, Agrarpolitik, Sozial- und Raumplanung im NS-Staat onto the market*. In it, the author elaborates on the Third Reich's 'Siedlungspolitik' in eastern Europe. More biographical, but no less interesting is Hans-Ulrich Seidt's work, *Berlin, Kabul, Moskau. Oskar Ritter von Niedermayer und Deutschlands Geopolitik*. This book, published by Universitas publishers in 2002, traces German politics in central Europe through Ritter von Niedermayer's work. That traces of German geopolitics eastward can still be felt was demonstrated through a remark by President Hamid Karzai of Afghanistan, who commented that the German-Afghan friendship began with 'the arrival of Oskar Ritter von Niedermayer and his people'. Finally, I would like to point to the monumental work by Mechtild Rössler and Sabine Schleiermacher (hg.), *Der Generalplan Ost. Hauptlinien der nationalsozialistischen Planunungs und Vernichtungspolitik*, which was published by Akademie Verlag. It was published earlier, but complements this one.

Furthermore, the appearance of the first edition of *Hitler's Lebensraum* in 1999 had implications for the author's own pen. In fact, the present book was born from an earlier study (1995). Then *Hungary*

1904-1945, the forgotten tragedy, was published. This book dealt with the final struggle in Hungary; which in many ways was the final piece of Hitler's policy. As German historian Eberhard Jaeckel emphasised, Hitler's policy was determined by two facets: his racial doctrine, resulting in the persecution of Jews, among other things, and the pursuit of *Lebensraum*. Due to a lack of resources, the latter policy was mainly driven by geo-economic interests. In Hungary, in March 1945, the German army still launched a large-scale offensive (operation 'Frühlingserwachen') eastwards, with the aim of recapturing the Romanian oil fields near Ploesti, as well as securing the Hungarian oil fields south of Lake Balaton. This study was followed in 2006 by the dissertation *Karl Haushofer en het Nationaal-Socialisme. Tijd, werk en invloed*, under the supervision of supervisor Prof Dr H.J.G.Beunders. Haushofer was in many ways the figurehead of German geopolitics in this period. The introduction to this thesis dwells on the history of geopolitics in Germany and is therefore of interest here as well: Geopolitics, as geopoliticologists Richard Hennig and Leo Koerholz described, seeks to fathom the influence of geography on the population and governance of a country and examine it for laws.[i] In his *Dictionary of Geopolitics (1994)*, author John O'Loughlin concluded that *Geopolitik* was primarily a political weapon, spiritual ammunition, from which German expansionism and hegonomy ideas emerged.[ii]

In the German-speaking world, the doctrine was initiated by Friedrich Ratzel, theoretically expanded by the Swede Rudolf Kjellén and, after World War I, put forward by Karl Haushofer as one of the necessary engines of German foreign policy. O'Loughlin rightly argued that there were great dangers in this. Not only was the discipline under the shadow of the traumatic First World War but it also used almost indefinable and intangible concepts such as *Lebensraum* and *Heim ins Reich*, which the Nazis would elevate to pseudo-religious hobbyhorses, and which already had an important place in Hitler's earliest writings. *Geopolitics served as a pseudoscientific instrument for a war-promoting political propaganda*, O'Loughlin concluded.[iii]

The unfortunate Treaty of Versailles played an important role in the way geopolitical thinking developed in Germany. Haushofer believed he had to 'educate' the German people as a result of the tragedy of 1914-1918.[iv] David Thomas Murphy concluded in his 1977 book '*The Heroic Earth, Geopolitical Thought in Weimar Germany 1918-1933* that without the Treaty of Versailles, geopolitics would have remained a small obscure field.[v] The political will to obstruct and overhaul the challenged treaty gave German geopolitics the wind in its sails.

With the strong influence of the spirit of Versailles on the one hand, and scientific mores on the other, produced a major area of tension within German geopolitics from the 1920s onwards. The National Socialists were quick to recognise that geopolitics lend itself to legitimising and scientifically underpinning their expansionist plans. Murphy points out that geopolitics voiced its objections, in contrast to the mostly emotional reactions to Versailles.[vi]

For example, some geopoliticians argued that the Treaty of Versailles did not take into account natural borders, both of Germany and of (equally difficult to define) central Europe. Moreover, Versailles did not take geo-economic laws into account. Thus, the reparations that the Entente demanded from Germany would go against the economic cohesion of Europe.

Besides these rational objections, geopolitics in Germany was under the spell of the irrational zeitgeist that the Nazis were reaping rewards from. Thus, geopolitical ideas competed for precedence with the determinism that emanated from (physical) geography and the (racial) determinism of man (and his technology). Sometimes they went together, in a kind of romantic geodeterminism, for instance regarding the polar regions, which had to be explored and made usable for man. However, there was the aversion to certain technical advances, such as urbanisation, the big city, industrial development- which created a difficult split between science and technical *Vernunft* on the one hand and a romantic-defaitist vision of society on the other. In Spenglerian fashion, this saw state and society as an organism to be protected through geopolitical scenarios. In the words of Leni Riefenstahl, the 'triumph of the will'[vii], menkind, was sometimes at odds with the geodeterminism that emerged from natural science. This dilemma, which made O'Loughlin advocate scientific distance from German geopolitics, characterised the work and spirit of German politics of those days as well.

Murphy rightly pointed out that this difficult split was caused by the fact that the German cultural area was sandwiched between two clearly definable forces: Russian Byzantinism and the Western world. [viii] The Germans therefore believed that the German 'cultural soil' was under threat. In this area of tension, the German 'school' of geopolitics emerged. Within this school there were different emphases by scholars, but all variants were influenced by the zeitgeist outlined above and the associated dilemmas.

In *The Heroic Earth,* Murphy outlines the main exponents.[ix]

Albrecht Penck and Wilhelm Volz emphasised the importance of German language and territory becoming driving forces behind the *Deutscher Schutzbund,* which defended the interests of German speakers outside German territory after 1918. Wilhelminian geopoliticians Heinrich Schnee and Arthur Dix insisted on the importance of colonies for Germany in the traditional sense of overseas territories, pointing out the geopolitical consequences of their loss. Karl Wittfogel advocated the socialist variant of German geopolitics, legitimising his specific proletarian ideals with geopolitical arguments, just like Haushofer. Within the (organic) state, class factors also still played a role, according to Wittfogel, and he felt that the 'right-wing' geopoliticologists paid too little attention to this. He was supported by Joseph Bloch, who in his *Sozialistische Monatshefte* argued for a merger between the disciplines of anthropology and geography, topped with a socialist sauce.

Friedrich Burgdoerfer insisted above all on the importance of demographic factors, while Ewald Banse defied the scientific side of geopolitics with his views that the 'soul of the landscape' had to be taken into account. Accordingly, his theory was seen as 'aesthetic geography'.

Adolf Grabowsky was a defender of the establishment's geopolitical thinking during the Weimar Republic. His views went against the 'vulgar' geopolitics that Haushofer would advocate. Born in Berlin in 1880, Grabowsky worked under the motto 'stand right, think left' and concluded that the focus of the young German republic should lie with foreign policy, to which he subordinated geodeterminist considerations. As a result, Grabowksy made 'treaty boundaries' part of the discipline, while Haushofer recognised only 'natural boundaries', which had major political and military consequences. Within German geopolitics, Manfred Langhaus-Ratzeburg was mainly concerned with the legal consequences of the discipline, while Walther Vogel focused on the historicisation of geopolitics, where explanation and legitimisation went hand in hand and the undertone was the pursuit of ethnic homogeneity.

G.R. Sloan has classified these various sub-aspects of geopolitics, as discussed above, into the various sub-areas in the 1980s:

– topopolitics: the topography of the area
– morphopolitics: the way the area is shaped
– pshychopolitics: the 'psyche' of the area and its inhabitants
– ecopolitics: the economic situation in the area
– demopolitics: the deomographic situtation in the area
– sociopolitics: the social conditions in the area
– cratopolitics: the legal basis for the area.[x]

The development of the discipline of geopolitics in Germany was not isolated, although nowhere was it as topical as there, due to the specific German circumstances. Internationally, everyone was actually indebted to the same thinkers: Friedrich Ratzel, Rudolf Kjellén and Sir Halford Mackinder. From the point of view of the Anglo-Saxon world, it is worth dwelling on the latter. The Oxford-based Mackinder, in his *heartland theory*, believed that a power-political confrontation over Europe could not be avoided in the future. In this sense, Mackinder had the same deterministic vision as Hitler's geopolitics. Unlike the Nazis, he put his cards on Russia, rather than Germany, as the power that would come to dominate Western Europe and Eurasia. Mackinder's vision was partly underlined by other geopolitical thinkers of the Western world, such as N.J. Spykman, who expressed fears that modern large nation-states could pursue world domination as well. As a geopoliticologist, the latter did emphasise that even for the most powerful nation-states, geographical factors were always present; passive and unchanging. According to Spykman, it was precisely this manifest presence that made the pursuit of great nations predictable and calculable. Indeed, over the centuries, geographical conditions had to be taken into account, creating a pattern in the actions of states. The Russian pursuit of warm seaports could serve as an example. This had been an immutable course of Russian foreign policy since Peter the Great, no matter who was on the Russian throne. Mackinder's influence on his generation was also evident in the block division of the world that Spykman thought he had identified: North and South America on the one hand, Western Europe and Eurasia on the other.[xi]

Within the Western world, the thinkers Admiral Alfred Thayer Mahan and General Homer Lea were important too. Mahan emphasised the geographical pattern in the political history of the world, assigning a particularly important role to the sea. Mahan saw the US above all as a maritime nation and, influenced by the Swiss strategist Baron Antoine-Henri Jomini (who had made a study of land warfare and geography), he emphasised that things were no different at sea. Possession of, say, a Panama Canal was of inestimable strategic and geopolitical value. Lea, like a number of German geopoliticologists, saw the state as a living organism. In addition, the general incorporated the two conflicting elements that flogged geopolitics, ethnic racial ideas, versus geographical determinisms. For Japan, Lea concluded that its expansion was a logical consequence of technology and the nature and character of population and regime, but that Pacific expansion was an entirely logical 'law of nature' as well.[xii]

The influence of Western geopoliticians on different governments was smaller than that of their professional counterparts in Germany. US strategy concentrated on the Western Hemisphere for a long time and was thus removed from the main flashpoints. The US becoming a superpower has sometimes been characterised as an 'accidental empire'[xiii], typifying that its becoming a superpower was not the result of an ironclad playbook but of circumstances. How different it was in Germany, which in 1914 had a roadmap for its preservation in which political and military measures were calculated down to the hour.

The actions of the main Western power in the making, the United States, were rather tentative and initially characterised by now almost forgotten conflicts, such as the war against Spain. In the Pacific, there were feelers towards China ('open door' policy). The passive US role was caused by a geographical determinism, Sloan believes.[xiv] There was simply too great a geographical distance between Europe and the US. As a result, the US was primarily focused on the Western Hemisphere as a matter of course. The rise of technology and international economic interests increasingly involved the US in areas beyond. With the growing strength of the US and the British weakening that had already set in before World War II, the US often took the lead in areas where the British had previously been influential.[xv]

With the arrival of President Wilson in 1913, the US added a strong metaphysical-romantic optic to its 'grand policy'. Wilson, of Irish-Scottish descent, was more involved in Europe and he believed that there was an 'American mission' in the world, involving religious elements. The victory of the Republicans in elections in November 1918 reduced the possibilities for Wilson to implement his ideas; ideas that would greatly increase American influence outside the Western Hemisphere. Now the US was once again retreating to its own continent. However, Franklin Roosevelt, who took the helm in 1932, had understood Mahan's lesson. US strategic borders were not only in the Pacific but also in the Atlantic,[xvi] and these borders would soon be violated by the violence of the Axis powers. The days of vacillating between isiolationism and internationalism were gone forever, in his view.

At the same time, a Marxist version of geopolitics emerged. This took a strongly polemical stance against non-Marxist theses. German geopolitics was the product of 'imperialism, militarism, fascism' and through 'revanche' politics (at Versailles) set on a war course to serve the interests 'of the monopoly capital'. The Anglo-Saxon powers were also exposed to great criticism. They did all they could to push Nazi Germany as a bulwark against Bolshevism. The Marxists naturally believed the Soviet Union's intentions to be much friendlier. The Soviet Union had managed to place 'man's free will' between the two frictions of 'subjective idealism' and geographical determinism. This free will consisted of the views of Marx and Engels, who believed that the influence of geographical determinism was above all of a social and economic nature. Since the discovery of America (1492), the discovery of the sea route to the Indies (1498), and the circumnavigation of the globe (1519-1522), the earth had suddenly increased tenfold in size. This had enormous consequences for the productive development of the economy and almost automatically propelled history towards the tenets of Marxism. In this, nature had mainly been reduced to a supplier of raw materials.[xvii]

That this was not entirely at odds with Hitler's geopolitics will be shown in this study. Central to this book is the question of what ideas formed the spiritual fuel behind operation 'Barbarossa', the German campaign against Russia. The answer reveals a wide range of people and arguments. Some of heartless rationality, others of racial and völkisch origin from the Orpheus underworld of National Socialism. Together they formed the geopolitics of the Third Reich.

Dr Perry Pierik
Soesterberg 2012

[i] Richard Hennig/Leo Koerholz, *Einführung in die Geopolitik*. Leipzig/Berlin 1935 p. 6. As we shall see later, different definitions were possible. Karl and Albrecht Haushofer stayed closest to Rudolf Kjellén's formulation, which we will discuss later in the book.

[ii] John O'Loughlin (ed.), *Dictionary of Geopolitics*. 1994, pp.92-94. Walter Theimer, in *The Penguin Political Dictionary, an ABC of International Affairs* (London 1939).

[iii] *Dictionary of Geopolitics* p 93.

[iv] See Haushofer's *Einführung in den Plan der deutschen Akademie* as an appendix in the *Gründungsaufruf des Akademie zur wissenschaftlichen Erforschung und zur Pflege des Deutschtums. Deutsche Akademie*, of 4 April 1925. In: Hans-Adolf Jacobsen, *Schriften des Bundesarchivs 24/II, Karl Haushofer -Leben und Werk- Band II Ausgewählter Schriftwechsel 1917-1946* Boppard am Rhein 1979 pp. 46-52.

[v] David Thomas Murphy, *The Heroic Earth. Geopolitical Thought in Weimar Germany 1918-1933* Kent 1977 p 46.

[vi] *The Heroic Earth* p 46.

[vii] *Triumpf des Willens*, film by cinematographer Leni Riefenstahl about the NSDAP-day in Nuremberg in the 1930s. On Leni Riefenstahl see, among others, Thomas Leeflang, *Gevallen voor de Führer. Leven en werk van Leni Riefenstahl* Soesterberg 2003 and Jean-Paul E. Ipema, *De film als propagandamiddel in het Derde Rijk in Perry Pierik/Martin Ros (red.)., Tweede Bulletin Tweede Wereldoorlog* Soesterberg 2001.

[viii] *The Heroic Earth* p 55

[ix] The examples are from *The Heroic Earth* pp. 64-120. For additions see also G.R. Sloan, the chapter *The Origions and Aims of German Geoplitics* in: Spykman (ed.), *Geopolitics in United States Strategic Policy 1890-1987* Brighton 1988 pp. 23-56/ Adolf Grabowsky, *Raum, Staat und Geschichte. Grundlegung der Geopolitik* Köln/Berlin 1960/Jan Wiktor Tkaczynski, *Die Geopolitik. Eine Studie über geographische Determinanten und politisches Wunschdenken am Beispiel Deutschlands und Polens* München 1993/Pierre Behar, *Zentral Europa im Brennpunkt*,

Analysen und Perspektiven einer kontinentalen Geopolitik [1991] Wien 1994.

[x] *Geopolitics in the United States. Strategic Policy 1890-1987* pp. 4,5.

[xi] For Spykman's theory see: *Geopolitics in the United States. Strategic Policy 1890-1987* pp.16-20.

[xii] *Geopolitics in the United States. Strategic Policy 1890-1987* pp. 80-126.

[xiii] On the origins of the accidental global empire, see, among others, Stephen E.Ambrose, *Rise to Globalism. American Foreign Policy since 1938 (*4th edition) 1985/ Erich Angermann, *Die Vereinigten Staaten von Amerika seit 1917* [1966] Munich 1995/ Maarten van Rossem, *De Verenigde Staten in de twintigste eeuw (derde druk) The Hague 2001.*

[xiv] *Geopolitics in United States. Strategic Policy 1890-1987* p 110.

[xv] *Rise to Globalism* pp. 6, 7.

[xvi] *Geopolitics in United States. Strategic Policy 1890-1987* p 110.

[xvii] Gunter Heyden, *Kritik der deutschen Geopolitik. Wesen und soziale Funktion einer reaktionaren soziologischen Schule* Berlin 1958/Massimo Quaini, *Marxism and Geography* [1974] 1977.

Content

Chapter 1 27

LEBENSRAUM: THE CONTINENTAL EMPIRE OF ADOLF HITLER

Bismarck and the young generation - Wilhelm II, Von Bülow and Tirpitz, the troubled superpower - Lebensraum, a black hole in historiography - The OSS's secret study of Hitler's brain - Communists see through National Socialism - Analyses of predictors: how long can Hitler wage war? - Postwar historiography discovers Hitler's Weltanschauung - *Mein Kampf* and Hitlerism - Lebensraum or Innere Kolonisation - Russia as an example of a continental empire - Das Dritte Reich - Russia and Hitler's anti-Semitism: was the Bolshevik revolution a Jewish plot? - Judophobia - Controversy Pipes-Haffner: communism and the holocaust, a debate on cause and effect - The German 'revolutionisation' of Russia - Eternal Jew, eternal scapegoat: Babi Jar - Nolte versus Goldhagen, the delusion of the day and the spiritual Umfeld of the Lebensraum field trip

Chapter 2 75

THE SCHREIBTISCH CONQUERORS.

Karl Haushofer, geopoliticologist, frequent writer and inspirer of the Lebensraum idea - Evil magician? - Thule - *Erfüllungspolitik* - *Meereskunde* and the eternal struggle against water - Britain, Venice and Japan - Plan Goergel, the draining of the Mediterranean - *Mitteleuropa*, Kjellén and the Berlin-Baghdad-Bombay land bridge - Where is

Central Europe? What is Europe? - *Verstümmelung, Versklavung, Einkreisung* - The natural unity of Russia - Devil's belt and natural rights - Hess, Landsberg am Lech and *Mein Kampf* - Hitler a Clausewitz connoisseur? - Haushofer's mental ammunition - The conquerors from the plains - Hess flies to Britain - Dachau - Haushofer and Brzezinski - Mediocre minds - Suicide - Mackinder's empire blocks - Lebensraum, *Kernraum* - Descent theories and myths for legitimisation and supremacy - Pax Romana versus Germania - *Grosswirtschaftsraum* - Apocalyptic coercive theory: Lebensraum or *Weltuntergang*

Chapter 3   101

REICH AND ROMANCE

Paul de Lagarde, Julius Langbehn and *völkische* thinking - A harmonic romantic myth disturbed - Rembrandt's organic masterpiece - Wagner and aesthetic man - Modernism as Fall - Lebensraum, a völkische catch-up manoeuvre? - Rosenberg's *Mythus and Kulturkampf* - 'The new age' - Christianity versus Rosenberg - Atlantis and the creative Atlantic man - Swan neck boats and the tombs of Thebes - Poliakov and Aryan descent - *Untermenschen*, race war - Houston Stewart Chamberlain - Nomocracy, the Jewish era - Wagner, Bayreuth and the Festival - National salvation plan - The Soviet Union and the *Protocols of Zion* - Rosenberg's anti-communist diplomacy - Bestseller - The 87 nationalities of Russia - Rosenberg's influence on Hitler - Origin of ideas - Russian migrants - *Mission civilisatrice* - Apprentice, teacher, follower - The Jewish intellectuals of the Russian revolution - Brandoffer - Dietrich Eckart - The sound of machine guns - Thule Society - Von Sebottendorff - Blavatsky and theosophy - Vienna and ariosophy - List and Lanz von Liebenfels - Germanic order - NSDAP - The wet poodle, Hitler discovered as an orator - *Ostara* - Madagascar - Wewelsburg as centre of the world and fortress against the new Huns - The cursed family of Wiligut - Carnuntum

Chapter 4   159

THE ESTABLISHED ORDER AND THE NEW ORDER

Central Europe's geopolitical dilemma - The eternal loyalty of the *Reichswehr* - *Blumenkrieg* and *Blitzkrieg* - *Draufgänger* officers - The apolitical soldiers and von Rundstedt philosophy - The trauma of World War I - *Überstaatliche* powers and the stab-in-the-back myth - Ludendorff and Mathilde von Kemnitz, the 'German Blavatsky' - Völkische Prussia and the generals - German-Polish relations - The ethnic cleansing of Bromberg - The German wizards and the *Kulturträgertum* - Nobility and soldiers' peasants - Horthy's heroic union and Darré's new nobility - *'Das sind wir!'* - Prussian generals and the 20th of July - Traditions, obedience, bravery - *Weltanschauungskrieg* - Imposed discipline - Obedience a racial issue, the new stab-in-the-back myth - *Bewährungstruppe* - 50.000 death sentences - Hitler sacrifices the SA - 'Bourgeoisie' field lord - Gallo, Göring and the Solstice at Karinhall - Siedlungen - Heinz Guderian's knightly estate - Land for a Ritterkreuz

Chapter 5   215

SWASTIKA REPLACES CROSS

Battle of the dogmas - Ernst Niekisch and the demons of the Third Reich - Bachelor Hitler - Rosenberg and the index of banned books - The authencity of primordial Christianity - *Artgeist* and *Artseele* - The nation between myth and utopia - The Conservative Revolution and nationalism as *Ersatzreligie* - *Die Geächteten* - *Deutscher Gottglauben* - Religious experience of the SS - Being versus thinking - Paul Hausser, Felix Steiner and the new crusaders - Der neue Gott - Otto Rahn and the quest for the grail - Cathars - Wolfhounds - Von Stuck - Gaius Cassius - Barbarossa and the eagle's nest - Goldhagen, Luther and the continuity thesis - Church fear of communism - Hochhuth and postwar criticism - Hudal, cic, Barbie and Draganovic - Murder of Polish priests

Chapter 6   241

GROSSWIRTSCHAFTSRAUM EUROPA: THE REALM OF THE UNLIMITED POSSIBILITIES

The meaning of the Hitler salute - The US war potential - Baku oil - Soviet production figures - *Lehrtruppen* in Romania - Ploesti fields - Danube, the river of the future - Soviet armament - Resource ratio 1:100 - Economic goals and *Führerweisungen* - Berlin-Baghdad - Finland, Romania, Hungary and Operation Barbarossa - The patchwork of the Caucasus - Von Pannwitz and Vlassov - Ploesti and *Frühlingserwachen* - Ribbentrop and *Lebensräume* - Görings four-year plans - The autarky idea - Herr Reaktion - Hitler and the big industrialists - *Unterschiedliche Intentionen* - Crisis - Practice of a *Grosswirtschaftsraum* - Divide and rule - Bureaucrats vs, Speer, Funk and Ley - *Arbeitsstab Russland* - Kriwoj Rog and Nikopol - Blast furnaces and coal mines - The soot-blackened miners of the Donets coal basin - Involvement of German heavy industry - Red Army's 1943 summer offensive - Scorched earth again - The boned-out East, slavery, famine, holocaust

Chapter 7   279

JOURNEY TO THE UNDERWORLD

Word of thanks   290

Notes   292

Literature   328

INTRODUCTION

There is a certain fear of actually studying the major, destructive ideologies of this century to their essence. This is above all due to the bloody and repressive nature of National Socialism (as well as Communism) that runs like a fault line through the 20th century. Inability and aversion to understand evil has taken refuge in tabooing it. After all, wanting to examine the motives of Hitler and the Nazis, to truly understand evil, makes the historian vulnerable. In his analyses, he should take the Nazis' *Weltanschauung* seriously, read and reread, analyse and explain their writings, risking being identified by the outside world with that which he wants to uncover. But he has no choice. History can only be exposed through the arduous and cumbersome route of knowing, understanding and unmasking. On this path, the historian must possess quality that a normal human being attributes only to God: namely, knowing the truth. The first casualty of any war is always truth. Analogous to the ancient legendary ancient poet Orpheus of Thrace, the historian will have to descend to the underworld to reclaim it, so that after analysis, the *Geschichtsbewältigung* can actually begin.

The historiography of the Third Reich is unbalanced. This may surprise readers, who understandably struggle to cope with the sheer volume of publications. Yet, anyone who frequently consults bookshops on the historical terrain of the interwar period and World War II knows that there is much of the same, and that the proclaimed end of the book flow - Book Week March 1995 - made for a nice *one-liner* in the newspaper but is far from reality. As a result of the miracle year of 1989, archives in central and eastern Europe have opened up and valuable additions to western historiography can be obtained.

Still, we don't even have to look that far to stumble upon the imbalance. In fact, the imbalance has existed since the late 1960s. Zealous study of Hitler's goals, his *grand strategy*, at that time first exposed what was now the core of Hitler's politics. Influenced by historians Walther Hofer and Eberhard Jäckel, the image of Hermann Rauschning depicting Hitler's rise to power as a 'nihilistic revolution' was finally done away with. Historians discovered *Mein Kampf* 45 years after the book was written, and with it the spiritual roots of Hitler's *Weltanschauung*. Crystallised, this provided a very enlightening picture of Hitler's main endeavour: his racial theories, subsequent racial politics and holocaust, and the plan to conquer Lebensraum. Through *Mein Kampf*, but also from other writings by Hitler, who recorded his thoughts on several occasions over the years, as well as from the practical political course of events, we know that since his first fledgling political steps, Hitler set out on the winding path that led to the implementation of these drastic plans: the destruction of the Jewish community, the conquest of Lebensraum in the East and the subjugation and exploitation of the Slavic population.

The strange thing is that since this discovery in the 1960s - which incidentally paralleled the first three major holocaust studies by Hilberg, Poliakov and Reitlinger - the study of the facet of Lebensraum has been completely subsumed by the study of the holocaust. Literally thousands of titles appeared after the pioneering work of Hilberg and his colleagues. The works varied widely, from standard works and attempts at them, to *oral histories* and small tragedies that brought the enormous tragedy of Hitler's racial concept back to life. As abundant as interest in the Holocaust and Nazi racial politics was, the field of Lebensraum, that other pillar of Hitler's Weltanschauung, remained empty and unexplored. Anyone who would take the trouble to walk into the Library of Literature in Utrecht, one of the largest in Europe, and type the term Lebensraum into the computer system there, will have to conclude, to their astonishment, that it does not yield a single title that actually deals with this topic. There is a gap in historiography.

The omission is astonishing for more than one reason. First and foremost, because Hitler's pursuit of Lebensraum, more than any other goal of his, was most intertwined with his racial theories. Indeed, Hitler's pursuit of Lebensraum, its politics and the campaigns that stemmed from it, were fuelled by and founded on the racial supremacy feeling that Germany had to rule over the peoples of the East. Besides the practical implementation of the holocaust, the campaign for Lebensraum, especially the attack on the Soviet Union (operation 'Barbarossa'), was the ultimate result of Hitler's racial theory with consequences, when looking at the number of victims, of an even greater dimension than the holocaust. The omission can most likely be explained by the fact that evidently the suffering that resulted from the Lebensraum field trip is largely still unconsciously seen as the general suffering of war, as any conflict has. The holocaust, on the other hand, represented the 'real face' of Nazi Germany. The war in Eastern Europe, where Hitler sought his Lebensraum, was thus relegated to an area above all of interest to military historians. Consequently, much and pioneering research has been carried out in the latter field. A case in point is Dr F.P. ten Kate's two-volume Dutch study, *De Duitse aanval op de Sovjet-Unie in 1941 (The German Attack on the Soviet Union in 1941)*. This book deals extensively with the armed forces and military plans on both sides. Only very briefly is the purpose of Operation Barbarossa discussed, and where it is, ten Kate does so on the basis of rational, power-political considerations. The imbalance in the historiography consists of the fact that this is only a martial study, as almost all books on the subject are, while the political, ideological and historical roots, often irrational in nature, are left out. Typical of this imbalance, for instance, is that the originator of the term Lebensraum, Professor Karl Haushofer, is mentioned only once and in passing. Haushofer's books are therefore missing from the bibliography. That Hilberg and Reitlinger are not missing is unsurprising given the gap outlined above.

Ignoring the political and historical context in which the idea for conquest of Lebensraum could arise may have had the same cause as the late discovery of the Holocaust. Although there is now a flood of books on the persecution of the Jews, this was not always the case either. We have just seen that the first serious studies appeared only in the late 1960s. Until then, no major research had been done, which may still be called remarkable. Indeed, Raul Hilberg had the greatest difficulty in getting his now standard work published. In part, he ruined his university career with it.

It seems that modern historians, living in a rational, transparent Western society, have difficulty 'empathising' with the roots of something as vast, destructive and irrational as National Socialism. The late discovery of Hitler's real aims and the slow research into the Holocaust and its lack of research into his Lebensraum theories show that Hitler was underestimated as a political thinker and ignored for a long time, that *Mein Kampf* remained unread even after the war, and that National Socialism remained misunderstood for a long time as a result. The German historian Bracher once formulated it in the words: 'The history of Hitler and National Socialism is the history of his underestimation.' It has become a guiding principle in my book.

Historically, hardly any books have been written that fill a historiographical gap with a single work. I have no such pretensions with this book. I have, however, tried to make a start for the Dutch-speaking region to expose the second pillar of the Third Reich: that of the conquest of Lebensraum, through which Hitler wanted to turn Germany into a *Kontinentalimperium*, which could survive as an economic autarchy and claim its position as a world power.

In studying this subject, I have chosen not to emphasise the practical implementation of this political and military endeavour or the description of the day-to-day official, economic, military and moral problems posed by the exploitative policy of Lebensraum in the East. The focus of the study is on the spiritual and historical roots of the Lebensraum idea, how it was able to emerge, where this German feeling of supremacy came from, which myths and thoughts played a role in it, and who helped develop and legitimise this 'legacy' into practical politics with which Hitler was able to embark on the greatest conquest field trip of all time: operation 'Barbarossa'.

This way of working entails that the reader will be drawn into the cool, power-political and rational planning that led to the Lebensraum field trip, but will also descend into the irrational undercurrent, the bubbling *völkische* underbelly of National Socialism, in an attempt to get a *feel*, from our Western perspective, for that which we have always left aside: Orpheus' underworld.

The historical roots will take us to Bismarck, Bülow, Tirpitz and Wilhelm II's *Realpolitik* of blood and iron. We will reflect on the roles thart the young science of geopolitics and Haushofer, Mackinder and Kjellén played in this. Just as the Holocaust had its *Schreibtisch* murderers like Adolf Eichmann - who himself never killed a human being - Nazi Germany also had its Schreibtisch conquerors, who drew the lines on the map and determined the directions of thrust, sometimes with uncanny foresight. We will dwell on the (Prussian) generals, the 'von Rundstedt philosophy', the feelings in the primal Prussian, Polish-German borderland. The Vatican's state raison d'etre. The *Rerum Novarum* will demand our attention as well as the economists' statistics, the mercantilist autarky idea, and the *Grosswirtschaftsraum* to be created.

Furthermore, we will try to shine light into the caverns of the German soul, the irrational undercurrent that had pseudo-religious and even occult traits. We will dwell on the earliest investigations into Hitler's thinking and actions; and immediately stumble upon the connection between Hitler's two fundamental ideas: holocaust and Lebensraum. For Hitler, Judaism and Bolshevism - which played an important role in his orientation towards the East - were closely intertwined. In addressing this theme, I will elaborate on the main controversies and theories in that area, from Margolina, Nolte and Pipes to Goldhagen. Germanic *Urgeschichte* will be discussed, or should I say Germanic descent myths? The völkisch thinkers will receive ample attention as a strong legitimising factor in the whole. The three völkisch centres, Vienna, Bayreuth and Munich will take us along the whimsical and absurdist path of 'ariosophy', the mythical-völkisch belief in German-Germanic-Aryan supremacy, the fairytale image of German unification, the failed scenic idyll, a tour past the tombs of Thebes, the ruins of Carnuntum to the Wewelsburg of the Reichsführer-ss Heinrich Himmler. Men of all walks of life, from *Schreibtisch* conquerors, to *Stammtisch* philosophers and downright idiots paved the winding path to 'Barbarossa' via Russian migrants, protocols, *Ostara*, Thule and Blavatsky, the mother of the New Age movement.

This book is a first attempt to create a foundation on which the second pillar - or should we maybe even say the first pillar, given the enormous dimension of the Lebensraum philosophy - of Hitler's Weltanschauung could take shape. It is the exploration of a thought, an idea, a feeling that 'hung in the air' and could take shape in Nazi Germany. This feeling was no accident; it was the product of the sum of many working lives in which wandering souls gave their energies to this destructive ideal, this evil myth that could become reality under Hitler.

That the rationale behind this is worth exploring is beyond dispute. No leader can operate entirely outside the framework of norms and values of his time. Hitler too was the product of his times, of thoughts that lived during his poor years in Vienna, his political rise in Munich and his annual pilgrimage to Bayreuth. Hitler's ideas were not even original; there was an *Umfeld* of thoughts and persons within which Hitler could flourish. Remarkably, the various interacting forces often had no more than partial interests in common. Each time, however, they were just big enough to take the next step towards the disastrous reality of 'Barbarossa'. I have tried to paint the underlying forces, rational and irrational, in this book. In doing so, to save space, I have assumed many historical facts to be known. May this book shed light on this forgotten pillar of National Socialism.

Perry Pierik
Soesterberg, spring 1999

'I think, the whole Nazi regime and everything Hitler decided was an attempt to achieve the ultimate. This is what an artist strives for. 'Etwas unmittelbar zum Gottes', to quote Rancke, That is exactly what the Nazis were trying to do.

Raul Hilberg (interview 1991)

'Is this man sincere in his undertakings or is he a fraud?'

(Secret War Time Report Oss 1943)

*'Son of the magnanimous Tydeus,
why are you asking about my origins?
'It goes with the race of men as with that of leaves.'*

Iliad, vi, 145-146 quoted from Marguerite Yourcenar, 'Archives from the North' (1977)

'Das Germanische Reich Deutscher Nation ist greifbar geworden ... Uns hat die Vorsehung die letzte Möglichkeit gegeben, das Reich zu vollenden. Die Würfel fallen jetzt, und die Würfel fallen auf ein Jahrtausend.'

Friedrich Schmidt in 'Das Reich als Aufgabe' (1940)

*'Im ewigen Kampf ist die Menschheit gross geworden
im ewigen Frieden geht sie zugrunde.'*

Adolf Hitler, 'Mein Kampf' (1924)

'So sah ich... im Marxismus die endgültige Lösung der Judenfrage, die mich von Kindheit an verfolgte.'

Leopold Trepper, Chef Roten Kapelle in his autobiography (1975)

Chapter 1

Lebensraum: the continental empire of Adolf Hitler

Bismarck and the young nation - Wilhelm II, von Bülow and Tirpitz, the troubled superpower - Lebensraum, a black hole in historiography - The oss's secret study of Hitler's brain - Communists see through National Socialism - Analysis of predictors: how long can Hitler wage war? - Postwar historiography discovers Hitler's *Weltanschauung* - *Mein Kampf* and Hitlerism - Lebensraum or *Innere Kolonisation* - Russia as an example of continental empire - *Das Dritte Reich* - Russia and Hitler's anti-Semitism: was the Bolshevik revolution a Jewish plot? - Judophobia - Controversy Pipes-Haffner: communism and holocaust, a debate on cause and effect - The German 'revolutionisation' of Russia - Eternal Jew, eternal scapegoat: Babi Jar - Nolte versus Goldhagen, the delusion of the day and the spiritual *Umfeld* of the Lebensraum field trip

The foreign policy of Germany is young, the emergence of a German world politics younger. Bismarck, under whose leadership the German Empire was born in 1871, concentrated above all on the political chess field of central Europe in the narrowest sense. Bismarck was a strategist. He made his political moves with great caution, prepared his moves carefully, and when he played he usually won. Such a politician did not get involved in adventures far overseas, or military missions to the east. Nevertheless, the foundation of German world politics was laid in the last phase of the Bismarck period.

In 1879, Friedrich Fabri wrote his book *Bedarf Deutschland der Kolonien?* The question was posed only to be answered in the affirmative. Germany needed *Brot und Ehre*! At the end of the 19th century, an era full of hubris, the urge to own overseas territories grew in Germany, as a form of recognition of Germany's place under the sun. French historian Raymond Poidevin therefore characterises this drive not only as an economic interest, but also as an opportunity to export social problems, as it were.[1] Nevertheless, expectations were high. Eberhard Jäckel wrote retrospectively that 'the German century' had arrived.[2]

Who supported thoughts of German colonies and a German world politics? First of all, business played a role. At the invitation of major trading firms in Hamburg and Bremen, Bismarck was confronted with the concerns of Germany's rapidly growing industry. The big trading firms wanted the German government to support them more, especially since British and French competitors, actively supported by their governments, were making German trade difficult.

Besides the trading firms, there was growing pressure on Bismarck domestically politically to go 'overseas'. A large number of associations had been formed with the aim of bringing 'German culture' overseas. The main exponent of this movement was the *Kolonialverein* founded in 1882, named *Deutsche Kolonialgesellschaft* in 1887. Its members consisted of prominent Germans, including professors, geographers, industrialists and officers. Owning colonies would enhance the prestige of the young German state. Another driving force for these thoughts was the *Alldeutsche Verband*, formed around Dr Alfred Leher, Dr Alfred Hugenberg and Prof Ernst Hase, and

General Ritter von Epp's *Reichskolonialbund*. Following the example of German historian Heinrich von Treitschke (1834-1896), who warned of 300 million English speakers in the future, these organisations advocated global support for the German *Volkstum*. Germans abroad were not allowed to forget their 'Germanness'; newspapers and schools promoting it were supported. *'Deutschland wach auf!*' was a cry from these folks, which would be used by the Nazis in their Jew policy. Under the presidency of Ernst Hase (1893-1908) and Heinrich Class (1908-1939), the *Alldeutsche Verband* grew from 20.000 members (one year after its founding) to 40.000 members.

A key idea of the *Deutsche Kolonialgesellschaft* and the Alldeutsche association was that, sandwiched between France and Russia, Germany had little room for manoeuvre and that overseas territories offered a solution. For trade, a world policy was attractive to Germany as well. All sorts of import and export restricting custums stood in the way of Germany's economic growth. Thereby, the German economy was plagued by a lack of raw materials and this was where world trade could provide. In 1888, raw material imports accounted for no less than 45 per cent of total imports. Another essential argument was that German agriculture was unable to feed the German population. Demographic expectations strengthened calls for new land and a world policy. Between 1871 and 1895, the German population had grown from 41 million to 52.3 million. In the process, Germans themselves had also become 'international', given that there had been a large emigration from Germany. Between 1881 and 1890, no fewer than 1 272 423 Germans had emigrated.

The counterarguments against world power politics, that it was a political diversion from social ills at home from the left, that the costs of a world empire would be counterproductive from the right, were dwarfed by the pathetic overidentification with the young nation. Hesitantly, then, under Bismarck, the first steps were taken to better represent German interests, especially in southwest Africa and Asia. In Bismarck's time, the total area of German colonies eventually reached 2.641.000 km^2 with a total population of 7.5 million.[3]

Bismarck's fledgling steps were reinforced by his key political successors. The three men who determined the face of German foreign policy in the following years were: German Kaiser Wilhelm II, Admiral von Tirpitz and Reichskanzler von Bülow.

The German Kaiser never doubted the historical mission Germany would have in the world. Germany had a 'cultural mission' and it went without saying that at the head of this mission would be the Kaiser in highest person. *'Volldampf-*Wilhelm II was very keen to put his own stamp on German ambitions and emerge from the shadow of Bismarck. Von Tirpitz was the man to deal with the practical consequences of building a German world politics. World politics without a fleet was not possible. In 1897, Germany had six battleships, the British on the other hand had 33, the French and Russians had 17 each, the Italians 13. To pursue a world policy, the German fleet had to meet two requirements: it had to have a fleet for overseas territory, and it had to have a fleet to tie the hands of the British if desired. Crucially, the consequences of this fleet policy in itself necessitated a change in the status quo. A fleet could only operate globally if there were sufficient support bases and coal stations along the world sea routes. Building up the German fleet was in line with the world view and self-image of the German Kaiser, who liked to present himself as the man of progress and modernism. Building up the fleet made him the *Bürger-Kaiser*, the man who would lead Germany into the great outside world with *felsenfester Überzeugung*. Just as the cavalry of feudal times had been superseded by the age of the machine gun, the mighty warships of the Reichsflotte provided a splendid substitute for it. *'Technik statt der Lyrik, Marine statt der Malerei.'* There was admiration for the own strength that had sprung up so suddenly. A people full of bubbling potentiality presented itself, an emperor who wanted to be the personification, the representative of this feeling.

'Nun mag Europa drohn!
Dich rief zum Kaiserthron
Germanias Thanks
Er, dem dein Herz geglaubt,
setze dir siegumlaubt
die Kaiserkron' aufs Haupt.
Heil, Kaiser, dir!'[24]

Finally, there was the support of von Bülow, secretary of state for foreign affairs in the Wilhelmstrassse, later Reichskanzler (1900-1909). His policy was characterised by three centres of gravity: industry, trade and shipping. 'We do not want to put anyone in the shade,' he mused, 'but we do want our own place under the sun.'

In the following years, economic developments reinforced the German drive for expansion. The German trade deficit was maintained between 1900 and 1913. The results of German world politics were also quite different. Some results were achieved in Asia, especially in China. Relations with the Ottoman Empire strengthened too. There were setbacks in Central and South Africa. However, much more serious was the fact that after Bismarck's departure, the German political leadership had become overconfident and neglected Germany's local-continental interests. From German *Vorherrschaft*, the German position shifted to that of *Einkreisung*. The outbreak of World War I was therefore above all a diplomatic fiasco by the Germans. Initially, this fiasco was brushed away by the military results of the German army, which was immediately followed by an ambitious, German political programme. Foreign policy gave way to a policy of conquest. The goals formulated by Chancellor Bethmann-Hollweg were annexation of important coal fields in Alsace-Lorraine and the creation of a series of buffer states in the east to keep Russia off Germany's border.[5]

The war ended disastrously for Germany. The goals in the west were by no means achieved. The goals in the east seemed reasonably realised with the peace of Brest-Litowsk after the outbreak of the Russian revolution in 1917. However, with the peace of Versailles, the gains were largely lost again. In the period from 1919 to 1932, Germany therefore worked mainly to re-establish its superpower status.

The peace of Versailles, although most Germans spoke of dictate, cut deep into the flesh in this regard. Germany had lost more than 10 per cent of its population (over six million inhabitants), 75 per cent of its iron ore mines and 25 per cent of its coal mines. As much as 10 to 15 per cent of Germany's agricultural production was lost and its army was reduced to a paltry 100.000 men. The once mighty *Hoch-*

seeflotte of von Tirpitz was reduced to a coast guard. In addition, Germany had to make reparations. The Weimar Republic, which had to take this war legacy on the shoulders of its young democracy, moved between the frustrations of 'diktat' and the political desirability of *Erfüllungspolitik*. And all this in an economically unstable Europe, where the Soviet revolution reigned supreme. In the east, the western victors turned a small blind eye in this regard. German Free Corps intervened in Latvia in late 1919 when Bolsheviks threatened to take over. In Oberschlesien, Poles and Germans clashed. Only in 1922 did things come to a 'final solution' when 7522 km^2 fell to Poland, including a million inhabitants.[6]

Broadly speaking, this was the situation Hitler faced when he came to power in January 1933. After Bismarck, Wilhelm II, von Tirpitz and von Bülow and the *Erfüllungspolitik, a* new phase in German foreign policy would now begin.

Much has been written about the Third Reich, but attention has not been evenly distributed. Remarkably, the persecution of the Jews was not initially very popular among historians. Attention was focused most on first 'standard works' as well as memoirs by allied war leaders. The founder of the serious study of the Holocaust, Raul Hilberg, can relate to this.

Hilberg, born in Vienna in 1927, fled to the United States in 1939. After the war, he studied political science and decided to specialise in the Holocaust. 'That will be your funeral,' mused his professor at Columbia University, by which he meant that Hilberg's career opportunities were dashed by his choice of subject. Hilberg, an individualist, was stubborn enough to disregard this advice and stuck to his choice. This made him an outsider in the academic world. He had great difficulty getting an academic post, which he eventually managed at the University of Vermont. Vermont may be a beautiful place, but the university is not known as a 'first choice' for talented scholars. After Hilberg was appointed in 1956, he was able to work assiduously on his study of the murder of the Jews - the term holocaust came into use only later - and completed it in 1964. Typical of the research climate was the fact that Hilberg had not only struggled to find a university appointment, but it also proved difficult to get his *The Destruction of the European Jews*⁷ published. In the end, it was the rather obscure publishing house Quadrangle books in Chicago that dared.

In retrospect, this, together with the books by Reitlinger (1953) and Poliakov (1954), published around the same time, was the start of a much larger-scale (and not always better) study of the Holocaust. Hilberg was the pioneer, along with the aforementioned authors, and after him a veritable tidal wave of studies began. By now, the amount of literature is barely manageable, although the number of really serious titles is somewhat disappointing and much of the work has the character of an *Oral History*, which, while strongly evocative, lends itself less to analysis. The publication flow sometimes got so 'out of hand' that in January 1979, when Gerald Greens TV series *Holocaust* appeared, *Der Spiegel* spoke of 'Black Friday' because of the sensationalism of many publications. German historian Martin Broszat pointed out that the holocaust was initially seen mainly as 'Jewish history' and only later was this subject picked up by the wider audience of historians and interested lay people. Broszat speaks of a *Nacherlebnis*.[8]

In fact, at the end of the twentieth century, a situation arose where, because of the enormous impact of this human tragedy, the attention paid to the Holocaust was so great that other subjects were overshadowed by it. Typical of this, for example, is a review of the most important literature on the Third Reich that appeared in the *Sixth Yearbook of the National Institute for War Documentation*, authored by Dick van Galen Last.[9] In his article, van Galen Last lists no fewer than 980 titles that can be considered the most important works on the Second World War. The selection is excellent and quite useful. Still, it is striking that the Holocaust is represented with 110 titles and plays an important role in dozens more. It is also striking that an important subject like Lebensraum does not have its own section, and indeed, cannot be listed as a 'specialist study' in the titles as such. Lebensraum is missing from bibliographies on the Third Reich as well, such as those by Michael Ruck and Helen Kehr.[10] For Hitler's Lebensraum concept, one has to consult books of a general nature on the character and motivations of the Third Reich.

The author cannot be blamed for failing to include these books in the lists. They are simply not available. From this, one can conclude that there is a historiographical backlog in the research into the geopolitical motivations and plans of Hitler Germany. The reason for this historiographical backlog can be explained by the fact that the image of the Third Reich was determined, for a very long time, by literally cutting this epoch out of German and European history and setting it apart as 'a dark enigma' - Fritz Fischer spoke of 'corporate accident'[11] - that descended over Europe and Germany. In the process, Hitler acquired demonic dimensions and the historical climate did not lend itself to systematic research into his motivations. Yet, much progress was made in this area in the late 1960s. However, the difference with the Holocaust is that the question of Hitler's motives, his *Weltanschauung* of which the Lebensraum philosophy is a part, as well as his hatred of Jews, never occupied the general public and was limited to a debate among historians. This is unfortunate, considering that Hitler's Lebensraum plans led to the biggest looting campaign in modern history: operation 'Barbarossa', the attack by Nazi Germany and allies on the Soviet Union. Historiographically, this campaign, more than any other geopolitical move by Hitler, was inspired by his racial beliefs. All the more reason to pay attention to this part of the Third Reich's politics. Some interesting stuff has been published on the day-to-day developments. Two well-designed books that show how Hitler built the road to his Lebensraum and *Grosswirtschaftsraum* are Norman Rich's work, *Hitler's War Aims* and *Der Generalplan Ost* by Mechtild Rössler and Sabine Schleiermacher.[12] The day-to-day political practice and Hitler's *Herrschaft* over Germany that was necessary for this are covered in detail herein. The latter authors also dwell on how *Raumordnung* was to take place in the East and what came of it. The spiritual, moral backgrounds of the conflict remain somewhat underexposed. Jochen Thies[13] should be mentioned here as well. He was one of the first to take a serious look at Hitler's *Endziele* and came to the conclusion that this was not *Zielloser Aktionismus*.

German historian Karl Dieter Bracher has sometimes typified the history of Hitler and his NSDAP as the history of his underestimation. The 'gap' in historiography noted above is clear evidence of this.

Serious study of Hitler's geopolitics and his Lebensraum philosophy would take off only a few years after the first serious study of the Holocaust, and even then remain limited in scope. We will discuss this in detail. Before then, relatively little material appeared, yet some studies are interesting enough to cover here, above all because these are the 'earliest works'.

The first to become convinced of the usefulness of such an in-depth investigation into Hitler and his political motives were, logically, his opponents. Still, they too, completely in line with Bracher's conclusion about Hitler's underestimation, went to work relatively late. Nevertheless, these studies were the first to show that Hitler's role was crucial within the policies and functioning of the NSDAP. Or as the historian Sebastian Haffner so aptly put it: 'Hitler was the Marx and Lenin of National Socialism in one person', and in his view, it was therefore no exaggeration to speak of a 'Hitlerism'.

One of the first really large-scale studies into Hitler's *Weltanschauung* was done by US authorities.[14] Given the fact that even today the discussion into Hitler's geopolitical views is not a widely held (public) debate, it should surprise no one that the first serious work was a *secret* study. In this secret study, the 'Office of Strategic Services' (OSS) was commissioned to scrutinise Hitler and his personality and ideas. Under the inspired leadership of the highly ambitious Colonel William J. Donovan, they decided to map out Hitler. The man hired to examine his psyche was psychiatrist Dr Walter C. Langer.

The choice of Langer was a shot in the arm for the OSS. Langer had long been personally interested in Hitler and the rise of the Nazis. This interest was partly explained by Langer's profession; on the other hand, Langer was in Europe at the time of the Nazi rise and personally experienced Hitler's first expansionist steps. Langer was in Austria in 1937 and 1938, witnessed the *Anschluss* between Berlin and Vienna and saw the Nazi troops move into the country. He tasted the atmosphere on the streets, saw the exuberant crowds. He witnessed a speech by Hitler and saw people's reactions. He also saw how the Nazi machinery operated, the anti-Jewish smear campaign conducted, and the many arrests.

The study became a huge task. The researchers collected books, articles and documents and talked to as many eyewitnesses and contemporaries as possible and also, if possible, to people who had known Hitler well personally. One interesting source was Otto Strasser, who had sought asylum in Montréal, Canada, after political struggles with Hitler in which his brother Gregor was killed. All the interviews conducted were meant to portray Hitler's relationship to his people and his politics and psyche. In total, the research yielded no less than 1,100 densely typed pages, which became known in the corridors as *The Hitler Source Book*. What caused Langer some concern was the fact that psychoanalysis was a 'therapeutic technique', where one worked directly with the source itself. In this case, however, he depended on secondary source material.

Nevertheless, the report came to interesting speculations. In the first chapter, 'As He Believes Himself to Be', Langer concludes that Hitler followed his politics 'with the certainty of a sleepwalker'. This formulation, quoted from an interview after Hitler Germany reoccupied the Rhineland in 1936, has since surfaced in several studies of the Third Reich, such as in John Toland's biography *Adolf Hitler*.[15] With this statement, the OSS made it clear that it believed Hitler could only be certain (like a sleepwalker) because he followed a fixed course. In other words: Hitler's politics were not a random manoeuvre, but part of a larger, structured plan. The OSS therefore concluded in its report, published in 1943 (too late!), that Hitler considered himself the man to redesign Europe, that it was he and not his generals who had to make these decisions, and that he listened to 'his inner voice'.

The latter raised speculation at the OSS. Were forces besides Hitler determining the course of the Third Reich? Names of astrologers had surfaced in the investigation. However, the OSS dismissed these esoteric backgrounds as rumours and gossip that stemmed (unintentionally) from an early study by Karl H. von Wiegand. Wiegand worked as a journalist for the Hearstpress and, along with Louis Lochner and H.V. Kaltenborn, was among the few non-German journalists who had had the opportunity to interview Hitler.[16] The fact that these rumours were dismissed by the OSS is not insignificant. Apparently, it was assumed that Hitler himself was hiding behind the (consistent) line of his politics. In formulating exactly which policy was responsible for this line, the OSS was left wanting. However, as usual in Freudian psychoanalysis, it did pay extensive attention to Hitler's childhood years, his sexual development and messiah complex (Hitler often compared himself to Jesus Christ), his vegetarianism and how it was that so many of his associates from the early years were homosexual. Finally, it is interesting to note that Langer took Hitler's suicide(!) into account.

Despite all its good intentions, the OSS could have saved itself a lot of work and found answers if it had taken note of the studies on Hitler and his politics already carried out by his opponents. As early as the 1930s, strikingly visionary works about the destructive role that Hitler-Germany would play in the European power constellation appeared from the left-wing perspective. American reticence towards these sources can possibly be explained by the often communist language used in this study. The jargon aside, such editions that saw the light of day through the French publisher Edition du Carrefour were highly relevant. The publishing house was run by a German emigrant and Soviet novelist, Willi Münzenberg.[17] In a series of books, he denounced the violent nature of the Third Reich. He did this through books on the Reichstag fire, in which the position of the accused Dimitroff was widely publicised, and by publishing a white paper on the 'Night of the Long Knives', 30 June 1934, which the publisher labelled as Germany's Bartholemy Night. More important were such editions as *Das Braune Netz* and Albert Schreiner's *Hitler treibt zum Krieg*.[18] In the preface to the former book (1935), Lord Listowel warned not only against the rearmament of Germany but above all against its ideological programme. As very dangerous, the author considered what he called the 'new German imperialism' that would follow the expansive path of Imperial Germany; '*Gleiches Blut im gleichen Reich*'. It was clear to him that the Nazis saw the limits of this *Reich* beyond the current status quo. New conquests were planned not so much in German East Africa, but above all in Eastern Europe: the Soviet Union. In fact, German emigrant writers observed, Germany was preparing for war. This was happening at all levels. Hitler had already described the coming war in *Mein Kampf*. The people, workers and youth were mobilised, as was science. The club around Münzenberg warned against the geopolitics of Karl Haushofer, who, inspired by Mackinder and Kjellén, philosophised and lectured on great border shifts.[19] Cartography, too, could take a hit. There was a veritable boom in hundreds of thousands of postcards showing Germany in its new borders. Here an uncanny distinction was made between *Volksboden* and *Einflussboden, which* would effortlessly bring millions of people suddenly under German rule.[20] Edition du Carrefour also charted propaganda, the Nazis' *Auslandarbeit* and violent mechanics towards opponents and Jews. *Brot und Ehre* had been replaced by *Blut und Ehre*. Among the earliest warners was Sebastian Haffner. In 1938, this young lawyer had emigrated to Britain with his Jewish girlfriend, where, after a brief internment, he wrote the visionary book *Germany, Jekyll & Hyde*[21] in which he mapped out the evil foundations of the Nazi empire.

Besides the psychoanalysts of the OSS and political opponents, Hitler's prophetic contemporaries were among the first to point out the grotesque and destructive that was about to happen. They tried to put their finger on Nazi plans based on lessons from the past and calculations from the present. *Can Europe Keep the Peace?*[22] asked Frank H. Simonds in 1932. He had no answer, although he feared the worst. His chapter two, 'Ethnic Europe'- a title that, by the way, would not have been out of place in the mid-1990s, at the height of the civil war in former Yugoslavia- referred to that. In his study, Simonds lists a whole list of problems - the consequences of the Versailles peace, the Polish corridor, Hungarian irredentism resulting from the Treaty of Trianon - that threatened the faltering peace. Even more interesting was the study by Fritz Sternberg, who no longer wondered whether there would be a Second World War, but how long it could be waged by Hitler. The book appeared in Dutch translation shortly before World War II broke out. In his study, Sternberg came to some very important conclusions that German strategic planners had better take to heart. A short-lived lightning war against

France was what Sternberg held possible. As for the Soviet Union, Sternberg called this idea an absolute utopia. Interestingly, the author pointed out that Germany did not possess raw materials for a long war as well. Hence the choice of the book's title: *How long could Hitler wage war?*[23]

Therein lies the deadly paradox in which Germany found itself. Germany went to war for Lebensraum in the east to obtain an autarkic economy, but did not possess the raw materials to wage such a war.

Although Hitler's contemporaries made interesting observations of Hitler's worldview and the motivations and goals of his actions, the true descent of Orpheus did not get underway until after the war. The best-known work that paid serious attention to Hitler's thought and gained notoriety appeared four years after Hilberg's life's work: Eberhard Jäckels' *Hitlers Weltanschauung*.[24] It should be noted that Walter Hofer had earlier reached the same conclusions as Jäckel, but put forward these theses in a somewhat more generally worded book.[25] Since Jäckel unfolded his theory in an overall survey of existing historiography, he thereby directly claimed his own place in the whole. In his book, Jäckel dealt harshly with the isolation of the Third Reich within German historiography. Hitler Germany had not appeared out of thin air; indeed, rarely in history had a leader described and told so precisely what he would do when he came to power. Where others mistook Hitler for a fool and did not take his thoughts and writings seriously, Jäckel studied Hitler's word and, above all, his writings. He discovered that Hitler did possess a *Weltanschauung*, which was engaged in a veritable *Kulturkampf* with competing ideologies. Initially, Jäckel believed, the image of Hitler was strongly defined by contemporaries of his, such as Hermann Rauschning, who in his book published in 1938 depicted National Socialism as a 'nihilistic revolution'.[26] Hitler, Rauschning believed, was an opportunist, a man without goals. Such theories were reinforced by Harold Laski (1942), who believed that Hitler was 'principle-less'. According to British historian Allan Bullock (1952), who relied on Rauschning more than once, Hitler was only about 'power for power's sake'. Georg Lukácz (1953) declared that Hitler 'had no closed system of ideas'. By then, the understanding had grown that Hitler's role in the whole process was crucial. Bullock was one of the first to make it clear that Hitler was not a 'pawn of shadow powers', but was following his own course, although Bullock, like the OSS at the time, did not yet see a line in it. Helmut Heiber finally made the leap to the view (1968) that National Socialism and Hitler were identical.[27]

With this observation, much was gained. Following this conclusion, it was logical to study Hitler's thought very seriously. The main source for this were Hitler's written works. An advantage was the fact that Hitler had put his thoughts on paper at various times during his life, so one could try to detect a pattern in his thinking. The first volume of *Mein Kampf* appeared in 1924, the second in 1926. In addition, one had the so-called *Zweite Buch*, which was never published and only surfaced after the war in 1961. Finally, there was Hitler's political testament from the Führerbunker in 1945. In all the works, Jäckel noted, Hitler's aims were discussed, so there could be talk of a multiple trial. In total, there are over 2.000 pages of text. In addition, there are Hitler's table talks that were meticulously minuted.

Closer examination revealed that the core of Hitler's ideology consisted of two components. On the one hand and, as we saw, the most well-known part: Hitler's racial theories. The conquest of Lebensraum is the other component of Hitler's ideology.[28] There has been some speculation as to which of the two elements of Hitler's worldview was the more important. John Lukacs, in his recent book *The Hitler of History*[29], believes that the race issue was the most important. In contrast, Swedish historian Alf W. Johansson believes that the Lebensraum question was the central goal of Hitler's worldview.[30] This discussion makes little sense. As we will see, the two elements were strongly linked and certainly did not compete for Hitler's attention.

Based on his findings, Jäckel rightly concluded that *Mein Kampf* was the most unread bestseller in world history. Only after his studies, through the work of Christian Zentner and Werner Maser, came detailed studies of *Mein Kampf* as the basis of Hitler's World View.[31] Old myths surrounding the book, such as that of Manuel Humbert (1936) who claimed that the book was a 'witch's bible', or merely a reaction to the Treaty of Versailles, no longer sufficed.[32] Even a historian like A.J.P. Taylor, who was inclined to interpret Hitler's foreign policy concept as that of a calculating rationalist, eventually believed that Hitler's irrational theories had to be taken seriously. 'Hitler believed unconditionally in the mess in his head,' he opined in *Europe: grandeur and decline*.[33]

The mistakes of historians and contemporaries are not surprising. Hitler was a man of many faces. He could be extremely gallant, friendly, the perfect host. He could talk animatedly. In his immediate circle, 'unpleasant topics', such as the fate of the Jews, were hardly ever touched upon. Contemporaries who knew him closely could, if they allowed themselves to, believe that there was no holocaust. On the other hand, he could be unexpectedly rude, which happened with the Hungarian regent Miklos Horthy. Horthy, like so many Europeans in the 1930s, was curious about the corporal who had enjoyed a career like a comet in Germany. Shortly after Hitler came to power, he paid a private visit to Hitler that was kept out of the press for political reasons. Although the conversation at the Berghof that followed was a one-way conversation - Hitler was talking for hours at a stretch as usual - the German host was courteous, and compassionate to his guest, especially where the peace of Trianon was concerned (Hungary had lost 63 per cent of its population and 72 per cent of its territory at this 'Versailles of the East'). 'I had no reason to contradict Hitler,' Horthy wrote in his memoirs after the war. He found Hitler understanding and intelligent. A few years later, he came to completely different views. During a visit to the naval port at Kiel, Hitler suddenly took him aside and made it clear to him that Germany was the superpower within Europe and that Czechoslovakia would be his first prey. In the event of resistance from that side, Hitler would not hesitate to raze Prague to the ground. Horthy was shocked. How could anyone talk about one of the most beautiful cities in Europe, if not the world, in such a way. 'I was not the only one who was wrong about Hitler,'[34] he noted in his memoirs, and that was a true word. The history of Hitler is the history of his underestimation. All the more reason to dwell on his thinking.

Hitler frankly admitted of himself that he 'was not a writer'. However, from a young age, he had nurtured the ambition to put his thoughts on paper one day. According to psychologist Robert G.L. Waite, this idea dated back to Hitler's Viennese years. He even designed the front cover for it, already adorned by a swastika. When he drafted the final text, years later, Hitler was said to be very 'wordy'. This is at least evident from the various printings of *Mein Kampf*. Hitler allowed the editors only minimal changes. This fear of change, incidentally, was not an isolated occurrence. Hitler's entire life and, as we shall see, his political decision-making as well, was caught in a mind-numbing monotony. His press chief Hanfstaengl complained after the war that living and working with Hitler amounted to a 'paralysing repetition'. Jäckel noted that Hitler had 'a panicked fear of changing his views'. Waite gives several examples of recurring patterns: Hitler always walked his dog by the same route; he always threw his dog's stick in the same direction. His personal grooming followed a set ritual every day. Hitler always wore the same clothes, year after year. He always played the same music and always chose the same seat.[35]

This monotony is very important for research. Hitler was very consistent in his thinking, and this reinforces the historical probative value of the policies he wrote down in *Mein Kampf* and that of his political testament of April 1945, which, in Waite's words, 'did not deviate by a single word from Hitler's earlier work'. About what Hitler eventually put on paper, Waite is also very clear. *Mein Kampf* went far beyond describing politics or the founding and *Werdegang* of a party. It is as Hitler himself said: 'We are not a movement, but a religion.' Indeed, we can observe that *Mein Kampf* acquired an almost religious status. In many German families, the book had literally replaced the Bible. Newlyweds were given *Mein Kampf* on their wedding day. Even in education, Hitler was compared to the Messiah. In an official dictation approved by the Ministry of Information and Propaganda from 1934, it was called:

'Jesus and Hitler. Just as Jesus freed people from sin and hell, Hitler freed the German people from ruin. Jesus and Hitler were persecuted, but while Jesus was crucified, Hitler was elevated to chancellor ... Jesus fought for heaven, Hitler for German earth.'[36]

The first part of *Mein Kampf* came into being in 1924, while Hitler bounced diagonally up and down the room, dictating his text, while listening to Richard Wagner, to Rudolf Hess and Emil Maurice. The second volume of *Mein Kampf* was written in Berchtesgaden, with the help of Max Amann and with (minuscule) text corrections by Father Bernard Stempfle. The former put the biggest editorial stamp on Hitler's work by convincing him that *Four and a Half Years of Fighting Lies, Stupidity and Cowardice* would not be the most effective title for the book and suggested *Mein Kampf*. And so it happened and the book appeared in at least 16 languages. Coming up with good titles was not Hitler's strong suit. Earlier, for instance, he wanted to write a book with the very presumptuous title: *Monumentalgeschichte der Menschheit*. From a historical point of view, it is unfortunate that this book never came about, but I am convinced that the guiding principle would have been equal to the two thousand pages we possess of Hitler, as well as the notes of conversations. The fact that Hitler believed he could write such a book - while he was of the opinion that he was not a great writer - reinforces the idea that the iron-clad racial laws he saw as a guiding principle should have provided the handholding to this monk's work. *Mein Kampf* - its circulation already exceeded 10 million copies by 1943 - made Hitler a rich man despite the fact that a tireless German researcher once calculated that there were as many as 164.000 errors and incorrect sentence structures in the book. This is the biggest confirmation that the editors had little to say about the work and at the same time increases the historical value of the book.[37]

It is clear from Hitler's writings that he had little regard for the geopolitical line of the German Kaiser, von Bülow and von Tirpitz. He was especially harsh about alliance politics. Although Hitler had more respect for Bismarck, he held an idiosyncratic view on alliances. He saw the German coalition with the Habsburg Empire in World War I as detrimental to Germany. The Germans, Hitler wrote in *Mein Kampf*, had entered into the alliance out of gullibility and stupidity.[38] Hitler no longer wanted Germany to depend on anyone. In the second volume of *Mein Kampf*, Hitler writes in a remarkable conclusion what, in his opinion, foreign policy should be:

'The foreign policy of the state should make the existence of its people possible by establishing between the numerical strength and growing power of the people, on the one hand, and the quantity and quality of its territory, on the other, such a healthy balance that this people can exist.'

Hitler considered as 'healthy' the situation when the people were able to obtain their total nutrition from their own soil and territory. Any other situation he considered unhealthy and he added for completeness: 'Only a living space of sufficient dimensions can guarantee a people freedom of existence.'[39]

In the first volume of *Mein Kampf*, Hitler clarifies in more detail what he meant by this definition in *'Die vier Wege deutscher Politik'*. For the Lebensraum issue, this is an important passage. Here, Hitler expresses his concern about the ever-increasing population pressure on German soil. The problem of overpopulation occupied him immensely. There were several solutions: the first was population regulation, which Hitler resented. Second, the concept of *Innere Kolonisation* came up, which amounted to intensification and rationalisation of the amount of land already available in order to achieve greater food production to cover growing needs. Thirdly, Hitler raised the suggestion of obtaining new territory where the millions of new inhabitants of Germany could settle in the future. Lastly, he wrote about colonial and trade policy.

While the first option was immediately dismissed as 'un-German', Hitler paid more attention to innere Kolonisation. The rationalisation of agriculture, something that certainly had good chances in highly educated Germany, was a serious rival to Hitler's Lebensraum views. He therefore insisted that the idea of innere Kolonisation implied too much of a pacifist attitude to life. The idea relied far too much on existing borders and self-imposed restrictions that Hitler dismissed as 'unnatural'. Territories are not predestined by nature to certain peoples, he believed in *Mein Kampf*, but are for that people who possess the strength to conquer it and are diligent enough to cultivate it. Nature knows no political boundaries; they were an invention of the human imagination. Another danger of *innere Kolo-*

nisation was that other peoples and races, who did have *grösseren Bodenflächen* at their disposal, would nevertheless multiply faster in the long run and eventually pose a danger to the 'culture races' whose expansion was limited by their pacifism.

Further danger of innere Kolonisation was that it had to be, as Hitler wrote, *'erarbeitet'*. The rationalisation of German agriculture was an inward-looking process. With this development, Hitler noted, German foreign policy was being buried and with it the future of the German people.

The fourth solution, trade and colonial policy, on which Kaiser Wilhelm II, von Bülow and von Tirpitz had worked diligently, did not have Hitler's sympathies either. Hitler saw the colonial empires as 'inverted pyramids'. By this he meant that their European territory was laughably small and the vast majority of their territory was in the colonies. The danger posed by this development was that the *Spitze* was in Europe and the *Basis* in the whole world. This made the colonial powers very weak in practice. A much better example of a healthy power base, therefore, Hitler saw in the USA, where the pyramid was exactly the other way around. The base was in the US continent itself, the striker stuck out, into the world.

The third solution had his genuine interest. The place under the sun, which Germany had long sought, Hitler wanted to shape within a continental empire. New land had to be obtained to give Lebensraum to the millions of Germans of the future. In defence of these plans of conquest, Hitler appealed to religious motives in *Mein Kampf*. According to God, the earth was for life, not for certain peoples. The race and nation that was strongest was allowed to appropriate the territory. This struggle could only take place in the *Heimatkontinent* and could only be through struggle. This struggle, according to Hitler, had to be faced *'ruhig und gefasst'* as something inevitable. He saw the democratic system of Weimar that ruled at the time he wrote *Mein Kampf* as unfit to carry out this historical mission. Democracy was based on the law of the majority, the numerically stronger races would win as a result. Hitler's thinking followed 'natural' laws. The most brutal and aggressive peoples would rule, not those who practised *'Selbstbeschränkung'*.[40]

The conquest of Lebensraum could only come at the expense of Russia, Hitler mused in *Mein Kampf*. Already in 1924, this had sown the seeds for Operation 'Barbarossa', the June 1941 attack on the Soviet Union. The new empire, Hitler believed, had to follow the old path of the *'Ordensritter'*. The German sword and the German plough had to go hand in hand and provide the daily bread for the nation. Only one ally qualified for the policy of conquest, and in Hitler's eyes that was Britain. The British could give the Germans backing during their new *'Germanenzug'*.[41]

Interestingly, such far-reaching conclusions were confirmed in Hitler's so-called *second book*.[42] This is a manuscript of a never-published book by Hitler that turned up in the archives in Washington under the signature eap 105/40. It immediately caused a sensation among historians. The manuscript was uncorrected (the erasures are still in the manuscript) and dictated directly to Max Amann. The sensation was that the book had been written in 1928, quite a few years later than *Mein Kampf*, at a time when Hitler's power was much more considerable. That is probably also why it never made it to publication. Hitler allowed himself to be too caught up. Later in the war, Hitler confessed to von Ribbentrop that his biggest mistake had been to publish his foreign policy in *Mein Kampf*.[43]

Of particular importance to the research is the consistency that emanates from the work in relation to the earlier claims in *Mein Kampf*. The chapter *'Von der Reichseinigung zur Raumpolitik'* shows conclusively that Hitler stuck to his definition of foreign policy. Domestic politics was nothing more than the plan to prepare Germany for a successful operation in the foreign policy field. Foreign policy consisted of dealing with Germany's 'impossible' ground surface. That this was no ordinary conquest becomes clear immediately. Hitler warned in his second book that one should not make the mistake of turning the subjugated Poles into Germans, for example. The 'racially alien elements' had to be encapsulated or simply 'removed', leaving the freed-up soil available for völkische redevelopment.[44]

In the execution of his politics, moreover, Hitler was much more subtle than in its formulation. The written work constituted Hitler's 'secret agenda'. The practical implementation showed a much more erratic and less clear-cut character. Hitler had no hesitation in pretending to be different from what he was, seeking rapprochements and forging alliances, only to sacrifice them just as easily to his strategic goals.⁴⁵

For Hitler, these were normal reasonings. He believed that his opponents viewed the world in this way too, above all Joseph Stalin, whom he therefore greatly admired. In general, he had the highest praise for Stalin, whom he often called 'the cunning Caucasian', who 'commanded unconditional esteem' and was 'a great man'. In Hitler's eyes, Stalin, like himself, had well understood the lessons of the past. Stalin knew his examples, Hitler believed, referring to Ghengis Khan. In his eyes, Bolshevism was just a tool, a disguise, through which the age-old clash between the Slavs and the Germanic and Latin peoples would be conducted.⁴⁶

Even in terms of Hitler's thinking on continental empire, Russia was in some ways a model for Hitler. James Joll, in his standard work *Europe since 1870,* rightly notes that Russia was in fact the most successful imperialist power of the nineteenth century. While other countries like Britain and France sought their empire overseas, Russia chose to expand eastward, on the continent. In the nineteenth century, Russia hereby subjugated central Asia and Siberia. The new territories were brought under Russian administration and the Trans-Siberian Railway exposed the area economically and militarily. As far as the Siberian port of Vladivostok and Port-Arthur on the coast of northern China, a huge area was opened up by Moscow. This was immediately followed by the policy of 'Russification' of the population, which peaked in 1907-1909 when half a million *setllers* settled in Siberia as pioneers.⁴⁷

The conclusion Hitler drew from the above reasoning was that state borders were man-made and therefore could and should be broken by them. Germany had to prepare to become a world power or perish. This was typical Hitler reasoning. As a politician, he had the attitude of a gambler: 'all or nothing'; he wrote these words in the 1920s. Until 1945, key speeches by Hitler would always feature this element again. 'Final victory' or *'Weltuntergang'*, world empire, or downfall of the German people, were eternally recurring elements. Here, too, we see Hitler's fear of change. His thoughts were polarised into a few fundamental points, which Jäckel put into words: the conquest of Lebensraum - with the underlying idea of world power or downfall - and the racial struggle, which Hitler saw as a 'war' to be won or lost, as we will see later.

Eastern Europe, and Bolshevik Russia in particular, had to provide Hitler with his Lebensraum. He saw no objection to this war of conquest. On the one hand, he points out in Chapter 14 of *Mein Kampf* that even religion offered no resistance to a war for bare existence: such a conflict was the only reason for bloodshed. On the other hand, Hitler's historical view of Eastern Europe and the Slavic peoples strengthened his conviction as well. The Russian, Slavic peoples were capable of little in Hitler's eyes. The state-building elements in these peoples were, he believed, of German (Germanic/Nordic) origin. Following this reasoning, Eastern Europe had actually been under German leadership throughout the centuries. However, this Aryan core had been massacred as a result of the Russian revolution, allowing Slavs and Jews to plot against Germany. Legend had it that the incarcerated tsarina in Yekaterinburg spent her days in front of the attic window, looking out over the beautiful gardens. Where she always sat, she had carved a swastika (swastika) in the wood. Next to it, she had written the date of her arrival: 17 April 1918. More than ever, in Hitler's eyes, there was a 'historical necessity' to intervene in 'Germany's geopolitical backyard'.[48]

Incidentally, Hitler made no secret of this intervention. When US President Roosevelt asked Hitler and Mussolini on 14 April 1939 to rein things in and leave neutral independent states alone, Hitler's reply was very firm. On 28 April, Hitler said that any such criticism from Germany regarding US interference towards Latin America would immediately invoke the monroe doctrine. Washington would see this as interference in the Americas. The same monroe doctrine existed in Hitler's eyes for German interests in Europe.[49]

This capitalisation on the monroe doctrine was adopted by the German Foreign Ministry. In front of American diplomats, von Ribbentrop made it clear in Berlin on 1 March 1940 that 'Germany too had its monroe doctrine'. This doctrine implied on the European continent that Germany had 'interests in Eastern Europe and that France, Britain and every other Western country should not interfere'.[50] On 9 June 1940, Hitler believed that in the mutual recognition of US and European (read German) of the monroe doctrine there possible lay the key to world peace. Should the USA recognise Germany's monroe doctrine, a final battle with the US could possibly be prevented. However, it had to be clear that the USA should not interfere in Germany's Lebensraum policy. Mutual recognition of the monroe doctrine could guarantee long-term stability between the major power blocs. Here, Hitler also referred to the Japanese share. Tokyo, Hitler believed, was also building its Asia Monroeshugi, the Japanese monroe doctrine.[51]

Fencing with the monroe doctrine was little more than a political argument in the geopolitical jousting game. The real motives and drives lay deeper. The historical 'necessity' and appeal to history that the Nazis used can already be seen in the term 'Third Reich'. The historian Waldemar Besson rightly noted that the term *empire* has a special ring to it among all peoples. It reminds us of the kingdom of God. Christians, since Joachim von Fiore (1202), spoke of the first, second and third realms, the realms of the father, son and holy spirit. Furthermore, 'empire' reminds us of the Roman empire: the Imperium Romanum; an empire that for its inhabitants was a 'world empire'. The empire tradition was revived at the end of the 15th century, with the *'Heiliges Römisches Reich Deutscher Nation'*. On 18 January 1871, the empire tradition continued, with the proclamation of the German Empire in the hall of mirrors at Versailles. Called the second empire, it also had ambitions to ascend to world power, as did Adolf Hitler's Third Reich.[52] Of course, there was no real connection between the different empires, and Hitler, although he copied many outward displays from the past (including the Romans), was definitely not a man in the footsteps of older powers and forces that could legitimise his *Werdegang* and Germany's *Alleingang*. Still, forgetting or misinterpreting the past is historically essential to the process of national awareness and *nation building*. The fantasies that were rampant within the National Socialist camp will be discussed in more detail.[53]

More important than fencing with monroe doctrine or referring back to the old empire, was Hitler's racial view of the Lebensraum question. Hitler saw the disappearance of the 'Aryan core' in Russia as the final stage before the country's total collapse as a great power. The German invasion would accelerate that process. That this war would require passing through Polish territory was no objection to Hitler. 'Poland is entirely in French hands,' Hitler already mused in *Mein Kampf*. And tensions with France were inevitable. France was the hereditary enemy from 1914 to 1918, the victorious power and spiritual father of Versailles, the occupier of German territory.

In Hitler's eyes, Russia was not only the future supplier of Lebensraum, but the stronghold of the Slavs and Jews he so hated as well. 'The international Jew rules in Russia,' he wrote in *Mein Kampf*. As a result, in the campaign to the east, both these axes of Hitler's *Weltanschauung* came together.

Hitler's anti-Semitism was not original. It had existed for centuries. But in the nineteenth century, anti-Semitism had been greatly fuelled by a host of processes that dealt with the European power, the power system of the post-napoleonic era, and the Congress of Vienna. The middle and especially the late nineteenth and early twentieth centuries were periods of upheaval and change. The era of colonialism and imperialism was in its last - bloody - convulsions, liberal democracy was in crisis, however, on the other hand young, nascent and promising too. Capitalism was on the rise, socialism was vying for world domination, emancipatory movements (Theodor Herzl, *The Jewish State*) were emerging, social changes were having their impact on society. Science contributed new theories that lend themselves to abuse, such as Charles Darwin's *On the Origin of Spieces* (1859) and British philosopher Herbert Spencer, the inventor of the '*Survival of the fittest*'. Nationalism and racism were other powerful forces, fuelled by World War I and its consequences. Between the two intolerant ideological extremes, totalitarian nationalism and totalitarian Marxism was, as Hugh Seton Watson described it, a veritable showdown.[54]

As we have already seen in the above theories from Hitler's *Mein Kampf*, Hitler actually abhorred all the movements that emerged in his time and clung frantically to his own nationalist-racialist outlook on life. At first, Hitler's anti-Semitism was a kind of 'liberal anti-Semitism' where Jews were mainly looked at for their 'status apart' and their isolation from society. After World War I, völkisch/ariosophical anti-Semitism slid over this, assuming conspiracies, protocols and Jewish-Bolshevism.[55] Characteristic of Hitler's anti-Semitism was that he saw all other factors, capitalism, the emancipatory movements but especially Marxism, as Jewish inventions. Where he criticised colonialist and imperialist policies, it was because the racial element was not sufficiently included in them. This narrowing of world affairs formed the foundation of the Third Reich and its foreign policy. Or as Hitler himself saw it, domestic politics consisted of little else but getting ready for the big confrontation with the evil outside world.

In his aversion to the many changes, Hitler was not alone. It was the time of Oswald Spengler's *Der Untergang des Abendlandes*, which believed that German culture was in its terminal phase. 'Herstellers' tried to turn the tide, from *Jungkonservativen* (Arthur Moeller van den Bruck, Ernst Jünger) to völkische thinkers (Paul de Lagarde, Julius Langbehn) and National Socialists. In fact, the rise of National Socialism was partly the rise of provincialism, the village against the city. This sentiment also resonates with one of the Nazi party's key ideologues, Richard Walther Darré, who - in agreement with the völkischen - saw the future of the German Reich in the 'rural' rather than the 'decadent-urban'. To this, Darré linked the issue of *'Blut und Boden'*. Or as he described it in a brochure for the Ministry of Health in 1936: 'The racial question is the linchpin of all the political questions of National Socialism.' Darré was full of the racial theories of Freiburg professor of racial studies Hans Friedrich Karl Günther. This *Rassenpapst*, who sold his 'scientific' race theories by the hundreds of thousands through Lehmann-Verlag and was heavily inspired by Arthur Gobineau, Houston Stewart Chamberlain and the anthropologists Otto Ammon and Georges Vacher de Lapouge - who specialised in natural selection and Aryan thought - helped Darré connect the Aryan myth to the landscape idyll.[56] One of Germany's fiercest anti-Semites also had agrarian roots: *Hammer publisher* and author of the *Handbuch der Judenfrage*, Theodor Fritsch. Fritsch had spent years campaigning for the interests of small farmers whose livelihoods were threatened by economies of scale in agriculture. From 1902 he devoted himself to his anti-Semitic writings in which he attributed just about all the evils of the world to the Jews. In his view, no distinction needed to be made between Bolshevism and socialism; both had the same destructive aim and were typically Jewish. His publications resulted in many a trial in which he had to serve prison sentences twice. He died in September 1933 at the age of 81, mere months after Hitler seized power. Yet, his ideas seeped into the brown, revolutionary movement that came to life on the völkisch rebirth.[57]

Little attention has so far been paid to a fundamental discrepancy in the völkisch rural idyll. Towards the 'decadent' metropolitan (Western) liberalism underlined the rural roots of the Nazis as a paradisiacal idyll. Against the East, on the other hand, it spoke with undisguised contempt of Slavic peasantry and underlined the cultural content of the German mission by pointing to German urbanism. These contradictory elements make it clear that thoughts about German positioning between east and west were based on feelings rather than facts. The whole expressed both naivety and uncertainty and delusions of grandeur, which we will discuss in detail in Chapter 3.[58]

Hitler was a typical product of German romanticism, with a völkisch and ariosophical self-image and self-pity, but with the aggression of the totalitarian twentieth century. Alongside the myth of the agrarian idyll stood the racial optic. Due to the strongly emotive nature of anti-Semitism, the German social democrat August Bebel had sometimes called anti-Semitism the 'socialism of stupid men'. Still, the Germans were not alone in their anti-Semitic tradition and *Alltag*. There was a wave of anti-Semitism in France in the nineteenth century as well, culminating in the Dreyfus affair. Russia was notorious for its pogroms, in Poland politicians like Josef Beck openly advocated deporting Jews to Madagascar, Hungary had its numerus clausus for Jews.[59] Unfortunately, in the Habsburg Empire and Germany, it took on more political forms and would lead straight to Auschwitz in the Third Reich.

This is not the place to dwell in detail on the roots of Hitler's anti-Semitism, but that racial doctrine played a strong 'legitimising' role in the creation and defence of the Lebensraum question is a fact. However, more important is the relationship that Hitler established between Judaism and Bolshevism, which involved Karl Marx's Jewish background, as well as his experiences with the *'Austromarxism'* of the *Rote Wien* of his youth and the anti-Semitic tradition of mayor Dr Karl Lueger and aristocrat Georg von Schönerer. Hitler was convinced that Bolshevism was a Jewish coup that had driven out the Aryan core of Russia. The role of Jews in the Soviet Union was viewed with suspicion, in 1939 their number was 3,020.141, making them the seventh largest ethnic group (after territory expansion in 1941, the number of Jews in the Soviet Union was 5,300.000).[60]

The relationship between Judaism and communism is fraught. Groundbreaking work has been done by Russian-Jewish writer Sonja Margolina in her *Das Ende der Lügen, Russland und die Juden im 20. Jahrhundert*.[61] To better understand the role of Jews in Russia, we will have to take a step back in history, as there were originally no Jews there at all. They arrived only at the end of the 18th century, as a result of the second partition of Poland. Even then, Jews were characterised by their special role in society. This was mainly due to the developments the community had undergone in Poland, where it formed a separate class between Polish farmers and artisans and the Polish feudal nobility. Jews largely constituted the city dwellers (they were not allowed to own land), and the bourgeois element in Poland. Their cross-border contacts with fellow believers in the west put them in a privileged position, which they exploited by building trade contacts and financing activities. Margolina calls the 16th and 17th centuries the 'Golden Age' for Polish Jews, during which they prospered greatly. Local anti-Semitism dates back to that time, when Jews acted as tax inspectors for the Polish nobility, came to dominate banking and offered fierce competition to Polish artisans. Given their different religious orientation and cross-border contacts, they were also considered 'Western' and seen as strangers.

In this, the seeds of prejudice were sown. The Jews, as money lenders, were said to have had a hand in the birth of capitalism, which

Hitler too, as well as communism, saw as a Jewish conspiracy. In reality, it was not the Jews who steered the historical processes. Margolina very rightly noted that no matter how much money the Jews may have had, they were never in power in European history. They were always the more or less successful servants of power. The emergence of the third estate and the rise of industrialisation and modern capitalism meant emancipatory opportunities for Jews, and so much of the western, Jewish communities supported the rise of capitalism, that made them equal citizens in the nineteenth century.

Equalisation in the east was more difficult. After the assassination of the Russian tsar in 1881, there was a setback in the emancipatory process. In 1892, Jews were largely expelled from Moscow, and thousands had to pack their bags in St Petersburg as well. Jews were restricted in their mobility and faced professional bans. Jews lived concentrated in a number of cities where they formed an inverted occupational pyramid. While 70 per cent of the Russian population lived and worked in the fields, this was only 3.5 per cent among Jews. 70 per cent of the Jews lived off trade and industry, and this made them the vanguard of capitalism blown over from the West, which the Russian villagers as well as the feudal nobility were deeply suspicious of.

The Jewish role in Russia's modernisation was important. Russian feudals, however, driven by negative feelings towards Jews, understood since the Crimean War that they could no longer lag behind the West. Social changes were therefore slow in coming, such as the abolition of serfdom in 1861. The Jews, strong in their international contacts and in banking, became the major financiers of emerging capitalism in Russia. A significant part of the banking system in St Petersburg and Moscow belonged to them, railways were built with Jewish money. Foreign Jewish money (from the Rothschilds) financed the exploitation of Russia's oil fields. The textile industry and even grain exports - a traditional Russian export product that was very sensitive - also came largely into Jewish hands. Some of the Jews benefited from this, but as industry flourished, the reward for Jews, assimilation as in the West, failed to materialise. Jews were still geographically tied to small areas and could not travel to the industrial areas that were being developed. The cities were overcrowded and too small to keep up with the new capitalism. As a result, a large proportion of Jews became victims of the 'progress' they had helped initiate. As a result, Eastern European Jews went through a different development from Western European Jews. While Western European Jews increasingly adopted the identity of the country where they lived, in Russia they remained 'stateless' and partly sought their way out in international socialism.

Margolina uses for Jews the term *überflüssige Menschen*, in Russian *lishny chelovek*, surplus human beings.[62] People with talent, hopes and expectations, but without a future. They could only take refuge in alcohol or in dreams of great changes. These changes presented themselves with the growing unrest in tsarist Russia, at the beginning of the 20th century. When revolutionary unrest broke out in 1905 in response to the disastrous Russo-Japanese war, as many as 37 per cent of the arrested revolutionaries turned out to be Jewish. In part, this could be explained by the anti-Semitic attitude of the Russian authorities, who arrested Jews a little too eagerly; on the other hand, Jews were indeed over-represented and were, as Richard Graf Coudenhove-Kalergi put it, 'embittered enemies of tsarism'.[63]

After World War I broke out in August 1914, tensions among the Jewish community in Russia continued to rise. As the first defeats against the German army emerged, the anti-Semitic smear campaign again took on greater proportions. Jews, with their traditionally Western contacts, were now seen as 'German spies', and murdered or deported during pogroms.[64] The Jewish community therefore eagerly awaited the new developments in early 1917. The revolution broke out in February, followed by a new law that came into force on 22 March 1917. In it, the revolutionary government promised equal rights for all citizens of the country.

The result was a sense of euphoria among a significant part of the Jewish community. Typical of the joy, according to Margolina, was the statement by the prominent Russian Jewish historian Simon Dubnow, who wrote that 'a 40-year-old dream of life had been fulfilled'. 'Society,' he commented, 'was between the dawn of freedom and the Bartholomew's Night of Pogroms.'[65]

In response to revolutionary developments, a large number of Jews chose to flee to the front. There was relatively little talented intellectual potential in the Russian cities where the Bolshevik revolution first took hold. So the new rulers had to make use of Jewish services. Jews, traditionally obedient and loyal, joined the vacant seats in the tsarist administration. For the first time in their Russian history, this turned Jews from victims to perpetrators, Margolina believed. Within Russian history, granting power to outsiders was not unusual. More than any other European power, Russia had historically been ruled by 'outsiders'. This went back to Peter the Great and the most famous example was Catherine II, who was of German origin and included many German and British decision-makers in her government. These facts helped form the basis of Hitler's claim that Russia 'could not lead itself' and had 'always known Aryan rulers'. Besides the Jews, the revolutionaries also took advantage of other minorities who had chosen to flee to the front or wanted to get a piece of the pie for purely opportunistic reasons. An example of large-scale sympathy for the revolution occurred among the Latvians, who were mostly used for 'dirty work'. Yet all sorts of groups and factions participated - time documents even mention Chinese execution units (including in an expedition against the Machno movement) - all for their own reasons.

Still, it was the Jewish image of revolution that persisted. The 'new man' in the East was a Mauser pistol-equipped man in leather jacket who spoke a broken Russian (Jewish) dialect.[66] This mistrust was reinforced as Jews fared better after the communist revolution than before. In 1938, for example, there were five Yiddish magazines, 14 Yiddish newspapers, 372 Yiddish books and Yiddish theatres published in the Soviet Union while before that Jews had been practically gagged. In 1941, 40 per cent of Jews in the Soviet Union lived in areas where the tsar did not allow them to live. This was a completely different situation from before the Russian Revolution.[67]

Despite this, there soon were warnings, including from the Jewish community, regarding the pioneering role Jews played in the communist revolution. This pioneering role could well turn like a huge boomerang against the Jews. On the other hand, some believed that malicious intent was at play. The Jews, Russian cultural historian Boris Paramonow proclaimed, had been 'framed'. Should the revolution fail, the revolutionaries could blame the Jews and sacrifice them to save their own skin. Maxim Gorki saw little in this conspiracy theory and believed that the revolutionaries rather wanted to compromise the Jews by making them do dirty jobs in the Tscheka in order to remain sure of their loyalty this way.[68] The unrest that the revolution brought and the civil war that followed convinced much of the Jewish community that they could not go back. As soon as the noose would loosen slightly, the revenants knew they had to march to the Kremlin to get the perpetrators on the scaffold. Although in the early years, of the 24,000 communists, 1,000 had a Jewish-ethnic background[69] (which is an over-representation, but therefore by no means an entirely Jewish affair), the image of the leading Jewish role in communism had emerged.

The civil war that followed the revolution was accompanied by extremely cruel anti-Semitism. In the Ukraine, pogroms took such bloody forms that they were the worst since Hetman Bohdan Chmielnicki's Cossack terror three centuries earlier. Russians had never seen Jews in public office and now, in the eyes of the people, Jews had suddenly become judges and executioners and omnipresent. In their eyes, Jews were the *mastermind* behind the revolution, which led to 'judophobia' and anti-Semitism. Anti-Semitism was so pervasive in Russia that even liberal thinkers could not entirely escape animosity towards the Jews. In this climate, the *Protocols of the Wise Men of Zion*, a pamphlet exposing a Jewish world conspiracy, could flourish.

The *Protocols* got their first printing in Russia in 1903. It was a tome consisting of 24 chapters that all had the same theme: Jewish world domination. It would comprise the text from a Jewish leader to his most loyal followers, about the method of international Jews to obtain world power. By spreading the message of the French Revolution - liberty, equality, fraternity - propagating liberalism, human rights and atheism (and keeping far away from them themselves), that world power would fall to them.[70] The protocols were probably a tsarist forgery, but they suddenly gained global attention. The communists did what they could to curb anti-Semitism, for they realised only too well that anti-Semitism was tantamount to anti-communism in the eyes of many. When the 'white' forces proved on the losing side in the civil war, the *Protocols* emigrated with them to the Weimar Republic. By then, at least 100,000 Jews had been killed in the pogroms in Russia.[71]

The identification of communism and Judaism would remain an important factor in the ideological thinking of the Nazis. According to the Nazis, there was a great affinity between Semiticism and communist ideology. Indeed, communism opposed property and this property was found in the cities and the Nazi agrarian ideologue on the farms, Darré stressed. The semite was originally a nomad who opposed the unlawful appropriation of land by settlers. Communism/Bolshevism was therefore sometimes presented as a 'atatised Marxism'. In *Rusland tussen Azië en Europa (Russia between Asia and Europe)*, F.J. Los describes this semitic-nomadic slant as the 'Scythian element' of Russia. The choice of Scythians is no accident; more than with any other people, this illiterate people's alleged looting and plundering was an unctuous horror anecdote about dark days of yore that captured the imagination. 'If the Scythians saw even a speck on the horizon,' Los mused, 'they rushed to destroy it.' The Scythian passion was for the barren plains, the endless distances, nature in its nakedness. According to this line of thinking, the Bolshevik state of mind was reducible to ancient, nomadic instincts. The leaders of the Bolshevik revolution would carry the outward traces of this with them. Of Lenin, according to Los, it was clear to see that he was a 'full-blooded Asian, half Mongol, with its typical traits: a balanced character and ascetic attitude to life'. He hardly needed anything for himself: 'a typical nomad'. Other Bolshevik leaders, such as Trotsky, were also described in this way, emphasising his Jewish background (Bronstein). Hitler, Nazi propaganda and the geopolitical thinkers behind the Lebensraum question would continue to appeal to comparisons of this kind throughout the Third Reich. The *Bauerntum*, Hitler believed, was the stronghold of the (Germanic) peoples and its destruction 'the condition of Jewish world domination'.[72]

Such theses were not merely recorded in private among confidants from Hitler's mouth but found their way into *Der Nationalsozialis-*

tische Führungsoffizier, a *Schulungs-blad* for internal use in the Wehrmacht. From this point of view, Jewish sources were also gratefully quoted, such as the 1919 *Jewish Chronicle* where this thesis was underlined: 'Of great significance is the fact ... that so many Jews are Bolshevists ... that the ideals of Bolshevism correspond in many respects to the highest ideals of Judaism.' As additional 'proof' of the Jewish leading role in the genesis of Bolshevism, it was also put forward that the symbol of Bolshevism, the star, was also the Jewish symbol: the star of David.[73]

The Jewish-Bolshevik unity thesis was frequently embraced within spiritual circles too. In his *Grundlagen des Nationalsozialismus,* Bishop Dr Alois Hudal believed that wherever Bolshevism (Hudal speaks of Marxism) came to power, it deliberately used its positions to favour the local Jewish population. In return, the Jews gave great (financial) support. Hudal specifically mentioned Jewish support for the *Umsturzparteien* in Austria, Germany and Hungary.[74]

From Yiddish there was a translated novel by M. Alberton, which reported on an autonomous Jewish Soviet republic in the east around the town of Birobidschan, formerly Tichonkaya. 8,000 kilometres east of Moscow and 1,000 kilometres from Vladivostok, a Jewish republic, larger than Belgium, twice the size of Palestine, was supposed to emerge on 3,862.682 hectares of land. The area, 60 per cent mountainous, was bisected 392 kilometres by the Trans-Siberian railway and was barely inhabited except for some 18,000 Cossacks and some (White) Russians. In beautiful prose, Alberton described the unprecedented opportunities for Jews in this area. There was rich flora, raw materials and fish in the Amur River. With its six sovchos and factories, Birobidschan could become a model example of the Soviet republics. For the Nazis, *Birobidschan, die Judenrepublik* was yet another 'proof' of the direct connection between Bolshevism and Judaism. In practice, as is evident when we read Albertton, the Jewish-Russian relationship was anything but easy. Russians were addressed with the teasing *'kazap'*; for the Ukrainians, the abusive term *'chochol'* applied.[75]

Incidentally, it was not only the Nazis who were sensitive to the alleged Jewish-Bolshevik links. The Nazis' henchmen in Western and especially Eastern Europe - the latter of which often carried out eager executioner work - shared this view. What the Latvian historian and journalist Professor Mavriks Vulfsons in Riga said about this in 1944 is interesting. The Jews, he argued, were primarily accused of being favourably disposed to the Soviet occupation of Latvia in the summer of 1940. Vulfsons could not deny this, but at the same time acknowledged that the Jews also had little choice. In fact, they had to choose between death or Stalinism. Vulfsons' argument was Margolina's thesis in a nutshell.[76] Welcome help for the Nazis came from neutral side, the Swedish frequent writer, explorer and geographer Sven Hedin, who in *Duitschland en de wereldvrede* (*Germany and World Peace*, 1937) did not approve of the anti-Jewish hatred in Germany but found it understandable because of the Bolshevik threat. Remarkably, Hedin made no distinction between the council revolutionaries and the (social-democratic) rulers of the Weimar Republic. For him, both were communist and Jews played an evil role in these political movements. In a kind of early-Nolte-like attitude, he characterised Hitler's counter-reaction as a kind of pre-emptive response; hardly tactical but inevitable. The fact that Hedin himself had Jewish blood in his veins, and was not secretive about it, made his thesis even more piquant.[77]

The Nazis' narrow focus on Jewish-Communist relations was a simplification of reality. Sonja Margolina made it clear how complex Jewish-communist relations actually were. The Nazi camp showed itself blind to the right eye as well, where Jews had played an important role in the conservative camp. For instance, one of the founders of Prussian conservatism, Julius Stahl, was of Jewish origin, and Eduard Simson played an important role in the German-national movement. Jewish efforts on the German side in World War I - 12,000 of them died in the trenches - were also ignored or denied.[78]

Therefore, the harshness of German anti-Semitism and their belief in a Jewish-Communist conspiracy and even a world conspiracy goes back further than the Communist revolution in Russia. Groundbreaking research on this has been done by Norman Cohn[79], who investigated the roots of the *Protocols of Zion*. Cohn sees political anti-Semitism - the belief in a Jewish world conspiracy - as the successor to ancient Christian anti-Semitism, which depicted Jews as devil-worshippers. Political anti-Semitism painted Jews as a people with a secret government with global ramifications, networks and organisations through which government leaders, parties, banks and the economy were covertly directed. The ultimate goal was world domination and, it was said, that moment was almost upon us.

The *Protocols* was just one of the many works in which the 'conspiracy' was revealed. The earliest trail leads to France, to Abbé Barruel, *Memoire pour servir á l'histoire de Jacobisme*. Barruel wrote this book out of horror for the French Revolution that had overthrown the old, familiar order. According to the French cleric, the French Revolution was the result of a diabolical conspiracy in which Templars, Jews and Freemasons reached out to each other. The Templars, Barruel claimed, had not disbanded in 1314 but had gone underground and infiltrated Jews. Their aim had been to destroy the papacy, overthrow the monarchies and establish the world republic over which they would rule. In the 18th century, the conspirators had subjugated the Freemasons and had infiltrated several monarchies. They had established a literary academy to which Voltaire, Diderot, d'Alembert and Turgot belonged, secretly undermining the authority of the monarchies. By 1776, a huge revolutionary apparatus of about half a million men, the later Jacobins, had been put in place. The French Revolution they launched was a first step towards world domination. With Abbé Barruel, the myth of the Jewish world conspiracy was born, the transition from a religious anti-Semitism to a political anti-Semitism made. A first step towards what Goldhagen would eventually characterise as 'eliminationist anti-Semitism'. Other similar works soon followed, including by Scottish mathematician John Robinson, Herman Goedsche and Biarritz, who named one of his chapters *'Auf dem Judenkirchhof in Prag'* - the similarity to the *Protocols* is remarkable.[80]

It is interesting to reflect on Coudenhove-Kalegri, who pointed out the one-dimensional nature of the conspiracy theory as early as the mid-1930s. According to Coudenhove-Kalegri, anti-Semitism did not stem from the French Revolution and its consequences, but rather from the *slow ebbing away* of the ideals of the French Revolution causing old prejudices to take over again. This brought him fierce criticism from the Völkisch camp, which was also critical of the *Pan-Europa-Bewegung* behind which Coudenhove was the driving force. Above all, his statement that the 'coming man' would be a '*Mischling*' stung them.[81]

The impact of the perception that Jews and communists, and the revolutionary plans linked to them, were two hands in the same belly is still part of debate. Notable and most far-reaching in his conclusion on this is undoubtedly Richard Pipes. The latter argues in his *Russia under the Bolshevik Regime* that the Holocaust was one of the unexpected *consequences* of the Russian revolution.[82] Pipes is supported in this by Ernst Nolte, who has increasingly come to see National Socialism as a *reaction* to communism, indeed, ultimately saw the holocaust as a *consequence* of the Jewish 'declaration of war' on Nazi Germany. Now, in this respect, Nolte is a research subject in his own right. Over the years, he has put forward no fewer than eight different theories from which the holocaust is alleged to have emerged: fallout, Jewish declaration of war on Germany, as a punitive measure against partisan activities and in support of occupation politics, as revenge for Stalin's deportation of the Wolga Germans, as a fight against communism, the holocaust as an imitation of Marxist mass murders, the holocaust as a reckoning with the political left, and the holocaust as an act of anti-intellectualism. So Nolte is not very consistent in his views.[83]

Even earlier work, such as Emil Franzel in his *Das Reich der braunen Jakobiner*, pointed to a certain exemplary role of Soviet Russia for Nazi Germany. Before 1933, pogroms were an unknown concept in Western Europe and occurred only in Eastern Europe. Franzel further believes that indeed a large proportion of Jews were favourably disposed towards the left wing of politics, which is not surprising given the arguments Margolina puts forward. What is remarkable is Franzel's assertion that the hundreds of years old Talmud schooling of the Jews played a role in this. The talmudic schools were known for their abstract thinking, which 'fitted in well' with the thought pattern of Marxism.[84]

Indeed there are similarities between the ruthless methods of communists and National Socialists, noting that communism effortlessly dwarfed the crimes of National Socialism. In two thorough studies, Robert Conquest has explained the ways in which communists got rid of political opponents. In *The Great Terror*, Conquest calculated that in Ukraine alone, 18.3 per cent of the population was murdered by the communists. Even before one shot of World War II had sounded, 13.5 million Soviet citizens had already fallen victim to red terror. Even in its political promise (promising everyone what they wanted), the Soviet state seemed a worthy precursor of Nazi Germany. In a recent study, Russia experts Marcel van Hamersveld and Michiel Klinkhamer pointed out that communism was a 'messianism without compassion' in which Lenin and consorts killed entire classes.[85]

Not only methodically but ideologically and electorally as well, there were remarkable similarities between communism and National Socialism. A great example is the book *Der verratene Sozialismus* by K.I. Albrecht, which was sold by hundreds of thousands just before and during the war in Germany. The book had been written by a 'communist regretting' optimist and the book title alone spoke volumes. The preface to the *Volksausgabe referred to* Operation Barbarossa, the attack on the Soviet Union, the fight *for* socialism, *against* Bolshevism.[86] Here we see the swerving policy of the Nazis: now emphasising their right-wing, völkisch side, and then appealing to their left-wing 'socialist' sides. In the monumental Goebbels biography by British historian Irving, who studied the propaganda minister's secret diaries in Moscow, the often inner ideological struggle of high-ranking Nazis between their socialist ideals and their national sentiments and völkisch ideas becomes clear. This then led to painful choices and deep conflicts, such as between Goebbels and the Strasser brothers.[87]

Historian Gunnar Heinsohn attributes the lack of consistency in explanations of the Holocaust to the 'desperation' of the world after Auschwitz. It seems as if the enormous dimension of genocide cannot be captured in a conclusive theory. Heinsohn inventoried the various explanations why Auschwitz could exist and came up with 42 different theories.[88] The current debate pits a number of theories against each other. The best works, such as by Raul Hilberg[89] and Arno J.

Mayer,[90] point out that, on the one hand, the Holocaust had strong ideological, worldview roots and stemmed from anti-Semitic sentiments of various backgrounds; on the other hand, as the *Funktionalists* (such as Martin Broszat, for example) rightly point out in the debate, Auschwitz was a *zwangsläufiges Zufallsprodukt*, as well as, as the *Intentionalists* (Christopher Browning, for example) claim, something that could only have taken place at Hitler's command. The controversial British historian David Irving oscillates between the two camps and revisionism.[91]

This lack of a simple explanation partly leads to the tense atmosphere in which the debate on Jewish-Communist relations is conducted. In his article *Der Jude als Bolschewist: Die Wiedererlebung eines Stereotyps* by Daniel Gerson in *Antisemitismus in Deutschland, Zur Aktualität eines Vorurteils*[92] , Gerson blames the weekly *Die Zeit for* the positive review of Margolina's book. According to Gerson, such books risk reviving the old stereotype of the Jewish Bolshevik. The emphasis on Jewish involvement in communism turns Jews into 'perpetrators' within communism and ('deserved') victims of 'reactive' Nazism. In his defence of this, Gerson largely proceeds to *deny* the Jewish-communist relationship. Yet, even this does not serve the truth. The reality is that there is no black-and-white proposition here. The Jews played a not insignificant role within communism, which, as we have seen, is also quite explainable, but they were not identical to communists.[93]

Jews were also victims of communism. Recent research by Richard Pipes, published in *The Unknown Lenin*,[94] shows Lenin's icy indifference to the fate of Jews. Where he could recruit them for the dirty work, he took shameless advantage of their flight to the front. When alarming reports were submitted to Lenin by Jewish communists about anti-Semitic pogroms by the Red Army on their retreat from Poland, Lenin prefaced them with the short phrase 'for the archive' and let the murderers go free.[95]

Recently, more has come to light about Stalin's anti-Semitism. Based on newly released material in his book *Stalin against the Jews*, Russian journalist Arkady Vaksberg concludes that Stalin was a heartfelt anti-Semite. Although he grew up in Georgia, which had 'only' mild anti-Semitism, Stalin soon adopted the brash, Russian anti-Semitism. The reasons for this lay in his hatred of Jewish power within the Communist Party. Stalin was treated rather paternalistically by Jewish 'comrades' who had a much better education, which produced a brewing inferiority complex. In addition, Jews like Lev Kamenev (Rozenfeld), Filipp Goloschekin and Yakov Sverdlov were direct competitors of his. Stalin, according to Vaksberg, always hid his anti-Semitism in a sophisticated way. For this purpose, among others, both his secretaries, Lev Mekhlis and Grigori Kanner, were Jewish. However, wherever he could, he dealt mercilessly with his Jewish competitors. In the military purges of the 1930s, almost all Jewish officers in the Red Army were murdered. Towards the end of his life, Stalin's public displays of anti-Semitism grew stronger and stronger. In addition to his work-related anti-Semitism, Stalin was also not insensitive to the more mystical popular anti-Semitism prevalent in the Soviet Union, according to Vaksberg. He points here to the case of the Jew Mendel Beilis, suspected of the kabbalistic, ritualistic murder of 13-year-old Andrei Yushchinsky in Kiev in March 1911. This case triggered a fierce anti-Semitic wave through the country which was similar to the French Dreyfus case, led to international protest and evoked similarities with the 'ritual murder' of Esther Solymosi from Hungarian Tiszaeszlár of which the Jew Josef Scharf was suspected.[96]

While Pipes paints the holocaust as a reaction to the communist revolution and Nolte and Gerson get worked up about it, Sebastian Haffner underlines a not unimportant sideline in this discussion, namely that communism could only succeed in Russia as a result of German superpower drive. In doing so, he places cause and effect back in history in reverse order. In his introductory chapter of *The Devil's Pact*, Haffner states that everyone knows that the Bolshevik October Revolution was the work of Lenin, who had travelled to Russia from his Swiss exile in April 1917. Much less known is the fact that this trip was on German initiative and that the 'decision' to send Lenin had been taken by the highest German authorities, the Chancellor, the Supreme Command of the Armed Forces, the Foreign Ministry and several German ambassadors. This had to do with the fact that Germany had decided to 'revolutionise' the war on the Eastern Front - where a militarily decisive turn of events was not in sight. This is a remarkable decision, because until then, Europe had been a more or less homogeneous European community of states despite all its disagreements and conflicts, with feudal rulers forming an exclusive club who did fight each other but also had a common interest in the survival of the system. Nevertheless, after seriously studying Lenin, his supporters in Russia and his writings, the Germans decided to put their cards on the 'revolutionisation' of Russia, which was a 'revolutionary' decision. As early as February 1915, the Archduke of Hesse, brother-in-law of the tsar, had stressed the need for peace in the east and concentration on the front in the west. 'Surely it should not be difficult to come to an agreement with the tsar,' he mused. That was right. At the time, the eastern front had stiffened on Russia's border with Poland and the Baltic states, and in the process Russia had no real war aims in Germany, and where it did have them, they were directed above all against the Habsburg Empire and Turkey. The reason why the German political leadership did not respond to this was because a 'status quo' peace was rejected. In September 1914, Bethmann-Hollweg had formulated the German war aims and had come to the conclusion that Germany had to be freed from her encirclement once and for all. That meant weakening France to the point where it would never again be a superpower. Russia had to be kept off the eastern border of the empire by breaking Russian rule over the vassal states to the east. In fact, the undersecretary for foreign affairs, Arthur Zimmermann, formulated the Eastern Europe policy as early as November 1914: 'If we do not now thoroughly deal with our eastern neighbour, we must with certainty prepare ourselves for new difficulties and for another war with him, perhaps already within a few years.'

Since Germany set itself such far-reaching goals, the 'rules' of the diplomatic and political game were violated. With Russia, not only was peace to be made, Russia had to be truly defeated. Since this could not be expected on the battlefield, the option chosen was the revolutionisation of tsarist Russia, despite the fact that the German imperial authorities had little sympathy for the dangerously utopian ideas of the Marxists. As a result of this process, a garland of states of core Russia had to be vacated: Finland, the Baltic States, Poland, Ukraine and the Caucasus. To achieve this, a Pandora's box was opened. The Third Reich would last for 12 years, but the spectre of communism would dominate Russia for more than 70 years, still forming a shroud over central and eastern Europe. The Germans had indeed made, as Sebastian Haffner so eloquently describes it, 'a pact with the devil'. Haffner rightly sees this as one of the greatest and dramatic mortal sins committed by the Wilhelmine Empire.[97] Combating the legacy that resulted from this pact constituted one of Hitler's main political goals.

The German role in the revolutionisation of Russia, incidentally, again led to myth-making in Poland. Antipathies against Jews and Germans had long been pooled in Poland. Indeed, in the eyes of nationalist Poles, both groups claimed exclusivity: the Jews by virtue of the fact that, unlike in Western Europe, they had remained largely Orthodox. The Germans appealed to their völkisch worldview, still seeing themselves as a vanguard of the *Deutschtum* in the East. In this, the Jews were cynically seen by the Poles as a 'German vanguard' in their country. After all, they spoke a kind of 'flawed German', came from the West and had many contacts with the West. Additionally, it was the German Jew Karl Marx whose ideas with German money had caused the revolution in Russia. When the Soviets invaded Poland in 1920, there was soon talk of a fifth column composed of Jews and Germans.[98]

Contrary to conspiracy theories about the role of Jews in communism, they fell between two stools, as had been the case previously in Russian history. Turning away from communism had become impossible. If the noose became looser, they would fall victim to an axe. On the other hand, non-Jewish communists kept eternal anti-Semitism up their sleeves as a secret card and, if necessary, played it against them.[99] By the way, such noises are still not a thing of the past in Eastern Europe, given the perils surrounding Auschwitz in Poland, where the murder of Poles (not Jews) is still systematically talked about.[100]

Of course, the Nazis and Hitler had no regard for this complicated reality of the Jews in Russia or the German role in the success of the

Russian revolution and the many similarities between the repressive, communist system and National Socialism. The Jewish double role of victim and perpetrator and hand-in-hand, did not fit their racial views. Nor did Hitler seem to see the fact that Jews had played a significantly larger role above all in the early years in Soviet Russia (until 1922) than afterwards.[101] According to him, Jews were the evil mastermind behind communism, which in turn was a plot to subjugate the Aryan world as once the Huns had done. These views were reinforced by the fact that after the debacle of World War I, the council republic and communism permeated Germany. Consequently, the revolution of 9 November 1918 made a deep impression on Hitler. In Germany, Karl Liebknecht proclaimed the 'free socialist republic'; the Kaiser fled to the Netherlands.

Major tensions persisted from 1919 to 1923, the year Hitler committed his Putsch. During this time of 'consolidation', there was an extremely fierce polarisation of political views. In fact, there was only a choice between two models: western democracy and the council society as it was shaped in the young Soviet Union.[102] Ultimately, it was this ongoing polarisation that paved the way for a 'third way': National Socialism.

Internal German documents show that the Nazis did take the Soviet Union and Bolshevism seriously as a danger, despite Hitler's haughtiness about the impending collapse. This was clearly reflected in the important document *Allgemeine Richtlinien für die politische und wirtschaftliche Verwaltung der besetzten Ostgebiete, which* was prepared for operation 'Barbarossa'. The guidelines systematically listed the main geopolitical factors:

- the Soviet Union has aggressive intentions and has never made a secret of it;
- the Soviet Union's entire industry was set up for war production;
- the communist international is an umbrella organisation for communist parties worldwide;
- communist parties worldwide are undermining the regimes of the countries in which they exist and trying to spark civil war;
- in case of war between two nations, communists will turn their

weapons on their own officers;
- in the newly occupied territories of eastern Europe (Poland, parts of Finland, the Baltic States, Bessarabia), the Soviet Union amassed so much weaponry that it became an arsenal that posed a direct threat to Germany's borders.[103]

For this dilemma, it offered two solutions. Germany could join the arms race with the Soviet Union and adopt a defensive posture. On the other hand, Germany could try to deal with the *Ostproblem* once and for all.

In concrete terms, this meant:

- destruction of the Red Army;
- rearrangement of the country according to völkisch insights;
- connection of border areas to the *Reich* (as, for example, with the Warthegau);
- exploit Ukraine and the Caucasus for Germany in such a way that the German empire would become *Blockadefest* - i.e. autarkic and impervious to hunger blockades as in World War I - and militarily so great and strong that it would be unbeatable.[104]

It concluded that the second option, the offensive, was preferable to the arms race, given that it could be 'endless' and gave no real guarantee of stability. The result of this thinking was that Hitler saw Eastern Europe, and Russia in particular, as ripe for German invasion. The Jewish-Bolshevik leadership would have turned tsarist Russia into chaos, and 'one only had to kick in the door and the whole rotten edifice', Hitler told himself, 'would collapse'. This notion was reinforced by the weak performance of the Soviet army in the war against Finland, which had only 10 divisions and hardly any heavy equipment. In the winter war of 1939-1940, the Soviet Union, which threw 26 divisions into battle, lost 1,500 tanks and 3,000 aircrafts, hundreds of thousands of soldiers and achieved remarkably little success. The Germans had seen the defeat of the 163rd and 44th infantry divisions at Suomussalmi and the 139th and 75th divisions at Tolvajärvi, which were ruthlessly slaughtered by Finnish officers Talvela and Siilasvuo, as symptomatic of having 'feet on clay'. The Red Army was powerful in numbers but poorly led. The Red Army's earlier successes, the destruction of the 6th Japanese Kwantung Army near the Halha River (Khalkin-Gol) in August 1939 by Georgi Zhukov, were overlooked. In the process, the weak performance hardly affected the totally controlled public opinion in the Soviet Union, as it knew no better than that a victory had been won. Nikita Khrushchev later confessed that it had been the Soviet Union's deepest moral defeat, but it slipped away from the Soviet people like an angry shadow.

A few months after the invasion, when dozens of Russian divisions had already been destroyed but new ones were being discovered at every turn, Hitler mused that he 'would never have started it if he had known how strong the Red Army was'. He had ignored the advice of the directive that recommended exploiting anti-communist sympathies in Belarus and Ukraine in particular, which could win him the support of eighty million people. In particular, the support of the peasantry was vital to bring in the harvest. The German occupation army of 1917/1918, 750,000 strong, had failed to circumvent the passive resistance of the Ukrainian peasants to turn in the harvest. Russian terror had been unprecedentedly bloody, but it had also failed to give Moscow what it wanted.[105] However, Hitler took a rigid and inflexible stance. Operation 'Barbarossa', more than any other battle, was his war: that of the new Germanism against the Jewish-Slavic, Bolshevik East. Compromises were not made in the process.

Only on the darkest aspect did he join hands with the locals. The propaganda of the Jewish-Bolshevik synthesis coupled with long-standing, traditional anti-Semitism made the locals support the *Einsatzgruppen* and the SS in their bloody work. In the same Ukraine where the 'whites' had raged in the civil war, Ukrainian militias emerged and eagerly assisted the German executioners.[106] The identification Jew-Bolshevik appealed to the worldview of part of the population of the occupied territories. The poison also seeped into the German army. On 12-09-1941, for instance, the Chief OKW reported that 'the fight against Bolshevism had to be pursued hard and energetically and that, above all, Jews had to be targeted because they were the *Hauptträger* of Bolshevism'. Other documents from that time - even before the Holocaust was ordered in the Wannsee Conference - breathed this atmosphere too.[107]

From the above, we can conclude that the Nazis' Lebensraum philosophy went hand in hand with racial doctrine and formed the very basis of the Third Reich's worldview. They were the drivers of Hitler's actions, the drivers behind the outbreak of World War II. An 'outbreak' that Walter Hofer quite rightly described not as an 'outbreak' but as an 'unleashing'. For this unleashing, Germany bore primary responsibility.[108] Here, the facets of Lebensraum and racial theory were intertwined and had another similarity: they both went down in 1945. The German Empire collapsed after 12 destructive years, National Socialism disappeared as an ideology. Most European Jews had been killed; the Nazis had 'won' this war.

The consequences of these events continue to affect us to this day. The constantly resurgent *Historikerstreit*, as well as the relatively late discovery of Hitler's motivations, both in terms of the Holocaust and Lebensraum, are characteristic of this. In 1996, new facets were added again to this ongoing debate. A year after the 50th anniversary, the *Historikerstreit* was once more in the spotlight due to the Daniel Jonah Goldhagen discussion. According to this young Harvard professor, in his *Hitler's Willing Executioners*[109], just about every German is guilty of the Holocaust. However, Ernst Nolte's view opposes this; he narrows the discussion of Nazi Germany by arguing that fascism can *only* be understood *through Hitler's writings*. Both views have a grain of truth in them: National Socialism could only be carried out and implement its grand and destructive plans if a large part of the German and even European population was willing to cooperate. Yet, on the other hand, National Socialism was the work of a handful of fanatics. Hitler took 10 years to fight his way to power and National Socialism was inconceivable without him. Like all great dictators and totalitarian rulers, Hitler toyed with the masses, coquetted with their attention, had supporters, but was lonely at the same time.

The downside of Nolte and Goldhagen's overly polarised theses is that they are not only historically unbalanced, but they also miss the mark. By declaring everyone 'guilty', as Goldhagen does, he is effectively declaring everyone collectively innocent simultaniously. After all, what then is the difference between the law-abiding bourgeois who tried to survive between 1933 and 1945 and an Adolf Eichmann, a 'Schreibtisch' murderer who, in his own words, 'was only carrying out orders'? With Nolte, too, there is this imbalance. By placing fascism - or rather National Socialism - so strongly in Hitler's shoes, he leaves the German people and collaborators in other countries more innocent than they are. That too is a *Verharmlosung* of history.

In addition, both views are driven too much by the delusion of the day, the political correctness of the moment.[110] It is better to concentrate on how a certain frame of mind was able to emerge that made a Lebensraum field trip possible, that set the Auschwitz machinery in motion. For more than holding any one person or group of people responsible for it, it was this state of mind that laid the foundation for Hitler's 12-year rule. During this time, from 1933 to 1945, this mindset was created for the general public, introduced, cultivated, institutionalised and finally transformed into a vital, driving force behind campaign and destruction: Stalingrad and Auschwitz.

In the following chapters, it is therefore important to chart the zeitgeist, the elusive spiritual *Umfeld* of the Lebensraum field trip. Not one man, or a particular group provided the ingredients. They were of all sorts: politicians and military personnel, university students and geopoliticologists, philosophers and Stammtisch scholars, völkisch writers, racists and anti-Semites, romantics and downright idiots.

*'Sie haben uns den Raum gestohlen.
Wir haben uns den Raum stehlen lassen.'*

Hans Grimm in 'Volk ohne Raum'

'In Germany, Traum and Trauma differ by only one letter.'

Henri Beunders in the nrc-Handelsblad 04-05-1996

*'Deutschland, aber wo liegt es?
Ich weiss das Land nicht zu finden.
Wodas Gelehrte beginnt, hört das Politische auf.'*

Friedrich Schiller

Chapter 2

The Schreibtisch conquerors

Karl Haushofer, geopoliticologist, frequent writer and inspirer of the Lebensraum idea - Evil magician? - Thule - *Erfüllungspolitik* - *Meereskunde* and the eternal struggle against water - Britain, Venice and Japan - Plan Goergel, the draining of the Mediterranean - Mitteleuropa, Kjellén and the Berlin-Baghdad-Bombay land bridge - Where is Central Europe? What is Europe? - *Verstümelung, Versklavung, Einkreisung* - The natural unity of Russia - Devil's belt and natural rights - Hess, Landsberg am Lech and *Mein Kampf* - Hitler a Clausewitz connoisseur? - Haushofer's mental ammunition - The conquerors from the plains - Hess flies to Britain - Dachau - Haushofer and Brzezinski - Mediocre minds - Suicide - Mackinder's empire blocks - Lebensraum, *Kernraum* - Descent theories and myths for legitimisation and supremacy - Pax Romana versus Germania - Grosswirtschaftsraum - Apocalyptic coercive theory: Lebensraum or *Weltuntergang*

Karl Haushofer was the figurehead of the young discipline of geopolitics. Geopolitics is the science that investigates whether there are laws that apply to inter-state relations. Given the greatly changed power-political constellation in Europe as a result of World War I, the new field attracted warm interest from students and media. Geopolitics made a huge splash in the mid-1920s. Professors of geography and history looked with envy at Haushofer's packed lecture halls, where sometimes as many as four hundred students were crammed in to not miss a word of his lecture, in which Stresemann's *Erfüllungspolitik* was given a run for its money. Haushofer's popularity meant that many of his fellow professors kept him quiet. They would have been better off replying to him and entering into discussion with him. Still, Haushofer had the tide with him and nobody seemed willing to stick their necks out to comment on Haushofer's harsh criticism of the geopolitics of the Weimar Republic. And so he lectured his students on what the optimal Germany should look like, how much area a 'growing empire' needed, what the ratio of raw materials to industry should be, and how many divisions of soldiers you could get out of a million citizens. Only from abroad, through Frenchman Jacques Ancel, came subject-oriented commentary. Ancel criticised the methods Haushofer used. In doing so, he rightly worried about the side effects of Haushofer's thinking, and the influence his writings would have on pan-Germanism. This concern was not unjustified. Accordingly, agronomist Konrad Meyer would later draft, with other scholars, the so-called *Generalplan Ost*, the geographic-demographic and political roadmap of the plundering and reshaping of Eastern Europe. In academia, the voices were silent.

This was mainly due to the fact that there was a general feeling of dissatisfaction with the German place under the sun. This thought was particularly prevalent in the völkisch movement, which sentimentally emphasised Germanness. To illustrate the broad-based German dissatisfaction with the new geopolitical power constellation, it is worth recalling the huge box-office success of Hans Grimm's *Volk ohne Raum*.[1] In this melancholic, monumental work of 1353 pages, Grimm sketches the *Werdegang* of Cornelius Friebott. Friebott leaves Germany as a young man and emigrates to Africa. There, after World

War I, he is forced by the British to return to his homeland. There is no place for Germans in the 'overseas'. However, the homeland also lacks the *'Raum'*. Hemmed in between Wasgen and Böhmerwald, Baltic Sea and Russia, Friebott- and with him the German nation- petered out. *Volk ohne Raum* became a mega-bestseller. Published in 1926, the book was reprinted at least 68 times over the years. The book apparently impressed Hitler so much that he used the title ver- batim in an interview with journalist Ward Price in the *Daily Mail*. Asked about the German position on the Danzig corridor, Hitler complained that the Germans were a *'Volk ohne Raum'*.[2] Haushofer's new science seemed to be able to provide answers to the questions of the people without space. For Hitler, this was of particular impor- tance.

Karl Haushofer owed his success mainly to the large number of publications. He discovered the writing profession relatively late. After a career as a senior military officer, he had started writing later in life. His penmanship was something of a catch-up for him. In total, he delivered no less than five hundred texts, all *'Bausteine zur Geopolitik'*, as he called one of his works. Hauhofer published for various magazines such as *Deutsche Rundschau, Deutsche Allgemeine Zeitung, Das Neue Reich, Münchener Neueste Nachrichten* and the magazine *Führerschaft* of the veterans' organisation 'Stahlhelm'. Linked to his books and articles was a journal of geopolitics, which grew to 12,000 subscriptions over the years. In addition, Haushofer could be heard monthly on the radio with his *Weltpolitischer Monats- bericht*. Haushofer was a member of the 'ns-Dozentenbund' and the 'ns-Lehrerbund'. He was in several völkisch-nationalist organisations that demanded a revision of the Versailles Treaty, such as Karl C. Loesch's *Deutsche Schutzbund,* which advocated *Volkstumsarbeit* out- side the borders of the *Reich* and was in favour of *'ein deutsches Reich, das alle geschlossene deutsche Siedlungsgebiete umfasst'*. These ideas cor- responded to the pan-Germanist ideas of the *Alldeutscher Verband,* which effortlessly saw the Netherlands and Flanders, as well as Swit- zerland (and Austria), as part of the *Deutschtum*. Haushofer was affil- iated with both the 'Volksbund für das deutschtum im Ausland' and the reactionary *Deutsche Akademie* in Munich. In addition, he held lectures for *Stahlhelm*, *Wehrwolf* and the *Bund Deutscher Osten*. Conservative big industrialists could also count on a lecture from Haushofer, such as the Opel factories and I.G. Farben. Haushofer was geopolitical adviser to the Freikorps 'Oberland', later the 'Bund Oberland'. In Haushofer's wake followed other geopolitical thinkers of his time, such as Erich Obst, Hermann Lautensach, Otto Maul, Hugo Hassinger and Swedish geopolitical scientist Rudolf Kjellén.[3]

Haushofer liked to dedicate his work to military men, such as German admirals Paul Behnke and Carl Holweg, and had a predilection for *'volkstümliche politische Meereskunde'*, in which conquest and racism approached each other. Haushofer's two great examples were the British empire and the city of Venice- as the exclusive synthesis between land and water. Haushofer had a fear of confined and bounded space. The world sea, he believed, had to become free. Free, incidentally, in his interpretation meant an open sea for the 'three-power pact': Germany, Italy and Japan. The seas and the new borders would mean conquerors should prevent countries from otherwise *'kleinräumig verkümmerten'*. Navigating the world's seas and the conquest it entailed would be very instructive for a nation, Haushofer believed. The sea was the best teacher for man because it was so demanding. Indeed, the power of the sea was infinite and peoples who defied its power would remain in eternal struggle and strengthen themselves as a result. As the best example of the good qualities that battle with the sea brought, Haushofer cited the British empire. According to him, the British were able to conquer the world with a handful of people because their country was born from the children of seafarers. The British were the direct descendants of Romans, Angles, Saxons, Danes and Normans, adventurers, heroes and conquerors, the best of their kind. To such men the world belonged, according to Haushofer.[4]

Opinions about Haushofer still vary widely. Some see him primarily as the spiritual father of a strong united German empire; a champion and builder of German unity, while others see him as an evil magician, the man who invented the swastika and instilled Hitler's dangerous Lebensraum philosophies. They point out that he would be a member of the secret racial Thule Society. Such a connection would put Haushofer in the camp of dangerous 'ariosophical' dreamers. British Trevor Ravenscroft went a step further and even believed that Haushofer was the man who initiated Hitler into 'the secret teachings' on Aryan descent theories. These teachings bear a strong resemblance to Blavatsky's theosophy. Anti-fascists around Münzenberg emphasised above all the criminal aspects of Haushofer's geopolitical lectures and saw him as the important founder of later Nazi aggression. Others thought of him more innocently and spoke of Haushofer as an unrestrained fantasist. His enemies in his own camp, such as Gauleiter of Halle and Magdeburg Rudolf Jordan, called Haushofer a 'cultist' who had instigated Hess's 'mad plan' to his 'mad flight' to Britain.[5]

The Haushofer controversy is attracting growing interest today. A recent study by Paul Heller and Anton Maegerle distances itself from the claim that Haushofer was a member of the Thule Society. Nor are such claims (true or not) at all necessary to demonstrate Haushofer's influence. There are plenty of sources showing the importance of Haushofer's ideas.

The main similarity between Haushofer and Hitler was the role of the East in both their theories. Haushofer advocated German supremacy in central Europe. Geographers and anti-Germanists raised eyebrows over the exact extent of this 'German East'. It was unclear where Central Europe would merge into Eastern Europe. They also wondered how this supremacy was to be established. Haushofer did not specify precise boundaries, which in this respect puts him on a par with the Völkisch thinkers, who separated the idea of 'nation and state' and assumed 'people and state'.

The agrarian interpretation of this theory was no accident. According to historians Corni and Goes, Nazi Germany was suffering from a blockade syndrome. The war experiences of World War I had left deep marks in the national consciousness. Germany had already lost World War I for agricultural reasons in the spring of 1916. Between 1901 and 1912, Germany's dependence on food imports had almost doubled. Despite this, the empire had entered World War I without a clear food strategy. When the *Kriegsernährungsamt* under Freiherr von Batocki was established in May 1916, it was already too late. The cattle herd had shrunk from 20,9 million to 16,4 million, the pig herd from 25,6 to 9 million. Crops had declined from 20 to 22 per cent. This was mainly due to the large recruitment of rural boys for the front and the switch from civilian industry to the war economy. For instance, this had completely halted the chemical industry's production of fertiliser in favour of production for the armed forces. As a result, the standard of consumption of the German population had fallen dramatically. Herman Reischle calculated that compared to the British, the German population had only 46,1 per cent meat, 50 per cent fat and 68 per cent flour available in 1917. In total, it was estimated that this cost the lives of between 600,000 and 800,000 Germans. Above all, the Nazis wanted to prevent a repeat of this traumatic experience. Lebensraum was to provide a solution to this.[6]

That Haushofer assumed hard power politics in his creation of a German *Mitteleuropa* can be inferred from his admiration for the Swedish geopolitical philosopher Rudolf Kjellén, whose theories we will discuss later. Kjellén advocated *Herrschaftspolitik* for the preservation of *Raum* and very specifically - and this gives some insight into the geographical consequences of the Lebensraum philosophy - advocated a direct land link between Berlin and Baghdad. By this, Kjellén meant a rail link between the two capitals, running entirely over German territory. Kjellén, incidentally, was not alone in such grotesque claims. Franz von Papen also expressed himself in this way in May 1939. On the eve of World War II, he believed, in a *Denkschrift* on the *'deutsche Weltmachtstellung'*, that in order to resist Britain and India, Germany should have a Berlin-Baghdad-Bombay land bridge.[7]

These 'railway thoughts' intrigued Hitler. Railways, like all modern transport technologies that allowed him to move around his *Raum*, captured his imagination. Several times in his table talks, Hitler mused about the importance of great railway routes over which entirely newly designed, super-wide trains would run. Trains that would be equipped with complete libraries, so that the German '*Herrenvolk*' could travel from Berlin to the new German Riviera in Crimea while studying. And perhaps even a train route to Baghdad that would allow them to manage Baghdad's black gold and make

German Orient tourists enjoy the capital of 1001 nights. In any case, Hitler would not have let the vast distances deter him from such plans. His frenzied plan of the Norwegian 'Polar-Eisbahn', running from Fauske to Kirkenes, to secure Scandinavian steel, testifies to this.[8]

Studying Germany's place in Central Europe, even the very concept of Central Europe, was not uncontroversial. Western powers saw the concept as a strongly emerging Germany and preferred to avoid the term. This legacy plays out to this day. As a result of the post-World War II division of Europe, Central Europe once again disappeared from view. Not for nothing did a popular book by George Mikes on this region start with the humorous question *'Where are you, Central Europe?'* [9] Others started their geopolitical analysis of Central Europe after the *Wende* with an even more profound question *'What's Europe? Where is Europe?'*[10] Such conceptualisation was and is particularly important in the Central European region. Hans-Peter Burmeister rightly pointed out that in 'viel-völker'-rich Central Europe, the danger of 'loss of identity' was strong. Constant underlining of one's own identity, something the Nazis and their young state excelled at, was therefore necessary for *nation building*.[11] Hans Hecker called this Central Europe's powder keg position: 'I know of no country in the world that has as many neighbours as Germany.'[12] Only Rudolf Steiner pointed to the great, positive forces emanating from the region. He was primarily interested in the *'Mitteleuropäische Geistesart'*.[13]

Geopolitical thinking on the security and future of central Europe emerged from the military pacts of the First World War. By allying itself with the Habsburg Empire, Bulgaria and Turkey, Germany and its allies literally formed the 'centrals' in Europe. World War I reinforced the orientation towards the East in two more ways. First, because of the German Imperial Army's successes on the Eastern Front. When the Brest-Litowsk peace was signed on the Eastern Front on 3 March 1918, the Germans gained more than they dared hope for. No less than Poland, Finland, Estonia, Latvia, Lithuania and the Ukraine fell into German hands. Leading German journalist Ernst Jäckh, apparently little aware of the impending doom on the western front, triumphantly exclaimed that now the war only needed to end in the west to 'open the way to Asia'. He called the newly conquered territories 'a belt of fringe states' which he labelled 'Central Europe'. In November 1918, that same First World War caused the turnaround in mood and understanding. What had begun as a triumphant expansion ended as a geopolitical *Verstümmelung* and economic *Versklavung* of Germany. From expansion to the east, Germany's future image changed to the doom image of *Einkreisung*, encirclement. The Rhineland, Saar region, Alsace-Lorraine, Tyrol, Austria (Kärten, Südsteiermark, Burgenland), Sudetenland, Hultschinerland, Oberschlesien, Posen, parts of Prussia and Memelland were lost. In total, Germany lost 13 per cent of its territory and 5,350.000 inhabitants.[14] Initially, the success of Brest-Litowsk had convinced the Germans of their mission in the east, their natural supremacy. After the defeat of November 1918, the Germans were convinced of the need to break the chains of encirclement. Here, Haushofer looked primarily to central Europe, an area he dubbed the '*Teufelsgürtel*'.

For him, the diabolical element will no doubt have been in the enormous risks of the mission, which Haushofer, as an intelligent man, naturally did not overlook. Following Mackinder's lead, Haushofer believed in a final battle for *Raum* between Russia and Germany. Russia had every advantage in this respect; it was a *Grosswirtschaftsraum* by nature. Moscow, according to Haushofer, was the eye of origin of the rivers, which meandered like tentacles in all directions. In Germany, the rivers were in an awkward south-north direction (*Parallelschaltung*), which directly reflected the country's geopolitical 'imbalance' due to lack of space. Thereby, Russia, as a 'natural entity', was rich in people and resources and, along with the USA, in fact the only country in the world that could claim this luxury. The other major powers, such as France and Britain, got their treasures from overseas. Germany, along with Italy and Japan, belonged to the *Habenichts*.

This explained all the political tensions. Furthermore, Haushofer believed that the spiritual baggage of Germans was caught in the same geopolitical clamp in which the territory was trapped as well. Nietzsche still best represented the German spirit in this respect. The German philosopher rebelled against the East, (against Jews, Christians and 'Russianism'), but at the same time he also rebelled against the West (*common sense* and democracy). Whereas Nietzsche's sister Elisabeth, along with her racial crusader Bernard Förster fled to Paraguay for a *'Nuevo* Germania'[15] that was not possible in 'space-poor' Germany, Haushofer believed in Germans as the *'Mitteleuropäer'* of the future. Germans were Orientals as well as Westerners. Plagued by lack of space, lack of raw materials and *Volksdruck,* they had to strive for a *Grosswirtschaftsraum.* It was economic autarchy or destruction.

Haushofer's jargon such as 'languishing small states', is the type of jargon Hitler himself liked to use. Haushofer introduced the terms Lebensraum and *Heim ins Reich* and provided the geopolitical argumentation directly with them, tailored to his needs.

The racial background in Haushofer's thought is in line with Hitler's thinking too. By attributing the good qualities of the seafaring peoples in his *Weltmeere und Weltmächte* only to the North Germans and Polynesians, he reinforced the belief in Germanic hegemony.[16] The element of struggle was another fraternising element between Haushofer and Hitler. Whereas Haushofer believed that the eternal struggle between water and man brought out the best - the combative and heroic - in man, Hitler too believed that eternal struggle was an absolute necessity for the survival of mankind. The continental empire he envisaged would have 'open, burning borders' in the east, where the black corps of the SS would live in constant battle with 'barbarians' from the east to ensure purity and strength of the nation.[17]

Following on from this, it is important to note that there was another substantial unifying element between Hitler and Haushofer: they had the same conception of the state. Both saw the state as a 'form of life' to which they applied biological and racial laws, although Haushofer was more moderate regarding the latter. Hitler went so far in this that he even questioned the *survival* of the German people and the German state when it turned out that they were unable to win World War II for him. In his view, states could be 'healthy' - with a well-drilled *Hitler Youth* - or 'sick' and 'infected with bacilli', by fellow Jews. Of influence on Haushofer's and Hitler's idea of the state were the views of the already mentioned Swedish Uppsala professor, geopoliticologist and member of parliament Rudolf Kjellén (1864-

1922), to whose translations into German Haushofer collaborated.¹⁸ The biological interpretation of the concept of state was primarily his. Among his most important works were *Die Grossmächte der Gegenwart, Die politische Probleme des Weltkriegs* and the heavily theoretical *Der Staat als Lebensform*. In the latter book, Kjellén also emphasises race as a *'state bildender'* factor. The factors that (geo) politicians had to take into account regarding the security of the nation were loyalty, nationality, genealogical, linguistic and ethnic backgrounds and the people's psyche. In the last-mentioned book, Kjellén firmly outlined what he saw as an inescapably polemical worldview, in which pan-Germanism (pan-teutonism), pan-Anglicism, pan-Latinism and pan-Slavism fought each other to the death.¹⁹

Apparent contradictions between Haushofer and Hitler were smaller than is often thought. Haushofer's keen interest in naval affairs and Hitler's continental strategy were not as far apart as seemingly appears. It is often claimed of Hitler that fleet and geopolitical maritime concepts interested him little. This is incorrect. During his reign, continental conflict was his top priority. Yet anyone studying his geopolitical playbook will come across a new conflict that Hitler had in mind in the second half of the 20th century. In the 1980s, Hitler believed with foresight, the showdown with the United States would begin and the battle for Lebensraum would spread across the world's oceans. Until then, the Third Reich would confine itself to consolidating Europe from Gibraltar to the Urals and from North Africa to Nova Zembla. Hitler saw the importance of controlling the seas and the influence it gave Europe globally. He ascribed this role only to Britain and the British empire. Hitler spoke of the British with great awe and often repeated that he deeply regretted being at war with the British. He seems to have hated the war against Britain. It was the first and only front he never visited.

Another common element between Haushofer and Hitler was their admiration for Japan. Haushofer wrote a lot about Japan and admired the Japanese as well as the British for their seafaring mentality. Consequently, during the war years, Haushofer published the book *Der Kontinentalblock*, in which he involved the Japanese in the division of the world.²⁰ Haushofer's love for Asia stemmed from the years he himself had spent in Japan. In Germany, he kept in touch with attachés at the Japanese embassy. At German-Japanese diplomatic receptions, Haushofer could be found at the side of Imperial Admiral Yendo. He invited Japanese guests to Munich University and toured the country with them. He greatly appreciated Japanese courtesy. Haushofer repeatedly advocated that Japan was Nazi Germany's natural ally in the fight against the USA and Britain. His warm support for Japan increased even more after the Japanese-Russian fighting in Manchuria, 1938.

Besides admiration for Japan and the British empire, Haushofer and Hitler had their contempt for and underestimation of the USA in common as well. Hitler's December 1941 pointless and almost indifferent declaration of war on the USA- a country with more military economic potential than all other wartime nations put together- illustrates this blatantly. Haushauer's image of the USA oscillated between admiration on the one hand and antipathy on the other. In letters to acquaintances, he spoke of the 'sleepy eagle', the national symbol of the USA, and criticised the American rhetoric of 'the chosen people', a people who, in his view, were 'better off minding their own business'. At other times, he spoke of the USA as the most economically powerful country in the world. Haushofer should have listened better to his own rhetoric; after all, were not Americans too born of seafarers, adventurers and conquerors?[21]

Addtionally, what Haushofer had in common with Hitler was the fact that his dreams sometimes had absurd traits. In his *Weltmeere und Weltmächte,* Haushofer described the serious Goergel plan, provided with the so-called 'Panropa map'. This plan involved nothing less than the draining of the Mediterranean Sea; the closing of the Mediterranean Sea at Gibraltar after which the water surface was to be allowed to slowly dry up. This would create more *Raum* through a land connection between Africa and Asia (Middle East). The water that would be 'released' could be used to water the Sahara.[22] In fact, this was the thousand-fold reclamation of the Pontine Marshes, which Mussolini personally participated in in bared torso - something the prudish Hitler would never do. It was the consummation of the *mare nostrum*, the consummation even of Hitler's immense pincer operation in the Caucasus and North Africa, in which he wanted the German troops advancing south via Grozny, and Rommel's Afrika Korps, to make contact somewhere in Iraq.

We know fairly precisely how Haushofer's ideas got to Hitler. It was indirect, because the self-taught Hitler was never very fond of learned gentlemen. Rudolf Hess, as a student of Haushofer, played an important role in this. Although Hess was certainly not a brilliant student of his, the professor cherished sympathy for the modest Hess, with his bushy eyebrows and his dog-like loyalty. He often sat in the lecture hall with bandages around his head, having used his steel fists the night before against communists who had made it difficult for Hitler to speak in a beer hall. He was also charmed by Hess' sincere attempts to introduce his theories to Hitler.

The Hess-Haushofer relationship was close. Ernst Hanfstaengel even wrote in his memoirs after the war that Hess was mentally highly dependent on Haushofer.[23] Haushofer's intertwining with the Nazi leadership dated back to the early years of the NSDAP. When Hitler's Putsch broke up at the Feldherrnhalle in Munich in 1923, Hess, fleeing by bicycle, sought shelter with the Haushofers. Haushofer condemned the ridiculous plan for revolution but did help Hess go into hiding. When Hess was convicted along with Hitler in 1924 and imprisoned in Landsberg am Lech, Haushofer visited them at least eight times. On his visits, Haushofer brought books such as *Vom Kriege* by Carl von Clausewitz and *Politische Geographie* by Friedrich Ratzel.[24] The regime in prison was lenient. The judge had sentenced Hitler to five years and Hess to 18 months in prison. This was a low sentence considering the seriousness of the offence; Hitler had successfully used his oratorical talent in court. 'The trial,' wrote the *London Times*, 'has at least proved that in Bavaria a conspiracy against the constitution is not considered a serious crime'.[25]

Haushofer always stayed all morning and afternoon and then, of course, saw Hitler. This is an important fact. In these days, Rudolf Hess typed out *Mein Kampf* for him. Shortly after the war, a US government study was published in twentyfold, done by Dr Lemkin, who identified Haushofer as the spiritual father of *Mein Kampf*. The geopolitics pursued by Haushofer, Lemkin believed, was not confined merely to the college benches. It was a dynamic and driven plan for the conquest of Eurasia and world domination. The pan-Germanic endeavour, coupled with the alliance with Japan came directly from Haushofer's mind, according to the American.[26]

Moreover, the Americans noticed that Haushofer's work, as was reported in a letter to the Nuremberg court, had a prophetic character from time to time. On one of his geopolitical maps of the USA and the Pacific, Haushofer had noted just three place names: Pearl Harbor, Hong Kong and Singapore. The Allies' major defeats were lined up on Haushofer's map.[27]

Haushofer, on the other hand, complained that Hess and Hitler understood very little of his theories. If Hess, who was of good will, did understand the lessons, Hitler talked over them, much to Haushofer's annoyance, or gave his own interpretation of them. This was the reason, as Haushofer stated after the war, that he 'fed' Hitler and Hess *Vom Kriege*, the standard work by Prussian war philosopher Carl von Clausewitz.

Unfortunately, this message did not reach Hitler. In particular, the lesson of the miraculous trinity would have been invaluable to him. By the miraculous trinity, Clausewitz meant that decision-making in war should actually be borne by three social facets: prince, general of the field and people. In World War I, the German people had been stateless, and in August 1914 the politicians had put the fate of the country in the hands of the military. The consequences were catastrophic. In the Vietnam War, the war was initially carried only by the political and military leadership. When shocking film footage reached the public it acted correctively. However, World War II was not yet a *television war* like Vietnam. Goebbels' Propaganda Ministry played the German people and Hitler controlled the entire political field and, from 1941, the military field as well. A new catastrophe like 1914-1918 was therefore possible.

If Clausewitz influenced Hitler at all, it was in a negative way. Hitler, who always liked to read to see his own ideas confirmed, still sometimes used Clausewitz to bluff his generals. They had 'understood nothing of Clausewitz or *Vom Kriege*', he believed. What the war was really about, and Hitler was referring to his Lebensraum theory, was the war economy; raw materials for the Third Reich. How Germany was to obtain these was perfectly clear to Hitler after 'studying' Clausewitz, Moltke and Schlieffen. 'First defeat the enemy armies, then occupy the capital'.[28]

Although Haushofer himself was not satisfied with his influence on the Nazis, the Allies thought otherwise. Some of the US war crimes investigators adopted the Soviet view that Haushofer was among the war criminals. Sidney S. Alderman, working for the *Justice Jackson Office*, saw Hitler as 'the symbol of Haushofer's doctrine'. According to the American, Haushofer was therefore among the biggest war criminals known to Nazi Germany.[29] Lemkin and Alderman's views dovetailed with earlier publications outside Germany, about Haushofer and his alleged influence on Hess and Hitler. In the *Daily Express* in December 1939, G.M. Thompson called Haushofer 'the man behind Hitler's war aims'. Haushofer would provide Hitler with spiritual ammunition and characterised his activities as 'the gospel of boundless opportunism'. In Thompson's view, Haushofer also provided the spiritual fuel for Operation 'Barbarossa'. Indeed, confrontation with Russia was 'inevitable' according to Haushofer's theories. The future would be determined by the struggle between coastal states and continental states. The continental states would only be able to face this battle through a tie-up between Germany and Russia, which of course had to take place under German supremacy. Then the war of 'the plains' against 'the coasts' would take place. Suddenly Haushofer - opportunist that he was according to Thompson - seemed to have forgotten his seafaring theories here. The great conquerors, according to Haushofer, always came from the great plains: the Huns, the Vandals, Atilla, Ghengis Khan, Tamerlane.[30]

Although Haushofer declared under oath after the war that he had neither part nor share in *Mein Kampf*, at least some of his theories ended up in it in a perverted manner. Heinz Haushofer, son of the geopoliticologist, stated to a Dutch historian in 1962 that his father had indeed influenced *Mein Kampf*. Haushofer's influence was said to have been particularly strong with regard to Hitler's *Ostpolitik*, in which the Lebensraum philosophy was most expressed.[31]

The relationship between Hitler and the geopoliticologist was much warmer than Haushofer was willing to admit after the war. Haushofer addressed Hitler as Adolf and he brought flowers and books for him. They could talk at length about their mutual love of painting, which was an extremely important topic for Hitler - who himself had lived off painting in his Viennese years. Haushofer was a gifted storyteller and Hitler listened particularly attentively to his story about the Huns and Ghengis Khan. There was one moment, a crucial moment in World War II, when Ghengis Khan suddenly surfaced in Hitler's rhetoric. When Gehlen's *Abteilung Fremde Heere Ost* (the military intelligence service of the Eastern Front) reported to Hitler on the numbers of Soviet troops on the Weichsel River, Hitler dismissed it as 'the biggest lie since Ghengis Khan'. Since then, several biographers have pondered the question of *what* Hitler may have meant by this. Is it not conceivable that somewhere in the back of his mind Haushofer's stories about the Huns resonated? During a lecture in Landsberg am Lech, Haushofer explained that in their heyday, the Huns had barely had five thousand horsemen at their disposal and had nevertheless subdued Europe, and that their opponents had always exaggerated those numbers to justify their own failures.

That the bond between the Nazi top brass and Haushofer was warmer than Haushofer wanted known was evident from other things as well. When Hess moved into Munich's *Braune Haus*, the new headquarters of the NSDAP, in 1931, he proudly invited his old professor to his office on the first floor. His study was next to those of Hitler, Goebbels, Gregor Strasser and Ernst Röhm.[32] Hess had not forgotten his old professor who had helped him flee in 1923. From a letter, dated 21 August 1924, we know that Haushofer had sent Hess his complete series of the journal *Geopolitik* in prison at Landsberg am Lech. *'Es ist doch viel Feines drin,'* Hess wrote to Haushofer as a note of thanks. Hess signed the letter with *'Grüsst in alter treuer Freundschaft'*.[33]

There was the friendship between Hess and one of Haushofer's sons, the brilliant Georg Albrecht, too, with whom he shared a love of geopolitics and piano playing. Albrecht was strongly inspired by his father and had graduated summa cum laude in history on 5

March 1924. Besides history, Albrecht's interests included geography and he was a keen traveller. He visited Brazil, the United States, many countries in southern and eastern Europe, among others, and was a frequent visitor to London and Paris. Although the young Haushofer was Anglo-Saxon in outlook, he was also influenced by the theories of his father, who advocated German supremacy in Eastern Europe. In November 1941, he co-authored a remarkable compromise report with von Weissäcker, the secretary of state for foreign affairs. In his memorandum, Haushofer advocated ending the war but retaining the main German conquests in the East. With the other son, Heinz Haushofer, contact was less frequent. Heinz was particularly interested in agricultural science.[34]

Warm relations with the Nazis were strained by Hess's flight to England. The literature on this flight has increasingly given space to the role the Haushofers played in the remarkable decision to fly across the channel as a kind of peace apostle. Haushofer deplored the hostilities between Nazi Germany and Britain, and Albrecht was of the same opinion. Haushofer had also been instrumental in introducing prominent Britons, such as the Duke of Hamilton, to Hess, and it was to his support that Hess was seeking his remarkable flight. After the flight, relations between the Nazi leadership and Haushofer cooled. Joseph Goebbels wrote in his diary that the naive Hess had been influenced by the Haushofers: '*An Ihm ist Hopfer und Malz verloren*'.[35] Haushofer was arrested by the Gestapo on 18 May 1941 and interrogated for two days about his role in the Hess affair. A second round of interrogations took place from 7 to 10 June, 1941. Albrecht had had to report to Berchtesgaden and was also questioned. Indeed, Hess had indicated when he landed in Britain that he had undertaken his escape partly on Haushofer's instructions, and this had caused great embarrassment to the Nazi leadership.

The relationship cooled further in the aftermath of the Von Stauffenberg attack in 1944. After the attack at the Wolfsschanze, Haushofer was arrested and the Gestapo conducted searches. Nothing suspicious was found but Haushofer did end up in the Dachau concentration camp for some time. He gathered his courage and wrote a letter to Hitler, dated 31 August 1944. 'That Churchill, Eden and Roosevelt would lock me up and Stalin would give me a neck shot I can imagine,' he wrote. 'But that the NSDAP would put me in Dachau I had not thought possible.' Karl Haushofer was eventually released again. His son Georg Albrecht Haushofer was less fortunate. He found himself in resistance circles, befriended general Beck, von Hassel, Popitz, von Schulenburgg, Freiherr Yorck and others, and fled into the mountains. On 7 December 1944, he was arrested near Partenkirchen and killed by the SS through a neck shot on the night of 22-23 April 1945. Albert Haushofer, the other son, was detained for some time in Vienna and later released.[36]

Haushofer's rich and imaginative thinking had several roots. First and above all, Haushofer was a product of his time. Other intellectuals, such as the geographer Friedrich Ratzel (1844-1904), the Englishman Sir Halford J. Mackinder (1861-1945) and the Swede Rudolf Kjellén, inspired him, along with his military schooling and the bloody lessons of the First World War. The Dresdner Dr Robert Jannasch, a statistician, and his tutor the Basel economist Wilhelm Roscher, can also be counted among Haushofer's examples. Jannasch was a fierce advocate of a dual mission in German foreign policy in the early 20th century. He believed that ecclesiastical mission and a colonising secular power could go hand in hand. His was therefore the statement that 'a nation that no longer colonises was as dead as a church that no longer carried out a mission'. Roscher, forty years attached to the evangelical mission, was a strong advocate of colonies for the 'land-poor' Germans as well.[37]

The war had caused trauma in Germany, and the elements were traceable to Haushofer as well. About von Schlieffen, another great German geopolitical thinker, Dutch historian Geyl once wrote that he could define security policy purely in military terms.[38] Haushofer's work suffers to some extent from this shortcoming too. In *Der Kontinentalblock*, there are pages full of maps and arrows showing spheres of influence and directions of impact. Nor is it without reason that journalist Jan Reifenberg of the *Frankfurter Allgemeine Zeitung* once compared Jimmy Carter's security adviser Zbigniew Brzezinksi to Haushofer. Indeed, his office was filled from top to bottom with cartographic masterpieces showing interests and strategic directions of attack with thick, coloured arrows.[39]

Furthermore, Haushofer's thinking stemmed from his own wartime experiences. By ensuring sufficient *Raum*, Germany was independent of foreign countries and as a strong autarchy no longer vulnerable to the deadly hunger blockade that had hit Germany in World War I. As an officer in the 1. Bavarian Army Corps and the 8. Bavarian Reserve Division, Haushofer had fought on both the western and eastern fronts. The focus of his traumatic experiences was in the west, where he took part in the *Stahlgewitter* in the Vosges Mountains, at Verdun and on the Somme. In the latter battles, he took part in the firestorms of the summer of 1916, an unprecedented low in military history.

After the end of the war, Hess did his old teacher one last favour. When Haushofer had to appear at the Nuremberg trial as Lebensraum creator, Hess pretended not to recognise him. For Haushofer, that did not matter much anymore. He had lost his son Georg Albrecht in the war, and he had understood that his role as a geopolitical thinker was finished. He possibly carried the inevitable guilt with him as well, as he and his wife walked into the garden behind their house, sat down under their favourite tree and took their own lives.

Typical of the tragedy in Haushofer's life, from Lebensraum creator to outsider, were his own notes, looking back on his life. 'My life was like a big dinner,' he mused, 'but never came the moment when the real meal was served'. Mediocre minds - probably referring to his Lebensraum ideas perverted by Hitler - as well as unfortunate circumstances had prevented this. 'The Japanese have understood more of my theories than the Germans,' he mused not without derision. True happiness in his life, Haushofer, the man who dreamed of infinite space, world seas and strategic thrust directions, had finally found in the domestic sphere. Thoughts of his two sons, the tomcat Felix and his very happy marriage had given his life substance. *'Zu etwas ganzem nach Aussen ist es nicht gekommen. Immerhin aber sind Schicksale an mir vorbei gewirbelt!'*

With this, the curtain fell for Haushofer. Little of his spiritual legacy remained and the field of geopolitics did not recover from the wounds inflicted for a long time. Only in the 1970s did geopolitics return to the social and political arena.[40] Georg Albrecht Haushofer captured this sentiment in a sonnet found in the lining of his coat on his body murdered by the SS:

Das Erbe

In Schutt und Staub ist Babylon versunken,
ein Tempel blieb vom alten Theben fest,
von Ktesiphon zeugt einer Halle rest,
das grosse Angkor ist im Wald ertrunken -

auch unser ganzes Erbe sind Ruinen.
Noch kurze Weile zwischen toten Mauern
wird kümmerlicher Menschen Sorge dauern -
danach wird alles nur dem Efeu dienen.

Das Efeu des Vergessen wird sich ranken
um ein Jahrtausend hoher Blützezeit,
um dreissig Jahre mörderischen Streit.

Wir sind die Letzten. Unsere Gedanken
sind morgen tote Spreu, vom Wind verjagt.
und ohne Wert, wo jung der Morgen tagt.[41]

The British Sir Halford Mackinder (1861-1945) also tried to find solutions before his time. That Haushofer and Hitler were influenced by him is certain. Haushofer shared with Mackinder his fascination with the British empire and the world's oceans, which were inextricably linked to the legacy of Victorian England. The oceans, Mackinder reasoned, covered 9/12 of the earth's surface. Europe, Asia and Africa covered 2/12 of the remaining portion. The rest, 1/12, was for the two Americas and Australia.

Mackinder, in this division of the world into geographical empire blocks, immediately assumes the Europe-Asia-Africa camp (as if that would form a logical unit), versus America. We seem to hear Haushofer and even Goergel speaking. Underestimation of America resonates as we follow Mackinder further. Both the Americas and Australia relate to water as Britain relates to Europe. In fact, both are no more than 'islets in the sea'. Between these 'islets' and the old world, Mackinder saw an inevitable struggle, that of the *'World Island'* - German jargon spoke of *'Weltinsel'* - versus the *'Heartland'* - Germans spoke of *'Kernraum'*.

It only gets really interesting when we see exactly what Mackinder means by *Kernraum*. According to him, this includes the plains of Asia, the steppe of European Russia, right across Germany and the Netherlands to beyond Paris. Through the *Kernraum*, Mackinder continues, following Haushofer's theory of the *Parallelschaltung* of rivers, the most important and largest in the world, flowing into oceans or inland seas, such as the Caspian Sea and the Aral Sea. The grasslands - contrary to Haushofer's water theory - have always produced great warriors, as the plains were very suitable for mounted troops on horses and camels. The *Kernraum* is safe from invasion to the east by the sea and to the west the way opens up for equestrian attacks. The parallels with Haushofer are striking. In the *Kernraum*, an area from the Pyrenees to far beyond European Russia, we recognise Hitler's Lebensraum. Hitler was fascinated by the great European rivers too; the mythical Rhine and the Danube, the river of the future over which the treasures of the Lebensraum would flow westwards. On the banks of the Danube, Linz, city of Hitler's youth, was to become a 'pearl' that could rival Budapest (the anti-Semites mockingly spoke of 'Judapest' because of its large Jewish community). The architects Giesler and Frick were to build a *'Kraft durch Freude'* hotel, a NSDAP party temple and an Olympiastadion that was to make Linz one of the most important cities of the Third Reich.[42] The resemblance between Mackinder and Hitler takes on even stronger forms in Raymond Aron's three-sentence summary of Mackinder's work: 'Whoever controls Eastern Europe controls the Kernraum. Whoever controls the Kernraum controls the *Weltinsel*. Whoever controls the *Weltinsel*, controls the world.'[43]

The Nazis were happy to be inspired by the creators of Lebensraum and *Kernraum*, but faced a paradox. For both Haushofer and Mackinder, the fighting spirit of the peoples of the European *Raum* was emphasised by the proud horsemen, and these all came from the East. So how was this to go with the image of Germanic supremacy? In practice, there were two reactions to this from völkisch, nationalist thinking: either one identified with the horsemen, or one denied or negated the influence of those horsemen.

Unification with the heroic background of the cavalry nations took place in Hungary. Hurt by the Treaty of Trianon, which hit the Hungarians even harder than Germany was hit by Versailles, they sought support in *the finest hours* of the past. The Hungarian fascist Arrowcross leader, Ferenc Szálasi, identified Hungarians as descendants of Huns, Scythians and Parthians who were 'naturally' entitled to supremacy in the Carpathian Basin. The identification with the horsemen peoples went so far that Szálasi even claimed that Jesus was not actually a Jew but a Hungarian. Given that the *Old Testament* mentioned that Jesus came from the area south of Palestine, then Parthen land, Szálasi believed he could draw this conclusion. The equestrian descent of the Hungarians seemed to be underlined by Hitler: he called them 'that brave equestrian people'. After the debacle of Stalingrad, in which the Hungarians were also swept up and totally annihilated, Hitler withdrew this comparison: 'the Hungarians are no longer the *kühne Reitervolk* of old,' he mused, showing little gratitude for the Hungarian blood sacrifice.[44]

Germany chose the opposite attitude: denial. This manifested itself mostly by being outright silent about the invasions from the East and by highlighting its own völkisch, military and geopolitical feats. In Nazi Germany, people wrote and spoke with admiration about the conquest missions of the Teutonic knight orders to the East, which brought Western thought to barbarian peoples. Besides Teutonic colonisation, Hitler praised above all the geopolitical operations of Frederick the Great, who as a powerful strategist led little Prussia through the power poker game between east and west, claiming an important position for 'the Germanic people' in the heart of Europe. Hitler personally drew parallels between Frederick the Great and his own time. When Hitler stripped the Waffen-ss tank divisions of their honorary armband with divisional names after the failed spring offensive in Hungary in 1945, he argued this with the fact that Frederick the Great did not shy away from taking disciplinary punitive measures against failing elite units either. A painting of the Prussian monarch adorned his wall.[45]

In fact, the Nazis' answer to the question of who controlled European Kernraum was based on three foundations:

- a reckoning with Rome and the Roman Empire as Europe's sole cultural and power-political pillar;
- A reckoning with 'the myth' of the popular invasions of the savage horsemen;
- and the use of Germanic interpretations of history to legitimise the scenic trios of *Heim ins Reich* and Lebensraum.

We find an example of this with Kurt Pastenaci in his *From Jutland to Byzantium, the 500-year struggle of the Germanic people against Rome*. Pastenaci argues that in 'modern historiography' the 'peoples stirring role' of the Huns 'was given too great a role'. Neither Atilla's victorious campaigns nor the peoples' battle on the Catalan fields led the Germanic tribes to leave their homeland. The march of the Goths, a historical fact that even the Nazis could not ignore, was reinterpreted by underlining the fact that their king Theoderik had founded an empire of his own in Italy. Rather, according to Pastenaci, the Huns posed a problem for the Romans, who were weak after the death of Aëtius. 'They had lost out to the Teutons,' Pastenaci observed not without satisfaction. For Pastenaci, a Nazi historian and author of *Die Volksgeschichte der Germanen* and *Das viertausendjährige Reich*, the parallel with Hitler's Lebensraum theories was very thick. Pastenaci saw the Germanic victory as a victory of *Nordic* man and spirit that had to fight against west (Romans) and east (Huns) for a new order in Europe. 'An ordering,' says Pastenaci, 'that continues into our time.'[46]

Whereas Haushofer was still wavering between his preference for the island kingdoms versus the continental powers, Mackinder opted for the mainland. Admittedly, in his view, the islands had the advantage of being 'united' as opposed to the continent which was traditionally 'divided'; but should the continent unite, the island kingdoms stood no chance.

Geopolitical strategists like Napoleon and Hitler took this theory of Mackinder well to heart. In both cases, their attack on Russia was a response to their war with Britain. The armed union of the continent would cause the collapse of the archipelago. The continent would, in Mackinder's words, 'encircle' the island, as it were. Unlike Haushofer, Mackinder believed that France and Russia were the two superpowers on the European continent that would fight for supremacy over the *Kernraum*. In doing so, he put his cards on Russia. When World War II broke out and it became clear that the final battle would be between Germany and Russia, he again chose Russia as the most likely. In 1943, he wrote that not the Mongols or the Huns, but this time the Soviets in their tanks and armoured cars would subdue the *Kernraum*.[47]

A possibly even more important point in Mackinder's work that translates to the Third Reich was his strategic economic theory. Mackinder assumed that the island states based their power largely on their world trade. By contrast, the *Kernraum* had the economy of the future: *die Grossraumwirtschaft*. World trade was an outdated concept, dating from colonial times. The Victorian Empire was already past its prime, the Netherlands was barely feeding off its golden seventeenth century, the future lay in a large contiguous (economic) *Kernraum*.

Such ideas naturally legitimised the idea that maintaining the status quo would, in the long run, result in the economic downfall, and hence power-political downfall, of the (German) state. When asked exactly how big the empire should be then, Mackinder's expansionist ideas were soon linked to the concept of natural borders. This adds Mackinder to the list - Hitler, Haushofer and Rudolf Kjellén - of people who saw the state as a living organism. For Hitler, the border lay somewhere in the east as far as the Urals, in the west as far as the Pyrenees, whence Franco's phalangists would close the gate to the south. Raymond Aron, in his standard work *Paix et guerre entre les nations,* warned against this line of thinking. 'The only natural thing about a natural border,' he wrote in 1966, 'is the fact that it is easily defensible.'[48]

Incidentally, it is noteworthy that different border definitions played a role among German geopoliticologists. For instance, Haushofer's colleague Dr Kurt Trampler spoke of *'Volksboden'* and *'Einflussboden'*. By Volksboden, Trampler understood those areas where there was German 'linguistic and cultural influence'. Implementing a *Heim ins Reich policy* along this definition meant that the entire German-speaking part of Switzerland, Alsace, Lorraine, Eupen-Malmedy, Luxembourg, Austria, South Tyrol, the German-speaking areas in Hungary, the German-speaking areas in Croatia, large parts of Czechoslovakia, the (Danziger) corridor, the Memel region as well as North Schleswig would have to be annexed to the *Reich*. In total, these were areas in which 20 million people lived. There was also the *Einflussboden (sphere of influence)*, where as many as 150 million people lived. Trampler counted among these areas: all of European Russia, the Baltic states, Poland, Romania, Hungary, large parts of Yugoslavia, the Netherlands and almost all of Belgium.[49]

All this provided mental ammunition for Hitler's ambitions and had a self-reinforcing effect because within the world of Haushofer, Kjellén and Mackinder, there was only room for the element of struggle. The will to live became the will to conquer. The will to conquer became the need to conquer. The need to conquer perverted itself into the need for struggle. From necessity to struggle, the step is only a small one to the necessity to destroy, an apocalyptic coercive theory of the young discipline of geopolitics to Hitler's perverted Lebensraum idea. From Haushofer and Mackinder to Hitler at Landsberg, the entry into Sudetenland, the fall of Warsaw, the street battles of Stalingrad and even the gas chambers of Auschwitz.

Indeed, the same apocalyptic coercive theory is evident in the persecution of the Jews as well. In a recent study on the Holocaust, Wolfgang Sofsky[50] clarifies that the power structure of the Third Reich was characterised by the fact that Hitler was all about absolute power. This power was unprecedented and could not be compared to hitherto known forms of despotism or slavery. Indeed, despotism is characterised by arbitrariness, a lack of order and authority. The absolute power Hitler possessed was an organised power that did not need to legitimise itself and relied on organised terror, hierarchical structures and large-scale collaboration. The most direct and ultimate form of Hitler's power featured violence. Given that absolute power compulsively seeks more power, nothing was ultimately safe. The end was not reached, Sofsky believed, until there were no more exceptions. Hitler's power and aggression was directed against Jews and Gypsies, Jehovah's Witnesses and homosexuals, against the Slavic peoples and against the Western Allies, against the German people and ultimately against himself. That Hitler would commit suicide because of the failure of his geopolitics was never in question.[51] Hitler was a gambler, someone who - although initially often after long hesitation - chose all or nothing: Lebensraum or *Weltuntergang*. Almost literally, he uttered this message before his leading generals, just before the start of the Ardennes offensive.[52] When victory failed to materialise, the German people did not deserve their Führer and survival. He drew them into his grave full of ingratitude.

'Der Russe, allein in der Welt, habe keine einzige Idee in der Menge der menschheitsideen eingeführt, was er vom Forschritt erhalten habe, sei durch ihn verzerrt worden.'

Alfred Rosenberg

'I have a burning private grudge in this war against that twisted little dummy Adolf Hitler for ruining, perverting, misapplying and forever damning the noble Northern spirit, an outstanding contribution to Europe, which I have always loved and tried to present in its true light.'

J.R.R. Tolkien

Chapter 3

Reich and romance

Paul de Lagarde, Julius Langbehn and völkische thinking - A harmonic romantic myth disturbed - Rembrandt's organic masterpiece - Wagner and the aesthetic man - Modernism as Fall - Lebensraum, a völkische catch-up manoeuvre? - Rosenberg's *Mythus* and *Kulturkampf* - 'The new age' - Christianity versus Rosenberg - Atlantis and the creative Atlantic man - Swan neck boats and the tombs of Thebes - Poliakov and Aryan descent - *Untermenschen*, race war - Houston Stewart Chamberlain - Nomocracy, the Jewish era - Wagner, Bayreuth and the Festival - National salvation plan - The Soviet Union and the *Protocols of Zion* - Rosenberg's anti-communist diplomacy - Bestseller - The 87 nationalities of Russia - Rosenberg's influence on Hitler - Origin of ideas - Russian migrants - *'Mission civilisatrice'* - Apprentice, teacher, follower - The Jewish intellectuals of the Russian revolution - Brandoffer - Dietrich Eckart - The sound of machine guns - Thule Society - Von Sebottendorff - Blavatsky and theosophy - Vienna and ariosophy - List and Lanz von Liebenfels - Germanic order - NSDAP - The wet poodle, Hitler discovered as an orator - Ostara - Madagascar - Wewelsburg as centre of the world and fortress against the new Huns - The cursed family of Wiligut - Carnuntum

Besides geopoliticologists, philosophers and politicians, völkisch thinkers played an important role in the perception of Eastern Europe and Hitler's Lebensraum theories. If 'forefathers' of the völkisch movement can be named, Paul Böttischer, known as Paul de Lagarde and Julius Langbehn qualify. De Lagarde wrote his first völkisch writings in the second half of the nineteenth century. He was a grammar school teacher from Göttingen who opposed the way German unity, the empire, was developing. He summarised his criticism in *Deutsche Schriften*, published in 1878. Lagarde was annoyed that while the new German empire possessed its *physical* unity, *spiritual* unity was lacking.

The völkische thinkers emerged from Romanticism and were characterised by a tendency towards the irrational and the emotional. They focused on man and the world. The völkisch man felt mystically connected to his soil and to the ancient generations that had previously lived on this soil. The völkisch thinkers assumed that one was *hineinborn* in a country and that every people possessed its *Volksgeist*. Völkisch literature constantly referred back to the rhythms of nature, of sowing, harvesting, feasting and fasting. The individual played only a limited role in this vision, always surrounded by these natural elements, always in close proximity to village and community. Life, like the rhythm of the seasons, was also depicted as a cyclical, biological development. This idealistic yearning for perfect relations between nature and man created space for mental restriction and repression, and the Nazis were to make grateful use of this. History was reinterpreted and used for legitimisation. History became the identity-defining element.[1]

In this, Richard Wagner wrote about '*das Reinmenschliche*', the ideal of aesthetic man, living in harmony with nature. This romantic idea derived its significance mainly from its contrast with the modern world, which Wagner saw as a fall from grace. '*Meine ganze Politik ist nichts weiter mehr als der blutigste Hass unsererer ganzen Zivilisation,*' he wrote in 1851.[2] Many people were trapped in a gloomy *Alltag* and searching for the deeper meaning of existence. The völkische thinkers heroically harked back to Jahn, Arndt and Fichte who had given the concept of 'people' its lofty content during the Napoleonic Wars of

Liberation. Impressed by Napoleonic domination, Johann Gottlieb Fichte spoke pompously about the German nation that was to emerge. He called the war against France a *'Volkskrieg'*. He was already *enamoured of* the scenic idyll in which this German empire would emerge.³

The German unification that came about in 1871 had always been presented as an agrarian-romantic development. Yet, when it came, a time of urbanisation and industrialisation followed. During the nineteenth century, society had changed considerably. For instance, society had changed from a feudal system to a class society. Industry was on the rise, urbanisation took huge forms. After 1900, more than half of the German population lived in cities and two-thirds in larger cities with more than 20,000 inhabitants. This was a new social phenomenon, which Georg Simmel described as an 'ambivalent fascination between massiveness, freedom and individualism'.⁴

Lagarde argued in *Deutsche Schriften* for the restoration of the mythical link between soil and man. History, he believed, rather than religion or class consciousness had to become the binding element of the nation. Traditions had to be protected. 'Progress' was scary and threatening. The Jews, *Fremdkörper* in the German nation, represented the 'new age' in Lagarde's eyes. The Jews stood for liberalism and a 'state within the state' which disrupted the harmonic-romantic picture. Furthermore, the Jew was *rootless* and therefore could not go along with the historical anchoring between people and soil.⁵

Lagarde's pupil Langbehn went a step further. In his youth, looking out over the - then still - clear water near Kiel harbour, he mused about purity as the primal source of all life: *'Rein sein ist alles'*. Thoughts he would soon project not only onto nature, but onto human beings as well. 'Deep and clear,' that was how organic man was to look. He opposed the Darwinian view of life that man was constantly evolving. Langbehn, like many völkisch thinkers, reverted to (the myth of) an 'idyllic past'. The 'Adam-ideal-man' had always existed, but had been 'wounded and infected' over the years. Humanity needed to return to its origins, to the *'Originalmensch'*. A dangerous obstacle to this, in his view, were the Jews, although he saw them as a 'passing evil'. The 'real problem' for Germany lay in its own attitude of soul. *'Wir sind elende Geschöpfe,'* he believed, and he appealed to Germany's spiritual elite to change course for the masses. Painter Hans Thoma, who portrayed the young philosopher with an egg - as a sign of a new (re)birth - in his hand, called Langbehn the 'aristocrat of the mind' and 'childishly unwise'. Still, Langbehn was unstoppable, found a financier for his book *Rembrandt as Erzieher* and managed to get a bestseller on the market with it. He then travelled around to win supporters for his vision, visiting, among others, the politician (*Patriotic League*) and publicist Dr Edmund Joery, the Austrian parliamentarian and economist Alexander von Peez, and the economic prophet of doom Freiherr Bernhard von Bothmer. Friedrich Nietzsche, who also enjoyed Langbehn's warm interest, jumped around the young author's neck and passionately kissed him on both cheeks. At first, Langbehn thought he had won over 'the old master', but he later discovered that Nietzsche had by now been admitted to an insane asylum and was severely confused.

In *Rembrandt as Erzieher*, Langbehn harks back to intuition and mysticism as unifying elements. Less than Lagarde, he strained to make history the unifying element. What was especially important to him was the spirituality of the Germanic traditions, adding the mystical element to the völkisch movement. Langbehn's books were read by millions in his time. In Langbehn's vision, Rembrandt represented the organic romantic, the simple man, who created masterpieces using simple colours from nature. What is striking about Langbehn is that he sought his 'hero' *outside* German territory. With the introduction of the Germanic element in the völkisch movement, the völkisch mission became a European affair and would finally end up in world politics.[6]

For the Nazis, it was not difficult to pervert these idyllic thoughts into *Blut und Boden theories*. The conquest of Lebensraum could still satisfy these idyllic needs. Was not the creation of the 'farm of 700 by 700 kilometres' that Hitler and Himmler advocated in Eastern Europe the creation of the völkisch paradise envisioned by De Lagarde and Langbehn? Wasn't the creation a völkisch catch-up manoeuvre to make mythological images of bygone times become reality after all? The main spokesman of the völkisch camp was the Nazi ideologue

Alfred Rosenberg, whose *Blut und Boden* theories still sometimes passed Hitler on the right. He saw the beginning of the 20th century as the defining moment in history. Rosenberg, in his *Der Mythus des 20. Jahrhunderts*[7], speaks of a veritable '*Kulturkampf*' taking place in Germany and Europe. In this context, he speaks of a '*Ringen von Seelenwert gegen Seelenwert*'. At stake in this struggle were racial purity of the German people as well as Germany's geopolitical dominance. Among völkische thinkers, Haushofer and Mackinder's geopolitical thoughts were drawn into the shadowy realm of whole and half-truths, Germanic mysticism and mythology, occult plots and grotesque and sometimes clownish thoughts.

The *Kulturkampf* that took place in 1930s Germany was a particularly bitter one. The shadow of World War I and the resulting social, political and economic malaise provided the ingredients for a powerful clash of ideas. Communists, Spartakists and Marxists pointed to developments in the east: the Soviet Union - for the solution to the problems. Christian democrats stuck to their Biblical principles, liberals oriented themselves towards Anglo-Saxonism or stared blindly at the communist danger, while the far right wing sought refuge in the brown camp. Freikorps and other semi-military organisations dreamt of völkisch rebirth.

In general, Rosenberg's role in this *Kulturkampf* is seriously underestimated. There are few biographies on Rosenberg. However, he is often treated in passing. Typical is Walter Laqueur's portrayal of Rosenberg in his standard work on the Weimar Republic in which he mainly ridicules the dusty image of the Nazi ideologue and the dullness of his work. 'Rosenberg was incredibly dull,' Laqueur believes, 'without spiritual power, without charisma and without humour.' That he had managed to make it so far within the Nazi hierarchy was typical of the 'low level of the Nazi leadership'.[8] As for Rosenberg, Laqueur limits himself to the outside. It is very easy and therefore tempting for historians and scholars to dismiss völkisch theories in general, and Rosenberg's in particular, because of their irrationality also immediately as unimportant. This is too easy a conclusion. *Mein Kampf* is full of irrational theories but at the same time is one of the most important sources into the thought and experience of Hitler and the Nazis. Dutch polemicist J. de Kadt rightly noted as early as 1933 that *Der Mythus* is an extraordinarily frank book.[9] The psychoanalyst Wilhelm Reich, in his early work *Die Massen-psychologie des Faschismus* (1935), already warned against dismissing Nazi ideology too easily, as this would stand in the way of unmasking the true character of the Third Reich.[10] Nor is the 'dullness' of Rosenberg's writings emphasised by Laqueur a measure of the importance of his work. Numerous biographies trace how the many guests of Hitler's endless table and night talks could no longer keep their eyes open from boredom, but no one will deny that the notes of Hitler's monologues must be considered among the most important *inside sources* of Nazi Germany. Whereas Laqueur and with him many others make fun of the high fantasy level of Rosenberg's völkische writings, he would do better to acknowledge them as a serious measure of the mystical and irrational nature of the Nazis' spiritual heritage. This becomes even more compelling if we consider that Rosenberg was no loner in his views and that these ideas - according to Laqueur, a corollary of the 'low level' - should rather be interpreted as a totally different perception world from that of today's Western, rational (and transparent) society. A world view that emerged from the conservative revolution and was driven, shaped and perverted by the likes of De Lagarde, Langbehn, List, Lanz von Liebenfels, the Ludendorff couple, Eckart, Wagner, Chamberlain and von Fritsch, to name but a few. It should be noted, however, that Rosenberg was radical even by völkisch standards and that he never became entirely *socially acceptable*. His work was therefore mainly a catalyst of völkisch thought and an often unquoted source for other völkisch thinkers, writers and politicians.

Rosenberg's most important work is *Der Mythus des 20. Jahrhunderts*. The idea for this book went back to 1917. For his political activities and for his motivation to write, World War I and the looming German downfall played an important role. The book was eventually largely completed around 1925 and appeared in print in 1930. Rosenberg had dedicated it to the millions of German soldiers who had died for their homeland. For Rosenberg, World War I marked the end of a long-ago period. Rosenberg spoke on the first page of his book of 'the *new* age', the '*new* world revolution', the 'mythical sign', 'the *new* mission' and 'the *new* faith' that awaited Germany. Rosenberg and other völkisch thinkers proclaimed their ideas with pseudo-religious conviction; the madness of World War I, the millions of martyrs to make a *'new birth'* possible. This new birth would partly give birth to the campaign for Lebensraum.

Rosenberg's *Der Mythus* was a true revolution in thinking. Until then, people's political, social and spiritual lives had been determined by their class consciousness and religious beliefs. According to Rosenberg, the class struggle belonged to the past and religious dogmas were obsolete. It was no longer about these battle points but about 'blood against blood, race against race and people against people.' *'Amatory Orthodoxy'* had not yet realised that *'Deutschtum'* had begun its heyday via Luther, Goethe, Kant, Schopenhauer, Nietzsche and De Lagarde through National Socialism. Above all, Rosenberg condemned Marxism and variants thereof, as well as the Christian heritage that downplayed the Germans' 'true Germanic origin'. Rosenberg spent much of his *Der Mythus* fiercely attacking the Christian faith, which, like the Jewish faith, was a 'make-believe' in Rosenberg's eyes. He argued this with the fact that Christianity was full of Germanic symbolism, which was much older than Christianity itself. As an example, Rosenberg cited that the Christian resurrection was no different from the Germanic festival in honour of the fertility goddess Ostara (goddess of light) and that the birth of Jesus could be traced back to the winter solstice festival. The *Blut und* Boden *journal Odal* explained that Ostara was corrupted to *Ostern* (Easter), just as *Weihnachten* was a corruption of *Wihinächten*.[11] Although Christians since Boniface had tried nothing but to eradicate Germanism at its roots, Rosenberg could not come to any other conclusion than that Christianity, for all its symbolism, was actually a *Nordic* (Germanic) thing. And therein lies the rub, according to Rosenberg. For Christianity had not confined itself to the Nordic countries, so non-Germanic elements, such as compassion, had penetrated Germanic culture. The same applied to a concept like humanism, which was said to be an invention of freemasons. All this eroded the will to fight and survive, and this could hurt Germany and the Germanic race in the geopolitical joust of nations.

In Rosenberg's thinking, this was a serious matter because he claimed Jesus and the origins of Christianity for his people. Symbolic of the revolutionary nature of *Der Mythus* was the fact that Rosenberg made human civilisation begin in Atlantis. In fact, he was making an inverse argument with regard to the contemporary view of the course of history. The 'culture-bearing peoples' did not, as assumed in mainstream scholarship, originate in the Middle East but came from the Germanic area and went to the Middle East. Theatrically, Rosenberg described how the 'culture-bearing peoples' fanned out across the globe via the now sunken, legendary island kingdom of Atlantis (Thule[12] in German). The Nazi ideologist was unable to pinpoint a precise location for the vanished continent, but believed it was in the 'Nordic region' at a time when a completely different climate prevailed than in present times. In doing so, he concurred with the positioning given to the area by the Greek geographer Pytheas in the fourth century BC (above Scotland), which had since been recalled through the poems of the Roman Virgil (70-19 BC), the play *Medea* by the Spanish-Roman senator Seneca Jr. and Joost van den Vondel. The *Atlantic People* crossed the oceans in their dragon- and swan-necked boats, bringing knowledge, conquering territories and creating a new world. The Atlantic people migrated to the area of the Mediterranean, Africa, China and North America. Among others, the blond Atlantic people, the Nordic (Germanic) race, settled in the Middle East as well, such as in Syria, Egypt and Palestine. As evidence, Rosenberg cited the blond Berbers, hamites and blond Libyans, with blue eyes. Swan-necked boats were depicted on tombs and drawings at the tombs of Thebes indicated four races. In ancient legends, Queen Nitokris was described as blond. The 'Amoriter', a descendant people of the Atlantic adventurers, were the founders of Jerusalem, according to Rosenberg, and Jesus is said to have belonged to them.[13]

This Völkisch, ariosophical reinterpretation of Christianity was a key feature of Völkisch thought and is found in many Völkisch ideologues, such as H. St. Chamberlain and the Ludendorff couple. This struggle between *Germanentum* and *Christentum* was an important psychological factor in German supremacist thought and 'legitimised'

German (Atlantic/Germanic) pioneering and conquests. Such claims were not specific to the 20th century. It is known that, for example, the Antwerp physician Goropius Becanus was already asserting things at the time of the Eighty Years' War that would be counted as ariosophy at the beginning of the twentieth century. For instance, he believed with great firmness that Adam would have spoken a 'Germanic dialect'. Houston Stewart Chamberlain, who exerted considerable influence on Rosenberg, believed that *Urchristentum was* of Aryan origin and had been corrupted over the centuries into a Judaeo-Christianity. Chamberlain specifically pointed to the Aryan descent of Jesus.[14]

Contemporaries of Rosenberg went even further in the detail of their claims. A certain Dr Georg Traue, author of many religious books, thought he knew the name of Jesus' father in 1934: Josephus Pandera, a captain in the Roman army. Jesus' mother was said to have been a certain Miriam of Bethlehem, a Hebrew girl. 'Evidence' for Jesus' Aryan descent, according to Professor Haeckel, a contemporary of Traue, could be found in forty to fifty gospels that had been kept 'outside the Bible' as well. Haeckel called the election procedure for inclusion in the Bible selective. 'Aryan' variants of the 'Jesus story' were excluded.[15]

We know that Hitler too was concerned with the ethnic background of Jesus. Dr Henry Picker, the man who recorded Hitler's endless 'table talks' at the time, recalled how Benito Mussolini tried to convince Hitler of Jesus' Roman descent. Mussolini showed Hitler an effigy of Jesus from the first century in 1938. On it, in Mussolini's opinion, it was 'clearly visible' that Jesus did not have Jewish but Roman facial features. Mussolini then concluded that Jesus had to be the son of a Roman legionnaire.[16]

Such descent theories were more common in Germany than in other countries. French researcher Leon Poliakov attributes this to the fact that German descent theories differed from those of other European countries. The Völkisch Germans identified themselves with the Germanic people, and the history of the Germanic people can only be traced in the early stages through research on Goths, Franks and

Lombards. What these peoples have in common is that they lived outside 20th-century German territory. In fact, the Germanic primordial history of the Germans plays out across the entire European mainland. Because of this, Poliakov believes, Germans have always been looking for the Germanic element in other peoples. The descent dilemma also manifests itself in German historiography. The historiography of the early period is always characterised by the *germanic Frühzeit* and the *deutsche Frühzeit*, and no one can pinpoint the exact beginning. In addition, the fact that *deutsche Frühzeit* almost always begins outside German territory is frustrating. An example of this is by making the beginning of German history start with Clovis and Chilperik (i.e. on French territory), because they would have spoken a Germanic language. Interesting for the Lebensraum issue is Poliakov's assertion that Germans are in fact stuck with two 'dividing lines': the internal one (who they think they are descended from and where they belong) and the external one (the borders resulting from the current power constellation).[17]

The above observations are important because they provide insight into the Nazis' mystical-mythical belief in their own missionary tasks, pioneering role and its geographical positioning. In one of the first chapters of *Der Mythus,* Rosenberg writes that the blond race determined the 'spiritual face' of the earth through a population movement 'in several waves'. This theory contains the germ of the Lebensraum ideology. The existing *Raum* had been lost to the Nordic, Germanic race as Atlantis had sunk into the ocean. New territory had to be conquered. In the process, the Atlantic people penetrated into the mountains of India, 'explaining' the indo-Germanic link.[18]

Rosenberg's 'Atlantic theory' took on grotesque proportions with this statement. His theory was probably inspired by studying the Vedic era in India. This awe-inspiring land with its eternal snow on the Himalayas, with tropical heat and vast river plains was invaded in about 1600 BC by a people who called themselves the Aryas (Aryans). The word, according to German philosopher Hans Joachim Störig, meant 'noblemen' or 'peasants'. Their original language had kinship with European languages. The conquest took the invading tribe several centuries after which the Aryas, being of different skin colour, ruled over the original population. They introduced the four different sections of the Veda, a complex of scriptures six times the size of the Bible, and they protected their ethnic background by introducing the caste system through their privileged position of Brahmins (priests), followed by Kshatrias (princes, warriors), Vaisyas (freedmen), descending to Shudras and Pariahs (unfree) and the untouchables. During the Third Reich, in India, as well as among Nazis like Rosenberg, people were convinced that there was still a direct blood relationship between Western European Germanic (Aryan) man and the Aryan caste upper class in India who, Rosenberg believed, descended from Atlantis.[19]

In Rosenberg's view, the Atlantic peoples were constantly exposed to mixing with 'inferior races', so that the original area, Germanic-Nordic Europe, would ultimately remain the true cradle. The Atlantic-Indian link 'stiffened' by dark blood.[20] However, sympathies for India did remain in certain German circles, partly based on the above mythical and semi-scientific conceptions and origins suspicions. Importantly, Rosenberg concludes that the origin of the Germanic missionary task was due to racial qualities and the influence of the sun on Nordic culture. As the only area on earth with such distinctly changing seasons, the wheel of light was a great inspiration for Germanic culture. The symbol of the Nazi party, the swastika, referred to the sun. The right-turning legs indicated its power and dynamism. With this reasoning, Rosenberg built a bridge between the natural element of völkisch thought and his racial theories. Parallel to such theories, many popular scientific publications arose that 'confirmed' partial elements of this theory. Wilhelm Scheuermann, for example, wrote a study on the origin of the swastika, using archaeological finds of this symbol to confirm the link with India, as well as the entire (Atlantic) spread of this symbol. Rosenberg's view that the Germanic-Indian link stemmed from Western initiative was linguistically 'proved' in Guido (von) List-like fashion by pointing out that words like birch and beech existed in India - the sacred Germanic trees - while they did not occur in the Indian climate.[21]

Rosenberg's work generated fierce debates. It was suggested from religious quarters that Rosenberg should be put in a straight-jacket because *kaltstellen* would not help. 'The Balt,' a derogatory reference to Rosenberg's Baltic origins, 'had in fact experienced too many Russian winters to be *kaltgestelt*.' The work was said to be blasphemous, atheistic and people even spoke of *'Wotanismus'* and *'heidnischer Wotanskult'*. Rosenberg rebuked them. In *An die Dunkelmänner unserer Zeit,* he called Jesus a 'medicine man', receiving above all the ire of Cardinal and Archbishop of Bavaria Faulhaber. In Rosenberg's view, the term 'medicine man' was not an insult. He was merely trying to use it to show how close Jesus actually was to traditional, Germanic wise men and was actually one of them.[22] The *'Prälaten and Kardinäle'*, Rosenberg mockingly spoke of *'Moral Theologians'*, had taught Germany pacifism, were often anti-German, dangerous to the state, against the *'Deutschtum'* and, together with the Marxists, threatened to hand Germany over to the *'Untermenschen'*.[23]

In Rosenberg's view, these Untermenschen were represented primarily by Jews and the Slavic people. Given that in the process, the Russian revolution was also characterised as a Bolshevik-Jewish plot, the sting of both völkisch antipathies came together in the Kremlin in Moscow.

Rosenberg was, long before Hitler came to power, an advocate of German grand expansion to the east. In his *Der Mythus,* he succinctly presents his geopolitical concept for the constellation of power in Europe. He places the beginning of the revolutionary upheaval in 1914, when Germany stood a chance of conquering Europe. After the defeat in 1918 and the humiliating peace of Versailles in 1919, it became clear to him that something had to be done, now more than ever. *Raum* had to be created for the millions of Germans who would be born in the years to come. In this, he saw France as the big obstacle. France was a problem in two respects. The Germans and the French were in a geopolitical and racial conflict in Rosenberg's eyes. Geopolitically, France was the country that would try to checkmate Germany through military coalitions. This would prevent Germany from extending its dominance into eastern and central Europe. Secondly, in Rosenberg's eyes, France was a 'half-neglected' country. In practice, the French idea of pan-Europe was nothing more than a 'Franko-Judäa' plot to 'destroy' Nordic man and create a 'raceless' Europe. As a natural ally against this threat, Rosenberg followed the lead of geopoliticologists, who advocated an alliance with Britain as well. Rosenberg added the Scandinavian countries to this. This constellation of power was to neutralise France, save the Nordic race and enable Nordic supremacy over Central and Eastern Europe. In an emotional appeal in *Der Mythus,* he calls for a shift in the pattern of the migrations of people. Germany had to become again what the old Atlantic peoples had been in the past: the bringers of a new culture. When the migrations of peoples involved Mongols and Turkic peoples as far south as Bavaria, now the direction had to be shifted. The direction of the future was 'from west to east, from the Rhine to the Weichsel, from the Weichsel to Moscow'; Rosenberg saw this as a natural, rhythmic change in history. The future belonged to a Nordic Europe with a German Central Europe. Germany as the continent's central power, protector to the south and southwest. In the north protected by Britain and the Scandinavian states.[24]

Like Haushofer, Rosenberg harboured 'warm feelings' towards Britain. Nevertheless, his fondness for the British seems to have added to his earlier theories rather than being part of Rosenberg's geopolitical concept from the start. His biographer Kuusisto believes that Rosenberg became convinced of British importance only later. His growing admiration for Germany-adept Houston Stewart Chamberlain played an important role in this. In his early writings, Rosenberg always depicted Britain as a nation ruled by Freemasons. For him, the 1917 Balfour Declaration, which recognised Palestine as the home of the Jews, provided the best 'proof' of this assumption. Kuusisto observes a slow change in Rosenberg's view of Britain's position in the international power constellation from about 1927 onwards. Rosenberg at this time begins to discover Britain as an 'Aryan nation'. This is somewhat similar to Haushofer, who admired the British as tough seafarers and empire builders, along with Japanese and ancient Venice. Haushofer too added, albeit more discreetly, mythical, racial factors. Rosenberg increasingly began to see Britain as a 'racially pure nation par excellence', almost entirely descended from Anglo-Saxons and Normans. In doing so, he noted, the British labour movement was not very Marxist in orientation, he admired the British aristocracy and became an admirer of *Die Grundlagen des xix. Jahrhunderts* by the in 1855 born Briton Houston Stewart Chamberlain.

Chamberlain, according to philosopher Georg Lukács the 'true philosopher of racialism' and according to Georg Schott the 'seer' of the Third Reich[25], was the 'British fulcrum' of German nationalism. Married to a daughter of Richard Wagner, the composer revered by Hitler, Chamberlain devoted his life to völkisch writings. Inspired, among others, by the French diplomat Joseph Arthur Count Gobineau, who had written a four-volume work on race in the mid-nineteenth century and was a Renaissance expert, he wrote biographies on Immanuel Kant, Goethe, and Wagner. But his most important book work was *Grundlagen des xix. Jahrhunderts*[26] which sold massively in Germany. The book, whose first edition appeared in 1899, was characterised by the same inflated style as many other Völkisch works. The cover depicted no less than Plato, Aristotle, Jesus, Dante, Da Vinci, Shakespeare, Luther, Augustine, Kant, Goethe, Beethoven and Rembrandt. For those who took note, this choice by Chamberlain was obvious. The British Germany enthusiast took a stand for *abendländische* culture, which was 'threatened' by the Jews. German society, Chamberlain believed, was threatened by 'world Jewry'. Judaism was not a religion, not a state; it constituted a 'nomocracy', a racially pure group of 'chosen people' organised along a set of laws. The most important of these laws, according to Chamberlain, was that Jews pursued racial purity (through the female line), while further pursuing as much racial mixing among the other races as possible. As evidence, he cited the biblical *Deuteronomy*, which states that 'no bastard may join the congregation of Yahweh, even ten generations later'. By now, Chamberlain calculated, 150 generations had passed and only 300 non-Semites had joined the Jewish people worldwide by 1800. 'The small number of babies with birth defects,' Chamberlain argued, 'was due to the purity of the race.' The aim of the alleged nomocracy, in his view, was to obtain world power. In his *Grundlagen,* he outlined that the power of the Jews showed a strong upward trend in the nineteenth century. The world was surrendering itself 'like voluntary Slavs' to the 'Jewish usurers'.[27] In his view, it was not even an exaggeration to say that by the end of the nineteenth century people were living in 'the Jewish age'. With this formulation, according to pan-European Graf Richard Coudenhove-Kalergi, Chamberlain delivered the 'decisive formulation of anti-Semitism.' [28]

Interestingly, Chamberlain allowed this era to begin on the anniversary of Goethe's death. With Goethe's death, the 'last pillar of the Occident was buried'. The overly pacified Indo-European (as Chamberlain described his fellow Nordic citizens, as Rosenberg spoke of Atlantic people and Hitler spoke of Germanic people), had no answer to the rapid social rise of the semites who had been welcomed. By referring to Goethe, Chamberlain tried to get the great German writer into the anti-Semitic camp, which did not correspond to Goethe's ideas.[29]

Great inspiration for his thinking Chamberlain gained outside Gobineau, in Richard Wagner's Bayreuth. In 1882, Chamberlain attended one of the first performances of Wagner's *Parsifal* and from that day on Chamberlain was a Wagner-adept. With growing interest, he read his anti-Semitic tomes, listened to his music. It was in his Viennese years, the stronghold of ariosophy, that Chamberlain wrote his works on Goethe, Wagner and Kant and that *Die Grundlagen* saw the light of day. The worship of Wagner and his work eventually went so far that Chamberlain moved to Bayreuth, married a daughter of Wagner and opted for German citizenship when World War I broke out. Bayreuth embraced the British thinker and made him an honorary citizen of the city. Besides the Nazis, Kaiser Wilhelm II was also among his admirers.

Like Hitler and Rosenberg, Chamberlain saw Richard Wagner as the forerunner of völkisch Germany. Even Thomas Mann, a Wagner enthusiast, had to express regret that the Nazis had claimed Wagner for themselves. 'There is an unassailable connection between the Wagnerian atmosphere and the National Socialists,' he wrote in 1939. He felt that German cultural heritage lend itself very easily to abuse. He summed up this character of German culture in one sentence: *'Es ist groß, es ist herrlich, aber es ist gegen die Zivilisation'*.[30]

Mann's observation is correct. Wagner was in many ways a figurehead of the völkisch tendencies of his time. He was co-creator of what might be called the 'German national salvation plan', a puritanical opposition to modernism, with a rich interest in racial hygiene.[31] From 1933, the Wagner-Festspiele in Bayreuth were cultivated as an educational institution for young students and schoolchildren. Hitler was a child of Wagner's descendants; Wagner's grandchildren called Hitler 'Onkel Wolf'. In 1923, the year of the Hitler-Putsch, Hitler visited Houston Stewart Chamberlain, who was in a wheelchair and in the winter of his life after a brain haemorrhage. Chamberlain saw in the young Hitler, who had just given a speech in Jean Paul Square, Germany's new strongman and predicted a great future for him. Chamberlain was one of the first known 'Germans' to openly rally behind Hitler after the 1923 Hitler-Putsch at a time when the latter could well use the moral support. At the time, Chamberlain's days as a great writer were already over. From 1916, he had been ill - some of his supporters believed in a secret British plot against Chamberlain's health, others believed he had MS - and annually he was further weakened. He had squandered his capital in shares of the fallen Habsburg Empire. In these final years, he had devoted himself to studies such as *Mensch und Gott*, in which he placed the person Jesus at the centre. Chamberlain would not live to see the Third Reich. He did, however, get a taste of what was to come.

After his death, Chamberlain-inspired authors such as Alfred Rosenberg took up the banner. The now completely forgotten Dr Artur Dinter should not be missed here, who became best known mainly for his bestseller, the novel *Die Sünde wider das Blut*, which sprang from Chamberlain's philosophy. In his *Zeitroman*, Dinter glorifies völkisch rural life and paints its threat by Jewish usurers. Despite the fact that *Die Sünde* was a work of fiction, Dinter provided the book, published by Wolfverlag in Leipzig in 1918, with an elaborate set of notes through which he contrasted the fortunes of the protagonist Hermann Kämpfer with things that actually happened. The book was dedicated to *'dem* deutschen *Houston Stewart Chamberlain'*. Dinter was an obvious product of the first radical völkisch forces that manifested themselves in Nazi jargon and symbolism. The cover of *Die Sünde wider das Blut* was 'adorned' with a red swastika from which the treacherous snake (of Judaism) crawled in black.

Dinter, like Rosenberg, linked his criticism of Christianity to his anti-Semitism. His criticism focused above all on the *New Testament*, which he began to rewrite from an Aryan perspective from the *Geistchristliche Religionsgemeinschaft* founded in 1927. Inspired by Chamberlain, but also by Kant, Fichte and De Lagarde, he believed that the *New Testament* was a Jewish theology that had to be translated back to its Aryan primal roots. A *Dinter-Bund* was founded at Insterburg to complete the *Entjudung* of Christianity and Luther's Reformation as yet. In *Die Sünde wider den Geist* and *Die Sünde wider die Liebe* as well as the programmatic struggle journal *Unser Ziel* and a number of periodicals, the fight against '*Juda und Rom*' was launched. His activism was rewarded by Hitler with a leading role in building the National Socialist movement in eastern Germany. Dinter built up the Thuringian branch and organised the first NS party day in Weimar. Yet, his unbridled activism also produced tensions with friend and foe. Jewish aggrieved people dragged Dinter to court, which he reported in *Lichtstrahlen aus dem Talmud*. They believed that Dinter was a '*Sünde wider das Vaterland*'. His heartfelt aversion to Christianity posed an electoral risk for Hitler which, like Erich Ludendorff and, to a lesser extent, Alfred Rosenberg, eventually sidelined him.[32]

Like Dinter, Rosenberg's role was not limited to theoretical foundations. Under Chamberlain's influence, in the coming years, Britain became increasingly part of the *Zukunftsweg* der völkische thinkers that Rosenberg actively advocated. After a long period of obsession over Central and Eastern Europe, Rosenberg, as a self-proclaimed apostle of National Socialism, made contact with the island's 'Aryan brothers'. In doing so, he made use of an old Baltic acquaintance who was now a British citizen, Baron William (Wilhelm) de Ropp. De Ropp was a journalist for the *Times* in Germany and had served in the RAF in the First World War. Through these contacts, Rosenberg began networking to the German-British alliance against the Soviet Union and 'world Bolshevism'. Through articles, co-written with De Ropp, he tried to polish the image of National Socialism in Britain.

The British were troubled by Rosenberg's self-imposed mission. As we saw, *Der Mythus* as well as Rosenberg's other writings did not lie, so many politicians had great difficulty in openly welcoming this radical Nazi. From London, the British embassy in Berlin was warned not to publicise Rosenberg's planned visit to Britain. Open political contacts were best avoided. Nevertheless, through De Ropp, Rosenberg did manage to speak to a number of leading Britons. Among others, a conversation took place with British Defence Minister Lord Hailsham, who did not feel very comfortable during the conversation. He was worried that Rosenberg would later quote from their conversation and tried to keep his mouth shut for as long as possible, which he managed to do for more than an hour due to Rosenberg's water of speech. In the second part of the conversation, Hailsham mainly insisted that he was counting on 'everything being in private'.[33]

Rosenberg's attempts to align with the British remained as fruitless as von Ribbentrop's later attempts. The Nazis were revolutionaries, not diplomats. They were preparing a crusade, and that required different diplomatic gifts vis-à-vis the reserved British. German professional diplomats like Konstantin Freiherr von Neurath (the German foreign minister between 1932 and 1938) who had to work with the Nazi diplomats were particularly annoyed by their incompetence.[34]

For Rosenberg, the visit to London was just a prelude to the real showdown that was about to unfold on the continent: the war with the Soviet Union. In the east, Rosenberg believed, life and death was already being fought between the 'remnants of Germanic descendants' and the 'sea of inferior races'. Rosenberg was deeply concerned about the fate of *Germanised* populations and peoples, such as the Finns, Estonians, Latvians, Ruthenians and, of course, the *'Volksdeutschen'* in Eastern Europe who had been handed over to 'Jewish-Bolshevik chaos' and 'Slavic oppression'. In his view, the chaos of Bolshevism, by which Rosenberg was referring to the civil war that followed the revolution, was explained by racial issues. Rosenberg sought the explanation, among other things, in the racial descent of the Bolshevik leaders. Lenin was of Tatar and Kalmuk descent, Trotsky was a Jew and Stalin a Caucasian. For Rosenberg, there was no doubt that Nazi Germany faced the historic task of intervention. As we shall see later, Rosenberg was actually going to take part in this in a practical sense.

In examining Rosenberg's ideas, two questions arise. Did Rosenberg's thoughts influence German politics and where were the roots of his grotesque ideas?

The picture of the influence of Rosenberg's thought is clouded by the lack of empathy of contemporary historians and the criticism and envy of his peers and fellow Nazis. It is important to bear in mind that theorists and think tanks of politics generally do not have an overly large readership. *Geopolitik* by the influential Karl Haushofer and consorts could count on 'only' 12,000 subscribers in its peak years. Yet its influence has been considerable. Looking at the astronomical circulation of Rosenberg's work, these speak in his favour. The 104th edition of *Der Mythus* went to press in 1936, six years after its publication. By then, no fewer than 523,000 copies had crossed the counter. In 1939, the book's print run had already reached 783,000 copies and would grow to over 900,000. In the meantime, other books by Rosenberg had appeared too, such as *Blut und Ehre*, which already had 50,000 printed copies in 1935 (fifth edition). By 1939, this print run had reached 140,000 copies. Sales of Rosenberg's thought were thus colossal. It was 'compulsory reading', although many will never have read it. Sceptics will wonder what Rosenberg's influence could have been if the bulk of people did not read his books. The question is whether that makes so much difference to the influence of the ideas. Hitler's *Mein Kampf* was an unread bestseller as well, but the influence of the thinking noted in it was of a disastrous magnitude. Thereby, the titles mentioned above were only a small fragment of the enormous production of the author Rosenberg. We will quickly run through the most important titles.

First there was Rosenberg's journalistic work, including for the NSDAP newspaper *Völkische Beobachter*. In 1924, he started the magazine *Der Weltkampf*, which was succeeded in 1930 by the monthly publication of the *Nationalsozialistischen Monatshefte*. Besides *Der Mythus* and *Blut und Ehre,* many more of his books appeared in a relatively short time. Many of these were published by the Zentral Verlag of the NSDAP, including *Revolutionen in der bildenden Kunst* (a small rapid-fire journal), *Das Wesensgefüge des Nationalsozialismus* (on the origins of German 'rebirth' with a print run of at least 63,000), *Der Kampf um die Weltanschauung* (lectures at the Kroll opera, 24 pages, circulation of around 26,000), *Der deutsche Ordensstaat* (on the National Socialist ideas of the state), *Der Sumpf* on the 'excesses' of the Weimar Republic as well as many lectures and speeches published in book form (party days) and a booklet on one of Rosenberg's spiritual predecessors, Dietrich Eckart.[35]

In Rosenberg's early work *Russlandpest,* he made an initial advance on his later *Ostpolitik*. The main thesis of his book is that Russia was not a nation but a nationality state. In a rough division, the territory of the Soviet Union could be divided into five blocks: 'Greater Finland' (Grossfinland), the Baltic regions (Baltenland), the Ukraine, Caucasia and the core country of Russia. This last area he geographically bounded with St Petersburg (Leningrad), Moscow and the Urals. In Rosenberg's opinion, this was only a very superficial division. At a later stage, when war had already broken out, he mapped 87 nationalities. In *Russlandpest,* Rosenberg underestimated Bolshevism's chances of survival. He initially thought it would be a problem of 'temporary nature' that would be corrected 'from within'. Later, Rosenberg adjusted this view and believed only in changes from outside, i.e. an intervention by Germany.

In 1920, he translated Gougenot des Mousseaux's anti-Semitic book, *Der Jude, das Judentum und die Verjudung der christlichen Völker*. German historian Werner Maser sees Des Mousseaux as one of the most important anti-Semitic authors who, along with Otto Hauser, Werner Sombart, Henry Ford, Theodor Fritsch and Friedrich Delitzsch, could count on Hitler's warm interest.[36] In addition, Rosenberg was the man who widely introduced *Die Protokolle der Weissen von Zion (und die jüdische Weltpolitik)* in Germany. *Those Protokolle von Zion* were until then very popular with extreme-nationalist Russian organisations, such as 'Soyus Ruskowo Naroda' (Union of the Russian People) and were now beginning a second life in Bavaria. This allowed the translation of old-religious anti-Semitism into the new political anti-Semitism. This brilliant tome gave anti-Semitism a strong tailwind. In Canada, Adrien Arcand began advocating the book, Henry Ford, Charles E. Coughlin and Gerald B. Winrods in the United States, Martinez Zuviria in Argentina, Darquier de Pellepoix and Louis Ferdinand Céline in France, Giovanni Preziosi in Italy and László Endre in Hungary.[37]

The production of the author Rosenberg and the themes of his work, the visions exhibited as well as the fact that they were published by the NSDAP, reflect the enormous influence he had as a catalyst of all kinds of political sentiments: anti-Semitism, pan-Germanist thought and the glorification of the völkisch ideal, the 'legitimisation' of the Lebensraum idea and anti-Slavism. The group that could still best withstand its wrath was the 'enemy within': the Christians. The life span of the Third Reich was simply too short, otherwise they too would have had to pay with their blood the price that the Holocaust and the Lebensraum field trip demanded of the others.

Misleading for the study of Rosenberg's influence is the extent of his actual political power. Rosenberg was more of a theorist than a politician. His convenient political enemies eagerly exploited this by portraying him as a 'dreamer' and criticising him where his rabid racism and anti-clerical stance went too far for the official line. His main competitors in the practical political field were the sharp Dr Joseph Goebbels, the overambitious von Ribbentrop and the powerful Reichsführer-SS Heinrich Himmler - who 'implanted' one of his confidants, SS-Obergruppenführer and Chief of the SS-Hauptamt Gottlob Berger, as a spy in Rosenberg political organisation. This sinister company did not miss a chance to put a spanner in Rosenberg's wheel. The clumsy, behaviourally disturbed and dreamy image of Rosenberg that emerged as a result has been partly adopted by historians. This conveniently forgets Rosenberg's huge publication stream which was respectfully released under the auspices of the NSDAP. Of course, the jokes about Rosenberg also reached Hitler from time to time, who could laugh at them and make fun of the somewhat humourless and blood-serious Balt who bowed under his ariosophical *Weltschmerz*, but when push came to shove, he protected Rosenberg. In a detailed letter from May 1931, Hitler defended *Der Mythus* against criticism from those who felt that this book 'should never have been published'. Hitler parried this attack with a historical counter example. Goethe was widely criticised in his time for his anti-clerical stance as well. Yet he was free to write whatever he wanted. In defending Rosenberg, Hitler invoked freedom of speech, a freedom which the Nazis themselves did not do justice after 1933. Another typical case of Hitler's support towards Rosenberg's ideas can be seen when German pacifist Carl von Ossietzky was nominated for the Nobel Prize. Hitler subsequently considered creating his own German 'Nationalpreis', and as possible candidates for this prize he mentioned Alfred Rosenberg, Fritz Todt and Willy Messcherschmidt.[38]

From the spectrum of everyday power politics, this support from Hitler for Rosenberg was not obvious and was therefore all the more remarkable and indicative of the importance Hitler attached to him. After the failed Putsch at the Feldherrnhalle in 1923, Rosenberg was appointed by Hitler to lead the party into illegality. This role did not suit Rosenberg, a thinker rather than a doer. Hitler's party faced competition from other völkisch organisations, such as the *Grossdeutsche Volksgemeinschaft*, and Rosenberg had difficulty parrying this. When, as a result of internal squabbles, he, together with Gregor Strasser and Ernst Röhm, did not attend the reconstitution meeting of the NSDAP, it constituted a deep rift between Hitler and Rosenberg. Although Rosenberg recanted, unlike Röhm and Strasser who would both be harshly removed from the political arena, the bond never became as close as before.

Moreover, it has been said by some historians that Hitler would never have read Rosenberg's *Der Mythus*. The opposite is true. No doubt Hitler already had an insight into the work before its publication. There were, however, reasons why Hitler kept his distance from the book. He was aware of the Christian criticism of the work and did not (yet) want to alienate himself from this part of the electorate. Secondly, Hitler - apart from Dietrich Eckart - recognised no spiritual predecessors and would never openly adorn Rosenberg. Also, as with everyone around him, Hitler applied the divide-and-conquer strategy with Rosenberg, which did not always strengthen Rosenberg's position. When Joseph Goebbels and Alfred Rosenberg both ran for the post of minister of science and culture, Hitler gave the job to former Hanover Gauleiter Bernhard Rust.[39]

Typical of the confusion surrounding Rosenberg's position, is the thesis of German historian Werner Maser who calls Rosenberg a *disciple* of Hitler.[40] This does not seem to be an accurate description. On the other hand, Rosenberg was not a *teacher* of Hitler either. For Hitler, Rosenberg was an ariosophical-völkian thinker whom, for electoral reasons, he did not unwillingly follow from a certain distance. From his eternal divide-and-conquer strategy, Rosenberg was a useful pawn that he could deploy and drop at will against leftist and Christian forces in the brown camp. This explains Rosenberg's peculiar position within the political force field in occupied Central and Eastern Europe, where he was not without power but mostly fell between the cracks. Under the impressive title of *Reichsleiter*, he was allowed to head the NSDAP's *Aussenpolitisches Amt* (APA).

Rosenbergs main influence has been on the politics vis-à-vis Central and Eastern Europe, but even there more in a theoretical than in a practical sense. Interesting is what William Carr writes about this in his *Hitler, a study in personality and politics*. Rosenberg's influence, Carr believed, was greater than Haushofer's. Where Haushofer merely provided supplements to Hitler's Lebensraum philosophy, Rosenberg changed Hitler's view of Eastern Europe. After the debacle of 1914-1918, Hitler was preoccupied with the old enemy images France and Britain, and infected with old anti-Semitic sentiments from his Viennese days and the ariosophical climate in Munich. Rosenberg brought these elements together by portraying the Russian revolution as a Jewish-Bolshevik plot. Hitler adopted this theory from about 1922 and it became the main concept of his *Weltanschauung*.[41] Less fortunate was Rosenberg's performance. Even before the outbreak of the war, Rosenberg was a fierce advocate of German interests in the East. The *Auslandsdeutschen*, divided into *Reichsdeutschen* (German citizens outside the Reich border) and *Volksdeutschen* (Germans who were citizens of another state), saw their interests represented by various organisations. Rosenberg's *Aussenpolitisches Amt* (APA) tried to play a leading role in this. This political power game, in which he had to compete with, among others, the *Volksbund für das Deutschtum im Ausland*, did not go well for him. Rosenberg was no diplomat, so his plans to bring Germans living outside Germany into one *Bund Deutscher Osten* (BDO) led by Franz Lüdtke ran aground.

Heavy-handedly, Rosenberg had to concede to his rivals on his points of contention. Whereas he was concerned with the survival of traditional characteristics of peoples, Himmler was not interested in *Germanisierung* or preservation of existing cultures but planned *ethnic engineering* of the East, at the expense of the indigenous population. This difference repeatedly led to asymmetrical political policies of Rosenberg's agencies and the rival agencies with all the administrative chaos that ensued. More than the other Nazis, Rosenberg, himself from Eastern Europe, was interested in the fate of the small peoples and the *Volksdeutschen*. This made him a target of ridicule.

Nevertheless, Rosenberg's influence, as a radical exponent of the völkisch movement, will be clear. The völkisch movement was a hotchpotch of more and less radical currents and thoughts, with variants such as Ernst Jünger, who emerged from the conservative revolution, among the völkisch thinkers who can be counted amidst the founding fathers of National Socialism. In their theories, we all see partial elements that we saw in Rosenberg's work as well. Therefore, it is striking how many cross-links and cross-pollinations occurred in the dark early days of the Hitler movement. Pseudo-religious ideas, ariosophical supremacist thoughts mingled with political frustrations, flat anti-Semitism, fear and hatred for the Slavs and occult secret organisations working for the new Germany.

Some of the people in this shadowy *Umfeld* came from Eastern Europe, as did Rosenberg, who had been born in Reval in 1893. They were displaced people who had fled to the West after the dramatic downfall of the German empire and the collapse of tsarist rule. Many of them belonged to the white opposition, the aristocracy, and their wealth was as great as their aversion to the Bolsheviks. At the beginning of this chapter, we already discussed the völkisch thinkers' fear of modernism. Clearly, the revolutionary transformations in Russia and its embrace by part of the Western intelligentsia were considered very threatening by the conservative part of the population. The horror stories carried by the displaced people reinforced the sense of insecurity. History tells us that at every deep crisis in Europe, Russia was labelled as a danger: 1812 (defeat Napoleon), 1917 (World War I) and 1945 (the start of the Cold War). Russia and the later Soviet Union were great but unknown. The negative image of Russia was reinforced at the beginning of the 20th century by the reactions to the Russian revolution, which posed a danger to the entire power constellation in Europe. This reinforced the old image of the West being 'civilised' against the 'barbaric' East. In fact, this characterisation dates back to ancient Greece and was adopted by the Christian church. Homer was the first to use the word barbarians when talking about Eastern Europe. Russia's historically often weak economic position reinforced the image of Western superiority. According to many - Hitler included - the Russian state had no 'original civilisation'. The country was only a poor imitation of the West and also had no *mission civilisatrice*; and if there was one then only towards Asia. Opinions were also divided on the period of Tsar Peter the Great, generally seen as one of Russia's more 'enlightened' monarchs. Tsar Peter was known not only for his modesty, studiousness and simplicity but for his unprecedented cruelty as well.[42]

The Russian revolution reinforced the fear of the large, unknown country and its imperialist ambitions. Comparisons between Russia and the raids of the Huns were therefore frequent. Russia was the realm of darkness, or, as Ronald Reagan put it in our time, 'the realm of evil'. Werner Maser points out that Hitler constantly tended to use negative descent typologies for the peoples of the East. He repeatedly compared the Russians to Huns and Mongols who had threatened the German people 'since it had entered the magic circle of historical consciousness'. Hitler drew direct parallels between the Bolshevism of his time and the Hun threat of the past. He called Bolshevism a 'new organisation of Central Asian humanity' and feared new invasions. Hitler also compared the Czechs to the Mongols; he saw the Bulgarians as descendants of the Turkmen.[43] Above all this were the Jews, who were the linchpin of this world order that threatened völkisch Germany. 'All the intellectuals who supported the Russian revolution were Jewish. Jewish students read from the *Pravda* in the hospitals full of wounded soldiers from the front,' Alfred Rosenberg mused. More positive stereotypes were usually short-lived. Supporters of the Restoration, the reaction to the French Revolution and Napoleon, saw Alexander I as their hero in the anti-revolutionary war and listened with admiration to the ideas of the Holy Alliance. Still this *'miracle russe'*, as Voltaire called it, was always short-lived.

This idea formation played an eerily legitimising role in the emergence of the Nazis' supremacy idea over Eastern Europe and belongs to the prelude to the campaign for Lebensraum. On the other hand, we should note that the fear of the East was not unjustified. With the communist revolution, after the horrors of World War I, the 20th century had embarked on the bloodiest wallow in human history. From a historical point of view, we must conclude that the image of Russia after the Russian revolution was still too positive rather than too negative. The Russian revolution, partly watched with sympathy in the West, had more opponents killed in the first few months of its rule than Christianity had in its entire existence. In addition, recent research has shown that the Red Army was already planning to overrun Western Europe during the Polish-Russian War. Here the völkisch thinkers had correctly assessed the danger of communism, but that leaves the criticism of the inhuman aspects of their own ideology untouched. Fear of the abuses in Eastern Europe was used for their own bloody ideology and to legitimise their plans for conquest.[44]

Among the Eastern European connections in the early years of the Nazis was the influential Max Erwin von Scheubner-Richter, a wealthy man who financially assisted the Nazis on several occasions. Von Scheubner-Richter had served in Turkey in World War I in a half diplomatic, half military mission where he had attempted to save Armenians from genocide. In 1917, he served in Riga, where he was leader of the Press and Propaganda of the German headquarters. In 1919, he served as political adviser to the Social Democrat August Winnig, the Reich Commissioner of the Baltic territories. Later, von Scheubner-Richter was involved in the reactionary Kapp-Putsch in Berlin and after its failure he had moved to Munich. Von Scheubner-Richter shared Rosenberg's deep concern about developments in Central and Eastern Europe and the alleged Jewish-Bolshevik hand in it. The cross-pollination continued when Rosenberg introduced von Scheubner-Richter to Hitler in October 1920. The latter was very impressed by von Scheubner-Richter, who soon became an important key figure in the white-nationalist Russian community in Germany. He tied the white opposition, which Hitler said in *Mein Kampf* was the 'Germanic core' of Russia, to himself by publishing the *Wirtschaftspolitische Aufbau-Korrespondenz über Ostfragen.*

Von Scheubner-Richter organised a major nationalist-Russian manifestation in the spa town of Bad Reichenhall in June 1921. At the time of the Russian civil war, he had good contacts with the 'whites' and in particular with General Wrangel, whose troops initially controlled large parts of Belarus. Von Scheubner-Richter also had good contacts with wealthy Russian immegrés who often had huge assets from the Russian oil industry. They included such big names as Gukasov, Baron Koeppen, Lenison, Nobel and the Duke von Leuchtenberg. They were able to bolster the coffers of Hitler's party and, through von Scheubner-Richter's charm and diplomatic skills, did just that. This made Scheubner-Richter an important *grand seigneur* for Hitler, a respectable public relations man he needed to gain access to the higher circles. The good circles to which von Scheubner-Richter had access included not only wealthy industrialists like Fritz Thyssen or the white aristocracy, but the circle around First World War general Erich Ludendorff and his wife Dr Mathilde Ludendorff von Kemnitz as well. Around Ludendorff and his *Volkswarte* publishing *house*, a strong, mystically oriented völkische movement had developed that had many overlaps with Rosenberg's, Chamberlain's and Dinter's ideas. As in *Der Mythus,* Ludendorff agitated not only against Jews and Freemasons, but also against Christianity as an 'un-German' power, accusing the Jesuits in particular of plotting against the German national character. *'Ehr und Wehr'* were at risk as a result. Hitler's attitude towards Ludendorff was very similar to that towards Rosenberg and Dinter. He respected him but for electoral reasons kept his distance from his radical criticism of Christianity, which was akin to an 'unguided projectile'. Max Erwin von Scheubner-Richter's life came to an abrupt end when he was fatally struck by a bullet at the Hitler-Putsch at the Feldhernnhalle in 1923. Hitler was genuinely affected by this. 'We can replace everyone,' he mused, 'except von

Scheubner-Richter.' In the march to the Feldherrnhalle, von Scheubner-Richter had walked alongside Hitler and pulled him down to the ground in his fall.⁴⁵

Von Scheubner-Richter was just one of the Eastern Europeans who helped influence the Nazis. The number of Eastern Europeans who had fled to Germany as a result of the fall of the tsarist regime and the expansion of communism was considerable. Russian writer Vlasislv Khodasevitsch typified this by calling Berlin 'the stepmother of Russian cities'. However, Germany was not the only haven for Russian emigrants. Paris and Warsaw were also in demand. Nevertheless, hundreds of thousands found shelter in Germany. In 1923, Russians in Berlin numbered no less than 400,000 souls. These soon led completely separate, isolated lives. Within the emigrant community there were often fierce feuds over the situation in the homeland. After the Treaty of Rapallo, which strengthened ties between Berlin and Moscow, many pro-tsarist Russians travelled on to France. Striking was the fact, historian Matthias Vetter believes, that many Russian migrants were very anti-Semitic in outlook. Consequently, a large number of them felt at home in the völkisch camp. For instance, the Russian Grigory (Grogor) Schwartz-Bostunitsch made it to SS-Standartenführer. Others, on the other hand, including well-known authors Andrei Belyy and Alexei Tolstoi, the 'red count', eventually moved back to Russia, where the latter replaced Maxim Gorki as leader of the Russian writers' union.⁴⁶

The most important Bavarian exponent of völkisch thinking was the writer, poet, and philosopher Dietrich Eckart, born in 1868 in Neumarkt, Bavaria.

National Socialism was a pseudo-religion. In this pseudo-religion, with Hitler as Führer, there was very little room for the open recognition of teachers. Dietrich Eckart was an exception to this. On his deathbed, he is said to have whispered: 'Follow Hitler! He will dance! But it was I who set the tune. I initiated him into the secret doctrine, I gave him the visions and the means of communicating with the forces. Don't feel sorry for me, because I influenced history more than any German.'⁴⁷

The figure Eckart has gained recognition in post-war literature on the Third Reich because Hitler dedicated *Mein Kampf* to him. Yet for most researchers, he has remained a fringe figure, dying in 1923 before Hitler knew real power. The descriptions given of him are rather similar and usually emphasise his penchant for angular statements, Stammtisch philosophy and his astronomical alcohol (and drug?) consumption, from which he also eventually died. The general tenor is therefore that Eckart was a 'somewhat lapsed type' with 'a hint of talent'. A 'coffeehouse intellectual', the American Hitler biographer Toland believed, who 'divided his attention between politics and drinking'. Fest called him a 'primitive orator and a friend of good wine'. Such approaches carry the risk that Eckart's input is too much out of sight. It is true that Eckart enjoyed earthly temptations with somewhat too great relish, but Churchill too was a hearty drinker and no one will deny that he played a role of historical importance.

Other historians do emphasise Eckart's role within the völkisch camp. George L. Mosse, who of course noted that there is no decent biography on Eckart, believes that Eckart's influence is underestimated. Nolte emphasises Eckart's role in reinforcing Hitler's anti-Semitism, and Werner Maser and Gerhard Schreiber emphasise Eckart's role as a teacher.[48]

As reticent as some historians are about Eckart's role, so outspoken are his contemporaries. 'Eckart,' believes Hitler press chief Ernst Hanfstaengl in his memoirs, belonged to the *'engsten Vertrauensgruppe'* that existed around Hitler. He found Eckart a 'splendid specimen' and a living witness to 'old Bavaria'. 'We soon became good friends,' Hanfstaengl continues, praising his translation of Ibsen's *Peer Gynt*. Eckart had a 'heart for the cause' and was one of the people Hitler had 'taken under his wing'.[49] Another contemporary, Hitler's line photographer Heinrich Hoffmann, points to the so-called '*Hitlerwalze*' in one of the ex-combatants' tribal pubs, where hours were spent debating the political course to be followed.[50] Completely lyrical is the Eckart study Wilhelm Grün wrote for the University of Munich. While professors d'Ester, von Müller and (again) Karl Haushofer looked over his shoulder, Grün wrote Eckart to the skies. His *Auf gut deutsch* is 'the best thing Eckart ever wrote', he was 'a godsend from heaven', that 'fell from heaven in this hour of need' for Germany. Grün erected a statue of him in his *Dietrich Eckart as Publizist*. What is interesting here is that Eckart Grün had initially stood out as a living *Abwehr propaganda* against the communist council republic in Munich. Eckart was the figurehead of anti-Bolshevism, placing Bolshevism on the offensive and National Socialism on the defensive. This element would also be used by Hitler in his attack on the Soviet Union in 1941. The author was pleased that Eckart's work 'knocked Eisner, Toller and Leviené around the head' and that for once his study of Eckart was not written 'from a Talmudist point of view'. Characteristic of the book is its inclusion of Eckart's entire family tree. At the time of National Socialism, this was the most important footnote.[51]

The contemporaries and Hitler's brief in *Mein Kampf* leave no doubt, Eckart, with Rosenberg, was among the most important völkisch thinkers who helped pave the way for the NSDAP and its fatal course.

The two also knew each other well. Rosenberg appeared at Eckart's without announcing himself. The poet was impressed by his appearance in the doorway: 'a tense, deadly serious young man'. Rosenberg's first words were: 'Could you use a warrior against Jerusalem?' Eckart laughed. 'Of course!' Rosenberg then presented him with an article on the destructive forces of Judaism and Bolshevism in Russia. Soon Rosenberg began writing articles for Eckart's periodicals. The themes here were usually the same: the Zionists had started the world war, as well as the communist revolution, and were now plotting, together with the Freemasons, to take over world power.[52] The meeting between Rosenberg and Eckart triggered new cross-pollinations. While Eckart gave Rosenberg a stage and introduced him to the Bavarian Brown camp, Rosenberg brought Eckart into contact with Eastern European anti-Semites and anti-Communists, including Max Erwin von Scheubner-Richter and generals Skoropadski and Bishupski, both from Belarus and future members of the Thule Society.[53]

Eckart was one of the best-known key figures of völkisch Bavaria. In his long sessions in Bavarian beer halls, he had gathered around him the hard core of völkisch thinkers. This informal circle included Hitler, Hess, Rosenberg, Röhm, Streicher, Feder and Drexler. The central theme everyone was talking about was the Bavarian council republic following Bela Kun's council republic in Hungary and the Russian revolution. Even before Eckart knew Hitler, he had an idea of what Germany's new strongman should look like who should put order in his affairs. To safeguard Germany from communist domination, a 'man who could stand the sound of machine guns' was needed. The new leader could not be an officer, he believed; after the war debacle, they had lost the respect of the people. It was better for the new leader to come from the working class. It was also important that he was not at a loss for words. According to Eckart, it did not take much intellect to do politics. After all, politics was 'the stupidest profession in the world. Even the market women in Bavaria understood more about it than those people in Weimar'. The profile of the Führer had been sketched.[54]

An important key to Hitler's *Weltanschauung* and the influence of the *Hitlerwalze* forms an extremely remarkable and almost forgotten booklet: *Der Bolschewismus von Moses bis Lenin.*[55] This booklet, which one looks for in vain on the bibliography of most standard works on the Third Reich, is one of Adolf Hitler's most candid confessions. It shows his most rabid interpretation of Völkisch and Ariosophical thought and his one-dimensional worldview that displayed occult traits. The 'gap' between Rosenberg's and Hitler's thought that many contemporary historians believe they see is also immediately closed on closer examination of this volume. Eckart wrote *Der Bolschewismus von Moses bis Lenin* practically on his deathbed, greatly weakened by his imprisonment as a result of Hitler's failed Munich Putsch in 1923. Before the end of the year, Eckart would finally lay down his head, leaving the world his last publication in draft form. Yet this thin tome published in March 1924 is a startlingly frank two-way conversation between Eckart and Hitler in which Eckart chose a raw, direct and unpolished style. It is almost as if the reader can join the *Hitlerwalze*.

Like *Der Mythus*, the dialogue is characterised by the all-important race issue. Initially, they discuss the 'Jewish role' in the Munich council republic, in which 'Jewish homes were systematically spared', only to fall back to the days of Pontius Pilate who had already 'lost track pertaining the Jews'. Even in biblical days, they conclude in concert, there was hardly a place on earth where Jewish influence did not assert itself. The Jewish exodus from Egypt was the result of a kind of failed French Revolution in which the Jews were mistaken about the 'nationalism' of the Egyptians who then chased them out of their country. The entire history was characterised by a constant attempt by the Jews to dominate the other races by sidelining and murdering their aristocracy. According to Hitler, the *Old Testament* was the best proof of this. Under Trajan, mass killings of non-Jewish nobility took place in Babylonia, Egypt and Cyprus. From the dark days of antiquity, Eckart and Hitler extended the line of conspiracy to the present. 31 (Aryan) kings were murdered under Joshua alone, so in 1871 Jewish-infused Frenchmen stormed the homes of the rich in Paris. The palaces of the Rothschilds were spared in the process.[56]

As the title of the book indicates, Eckart and Hitler saw Bolshevism as the latest link in a long series of moves by Judaism to conquer the world. This made the Lebensraum conquest policy a step in the race war that Hitler considered inevitable. In this tirade, Hitler for once was frank about Christianity. He spoke of popes with Jewish blood, children's crusades set up by Jews. With foresight, he opined that the burning of synagogues would have little effect. Finally, he issued a final warning: the Jews pursued paradise by seeking to destroy the rest of humanity. By doing so, they 'called down upon themselves the tragedy of Lucifer'.[57]

Eckart's *Hitlerwalze* were not harmless *Stammtischgespräche*, over the years they formed a playbook that Hitler would unfold in the NSDAP, a meeting place of reactionaries, ariosophists and völkische thinkers who collectively produced the dangerous mixture of talent, guts and sentiment. Underneath the NSDAP's pragmatic and populist programme lay the foundation of the *Hitlerwalze* as a concrete foundation, allowing Eckart to rest his head with peace of mind. How the National Socialist revolution would take place was another story: a Putsch, a coup, a parliamentary election? Eckart travelled with Hitler to the Kapp-Putsch in Berlin, where they soaked up the political powder vapour. At the Bierhallen-Putsch, the first grab was made.

Furthermore, the 'concrete foundation' included ariosophical thought with its occult traits. In this, too, Eckart played an important role. In his final moments, Eckart spoke of Hitler's introduction to 'the forces' and the 'secret doctrine' he had taught Hitler. These were the same words the Russian medium Helena Petrovna Blavatsky had used to capture the essence of her theosophical thought.[58] Eckart's words also bear resemblance to one of the most occult ariosophical-völkian thinkers, Lanz von Liebenfels, who wrote to a friend that Hitler was 'one of his disciples' and that he would 'make the world hold its breath'.

Eckart, like Rosenberg, was a 'Guest' - an official title with a certain status - of the so-called Thule Society. The Thule Society was a mystical-occult movement founded in 1918 that dwelt on Aryan racial purity. On 9 November 1918, Rudolf von Sebottendorff had 'declared war' on Judaism at the Walterspiel brothers' Vier Jahreszeiten hotel in Munich. The organisation had been founded around von Sebottendorff (his real name was Adam Alfred Rudolf Glauer or Erwin Torre), Walter Nauhaus and Walter Deicke and had around 1,500 members. The Thule Society had an elitist outward appearance. This was due in no small part to the fact that many wealthy people had joined the organisation. It is believed that in addition to the aforementioned Sebottendorff, Rosenberg, Drexler and Hess, among others, Bavarian Justice Minister Franz Gurtner was a member of Thule society, as was Munich's police commissioner Pöhner and his right-hand man and later NS Interior Minister Wilhelm Frick. Other prominent or high-profile members included the later Poland executioner Hans Frank, publisher Julius F. Lehmann, Hans Georg Grassinger (*Münchener Beobachter*), Gustav Franz Maria Prinz von Thurn und Taxis, Baroness Adelheid von Mikusch, Wilhelm Freiherr von Wittenberg, Hans Hermann Freiherr von und zu Bodemann, Franz Karl Freiherr von Teuchert, Ernst Freiherr von Löffelholtz, Freiherr von Reitzenstein and Countess Heila von Westarp.[59]

At his speech on 9 November 1918, after the German military defeat, von Sebottendorff had directly articulated the ideological thinking of the secret organisation. 'My brothers and sisters,' he had begun the meeting, 'yesterday we experienced the collapse of everything that was familiar and of value to us. In the place of our blood-related monarch reigns our mortal enemy'. The motto of the alliance was: *'Dencke daran dass du ein Deutscher bist, halte dein Blut rein.'* These were not empty words. The assassination of Kurt Eisner (left and Jewish) on 21 February 1919 was carried out by Count Arco-Valley, a confidant of the Thule Society. It was one in a series of murders and attacks carried out by reactionaries in the final days of the November defeat. One of the best-known attacks was that on the politician Walther Rathenau, who, because of his wealth (his father was one of the founders of aeg), his Jewishness and his left-wing political beliefs, as well as his collaboration with the Allies and his 'dangerous' utopian political views expressed in *Von kommenden Dingen*, among others, was the textbook example of the 'anti-German' Jew for the right. His critical and highly psychological booklet on Kaiser Wilhelm II, *Der Kaiser, Eine Betrachtung was* not warmly received. This, his biographer Kessler believes, made him a kind of arch traitor in the eyes of millions of impoverished and starving Germans. *'Knallt ab den Walther Rathenau, die gottverdammte Judensau'* And so it happened. Reactionaries from the circle around Ernst von Salomon, who reported on the attack in *Die Geächteten,* Ritter von Epp and Ehrhardt, killed Rathenau with gunshots and a hand grenade. Other well-known 'leftists' who fell victim to völkisch violence were politicians Matthias Erzberger, Karl Gareis and publicist Maximilian Harden.[60]

The origins of the Thule Society's thinking went back to ariosophy, which had sprung from the theosophical movement. In the late nineteenth century and early twentieth century, there had been a huge revival of occultism and mysticism. Often this mysticism, even among the theosophical movement, was of an idealistic nature and the message it proclaimed was one of peace and mutual respect. In practice, however, much could go wrong with the elaboration and interpretations of these ideas.

The most important representative of the theosophical movement was Helena Petrovna Blavatsky. Her life story is as wondrous as it is interesting. The debate about her ideas and her life's journey persists to this day. Her work is still available in every major bookstore. To some, Blavatsky is an absolute saint, to others a fantastic impostor. We must suffice here with a brief sketch of the woman and her work, for the theosophical movement and the effect of their ideas on völkische thinkers is the focus here.

Blavatsky was born in August 1831 in Ekaterinoslav, present-day Dniepropetrovsk, Russia. She married early but soon divorced again and went through an adventurous time, travelling the world, which was not an everyday occurrence for a woman in the Victorian era. In July 1873, she set foot in the USA and founded the *Theosophical Society* there on 17 November 1875. Initially, they had wanted to call the organisation *Miracle Club*, with the aim of studying spiritualism. The main aim of the *Theosophical Society was formulated* as follows: 'To promote a sense of brotherhood among peoples and to render assistance.... by counsel, information to and cooperation with all worthy persons and associations, with the strict provison that no pecuniary gain should result for the Society.'[61] The sources of wisdom from which the association drew to provide its 'counsels and intelligence' were rather wonderful in nature. On one of her many travels, Blavatsky said she had been to the Himalayas. On the roof of the world lived 'the true princes', called mahatmas in Sanskrit. These 'adepts of the highest wisdom' had escaped samsara, the eternally spinning wheel of death and rebirth. Their minds ruled over the body. These mahatmas possessed unimaginable power, Blavatsky said, and developed further and further so that in the future, in a cloud of detached atoms, they could rule humanity and earth as Greek gods. For a long time, this special knowledge had remained hidden from the world, until Blavatsky was sent out by her masters to spread the message. 'I belong to the secret sect of the Druze of Mount Lebanon and was for a long time among Dervishes, Persian mullahs and mystics of all kinds,' she told of her own spiritual knowledge.[62]

The thrust of her message, in brief, was as follows. Across all cultural differences and religions, a secret alliance of initiates and adepts ruled over matter. Blavatsky saw it as her task to initiate people into the foundations of religious science so that the divine spark that resides in each of us would ignite. Blavatsky recorded her thinking in *Isis Unveiled* (1877) and *The Secret Doctrine* (1888).[63] Taken together, the books span more than three thousand pages and were followed by another endless series of speeches and articles. In the latter book, Blavatsky unfolds the essence of her secret wisdom as a messenger of the lodge. Never, according to theosophists, was a messenger or medium as candid as Blavatsky. In fact, her work constitutes an alternative creation story.[64]

The core of the creation story consists of a sequence of seven original races, tied to seven continents. The first race she traced to the North Pole consisted of beings without physical bodies. The second race extended over a large area, from Greenland to Kamchatka whom she called the 'hyperboraeans'; they were beings who made a first attempt to take on human forms. The third root race originated in Lemuria and formed the beginning of humanity. After Lemuria perished, the survivors settled in the mystical island kingdom of Atlantis. When Atlantis went down, the survivors fled to northern and central Europe and moved through that area to central Asia and the Gobi Desert (note the similarities with Rosenberg's *Der Mythus*). There, the fifth root race arose: the Aryans, with whom Blavatsky had arrived in the present age. Two more original races would follow, before man would complete his triumphant march to higher astral life.[65]

With Theosophy and Blavatsky came what Leon Poliakov has characterised as 'the Aryan myth', which would be the cradle for the emergence of a perverted interpretation of Blavatsky's racial theories. Although Blavatsky wanted to stir up anything but racial differences, an uncanny *Blut und Boden ideology* arose out of the theosophical notion that the present age was the age of the Aryan race, which culminated directly in the creation of such radical-racist organisations as the Germanic Order, the Thule Society and the Armanenschaft. This perversion of the theosophical view of the Aryan root race is generally referred to as ariosophy, although arism and germanomania are also mentioned.[66]

Ariosophy had its headquarters in Vienna. In *Mein Kampf*, Hitler already told us that 'the streets of Vienna had been his hardest and best teacher'. The influence of the Vienna years on Hitler was profound. He saw Vienna as '*die Verkörperung der Blutschande*' and spoke of a 'racial Babylon'. Through the city ran an invisible but palpable line between 'Germans' and 'Slavs'. Jews had been emancipated at the end of the nineteenth century and greatly outnumbered by migration. The industrial revolution presented itself and the Anschluss movement revived after the birth of the Austrian republic in 1918. Radical politicians, like Georg von Schönerer (1842-1921), advocated pan-Germanism. He had himself called Führer and was notorious for his anti-Semitism. This made the atmosphere tense and rich in historical processes. In von Schönerer's pan-Germanist Vienna, Herzl worked on his 'Jewish state'. Theodor Herzl was originally from Budapest and initially aligned himself with the nationalists and admirers of Bismarck. Increasing anti-Semitism in his student days made him more aware of his Jewishness, which eventually made him a Zionist. Thus, in Vienna, the capital of völkisch rebirth and Lebensraum, Herzl too dreamt of the 'promised land'. '*Wenn ihr wollt ist es kein Märchen,*' he mused in his 1902 novel *Altneuland*. On 2 July 1904, he died of exhaustion. Like Moses, he had initiated a return to Israel. On the first El Al flight between Vienna and Israel in 1949, his bones were flown over.[67]

In this turbulent climate, the ariosophical perversion of theosophy thrived. In fact, ariosophy formed the turbulent underbelly of an already turbulent and tense political climate. The ariosophists played on the fear of the sharpening multi-ethnic and multi-cultural divisions that emerged in the closing years of the Habsburg Empire, in a country transforming from an agrarian society to an industrial one. Drawing on cultural pessimism, a *century-Wende* with well overhanging changes and uncertainties, ariosophy got wind of the situation. In doing so, ariosophy played on a wishful thinking that is sometimes eagerly embraced in an ethnically divided society: one could belong to a group, and within those groups plead for purity and cleanliness. It had something elitist about it and, through theosophy, was also linked to the supernatural.

The best-known völkische thinkers of ariosophy were Guido von List and Lanz von Liebenfels. Guido Karl Anton von List - the 'von' he later secretly added - was a typical product of ariosophy. From an early age, List possessed a keen interest in mystical matters. His most vivid childhood memory involved visiting the underground catacombs of St Stephen's Cathedral in Vienna, where he was born on 5 October 1848. His parents were in business, but List wanted to become an artist from an early age. Above all, he wanted to escape settled life and travelled extensively through the enchantingly beautiful Habsburg Empire. He became a landscape admirer and became fascinated by mountains and the castles or ruins perched on them. List joined the Alpine Society and trekked across the country, often bivouacking at the foot of a castle. There is an interesting anecdote about him that has been frequently quoted. In 1875, he made a trip to the remains of Carnuntum on the Danube, where 1500 years earlier the Germanic tribes had inflicted a defeat on the Romans. In honour of this battle, he visited the site and, at the foot of the ruins, buried a number of empty wine bottles in the shape of the swastika. Thereupon, he solemnly promised to dedicate an ode to the Germanic achievements towards Rome by means of a book, which indeed saw the light of day in two volumes in 1888.

List was the first to synthesise ancient Germanic mythology and the Aryan theory of theosophy, referring to them as Ario-Germanic. Studying archaeological sources, texts and maps, List had come to the conclusion that there were remarkable similarities between theosophy based on Eastern philosophy and mysticism and the pre-Christian, Gnostic primordial culture of the Occident. Just as Blavatsky drew on ancient Eastern wisdom to determine the way forward in the present, so too did List delve into his own primordial history, which he believed had been snowed under by Christianity and Judaism. List discovered that in the Habsburg Empire there were all kinds of indications of the primal language that had fallen into oblivion as a result of the advent of Christianity. Near the town of Melk, famous for its monastery, he discovered an important 'Arman temple' of the Wodan priesthood. Inspired by the ancient writer Tacitus, List founded the so-called 'Armanenschaft', which aimed to return to the Germanic primal root of German-speaking culture. Through theosophical and ariosophical studies and occult séances - in a vision he had seen the battle for Carnuntum - List fought for the return of Aryo-Germanic folklore in the Habsburg Empire. This earned him a good name in völkisch circles and several books were published on his work and life, including one by Jörg Lanz von Liebenfels (again, the 'von' was smuggled in), a former monk from Heiligenkreuz who became one of the founders of ariosophy.

In 1958, a letter from (Dr Georg) Adolf (Jörg) Lan(c)z (von Liebenfels) - henceforth called Lanz von Liebenfels - surfaced with startling content. It was addressed to one of his kindred spirits. He wrote in the 'p.s.' of his letter:

'Du warst einer unserer Ersten *Anhänger und Tempelweisen! Weisst du dass* Hitler *einer unserer* Schüler *ist. Du wirst es noch erleben, dass er und dadurch auch wir siegen und eine Bewegung entfachen werden, die die Welt erzittern macht.*
Heil Dir![68]

Who was this man, who spoke of temple sages and of the fact that none other than Hitler was his disciple. Who said with foresight that Hitler would make the world tremble? They were almost the same words Hitler used when he invaded the Soviet Union: 'The world will hold its breath.'

The connection between Lanz von Liebenfels and Hitler was first made by Wilfried Daim in his book *Der Mann der Hitler die Ideen gab*.[69] Lanz von Liebenfels, like List influenced by a perverted form of theosophy, described in his book *Theozoologie oder die Kunde von den Soddom Aefflingen und die Götter Elektron* (1905) that non-arians, and above all Jews, were 'half-humans' and should therefore be segregated or deported, thinking of the island of Madagascar. Other terrible alternatives he proposed were to have Jews serve as burnt offerings (that is the literal meaning of the word holocaust) or be used as beasts of burden. To reinforce his ideas, Lanz von Liebenfels founded the 'Orden des Neuen Tempel' (Ordo Novi Templi, ont) with his brothers in 1900, where there was endless daydreaming about Teutonic knights and Templars and the preparation for the world domination of the Aryan race. In his journal *Ostara*, first published in 1905, Lanz von Liebenfels sang the praises of the blue-eyed blond Aryan (he often spoke of the *'arioheroic Mensch'*) who would seize world power under the leadership of a new Saviour. In his magazine, Lanz von Liebenfels frequently incorporated the symbolism of the later Third Reich, such as the swastika. He often referred to the 'inferior races' as the *'Urmenschenrasse'* or *'Tschandalen'* to which he conveniently included socialists and communists. Like Hitler, Lanz von Liebenfels evidently assumed that communism could only be the product of Jews and Slavs. One of the clearest examples of the connection he made between Judaism and communism appeared in a relatively late *Ostara*: (Vienna 1930 Nos 13 and 14) entitled: *'Der zoologische und talmudische Ursprung des Bolschewismus'*. In a very plastic way, *Ostara* depicted the Bolshevik danger as a huge, murdering, pillaging and raping gang. Lanz von Liebenfels possibly was inspired in this by his own experiences after World War I in Hungary, where he was almost executed by Bela Kun's terror. The ONT owned a temple in the form of a refurbished, old ruined church, Marienkamp-Szent Balázs, on Lake Balaton, where Lanz von Liebenfels could regularly be found. Later came another small temple at the foot of Vaskapuberg near Pilisszentkereszt.

Almost visionary articles appeared in *Ostara* by Lanz von Liebenfels, but by collaborators as well, such as Dresden-born Adolf Harpf, which had particular similarities with later Nazi ideology. For example, Harpf wrote about the 'völkische battle' that Europe was in, 'from the Baltic to the Adriatic coast'. The similarity with Rosenberg's *Kulturkampf* is major, including the previously noted dilemma of the struggle for an apparently limitless *Geistesreich* - where exactly did Germany begin and end? - reflected in the geographical definition from the Baltic to the Adriatic coast. Eastern Europe was thereby delineated as threatening in *Ostara*. *'Der ganze Osten bildet eine einzige Kampffront gegen das deutsche Volk!'* *Ostara* drew the following conclusion from this: *'Die Germans* (strikingly, *German is* now thus replaced by the geographically indefinable *Germanic*) *müssen das erste Kriegsvolk der Welt bleiben, wollen sie nicht den eigenen Untergang.'*

In summary, *Ostara* formed a collecting basin for völkisch, anti-Semitic articles, preaching that Germans were the *'Übervolk'*. Furthermore, *Ostara* was anti-parliamentarian and against a policy of reconciliation with the Slavic peoples; after all, fraternisation was racial mixing. It was also, unsurprisingly given Lanz von Liebenfels' Christian past at the Heiligenkreuz monastery, a revision of the Bible and Christianity. According to Lanz von Liebenfels, very important racial paragraphs had been left out of the Bible, which stressed the importance of racial purity. According to him, the castle Weferstein, which the ONT had acquired, was the 'old Grail castle' and members of the ont were therefore required to behave like (racially pure) Grail Knights.[70]

In the nearly thousand '*Ostara* publications[71], some of which were for insiders only, Lanz von Liebenfels designed a definition of the aryan that can be considered an outright precursor to the Nuremberg Race Laws. He defined the distinction between Aryans and non-Aryans in a points table, where one could score plus 12 points with blue eyes and minus 12 points with black eyes. Whoever got to the full hundred points was Aryan 'completely pure'. Those who stayed above zero points could count themselves Aryan. Those who got below that belonged to the non-arians. On his ideas regarding the future of the 'inferior races', Lanz von Liebenfels was very frank: '*Durch die Zertretung und Ausrottung des Ur- und Untermenschentums steht die höhere Rasse aus dem Grabe der Rassenmischung und Rassenentartung auf und steigt auf zum Gottmenschentum, zur Unsterblichkeit und Göttlichkeit in Keim und Rasse.*'[72]

In retrospect, we can characterise Lanz von Liebenfels as the forerunner of the most radical variant of *deutschen Biologie*; the perversion of biology on the basis of racial theory and 'Racial Hygiene'. The origin of his ideas can be partly explained by the enormous development that the view of the genesis of life and that of man in particular had undergone in recent history. Charles Darwin and Jean Baptiste de Lamarck had turned the static-Christian image of unchanging life completely upside down. The static picture had been changed by heredity theory, natural selection and the struggle for existence. The evolutionary theory this entailed was initially strongly Eurocentric (and German) inspired. After all, the first Neanderthal was discovered near Düsseldorf-Mettmann by Johann Carl Fuhlrott and Hermann Schaaffhausen. Germany was the cradle of human civilisation.

Here, 'German biology' took advantage of the lack of knowledge about primordial man and the confusion surrounding this research - the Piltdown man forgeries. We could not then have suspected the existence of 'Lucy', the startling, very oldest find from Hadar in Ethiopia from November 1974. Influenced by *The Origin of Species,* a strong popularisation of Darwinism took place in the second half of the nineteenth century. Since Darwinism was at odds with the Christian view, it was popular among opponents of the church, to which one could include Ariosophy. After all, it advocated a return to the natural-völkian life cycle instead of a life in the shadow of the Fall. Furthermore, the anti-Christian nature of Darwinism brought about a sense of 'progress thinking'.[73]

The ariosophical message of List, Lanz von Liebenfels and other radical völkisch thinkers was not confined to Austria. In Germany, humiliated by World War I, there was ear for the elitist and megalomaniacal appeal of ariosophy. The followers of ariosophical (or Theozoological) thought included the Thule Society. The writings of Thule leader Baron Rudolf von Sebottendorff (including on astrology and a small Turkish pocket dictionary), were published by the 'Theosophical Publishing House', underlining its connection with the ariosophical interpretation of Theosophy. Thereby, the name Thule was the German reference to Atlantis, the mysterious island kingdom that played an important role in Blavatsky's *The Secret Doctrine,* as well as in Rosenberg's *Der Mythus*. Even before the NSDAP, the Thule Society had the swastika as its symbol, the same swastika that we also find in theosophical writings[74] and that was already flying above the Werfenstein castle where Lanz von Liebenfels' ONT nested in 1907.

There are other important similarities. Earlier in this chapter, we expressed some surprise at Rosenberg's clownish ideas about his Atlantis, the Atlantic people's journey across the world and bringing civilisation to other continents. In perspective, it is clear that besides the Vedic influence mentioned earlier, Rosenberg derived his (ariosophical) contemplation largely from the ideas of Theosophy. Blavatsky's Aryan root race went from being bringers of the new hope, to being the occupiers and *Übermenschen* of tomorrow. As proof of the 'false Christian religion', Rosenberg, as we saw, cited the worship of Ostara among the Germanic people. Daim believes it is not proven that Rosenberg read *Ostara* by Lanz, but that he was in the *Umfeld* of this body of thought is certain.[75]

Striking too are the smaller similarities between the ariosophists and the Nazis, such as List and Lanz von Liebenfels' fascination with mountains and castles (Werfenstein, Marienkamp and Carnuntum). Hitler built his Berghof on the Obersalzberg in the thin air of the Bavarian Alps. Looking out high over the world, almost like a 'mahatma' on the roof of the world, he wanted to rule. The fascination with castles is also found in Nazi Germany. Important discourses relating to Eastern Europe often took place in Klessheim Castle near Salzburg. Himmler restored the Wewelsburg for special seances and sessions of the top of his SS empire. Castles and völkische mystique went back to the Napoleonic era. Berlin professor Friedrich Ludwig Jahn, foreman of the youth movement 'Burschenschaften', called in 1817 for foreign books that 'poison German culture' to be burned at the gates of the Wartburg.[76]

That the Thule Society was an ariosophical-based society is evident from the personal life history of Rudolf Freiherr (and also the stolen) *von* Sebottendorff. Born on 9 November 1875 in Hoyerswerda, Saxony, Sebottendorff had a fascinating life. After an unsuccessful relationship, he became a sailor and signed on to the deep sea. This took him to Australia where he tried his luck as a gold digger. Not much richer, he later ended up in Egypt (according to Blavatsky the cradle of civilisation) and Turkey, where he immersed himself in astrology. After several failed marriages, he eventually married a rich merchant's daughter in Vienna and returned to Germany in 1916, during the First World War. There, he immediately became a member of the so-called Germanic *Order*, an offshoot of the ariosophical movement founded by List, Lanz von Liebenfels, *Der Hammer publisher* and writer Theodor Fritsch (like Rosenberg, a Baltic German and, according to the historian Franzel, Germany's harshest anti-Semite), Philipp Stauff and Baron Wittgenberg, a man who had dedicated his life to 'unmasking' nobility of Jewish origin. The *Teutonic Order* wanted to form a secret society to combat secret Jewish organisations and lodges. Sebottendorff seemed to have finally found his peace and purpose in life. He became publisher and, for at least a year, also the sole financier of the Germanic journal *Die Runen, Zeitschrift für germanischen Geistesoffenbarungen und Wissenschaften*.[77] Like Rosenberg's work, *Die Runen* was full of references to 'biblical theft' from the Germanic traditions.

Sebottendorff set to work with great vigour and his efforts would have historical consequences. First of all, he worked to gain wide acceptance of ariosophical ideas within the wealthy circle. He did so fairly successfully. As the *Teutonic Order* and the Thule Society in Bavaria grew rapidly, Sebottendorff was officially appointed 'Meister' of the secret Teutonic Lodge Bavaria on 7 August 1918. In 1918, he bought a small, insignificant newspaper, the *Beobachter* from Verlag Franz Eher, which had led a languishing existence since 1868. The newspaper became the mouthpiece of ariosophical ideas and was the eventual forerunner of the famous Nazi newspaper the *Völkische Beobachter*, in which Eckart and Rosenberg praised Hitler's *Weltanschauung to* the skies. Furthermore, the indefatigable von Sebottendorff started the DAP (Deutsche Arbeiter Partei, the later NSDAP) the 'popular branch' of the Thule Society in December 1918, together with Thule member and railway worker Anton Drexler, to move ariosophical thought from the salons to the streets. Sports journalist Karl Harrer initially became chairman of the party and Drexler became second-in-command. The party's ideas, which Drexler painstakingly wrote down, were the strange mixture of ideas one would find in the NSDAP as well.

Hitler's introduction to the DAP took place through Sebottendorff's confidant Anton Drexler. At the time, Hitler was a military spy tasked with monitoring Bavaria's political parties because of the lurking spectre of communism. The Reichswehr was spooked by Rosa Luxemburg in Berlin, Bela Kun in Budapest and Trotsky, Zinojev and Kamenev in Moscow. Captain Karl Mayr, the commander of Hitler's unit, had picked his most reliable men to keep an eye on. Hitler, who had a good record, was among the men recruited for espionage work. For this task, they were specially drilled in a so-called indoctrination course taught by Professor Karl Alexander von Müller of the University of Munich. On one of the days of spying, 12 September 1919, Hitler was instructed to visit a political meeting of the DAP in a small beer house in Herrenstrasse. The speech was dull, but Hitler's attention was focused on the free discussion afterwards. A professor opined that Bavaria should secede from Prussia and go its own way. At that moment, the young Hitler jumped up and launched into a 15-minute tirade so brilliant that the 'professor skimmed off like a wet poodle'.[78] Anton Drexler, who was in the audience, was so impressed that, according to Hitler biographer John Toland, he whispered: 'We need this guy, we can use him.' At that, Drexler pressed into his hand a small book of his own, *Mein politisches Erwachen*, asking him to read it and come back again. When Hitler came to the second meeting of the DAP, he was already known as 'the Austrian with the big mouth'.

Normally, as a military man, Hitler was not allowed to join a political party, but since its message did not harm the Reichswehr, his superior, Captain Karl Mayr, decided to turn a blind eye, 'to please (the reactionary) Ludendorff', as he told himself. On this, Hitler joined the DAP and was instructed by Mayr, among other things, to investigate a possible 'Jewish threat' to Germany. The idea of a Jewish threat had increased in Bavaria due to the fact that a number of Jews held leading roles in the communist and anarchist camps. The successive Jewish 'reds' who 'threatened' Bavaria were Kurt Eisner, Ernst Toller and Eugen Leviné. Through the DAP, which monitored these forces from a völkisch perspective, the Bavarian Reichswehr hoped to gain more insight into the ins and outs of these revolutionaries. Hitler's 'insights' into the 'Jewish-Communist camp' grew rapidly, of course, since meeting Drexler, Eckart (who gave speeches to the DAP) and other Sebottendorff acquaintances. A few days later, Mayr already had a report from Hitler on his desk. Its contents were shocking. It was full of accusations against the Jews. 'He burrows into the democracies and sucks the blood of the benevolent masses, he grovels before the majesty of the people, but knows only the 'majesty of money'. His activities ended in a radical tuberculosis of the people'. As a solution, Hitler proposed legally depriving the Jews of certain rights because they were 'in fact of a different race'. Finally, he believed that the final goal should be irrevocable *'Entfernung'* of the Jews.[79]

How 'accidental' Hitler's acquaintance and subsequent membership with the DAP was, we will discuss in a later chapter. There are strong indications that Hitler was catapulted into politics, as it were, by reactionary forces from the military apparatus and völkisch-ariosophical political forces who were looking for a man who was 'not afraid of the sound of machine guns and who came from the people themselves', to quote Eckart.

By all accounts, Hitler's encounter with Anton Drexler and the DAP was not the first time Hitler had come into direct contact with völkisch-ariosophical thinkers. This line of thought was already familiar ever since his poor years in Vienna. As early as 1958, Wilfried Daim stated in his *Der Mann der Hitler die Ideen gab*, that Hitler met Lanz von Liebenfels personally. Lanz von Liebenfels was interviewed by Daim in 1950 (he died on 22 April 1954). In it, the then 77-year-old ariosopher said that the meeting with Hitler had taken place in 1909. Hitler had come to buy some missing volumes of *Ostara*, Lanz von Liebenfels's cheap ariosophical reading, in which he talked about the supremacy of blue-eyed people over the 'dark people'. Hitler looked so shabby at that meeting that Lanz von Liebenfels gave him the copies of *Ostara* for free, as well as a few crowns for public transport to travel back to central Vienna. Daim examined Lanz von Liebenfels' statements and confirms their authenticity in his book.[80] Goodrick-Clarck, a specialist on Nazi occultism, also believes the meeting actually took place.[81] British historian William Carr, who among other things studied Hitler's intellectual background, takes some issue with Daim's evidence, but underlines that magazines like *Ostara were* indeed influential.[82]

The magazine *Ostara* was popular in Austria, with some issues reaching a circulation of around 100,000 copies. Readers of Lanz von Liebenfeld's magazine included Dietrich Eckart and Mathilde Ludendorff von Kemnitz, as well as Karl Kraus (*Die Fackel*), Lenin and the British field marshal Lord Kitchener of Khartoum. Kitchener defended British interests as a field general in the colonies, which made him an advocate for the 'Aryan cause' for Lanz von Liebenfels. Lanz von

Liebenfels boasted that he very regularly received enthusiastic letters from the senior officer. When Russia fell into the grip of *Judäobolschewismus* (according to Lanz von Liebenfels, this revolution had been supported by the Jews Bethmann-Hollweg, Rathenau and other leading figures), Kitchener left for Russia to 'save czarism'. However, the cruiser Hampshire would never arrive and Lord Kitchener disappeared with the ship into the waves. Lanz von Liebenfels suspected a plot.[83]

The DAP's ariosophical rhetoric rested on an already laid hidden surface of sentiments from Hitler's Viennese years. Hitler's encounter with the DAP and the Thule Society struck him at a time when he was uncertain in life, demoralised after defeat at the front. 'When I first saw him, he looked like a jaded stray dog looking for a master,' Captain Mayr recalled Hitler in those days. He was under the impression that Hitler was ready to join 'anyone who would be just a little bit nice to him'.[84] The Thule Society, with its pseudo-religious theories of racial purity, provided an attractive refuge for Hitler, a man with no future but driven by an inner fire of rage, gained in the trenches and the pointless and purposeless years on the streets of Vienna.

Besides the two general guidelines of Hitler's *Weltanschauung* - persecution of Jews and Lebensraum - the ariosophical precursors seem to have helped influence certain decisions and plans of the Nazis in detail as well. Shockingly, Lanz von Liebenfels and other völkisch thinkers planned to deport the Jews to Madagascar. This idea was later adopted by the *Pan-arian Union, Weltbund der arischen, arianisierten und affiliierten Völker*, a völkisch sibling of the Thule Society founded in 1923-'24 by Georg de Pottere, born in Hungary in 1875, and Edwin Cooper, who came from Britain. Cooper was a member of Lanz von Liebenfels' ONT and, according to insiders, the originator of the so-called Madagascar plan.

This plan involved the exile of all Jews from Europe to Madagascar. The choice of this island was, the völkisch writer Paul de Lagarde believed, 'historically' and 'religiously' determined. Historical because of the fact that the island would have already been inhabited by Semitic peoples in the distant past, religious because the Jewish religion did not belong in Europe but in Africa. Above all, this had to do with a text from 'Genesis', in which after the flood, Noah's three sons Shem, Ham and Japhet were each assigned a continent of the world. Cham and his descendants (the Jews) were hereby assigned Africa. Deep into the Middle Ages, we find this division of continents on maps (*mappae mundi*) distributed by monasteries.[85] The Pan-Aryan Union disseminated the Madagascar plan worldwide through its *Weltdienst (*in three languages). The originator of this concept was Dietrich Eckart, and the leadership of the *Weltdienst fell to* Alfred Rosenberg from 1938 onwards. Later, the Madagascar plan was worked out again, this time by the SS and in particular by Eichmann's employee Theodor Dannecker, and seriously considered for its technical possibilities.[86] Once again, an idea from the ariosophical corner had become National Socialist reality: the Madagascar concept.

The Aryan idea, the connection between Bolshevism and Judaism, Tsarism as Russia's Aryan upper class, the purity ideal of the Grail Knights and the Madagascar Plan were all hobbyhorses that the Aryan philosopher Lanz von Liebenfels had in fact prepared for Nazi ideology. Interestingly, there were even direct contacts here, as in the case of Cooper, who was both a ONT-member and at the cradle of the Thule Society. ONT-member Rudolf John Gorsleben, who provided an Edda translation, was also a member of the Thule Society and was briefly held hostage by communists during the council republic. There were Eastern European connections too, such as ONT-member and senior lecturer Gregor Schwartz-Bostunitsch, who had many an anti-Communist article to his name and who, as an anti-Communist agigator in Kiev 1914, had collaborated with generals Denekin and Wrangel and later offered his services to Alfred Rosenberg. A key associate of the Reichsführer-SS, Karl Maria Wiligut, was introduced to the SS through an ONT-member. Through this again ran cross-links to Guido von List, such as the publisher Herbert Reichstein, who was both a 'pupil' of List and the ont.

The rationale promoted by Lanz gained a foothold in the NSDAP without giving him even a marginal role within the Nazi community. The völkische camp also drew on Lanz von Liebenfels' sources but otherwise abandoned the ONT, which resulted in an angry reaction by Lanz von Liebenfels to Ludendorff's *Volkswarte*, in which Ludendorff's wife Mathilde von Kemnitz quoted from Lanz von Liebenfels' work rather freely, as well as to *Der Hammer publisher* Theodor Fritsch, who indulged in plagiarism too. Lanz' ONT came under increasing scrutiny. Before the Nazi era, the judiciary was already watching him, preventing publication of a number of very interesting themes planned for Lanz's second series alongside *Ostara*, the so-called *Luzerner Briefe*: namely: (1) awakening Hungary, (2) the third Rome and Mussolini, (3) the Third Reich and Hitler and (4) the Freemasons, Jews and Jesuits and Ludendorff. Other publications that did go ahead, Lanz renumbered for security reasons, so that the publication date was no longer traceable. In the Nazi era, Hitler silenced him.[87]

We have already touched briefly on the relationship between Ariosophy and the Reichsführer-SS Heinrich Himmler. Ariosophy, with its purity, its missionary urge towards lesser peoples and its heroism was grist to the mill of Himmler, who was in charge of the black-uniformed SS. His main ariosophical adviser was Karl Maria Wiligut.

Wiligut was born in Vienna in 1866 - how could it be otherwise? Over the years, he developed into a kind of mentor to Himmler, which was reflected in his lightning career. Wiligut climbed from SS-Hauptsturmführer to SS-Brigadeführer, during which time he designed the SS's Totenkopfring, worked on the ss headquarters the Wewelsburg, preached ideas of racial purity, supremacy and advocated the conquest of Lebensraum. Wiligut considered himself one of the descendants of an ancient Germanic tribe which had produced such well-known heroic figures as Widukind and Cheruske. Furthermore, Wiligut could 'prove' this lineage, given that he had been initiated by his father into reading ancient runes that were completely illegible to others. By his own admission, Wiligut was the last man in Germany who could still tell stories from ancient times that had been handed down to him through his grandfather, Karl Wiligut (1794-1883). In the völkisch camp, Wiligut had gained great status through this special knowledge. One could compare him somewhat to Utrecht-born Hermann Wirth Roeper Bosch, whose völkisch-historical, linguistic and archaeological research in the 1920s led to the establishment of the *Herman Wirth Gesellschaft*, in fact the forerunner of the *SS-Ahnenerbe*, the scientific office of the Reichsführer-SS. Lanz von Liebenfels took an interest in Wiligut, and this love was mutual given that Wiligut was a reader of *Ostara*.

Theodor (Theoderich) Czepl, member (and successor?) of Lanz von Liebenfels ONT, was a long-time intermediary between the two lords and told that Wiligut was from an old, secret noble lineage. Wiligut had told him that 'his palace' stood in Goslar and that 'his sword was buried in a stone tomb near Steinamanger'. Wiligut's historical knowledge stretched back improbably far. Contemporaries like Czepl reported that Wiligut knew sagas that took place thousands of years before Christ. His ancestors, Wiligut proudly mused, were the founders of Jöruvallas (Goslar) in 78,000 BC. Much later, under Frankish pressure, the Wiliguts had to flee, moved to Russia and founded the city of Vilna, capital of the Greater Gothic Empire always denied by Russians and Christians. The attentive reader will immediately see in this, albeit with some other details, a new interpretation of Rosenberg's 'Atlantic expansionism'. In 1242 AD, the Wiligut family, pursued by angry Christians, fled to Hungary, where, as a result of chaotic conditions caused by Tatar invasions, they were able to escape pressure for a while. The Wiliguts were the personification of a competing philosophy of life at odds with Rome's interests, and they had to fear for their lives. In 1920, Wiligut still believed Catholics, Jews and Freemasons were hot on his heels. In 1924, the fuses blew. Wiligut was found schizophrenic, accused of trying to murder his (not understanding) wife and of dangerous occultism. He was locked up in a psychiatric clinic in Salzburg. Only in 1927 was he released again.

In 1932, he left Austria behind and settled in Munich, where he witnessed the rise to power of the Nazis in 1933. Wiligut had not yet been forgotten by his occult ariosophical friends. Richard Anders, an ONT member and Lanz von Liebenfels scholar, had made a career in the SS and introduced Wiligut to Himmler. In September 1933, Wiligut joined the *Schutzstaffel* under the name Karl Maria Weisthor. Wiligut concealed his stay in the mental institution but told his entire wonderful family history, including the details mentioned above, to the SS official who recorded his life history for protocol. The document has been preserved and is available for inspection at the Berlin Document Center. Interesting is the passage from Wiligut's 1918 recollections, in which he mentions a meeting with Legate Cardinal Ratti, - by the time the report was recorded (16 May 1937), he was now Pope - the Jesuit general Ledochovski and Bishop Pelopotszki. The meeting took place in a *Heimkehrerlager* near Lemberg, on the former Eastern Front of World War I where Wiligut was commander. After mass, Ledochovski walked out with Wiligut, asked him his name and whether he knew any old lore. In his suddenly rising hatred, the May 1937 report writes, Wiligut replied 'Yes!' Shocked, Ledokhovsky whispered to Ratti: *'Famiglia maladetta!'* Wiligut heard it and proudly replied: 'Yes, I am from the cursed family.'[88]

Such uncommonly fantastic stories were no obstacle to Wiligut's career in the SS. Quite the contrary. Wiligut became head of the *Rasse und Siedlungshauptamt* of the SS in Munich. In just one year, he managed to make a big impression on Himmler. This was above all because Wiligut juggled his 'ancient knowledge' in his correspondence. Himmler, a romantic, was charmed by his runic wisdom and knowledge of Gothic language and ancient history and was open to his knowledge and instructions.

Wiligut's greatest contribution to the SS empire was his role in the creation of the Wewelsburg. Himmler travelled through Westphalia in January 1933 and was impressed by this land of Widukind, the Germanic warrior Hermann and his pompous statue near Detmold and the misty forests of the Teutoburgerwald, where the Roman legions had once been defeated. It seemed like a good idea to him to establish a castle for the SS in these historical regions. Initially, Himmler had Schwalenburg in mind, but the owner, the headstrong Countess von Lippe, refused to rent the castle to the SS. She did not want a swastika flying on the towers of her castle. The solution was found in the small town of Wewelsburg near Paderborn. Crouched in the hilly landscape there was a dozing village with the Weser Renaissance castle the Wewelsburg, the only triangular castle in Europe, at its centre. In his book *Monumenta Paderbornesia*, Ferdinand von

Förstenberg, bishop of Paderborn, wrote in 1669 that the history of the Wewelsburg was 'obscure and uncertain'. In any case, it was clear that the castle was first mentioned in 1123 by the Saxon chronicler Arnold von Berge. In contemporary history, the castle would once again play a dark and mystical role in the ariosophical ideal of the SS. In November 1933, Himmler, accompanied by Gauleiter Dr Alfred Meyer and aristocrat specialist Dr Heinrich Glasmeier, visited Wewelsburg Castle, which was subsequently inaugurated as a museum for the SS. That was only the beginning of the Wewelsburg's significance. Under Wiligut's influence, the castle was placed directly under Himmler's staff in 1935. The reason for this was the fact that Wiligut had managed to convince Himmler that the Wewelsburg was an even more important symbol for the Nazis than just a historical legacy from the land of Germanic warrior Hermann. According to an old Westphalian saga, the story of 'The Battle of the Birch Tree', Wiligut drew on his primal memory, the Wewelsburg was destined to become a Germanic bastion for a massive battle between Europe and Asia. Wewelsburg was a bastion against 'new invasions of the Huns', Wiligut believed. Himmler's aide, Karl Wolff, said that Himmler was particularly impressed by this argument of Wiligut's, and from then on the worship around Wewelsburg took on occult traits.

In the enlarged north tower of the castle, Wiligut, who had become close friends with the castle lord Manfred von Knobelsdorf, planned a seance room, in which all the SS-rings of fallen SS officers would be kept and where uniform pieces of dead SS officers would adorn the walls. Furthermore, the castle was to be decorated with images from Nordic mythology, with depictions of Widukind, King Arthur and the Holy Grail, Heinrich der Löwe and others. These in themselves miraculous developments led to wild speculations about the Wewelsburg after the war. In trivial reading, the Wewelsburg was spoken of as the 'black Camelot', the 'grail castle' and 'Himmler's Walhalla'. According to documents from the Nuremberg trial, it was at this castle in 1941 that Heinrich Himmler, before 12 senior SS officers, including Erich von dem Bach-Zelewski, is said to have said for the first time that after Operation 'Barbarossa', 30 million Slavs should 'disappear'. Himmler biographer and historian Richard Breitman took this statement by Bach-Zelewski very seriously. He rightly noted that this von dem Bach-Zelewski statement did not benefit the trial. He also refers to a remarkable diary entry by Alfred Rosenberg - who was always more lenient towards the *Ostvölker* and apparently shocked - of 2 April 1941: '*Wass ich Heute nicht niederschreiben will, aber nie vergessen werde.*'[89]

Wewelsburg was much more than a *Karinhall*, Hermann Göring's luxurious outdoors. The Nazis themselves participated fully in the mystique surrounding the castle. According to Himmler, Wiligut and other 'believers', the castle dated back to the year 930 and had been built as a bulwark against the Magyars and Huns who had penetrated deep into Europe. In reality, archaeological excavations after the war revealed, the castle dated back to the time of the Saxons and received its current form in Renaissance style in the 17th century. Partly under Wiligut's influence, the castle was rebuilt under the direction of architect Herman Bartels with the help of kz workers (mostly Jehovah's Witnesses, who did their work in a highly disciplined manner) from camp Sachenhausen. Soon the castle was hosting mystical, völkisch research for the SS. Wilhelm Jordan from Merseburg joined the SS staff at Wewelsburg on 15 October 1935 and was entrusted with old archival and library records. When the Russia Field Campaign broke out, Himmler sent him as *Sonderbeauftragter* to the east, to Crimea and the Ukrainian city of Kharkov, to look for rare items for Himmler's ss archive. After the war, Jordan would remain active in the same industry, only as a museum assistant at the Roman-Germanic Museum in Mainz. Dr Hans Peter des Coudres (1905-1977) ran the SS library, which was soon given a place at the castle. Des Coudres was also employed by Alfred Rosenberg. He set to work with great energy. By April 1938, he had already collected 16,000 titles. The power of the Reichsführer-SS was liberally wielded in the process. The interest of the ss was largely in primeval history and (indo)Germanic studies. Universities helped bring the Wewelsburg's book stock up to standard as well. The University of Münster lend hundreds of rare volumes for the ten-year period because of an 'important study' of the Reichsführer-SS. The university praised the 'rich, Nordic spirit' of des Coudres' library. Dr Hans Illich became the specialist in medieval manuscripts. Illich also worked for Rosenberg's *Institut zur Erforschung der Judenfrage*. The castle housed an SS school, the *SS-Schule Haus Wewelsburg*, and the *Gesellschaft zur Förderung und Pflege deutscher Kulturdenkmäler e.V. (Society for the Promotion and Care of German Cultural Heritage)*. Robert Ley of the *Deutsche Arbeitsfront* (DAF) joked that Wewelsburg had become the 'high school of the Schutzstaffel'.

Renovations, the cost of which reached 11 million marks, made the castle a typical example of the Nazi building style of *Triumphalismus*. A green marble sun path symbolised the mythical power of the swastika. Near the officers' quarters hung an artwork showing warring SS troops, fertile fields conquered in the new land, and new villages where numerous Germanic children grew up, protected by German soldier-farmers. Where that new territory was to be conquered was abundantly clear. In SS school, *Gründung eines grossgermanischen Reiches und der Gewinnung von Siedlungsraum im Osten* was a regular topic. Michael Prawdin's books on the raids of the Huns were compulsory study material.[90]

Remarkably, Wiligut voluntarily resigned from the SS two days before World War II broke out, on 28 August 1939. It is not entirely clear what the reason for this was. On the one hand, Goodrick-Clark speculates whether it was Wiligut's poor health; on the other, there are rumours that Himmler had found out about Wiligut's psychiatric past. Wiligut withdrew from active service but Himmler did not lose sight of his 'Rasputin'. Elsa Baltrusch, from his personal staff, was appointed his housekeeper. Wiligut survived the war and died in Arolsen on 3 January 1946. He was the last initiate into his family secret.[91]

In addition, Wiligut brought other occultists into the SS, such as Günther Kirchhoff, a List-adept from the Baden-Baden area. Kirchhoff was above all interested in genealogy, prehistory and ancient legends, and nurtured ariosophical descent theories. According to one of Kirchhoff's essays, sent to Himmler and minister Walther Darré, Kirchhoff, relying heavily on List, mentions that there had been three primal families in ancient Europe: the Uiskunig of Goslar, King

Arthur of Stonehenge and Ermanrich of Vilna. They were the rulers of ancient Europe, the Europe that could thereby be 'claimed' for the Aryan race. We can safely say that such claims were eagerly heard by higher-ups in the Nazi party. Kirchhoff was given a research position in the SS's scientific institute, the *Ahnenerbe*. Cooperation with the SS scientists, incidentally, did not go smoothly. Even for them, Kirchhoff's claims were a bit 'too fantastic' and 'unscientific', although Himmler held his hand for a long time.[92]

Other völkische thinkers who were included in the Wewelsburg project were Otto Rahn and Knobelsdorff.

Otto Rahn was a young writer (1904-1939) who had caught Himmler's eye because of a remarkable book, *Kreuzzug gegen den Gral*, published in 1933. Rahn studied German primeval history and opposed the established historiography of ancient Rome. Himmler sent him to Iceland for research. Rahn plunged into the Völkisch-Germanic *Umdeutung* of Christianity, reintroduced Lucifer as the bringer of light in Germany and held a major lecture tour of Germany. 'A wealth of thought,' wrote reviewer Dr Wolff Heinrichsdorff in 1938 after a performance by Rahn at the 'Dietrich Eckart house' in Dortmund.[93] The Nazis thought so too, until the SS discovered that Rahn was homosexual. Rahn was expelled from the SS and died in the Alps in March 1939, as called officially 'from the effects of a heavy walk'.

A völkisch thinker, Knobelsdorff (1892-1965) came into contact with Himmler through his marriage to Ilse von Knobelsdorff-Darré, sister of the Reichsbauernführer Richard Walther Darré. Von Knobelsdorff initially worked as a representative for a perfume factory, but his study of the Germanic people around Detmold had not gone unnoticed by the Nazis. In 1936, Hitler showed his appreciation by granting Knobelsdorff the title of professor.

Besides the eccentrics around Wiligut and the Wewelsburg, Himmler made use of others with special knowledge in his order as well. Of interest to the research in this is another brief mention of the efforts of biologist-anthropologist Dr Ernst Schäfer, who was commissioned by the Reichsführer-SS even before the start of operation 'Barbarossa' to open up Tibet for the Nazis as a kind of first step towards the

Berlin-Baghdad-Bombay concept of the Nazis. Schäfer, like a kind of Lawrence of Arabia, was supposed to expose the East for the Nazis, which would allow work to begin on undermining the position of the Soviet Union and the British Empire (India).[94]

Wewelsburg, Wiligut's brainchild, partially collapsed on 31 March 1945 when Heinrich Himmler ordered its destruction as US units approached the area. A small *Sprengkommando* commanded by SS-officer and *Eichenlaub zum Ritterkreuzträger* Heinz Macher, the former company chief of the 16./ss-Pz.Gren.Rgt.3 Deutschland of the *Das Reich* division, had been personally ordered by Himmler not to let Wewelsburg fall into enemy hands undamaged. 'It was my most nonsensical order of the war,' Macher mused after 1945. Still, an order was an order and the SS troops set fire to the castle. As the flames leaked through the roof, the siren suddenly went off, cutting through marrow. On this, the nervous soldiers opened fire on the siren in a vain attempt to end the noise. The haunting image evoked memories of the 1815 fire, when the Wewelsburg's largest tower caught fire and burned down after being struck by lightning. Afterwards, the castle became the home of the Father of Wewelsburg, as no one else wanted to live in this 'unlucky castle'. The castle only partially burned down in 1945, and many Nazi relics, including hundreds of Totenkopfringen, fell into Allied hands. Nevertheless, Macher was promoted in rank for service rendered. The smoking remains were captured by US forces on 2 April 1945. It was left behind as the Carnuntum of the Third Reich.

The Wewelsburg still stands. Those who know the history of Wiligut, the saga of the battle of the birch tree and make their way through the Teutoburg Forest to Himmler's triangular castle, paint a picture of the structure in their minds. Alexander Kirchner's grail castle stood high on a hill, gleaming in the sun, and Wilhelm Stiehl's oil painting of the 1815 fire shows the Wewelsburg large and mighty. The last few kilometres of the winding road through the forest and there suddenly appears the tiny town of Wewelsburg. The visitor stretches his neck, looking for the mountain on which the castle should rise above the town. When the mountain fails to appear, one looks for the hill, but it too does not exist. Himmler's castle, the epicentre of the SS, lies in the middle of the town. Almost like a fortified farmstead, it is part of its surroundings. Had the automobile not made its appearance en masse, the farmyard chickens would have effortlessly defied the gates of the Wewelsburg. Anyone standing at the foot of the occult triangular castle here knows for sure. The Third Reich was the triumph of the province over the city, völkische thinking over modernism. The black Mercedes Benz that Himmler brought to his palatial castle was emblematic of the Third Reich's ambivalence. The gleaming bolide, Germany's industrial potential was a prerequisite for obtaining this idyllic splendour. Not in Germany, then in the East. A remnant from the Wewelsburg library shows the 1493 *Weltchronik*. In it, Michael Wohlgemuth shows on parchment the '*Totentanz*'. Four skeletons dance around the corpse of a human being. One blows the flute, the others follow him in their journey into the night.

Germans are the most militaristic people in the world

Adam Szelagowski

1911 ein Glutjahr
1912 ein Flutjahr
1913 ein Gutjahr
1914 ein Blutjahr

Hans Bächtold (1912)

Die deutsche Not hat nur ein Gebot: 'Schlagt tot!'

Ernst Röhm, in Geschichte eines Hochverräters (1934)

Chapter 4

The establishment and the new order

The geopolitical dilemma of Central Europe - The eternal loyalty of the Reichswehr - *Blumenkrieg* and *Blitzkrieg* - 'Draufgängerische' officers - The apolitical soldiers and the Von Rundstedt philosophy - The trauma of the First World War - *'Überstaatliche* powers and the stab-in-the-back myth - Ludendorff and Mathilde von Kemnitz, the 'German Blavatsky' - Völkische Prussia and the generals - German-Polish relations - The ethnic cleansing of Bromberg - The German wizards and the *'Kulturträgertum'* - Nobility and soldiers' peasants - Horthy's heroic union and Darré's new nobility - *'Das sind wir!'* - Prussian generals and the 20th of July - Traditions, obedience, bravery - *'Weltanschauungskrieg'* - Imposed discipline - Obedience a racial issue, the new stab-in-the-back myth - Bewährungstruppe - 50,000 death sentences - Hitler sacrifices the SA - 'Bourgeoisie' field lord - Gallo, Göring and the *Solstice* at Karinhall - *Siedlungen* - Heinz Guderian's knightly estate - Land for a Ritterkreuz

919. The smoke of World War I had barely cleared or the first signs were there that this war had given birth to a terrible child. Reactionary soldiers struggled with the stranglehold of defeat, the shame of the German nation's first lost war. Progressive journalist Kurt Tucholsky observed the brooding discontent with cynicism.

Feind im Land

Das Heil von aussen

Was wir bereits gestorben glaubten,
ist, hols der Teufel, wieder da:
die alten Achselstückberaubten
Kommis der Militaria

Das wandelte wie in alten Tagen,
for alles Neue gänzlich taub:
man trägt nur manches auf dem Kragen
und ist ein Kerl mit Eichenlaub.

Das sind doch alles Kleidermoden:
der Aermelschmuck und wie das heisst....
Man stellt sich einfach auf den Boden
der neuen Welt - im alten Geist.

Und haben wir den Krieg verloren:
die Herren, silberig besternt,
verschliessen ihre langen Ohren -
sie haben nichts dazugelernt.

Und nur ein Friede kann uns retten,
ein Friede, der dies Heer zerbricht,
zerbricht die alten Eisenketten -
Der Feind befreit uns von den Kletten.
Die Deutschen selber tun es nicht.[1]

The army was Hitler's main practical weapon to obtain Lebensraum. The armed forces appeared ready to fulfil this wish of Hitler's. The reasons for this are manifold. First, the army was entangled in a geopolitical and historical dilemma to which Hitler was listening and offering solutions. Second, the armed forces were wrestling with bitter experiences from World War I and the stab-in-the-back myth was tracing its path through Germany. *Überstaatliche* powers were held responsible by part of the officer corps and soldiers for the responsible for the downfall of the Wilhelmine Empire. In this, the army's inner structures, their appreciation of obedience and discipline, were elements that were not unworldly to the National Socialist state. Hitler, as we shall see, made the necessary concessions to the army. Here, too, he proved to be an extremely skilful political tightrope walker; the tightrope walker he would remain until he finally showed his true face with the invasion of the Soviet Union in June 1941. From then on, he became obstinate and immovable, only to sit out the war to the last man and bullet on utmost willpower.

The geopolitical, historical dilemma of the German switching position in Central Europe was firmly entrenched in German security thinking. It was relatively new for the Germans to take the initiative in this and force relations within the Central European power constellation. When they could get a taste of it, they did so lavishly. Since 1871, Germany interfered tensely in international geopolitics with the aim of gaining a place under the sun. Feeling empowered by historical injustice and the urge for autarchy, its politics became increasingly ambitious via the line of Bismarck, Wilhelm II, von Bülow and Tirpitz, until very soon it found itself in the First World War and overnight was at war with practically half the world.

This happened perhaps partly 'overnight' because of the fact that Germany had never before been in the luxury position of competing for superpower status, let alone world power. Indeed, German history is not a story of pompous greatness, flying banners and hegemony. Rather, the history of the German-speakers is one of particularism, partial alliances and eternal muddling through the hotly contested battlefields of central Europe.

The armed forces played a very important role in this particular German history. To survive, 'the German' depended on the functioning of his armed forces and these faced an almost impossible task. Illustrative of the German geopolitical problem, for example, was the geographical positioning of the territory of the Hohenzollerns. Near the Dutch border, they possessed a series of small principalities: Cleve, Mark, Ravensberg, Geldern, Moers, Linge und Tecklenburg. In central Germany, the Kurfürstendum Brandenburg and most of Pommern formed another important segment. Finally, in East Prussia were the knight's estates. In the hectic days of the time, it regularly happened that this territory was threatened by enemies to the west or east, often even at the same time. The main enemies were almost always the same: France in the west and Poland and Russia in the east. Facing such a constellation of power as a monarch required a very sophisticated survival strategy. The population had to be willing to pay the price for a good army, the army had to be effective and flexible, and politics had to be able to rudely break up alliances and enter into them where necessary.[2]

We find these necessary qualities in a number of German leaders. Frederick the Great was a classic example of a general-state leader who constantly walked a tightrope with the above geopolitical realities. Friedrich Wilhelm II tactically manoeuvred Prussia through the Napoleonic Wars. Bismarck too showed that he mastered geopolitical jousting to perfection. Nevertheless, Germany suffered from its geopolitical positioning. In his analysis of Germany's position at the heart of Europe, German historian Arnulf Baring points to the short span of time in which successive regimes faced their colossal problems: the Bismarck era 19 years, the Wilhelmine period 28 years, the Weimar Republic 15 years and the Third Reich as the record holder with only 12 years. All that time was spent fighting at the cutting edge.[3]

Always Germany had to provide back cover, keeping France and Russia apart. Hitler also broadly followed this strategy; skillfully played Moscow and Paris and London against each other on the backs of Poland, but single-handedly, through operation 'Barbarossa', put an end to this comfortable situation.

To understand this remarkable imprint of Hitler on this power play and thus on the armed forces, Hitler's insights and, above all, successes in manipulating and changing the constellation of power in Europe play an important role. The military slowly but surely advanced towards Hitler and he gradually offered more room for them, subordinating party interests in the military field.

First of all, Hitler had an ear for the most immediate interests of the German armed forces. He resisted the restrictive measures of Versailles, which limited the total size of the German land forces to 100,000 men - officers only. An army without soldiers was, of course, no army. Hitler understood that officers without soldiers were powerless. He ignored the victors of World War I and reintroduced conscription, to the relief of security thinkers in Germany. Even a moderate like Brüning suffered from the fear that Germany could be overrun by its neighbours. 'It takes the Polish cavalry divisions only 24 hours to get to Berlin,' he mused.[4]

General Curt Liebmann, commander of Berlin's famous Kriegsakademie, where Scharnhorst, Gneisenau and Clausewitz had once taught, thereupon promised Hitler 'eternal loyalty' from the armed forces. Not only did Hitler restore conscription, he also gave the army back its success and respect in the period of the *Blumenkrieg*, in which, with a lot of political sense, he led the neighbouring countries astray and blew them off by rejoining the Saar and Rhineland and Austria to the German Empire. In addition, the 'rapprochement' between politics and the army was worked on in the army. Committed soldiers, such as Wilhelm Keitel (nicknamed 'La Keitel') and Alfred Jodl (according to Abwehr chief Wilhelm Canaris an 'insufferable *nur-Soldat* and Hitler admirer') were to be given more and more space. Critical soldiers, such as Ludwig Beck, were gradually pushed into the background.

The *Blumenkrieg* was followed by the period of the *Blitzkriege*. Hitler's credit in the army grew rapidly. Nine months after the start of World War II, Germany owned Poland, Denmark, Norway, Belgium, Luxembourg and the Netherlands. Hitler had embarked on a veritable triumphal march. The cost of the campaign, including in human lives, was surprisingly low. It was unlike anything else in history, British historian A.J.P. Taylor opined. The unpleasant taste of November

1918 had disappeared. The supreme commander of the land forces, Generaloberst Walther von Brauchitsch, called Hitler 'the first soldier of the German Empire'. Indeed, one felt so strongly that contact was made with Britain with the aim of 'dividing the world'. The OKH's foreign specialist formulated it as follows: 'Britain should turn one of its blue eyes away from Europe and concentrate on its colonies. Then we will deal with the continent.' Historian Jürgen Förster noted that the admired Britain was now no longer even seen by the Nazis as an equal partner, but as a 'junior partner' of the Third Reich.[5] Britain, Hitler believed, would have its hands full protecting its overseas territories from the USA and Japan. By focusing on the east, Berlin gave London room to do so. On 19 July 1940, Hitler therefore made a peace offer to Britain, which, however, was answered negatively by Lord Halifax on 22 July.

The enormous successes of Hitler, who initially appeared to have as good a *Fingerspitzengefühl* for *das Militär* as for playing off his political opponents, increasingly silenced his opponents and critics in the army. Hitler followed the clever tactic of surrounding himself sufficiently with dedicated soldiers like the aforementioned Keitel and Jodl, so that he could determine strategy. In addition, he sent *draufgängerische* talents into the field (Rommel, Model, Friessner, Schörner) who could conduct his Blitzkriegen. Furthermore, he was smart enough to tolerate critical strategists (Guderian, von Manstein) and embrace their unorthodox ideas in some key cases. The resulting successes were used to create an image of Hitler as a great strategist. This 'Führer image' was inflated to pseudo-religious proportions by Goebbels' propaganda ministry. This image-building was done carefully. Abuses of the SS were also usually blamed by generals on Heinrich Himmler and the SS itself, and not on Hitler; he was above the parties. As a result, in the course of World War II, the chain of command changed as well, until Hitler himself pulled all the strings and had paladins in key posts. Someone has therefore once compared Führer's headquarters to a hall of mirrors, where Hitler was only reflected his own thoughts at the last. Of course, this is an exaggeration, but the fact is that the number of truly critical officers could be counted on one hand. Typical of this is what Percy Ernst Schramm said about this after the war. When asked what the political beliefs of the officers in the *Wehrmachtsführungsstab* were, he was unable to answer. He had no idea; everyone wisely kept their own views to themselves. Such was the image of the Führer state.[6]

The military exerted little influence on the political decision-making process. However, their influence on military policy was smaller than might be expected. Attempts, later in the war, to get Hitler to relinquish the military supreme command were tentative and half-hearted. Erich von Manstein describes such an attempt in his memoir *Verlorene Siege*. Hitler resolutely rejected any plan in that direction. 'Göring would never accept having a general as commander of the three army branches above him,' Hitler mused. And that was the end of the matter.[7]

German officers themselves also seemed to go along with the golden rules set by the Führer's court. To come to terms with themselves over the many abuses in the occupied territories, especially after the launch of Operation Barbarossa, they concentrated on the military-technical side of things. German general Hans Speidel, *Stabschef* to Africa Corps general Erwin Rommel in 1944 and supreme commander of the nato's land forces for the *Europa-Mitte* area from 1957 to 1963, notes in his memoirs that already after 1933, more and more German officers started playing 'dumb'. They posed as *nur-Soldat*. This parole was repeated endlessly, and its intention was clear. The generals wanted to pose as 'a-political' and distance themselves from the political decision-making of the Third Reich. An example of this occurred on 8 July 1941, in the Heeresgruppe Nord area. General von Roques reported to his Heeresgruppe commander because of the mass executions of Jews by Lithuanian killing gangs near Kowno. 'Stay away from it,' advised Generalfeldmarschall Ritter von Leeb von Roques, 'we have no influence over it.' Speidel classified this attitude under the heading of 'gullible' and above all 'easy' (in ignoring). Speidel explained this attitude partly by the fact that the generals had not acted decisively in their initial criticism of Hitler, taking Hitler's repressive measures against 'troublemakers' like von Schleicher and von Bredow for granted. When more serious opposition tried to make its case in 1938, it was too late.[8]

British military historian John Keegan has called this behaviour the 'Von Rundstedt philosophy'. Gerd von Rundstedt was in some ways the *grand old man* of the German army and the quintessential primal Prussian general. He was brave, calm, righteous and orthodox. However, his 'philosophy' assumed that he had to follow the orders of his masters, but also take care not to get involved in these politics in terms of content. At Nuremberg, they understandably struggled with this attitude.

In fact, the Schlieffen Plan is the best example of being a *nur-Soldat*. Count Alfred Schlieffen spent much of his military career figuring out how to achieve a quick victory over France. In the best version of this idea, he did not care about political reality. The outcome of this fact was that politicians were faced with a plan in which the advance would pass through neutral Belgium. Typical of German politics - and the supremacy of the military in World War I (as opposed to World War II, where the primacy lay with Hitler and thus politics) - was that German politics bowed its head and put the plan into action.[9] Another famous example of the *nur-Soldat* was General-oberst Hans von Seeckt who rearmed Germany after Versailles.[10]

By playing 'dumb', the German generals violated one of the wisest lessons of their talented predecessor Carl von Clausewitz: the miraculous trinity. In an earlier chapter, we briefly considered Clausewitz's thesis that decision-making in a war effort should be influenced by three factors: Sovereign (Hitler), field lord (OKW and OKH) and people. The ostrich politics described by Speidel in his memoirs precluded a healthy interaction between these forces. Joseph Goebbels' propaganda and *gleichgeschaltete* social life ensured that little critical note could be expected from the side of the people. The generals walked on the leash of politics. The Nazis had thus turned Germany into the weapon with which Lebensraum politics could be made the nation's foreign policy. This is remarkable considering that in World War I it was the other way round. When the cannons spoke in August 1914, it was the politicians who placed the fate of the nation in the hands of the military with almost blind faith. Hindenburg and Ludendorff were the men from 1914 to 1918. Unfortunately, the consequences of the lack of the miraculous trinity were still hard to see in

1941. After ten years of toil and failure in life, 12 years of staggering successes dawned for Hitler in 1933. It was hard to see that in the late summer of 1941, the top had been reached and a bottomless abyss lay ahead: four years of failures and catastrophes. Sebastian Haffner does not characterise this as a very striking historical break for nothing: 'Nowhere in history do we find anything comparable.'[11]

In 1941, Hitler-Germany's successes seemed unimaginable. In an extraordinarily short time, he had Europe at his feet and Britain, while not defeated, was isolated. A huge army was on the march and a decision had to be made whether to return the army to barracks or embark on the greatest campaign of all time. For those who knew *Mein Kampf*, the answer to the question of what Hitler would do with this power was a foregone conclusion. Operation 'Barbarossa' was Hitler's most wanted war: the völkisch countryside, the granary of Europe awaited there, the autarkic desire, the *Grosswirtschaftsraum* that Germany had been deprived of overseas.

The army followed Hitler, as Germany followed him. And once over the threshold, the crimes against the Soviet Union and its inhabitants had reached such proportions in a short time that soon there was no turning back either. World War II was a compromising war. The *Weltanschauungskrieg* had the character of what came to be called *ethnic engeneering* after the Yugoslav civil war in the late 20th century. Those who did not participate saw it with their own eyes or had heard of it. It must be admitted here that it was, of course, not always easy for officers and soldiers to protest against it either. Firstly, the war against the Soviet Union was of a very different character from that in the West from the start. The soldiers of the Red Army were tough opponents; the battle was brutal from the start. Initially some of the German soldiers were arrogant, surprised by the fact that the Russians dared to offer such tough resistance. Others, General Günther Blumentritt confessed after the war, feared the war from the first hour. Von Kluge, commander of the 10th army that was to fight for Moscow, had the history of Napoleon's army next to his cot and repeatedly compared himself to his Marshal Ney, brave but unable to turn an already lost war into a victory. This astonishment of the arrogant soldiers turned into great irritation and anger, and an ever-increasing sense of dread in the winter of 1941-1942. Pandora's Box had been opened and a nightmare awaited them. Secondly, the compromising killings suddenly went remarkably fast. American historian Christopher R. Browning calculated that by mid-March 1942, 75 to 80 per cent of all Holocaust victims were still alive. Just 11 months later, in mid-February 1943, 75 to 80 per cent of Holocaust victims had perished.[12]

As a result, there was little room for a different political line even for the armed forces. An example of the thinking within the armed forces at the time was army group commander Hans Friessner's reaction to the von Stauffenberg attack on Hitler in July 1944. He was shocked by this attack and immediately travelled to the front to gauge the mood among the military. People everywhere reacted with indignation and anger. Friessner attributes this to the fact that the German soldier had been 'long out of command' in the east.[13] Such observations indicate the deep realisation that a *Weltanschauungskrieg* was raging in full force here, that there was no turning back.

And where the army became more unreliable, Hitler increasingly relied on a specially created fourth army branch: the Waffen-ss. This ideologically drilled fighting force grew over the years into 38 major front units, most of them divisional in size, most of them reasonably to very well equipped and serving in the front's main flashpoints. After the army's debacle at Stalingrad, they were not missing from any major battle. In the last major German offensives of World War II, Tarnopol 1944, Normandy 1944, Ardennes 1944/1945, Alsace 1944/1945, Budapest 1945, Lake Balaton 1945, Vienna 1945, Arnswalde and Berlin 1945, they formed the hub of the German forces. Besides deviant uniforms and ranks, a blood-group tattoo under the armpit characterised the soldiers of the Waffen-ss. It was the ultimate form of the compromising politics of the NS regime. The fact that many Waffen-ss soldiers volunteered for service under the banner of 'the Crusade against Bolshevism' also underlined the ideological nature of the struggle.[14]

Another important element of fraternisation between the Nazis and the armed forces were the experiences of the First World War. World

War I was a traumatic experience. Despite the high morale, great self-confidence and conviction of the German right to a place under the sun, World War I degenerated into a great, German trauma. Wilhelm II had been unwise enough to drastically alter the course of his predecessors and break with the idea that a two-front war was to be avoided above all else. The nickname for the German-Austrian-Hungarian alliance, the Centrals, spoke volumes in that regard. Germany had 'locked' itself in the centre of Europe, surrounded by enemies. The 'solution' to this huge issue had been placed in the hands of the military by the German Kaiser and politicians.

The Schlieffen plan was not a sign of strength, but a sign of weakness. Schlieffen, the deviser, had spent his life figuring out the solution to the two-front war. Without having the actual (motorised) resources to do so, he devised a plan that could be termed an early version of the *Blitzkrieg*. Given that Tsarist Russia would take a long time to mobilise its huge armed forces, a quick offensive in the west was to force the war there into a German victory. After this victory, the German army would have to turn right around to the eastern front to face the threat from Moscow. The war should not last long, Schlieffen believed with foresight. The British fleet would ruin Germany economically. Therefore, there was no room or time for an *Ermattungsstrategie*. Any layman could understand that only very little needed to go wrong for the entire plan to fall apart. Time was a detrimental factor for the Germans. This was true not only on the military side, by the way, but on the economic side as well. Resource-poor Germany had relatively small strategic reserves. A quick end to the war was necessary but failed to materialise. In November 1918, the war was finally lost for imperial Germany.[15]

This reality, predictable with almost mathematical certainty, was unpalatable. Instead of facing up to its own political and military failures, there was a tendency to point to other 'causes'. The downfall in November was largely attributed to the stab-in-the-back myth. Germany was said not to have been defeated at the front but brought down by traitors from within. The influence of this myth created a climate that contributed significantly to closing the gap between the old military elite and the new elite of the Third Reich. Indeed, at the time of the Weimar Republic, the traditional enemy image of the German armed forces changed. No longer focused purely on the geopolitical reality of Germany as a power factor in central Europe, but increasingly on the spectre of the dark powers that were 'responsible' for the Dolkstoot (myth) too. As a result, the image of *überstateliche* powers, which was frequently encountered in the völkisch camp, crept into the perception of the army. Eventually, this crystallised into the 'concrete' finger pointing at Jewish Bolshevism, Communism and Marxism.

The enemy consisted of 'un-German' elements that threatened conservative values and norms. For the general staff, these 'secret enemies' posed an additional threat to their social position, above all in their Prussian homeland where many German generals had their roots. These sentiments are as old as mankind itself and serve a purpose. Christian Graf von Krockow examined 'German myths' and found that they were indispensable for self-definition. Enemy images belong to this, such as *'Sinn und Orientierungsbilder'*. After November 1918, people went in search of the 'lost enemy', with the social upheavals, the November Republic - soon referred to as *'Novemberverbrechern'* - as an 'un-German system' coming under heavy fire, as did the *'Ersatzkaiser'* who wielded the sceptre. Alongside the 'lost enemy' loomed the created enemy: the *überstateliche* powers. Where in the last few months the völkische forces had called for an all-out *levée en masse* to save the German homeland, this had 'turned' into a *Massen-Levi*.[16]

The shocking upheavals did not cause a stir only in the right-conservative camp. Social democrats such as August Winnig were also shocked by the blows to the *Deutschtum in* the months immediately following the First World War. Although Winnig advocated *Der Glaube an das Proletariat* on the one hand, he stuck to patriotic views, Haushofer-like 'Realpolitik' and völkische literary excursions in *Die ewig grünende Tanne* on the other. Winnig felt that the council republicans in Berlin were sacrificing *Deutschtum* in Poland and 'Baltenland', and even endangering East Prussia. The republic threatened to 'emasculate itself' he wrote in his book *Das Reich als Republik*. He argued for '*die Diktatur der Mitte*' in which the interests of both the country and the workers were kept in mind. None of this was an easy task under all the extreme forces at play. As politics polarised further, Winnig switched to the brown camp and warned against Jewish Bolshevism in his *Europa, Gedanken eines Deutschen*. Politics slid towards ever further radicalisation; concerned about the horrors of World War I and the adverse consequences of the Treaty of Versailles, former Italian prime minister Francesco Nitti spoke of the 'Balkanisation' of Europe. Germany, once the great driving force of life in Europe, Nitti believed, was being controlled, humiliated and robbed of its best assets. [17]

One of the most important interpreters of the stab-in-the-back myth - and who had roots at the border country of *the Deutschtum* (Posen/Poznan) as well - was General Erich Ludendorff, the right-hand man of Paul von Beneckendorff and Hindenburg (also born in Posen), the general duo who had commanded the German armed forces during most of World War I. New facts about Erich Friedrich Wilhelm Ludendorff have come to light in recent years. For instance, the scope of his military status has shrunk somewhat as a result of an upgrading of other German generals, such as the Hussars General von Mackensen, the man with the *Totenkopf fur* cap and the falcon eyes who, according to his biographer Theo Schwarzmüller, played a more important part in the victories of 1914 than for which he received credit. The American historian Asprey, in a recent double biography of Ludendorff and Hindenburg, pointed out the less attractive military sides of both lords of the field. Nevertheless, both men were the face of Germany at the time.[18] German historian Arthur Rosenberg in particular characterised Ludendorff's position of power as of dictatorial status.[19] For Ludendorff, who had fought for the German cause with heart and soul, the November defeat was unpalatable. He therefore simply denied it and had to undergo treatment by a neurologist.[20]

The German people had remained undefeated in the trenches, was his motto invariably. According to Asprey, Ludendorff was a man of iron principles and could not be moved from this position once taken. He therefore completely dismissed the final defeat as a plot against

Germany. Not surprisingly, Ludendorff was aware of the existence of the Thule Society and could regularly be found at the Hotel Vier Jahreszeiten, where von Sebottendorff's ariosophical organisation held its meetings. Ludendorff did not hide his disgust about the *überstateliche* powers. The following conversation arose between Ludendorff and British general Sir Neil Malcolm in the spring of 1919:

'You mean, that you were stabbed in the back?'
Ludendorff replied:
'That's it exactly, we were stabbed in the back - stabbed in the back'.[21]

Other testimonies have survived from the first period that report of Ludendorff's frustration. When Ludendorff left his military headquarters on 26 October 1918 and arrived at Potsdam railway station, he said: 'Hopefully the army will come home undefeated.' Major von Harbou, working in the Army's operations department, then whispered half to himself and half to the listeners: *'Wir sind ja an allen Fronten besiegt.'*[22]

As the German army, dressed in trench rags, stumbled back to the Rhine, Ludendorff made a speech in which he blamed the defeat on everyone but the armed forces. He did so with such theatrical feeling that tears streamed down the cheeks of the audience en masse. The 71-year-old Hindenburg, stoic as ever, looked on. 'With God's help, Germany will come out on top,' he muttered after the speech.[23] Incidentally, the stab-in-the-back myth was not limited to Ludendorff or a small number of officers. The myth was a pervasive thought and frustration. *'Ihr seid im Felde unbesiegt geblieben,'* Friedrich Ebert mused at a speech under the Brandenburg Gate.[24] This frustration is reflected in literature of the time as well, such as in Werner Beumelburg's mass-read works *Sperrfeuer um Deutschland* and *Deutschland in Ketten,* or Gustaf von Dickhuth-Harrach's *Im Felde unbesiegt* from Lehmann publishers. A literary battle soon arose between the völkisch-nationalist camp and the more national-critical camp, and before long the latter's work was being characterised by the former as *Dekadenzromane*. Beumelburg single-handedly opened the attack on Thomas Mann's *Der Zauberberg*, changing the name of the protagonist Castorp to Casdorp in his own novel *Gruppe Bosemüller* and turning Mann's (anti)hero into a cowardly opponent of the *Soldatentum*. He did the same with books by Arnold Zweig.[25] Worth mentioning here is Ernst Röhm's remark in his *Geschichte eines Hochverräters*, in which he reports that 94 per cent of active German officers in World War I had given their blood for the fatherland.[26] This remark is factually incorrect but emotionally completely spot on. How could a nation that had fought so hard and stood successfully against virtually the entire world now be defeated. The gaze went inward, to one's own country.

Ludendorff's frustrations only increased over time and with them his radicalism, with even someone like Beumelburg taking the rap for alleged 'Masonic contacts'. He felt the flight of the German Kaiser was shameful. A Swiss friend wrote to him: *'Die Deutschen sind als Sieger brutal, als Besiegte verächtlich.'*[27] In additon, Ludendorff was concerned about Bolshevism in Germany, which he felt should give even Britain, winner of 1914-1918, goose bumps. Furthermore, there were the Ruhroproer and the French sanctions. For a short time, to escape the pressure, Ludendorff diverted to Denmark and Sweden.

Ludendorff's völkische belief in *überstaatliche* powers brought him into contact with reactionary circles and with Hitler. A biographer of Ludendorff once pointed out that the mutual contact and cooperation was essentially based on a misunderstanding. Hitler saw in the excellency Ludendorff a form of legitimisation that could strengthen his movement and his own position and make him famous even outside Bavaria. Ludendorff saw in the charismatic speaker Hitler a man who could give him back his pre-war popularity and make him Germany's strongman. Yet this is a little too simplistic. Both men were in the völkisch camp and that was the real key to their pact. Ludendorff, along with Karl Haushofer, was among the club of intimates who regularly visited Hitler in prison at Landsberg am Lech during the time *Mein Kampf* was being written. Hitler particularly appreciated contact with Ludendorff. He always addressed him respectfully as *'Euere Exzellenz'*, i.e. in the third person. Ludendorff, who had participated in the Putsch, had been acquitted as a war hero.[28]

Ludendorff was so forthright in his political preferences that he passed Hitler politically on the right. Co-cause of all this was Ludendorff's marriage to a very special woman, a kind of German Blavatsky: Dr Mathilde von Kemnitz. This highly gifted and extremely serious woman (the physician Professor Kraepelin, called her 'one of the best students he had ever had') was a neurologist and ran a small practice in Tutzing on the Starnberger See. After a study period in abject poverty and an unhappy marriage in which her husband Gustav Adolf von Kemnitz died in a skiing accident, she had thrown herself into her work and the esotericism of *deutsche Gottglaube*. She saw in Ludendorff the only great general in German history, *Der ewige Recke*, the man who had fought for völkische Germany. Ludendorff in his place fell under the spell of the vast spiritual knowledge of von Kemnitz, who liked to engage in religious-philosophical reflections. The first meeting between Ludendorff and his future wife took place in Munich in October 1923. The man who introduced Dr Mathilde von Kemnitz to Ludendorff was Thulelid, Eckart friend and Nazi economist Gottfried Feder.

Feder has received little interest from historians but was, in my opinion, one of the most important figures in the early days of the völkisch movement. Not only did he know Hitler's military commander Mayr and taught Hitler during his political courses, he was also the man who brought Ernst Röhm, the later SA chief, into the NSDAP (then DAP), where he was among the first 60 members. He was intermediary between Röhm and Ludendorff when a personal crisis arose between them. In his book *Der Deutsche Staat*, Feder had embraced von Kemnitz's 'völkische, religieuze' perception and he strongly advised von Ludendorff to read her books. Partly because of Feder, Ludendorff's house was a meeting point of reactionary forces. A piquant detail: Heinrich Himmler, the later Reichsführer-ss, and Rudolf Höss, the later commander of Auschwitz, met at Ludendorff's home. Wolfgang Kapp was among the frequent visitors to the Ludendorff home as well.[29]

Hitler soon realised that von Kemnitz's theories, especially on Christianity, although on the völkisch line, went far beyond what the NSDAP could electorally support. Röhm described the views of Ludendorff and his wife in his memoirs as of 'rücksichtslose sharpness against Rome', and Hitler felt exactly the same way.[30] He therefore tried to put the brakes on von Kemnitz. 'If indeed *überstateliche* powers exist, they have sent her on our roof,' Hitler complained of von Kemnitz's growing influence. Here was a strong resemblance to Hitler's concerns about Rosenberg and Dinter, whose strong anti-clerical stance offended many Christians. Ludendorff was originally a Lutheran Christian but had never allowed himself the time to really delve into religious matters. Von Kemnitz convinced him, using religious texts, of 'the madness' of all religions. Christian doctrine, she claimed, did not stem from Christ at all, but from an ancient Indian Krishna legend. Jesus was a false Jewish prophet, von Kemnitz believed, and she rejected the word *religion*. *Believing* had to be replaced by *knowing*. The way to do this was the way of study, unlike the biblical lore, which assumed a wait-and-see attitude. The forgeries had been 'presented' to people by *überstateliche* powers: Jews, Freemasons, Jesuits, Rosicrucians. In a multitude of publications, including *Das grosse Entsetzen - Die Bibel nicht Gottes Wort*, the findings were revealed, to the shock of the church. The church institutions again responded with mass printed pamphlets, such as Dr Karl Piepers *Ludendorff und die heilige Schrift*, which 'demonstrated' the Ludendorffs' 'ignorance' on theological issues.[31]

The Ludendorffs' publications were not just about the biblical days or the postwar period. They saw a pattern running through the whole of history, especially German history, as is shown in Ludendorff-von Kemnitz's book *Hinter den Kulissen des Bismarckreiches*, in which the *überstate* powers were depicted rather plastically on the cover. Mathilde believed in the *Protocols of the Wisemen of Zion*, which had been introduced to Germany by Alfred Rosenberg, and she was a reader of Lanz von Liebenfels' *Ostara*. Von Kemnitz had put the core of her theories in writing in her *Triumph des Unsterblichkeitwillens* (1921) which she herself immediately considered the most important work of the last thousand years.

Ludendorff, living in the midst of the heated atmosphere of postwar Bavaria, was impressed by this 'creative and struggling woman', as he described her. At the time he met von Kemnitz, Ludendorff was already an anti-Semite - '*Die Beteiligung des Juden an unserem völkischen Untergang stand klar vor mir*' - but von Kemnitz pointed out to him the 'great connections'.[32] The salvation of the völkisch movement, she believed, lay in a revision of the faith on a völkisch basis, not with the Christian-Jewish faith or the 'sectarian' Freemasons or Rosicrucians. Regarding the latter, Ludendorff author German Nording reported that this was a 'Tibetan diversion' offering a romantic adventurous sham religion to the 'believers'.[33]

Von Kemnitz offered Ludendorff her services. She saw a separate role for women, which she propagated in the *Weltbund Nationaler Frauen* of which she was the delegate at congresses in Rome and Geneva. In her writings, such as *Das Weib und seine Bestimmung*, she spoke solemnly about the role and task of women in relation to their country and people. Nor did she forget the *Mutterschaftsaufgabe*.

The general was very impressed by the fact that she had actively contributed to the defeat of the council republic in Garmisch (1920) and the creation of the Freikorps Werdenfels. He was endeared by her desire to achieve her goals in a pacifist manner. In addition, Ludendorff greatly admired her medical qualities. Ludendorff, who had suffered from nerve attacks since World War I, was helped by her. She also diagnosed the general with a life-threatening occlusion of his airways. Ludendorff was getting more cramped by the week, but doctors dared not operate on him for fear of losing the famous general's life. Von Kemnitz, however, made a case for the operation, and after publicly taking responsibility for the medical treatment and consequences in the press, Ludendorff was operated on with success. He became quite the old man again, and was soon boasting about his eight- to 10-hour mountain hikes, which he made together with Mathilde. The good relationship between the two was sealed with marriage on 14 September 1926.

Ludendorff underlined his admiration for von Kemnitz by recommending to Hitler *Triumph des Unsterblichkeitwillens*. Von Kemnitz even visited Hitler in Landsberg prison, but Hitler was embarrassed by it. He made it clear that for electoral reasons he had to keep his distance from von Kemnitz's anti-Christian rhetoric in particular, and had to watch with regret as Ludendorff moved away from him and toured the country together with von Kemnitz with a large lecture series. Ludendorff and his wife streamlined their activities in the so-called *Tannenbergbund* (named after the legendary battle) and published many books, including *Deutscher Gottglaube* and *Das Geheimnis der Jesuitenmacht und ihr Ende* in which their anticlerical stance was clearly expressed. Besides the many books, several periodicals came out, such as *Am heiligen Quell deutscher Kraft* and *Ludendorff's Volkswarte*. Its following in its heyday was estimated at around 100,000 people. Karl Tschuppik, in his 1931 critical Ludendorff biography, saw in this movement the precursor of much doom. He saw Ludendorff's path as one of self-destruction. The völkische ideal, Tschuppik warned, did not in reality belong to German history at all, but was a wishful thinking that first had to be realised. As a military man, Ludendorff knew only one way to do this: battle. Although the völkisch movement and its ideals were sometimes laughed at in those days, Tschuppik underlined the dangers. 'The misunderstandings underlying Ludendorff's thinking live on in millions. They are productive, establish parties and armies and may one day become a power of significance.'

After 1933, when Hitler had his electoral blessing, relations between Hitler and Ludendorff improved. Hitler authorised the creation of the *Bund für Gotterkenntnis Ludendorff* on 30 March 1937, after they had first been proscribed as heretics. Nine months later, Ludendorff died. Hitler saw to it that the general was given a state funeral and spoke a few words himself at his grave: *'General Ludendorff! In Namen des geeinten deutschen Volkes lege ich in tiefer Dankbarkeit diesen Kranz vor Dir nieder!'* After the war, von Kemnitz continued her activities for the union until her death in 1966. The organisation, which still exists and has 240 members according to the German Verfassungsschutz, was banned several times because of *Blut und Boden theories*. Von Kemnitz's work is still published by publishing house Hohe Warte.[34]

It was rightly asked with some surprise by the historian Hellmuth Auerbach how on earth it could have been possible that Erich Ludendorff, an important military leader and symbolic figure, had suddenly emerged alongside the completely unknown Corporal Hitler, as the spearhead of the national movement in Germany, and that Hitler was apparently supported by other high-ranking military officers as well.

The relationship between Ludendorff and Hitler was one of the first clear signs that the military and the Nazis could find common ground in the völkisch-ariosophical myth of *überstateliche* powers. However, the origins went back even further. Hitler's immediate military superior, Hauptmann Karl Mayr, whom Hitler had spied for as a v-Mann (*Vertrauensmann*) shortly after World War I, was already intertwined in the völkisch camp. Mayr was commander of the *Nachrichten und Aufklärungsabteilung des Gruppenkommandos iv* Munich, which had to monitor the turbulent political climate in Bavaria. In the process, as mentioned, Hitler monitored the political activities of various organisations. His reports were outright anti-Semitic pamphlets that had the effect of raising Hitler in Mayr's esteem. It was no objection to Mayr that his Reichswehr soldier Hitler spoke at the first major post-World War I anti-Semitic meeting in Munich: the speech in the Kindl-Keller. Indeed, Mayr sent his soldiers to the lecture, and allowed Hitler to recruit soldiers for the DAP. Mayr's fanatical involvement in the political *Alltag* is endorsed by the memoirs of Ernst Röhm. In his *Geschichte eines Hochverräters*, Röhm reports that Mayr used his military position to support his political ideals. Röhm saw Mayr as one of the biggest supporters of the later Kapp-Putsch.[35]

The explanation for supporting Hitler lay in a similar rationale, namely that 'evil powers' determined the course of history and that they had to be fought at all costs. The principle of the völkisch movement echoed in this. Something had gone wrong with the long-awaited German empire that saw the light of day in 1871. It was the same driving force that had set in motion the pens of List and Lanz von Liebenfels, of Drexler and Sebottendorff, of Wagner and Chamberlain, of Rosenberg and of Eckart. They also stirred up Ludendorff; they had stirred up Karl Mayr. Mayr, as a purebred revolutionary, had even kept weapons ready for the 1923 Putsch, which was supposed to be the German 'march on Berlin', following the 'march on Rome'. In early 1923, Hitler and Göring had bought these weapons from a dealer near the abandoned Schliessheim airfield. After buying them, they had handed them over to Bavaria's military commander, von Lossow, with a request to watch over them in case communists made a grab for power.[36] The völkische basis idea lived on even among the judges who had to try the Hitler and Ludendorff's Beer Hall-Putsch conspirators. *'Doch ein kolossaler Kerl,'* one of them had it recorded about Hitler in the trial minutes.[37]

This *common interpretation and perception of history* has convinced some researchers that Hitler's espionage and later involvement in the DAP was no accident at all. The Reichswehr infiltrated the party and actively helped create a conservative-national political stronghold. This would have made Hitler a stooge of the völkisch forces in the military camp. We find such assumptions and claims mostly among Marxist-oriented historians. The title of Emil Carlebach's work, *Hitler war kein Betriebsunfall* - also the title of a book work by Fritz Fischer - speaks volumes in this regard. The late historian Reinhard Opitz, in his *Faschismus und Neofaschismus*, speaks openly of *'Hitler's Auftrag in der dap'*. In a recent Hitler biography, Manfred Weissbecker and Kurt Pätzold point out that Hitler's decision to become a politician in 1918 is based on legend. Hitler only became politically active after the council republic in Munich, when he joined Commander Mayr, in May 1919.[38]

These propositions are thought-provoking because they provide an answer to Auerbach's question. Still, they are dangerous propositions because they would once again underestimate Hitler's role and his personal perception of politics. We still remember Bracher's words. It is certainly not imaginary, but even probable that the reactionary military discovered Hitler as the man who appealed to the people and that in some kind of collusion or on the basis of the same rationale as the DAP, the völkisch-ariosophical Thule Society and the Germanic League, they put Hitler forward. In my opinion, the *common rationale* is preferable to conspiracy. If military and völkisch forces put Hitler forward in collusion, he never became their real stooge. People who could somewhat claim a guru-like role were gagged by Hitler after 1933. Hitler was too stubborn and obstinate. The well-known German historian Sebastian Haffner, who had fled to Britain with his

Jewish friend Erika Hirsch after Kristallnacht in 1938, noted as early as 1940 that Hitler had become the central figure. Others could only rule in his name.[39]

What is clear is the fact that Hitler's oratorical talent was discovered almost simultaneously by the völkisch camp (Anton Drexler) as well as by the military, where professor Karl Alexander von Müller pointed out to Hitler's superior Mayr the exceptional oratorical talent of the young soldier who was being groomed for political espionage with him. This did not fall on deaf ears: in the völkisch camp, Hitler's career after meeting Drexler was tolerated and encouraged by the army. Mayr used Hitler's oratorical talent by briefly employing him as a lecturer with the task - a piquant detail - warning soldiers of the communist danger.[40]

As in the political, völkisch camp, Hitler soon had his admirers among the reactionary military. These included Max Amann, the proofreader and publisher of *Mein Kampf*, his former company sergeant-major and Colonel Hermann Kriebel, military leader at the 1923 Putsch. The Hitler biographer Gisevius writes: 'He (Amann) must have so appreciated him (Hitler) as a soldier and human being that he joined him as early as 1920.'[41] Or was it exactly the other way round: did Amann notice how Hitler had been pushed forward by völkisch and reactionary forces and saw 'bread' in the young politician? The idea that Hitler was encouraged by völkische forces and the military authorities to launch his career politically is also echoed by Hans-Günter Richardi. In his *Hitler und seine Hintermänner*, he claims that although Hitler was already an anti-Semite, he was not initially dismissive of social democracy. This view is confirmed by Wolfram Meyer zu Uptrup as well, in a recent article in the *Zeitschrift für Geschichtswissenschaft*. Hitler was not clearly on the side of the Freikorps in the heat of the council republic days, something he was later accused of doing by his growing rival Ernst Röhm. Indeed, Hitler is said to have worn the revolutionaries' red strap. We know from a recent Hitler biography by Charles Bracelen Flood that this need hardly have political significance, however. Practically the entire unit from Hitler's Maximilian II barracks seems to have worn the strap 'for protection'. Hitler's real activities and sympathies are unclear.

What is clear is that he did not take part in the reactionary forces' 'white' counter-offensive on Munich.[42] Interestingly, Hitler's immediate commander Mayr sent the DAP's party programme to the putchist Wolfgang Kapp (more on this later) in Berlin (24 September 1920), saying that the DAP seemed to be the 'national shock troops they had hoped for'.[43]

We can therefore conclude that the völkisch element was not absent among senior military officers in post-World War I Bavaria. To a large extent, the secret völkisch organisations had the same rationale as the army. Meyer zu Uptrup comes with new, strong indications in this direction. According to the German historian, who investigated the origins of Hitler›s anti-Semitism, Hitler was initially not very active politically - possibly already anti-Semitic. His political activity increased after he received systematic political training from the Reichswehr. Meyer zu Uptrup points out that Gottfried Feder, a confidant of Mathilde Ludendorff and Dietrich Eckart, was a member of the Thule Society and, moreover, was one of the teachers of the espionage students alongside Karl Alexander von Müller. Besides Feder, Joseph Hofmiller and Karl Graf von Bothmer, all confidants of Eckart and affiliated to the anti-Semitic-Völkisch line, acted as referees as well. Hauptmann Mayr had Dietrich Eckart's *Auf gut deutsch* distributed in the lecture hall as teaching material. Hitler's military campus was steeped in völkisch-ariosophical thought.[44]

An interesting side note here is the question of whether Hitler was treated so kindly by the Bavarian judiciary after the 1923 Putsch partly because of this common ground between 'reactionaries' and 'völkischen'. Indeed, it is known that Bavarian justice minister Franz Gurtner, as well as police commissioner Ernst Pöhner and his right-hand man Wilhelm Frick (later interior minister under Hitler), were members of the Thule Society.[45] So it is not illogical to assume that they used their influence to spare Hitler. What is certain in any case is that Hitler got off graciously and was enabled to write *Mein Kampf in* Landsberg prison with the help of Hess and Haushofer. A recent study by Hans-Günter Richardi seems to support this thesis and portrays Pöhner as an enemy of the republic, who gave Nazis false passes to escape justice. Pöhner, along with Frick, kept Hitler free from state pressure as much as possible. Hitler thanked them for this in *Mein Kampf*.[46]

Meanwhile, pioneering research on this is being carried out by historians Lothar Gruchmann and Reinhard Weber in a four-volume study. The initial results are startling. The *Süddeutsche Zeitung* spoke of '*Das dümmste Gericht*'. The judiciary and Bavarian prime minister Eugen Ritter von Knilling reacted to the Feldhernnhalle-Putsch with a mixture of fear and sympathy. Von Knilling believed he should be lenient towards the Putchists, given that he could 'hardly entrench himself in a barracks for the rest of his life anyway'. Characteristic of the atmosphere in which the trial took place was the fact that the death of four policemen in the Putsch was never brought up during the court hearings.[47]

Another well-known soldier who supported Hitler from the very beginning was Eduard Dietl. Dietl would rise to general of mountain troops in World War II and create a furore with his capture and defence of Narvik (Norway) with 6,000 men against 20,000 British, between April and June 1940. Yet when Dietl met Hitler, the latter was only v-Mann and Dietl a professional soldier who had made it to battalion commander in the First World War. It was June 1919 in the *Munich Türkenkaserne* that the two men had their first conversation. It was a very important event for both of them. After an hour-long conversation, Dietl shook hands with Hitler and told him that from then on he would be Hitler's follower and supporter. He kept his word. Hitler saw in Dietl a soldier after his own heart, a *Gneisenau*, and was genuinely touched when he heard in 1944 that Dietl had died in a plane crash. Not only did Dietl provide genuine support from their first meeting (soldiers from his company provided the political speaker Hitler with 'hall protection' at the time when the SA was not so strong), but also, through Dietl, Hitler became even more closely associated with the hard core of reactionary professional soldiers who, instead of a republic, preferred to see a government of action.

Dietl was not an unimportant man in this camp. He was good friends with Freikorps leaders, such as Rudolf Berthold (Freikorps *Eiserne Schar*) from Bad Kissingen and Major Josef Bischoff, the former commander of the *Eiserne Division* (the cadre formed the remnants of the 8th Army) who had fought in the Kurland, among other places. This provided Hitler with another 'Baltic connection'. The reactionary officers felt connected to that area and considered the defence of the 'Baltenland' a matter of honour. In 1918, about 70,000 Volksdeutschen lived in Latvia, almost 20,000 in Estonia and 40,000 (excluding Memel area) in Lithuania. In total, Volksdeutschen made up about 8 per cent of the population of the Baltic states. Traditionally, they belonged to the wealthier part of the population, the large landowners. The relationship between the Germans and the Balts was strained because the Germans often called the shots in the past. Following the Treaty of Brest-Litowsk, the Baltic states had come under German control on 3 March 1918, but when the Treaty of Versailles dissolved the Brest-Litowsk treaty, the Red Army advanced towards them. This drove the Balts into German hands and a tense collaboration began.[48] When Russian troops had invaded in November 1918, the Germans had immediately deployed volunteer units. Fighting in the Baltic region culminated in a brutal and bloody conflict. In an atmosphere of chaos and 'hyper-nationalism', the idea arose among reactionary circles that the future of the German East stood or fell on the outcome of this showdown.

'Wenn das Vaterland es über sich bringen sollte, uns preiszugeben, dann gut, dann sind wir eben die letzten, die aus dem grossen Krieg ihr Pflicht und Ehrgefühl gerettet haben'.[49]

Riga and Mittau were stormed by the Baltic Landwehr (Baron Hans von Manteuffel), Reichsdeutschen volunteers (Hauptmann von Medem) artillery (Anna Berg veteran Albert Leo Schlageter), the 2.Garde Ref.Rgt. (Gruppe Plehwe) and the 'Kurland Feld.Art.bt.' (Hauptmann Tschocke). The 40,000 Freikorp soldiers who served in this conflict brought a blood-soaked legacy back to Germany and would play a lasting role in the reactionary camp. Their anti-Bolshevism, anti-Slavism and anti-Semitism played an important role in the 'black Reichswehr', the Kapp-Putsch and the Hitler-Putsch.[50]

Robert G.L. Waite conducted research in the early 1950s on the enormous influence of the Freikorpsmanship on the Völkisch movement and the Third Reich. In practice, the anti-communist Freikorps proved to be a lucrative stepping stone to a Nazi career. In *Vanguard of Nazism*, an all-telling title, Waite depicted a number of careers. For example, Freikorpser Herbert Albrecht worked for the '*Völkische Beobachter*' and became a delegate for the NSDAP to the 'Reichstag', and Friedrich Alpers became a member of SA, SS and minister of justice in Brunswick (1933). Willy Andreson, active in the Baltic region and a participant in the Kapp-Putsch, became director of the Gauleiter school; Benno von Arent, a member of the East Prussian von der Heyde Freikorps became an SS member; Hubertus von Aulock climbed to Brigadeführer with the NSDAP; Hans Baumann became Gauleiter; Robert Belding joined the SA; and Bergmann became Reichstag delegate, to name just a few. The most famous Freikorps members were Martin Bormann, (Freikorps Rossbach), Kurt Daluege (Rossbach), Hans Frank (von Epp-Freikorps), Rudolf Hess (Ehrhardt Brigade), Reinhard Heydrich (Maerckers Schutz und Trutzbund), Dietrich von Jagow (Erhardtbrigade), Erich Koch (Freikorps member in Opperschlezien), Röhm successor Viktor Lutze, paratrooper general Bernhard Ramcke (Freikorps Baltic area), Karl Wolff, Himmler's later adjutant and Emil Maurice, Hitler's driver. In all, Waite lists two hundred prominent Freikorps figures who would gain important positions in the Third Reich.[51]

In addition to Waite's study, the main influence of the Freikorps are exposed by period documents such as the memoirs written in 1934 by the iron fighter Ernst Röhm. In his *Geschichte eines Hochverräters,* Röhm describes the psychological, social process through which the front fighters of 1914-1918 went. The war had fundamentally changed the social perception of the combatants. The bourgeois structures of once had lost all their value as a result of the hardships suffered and the unpretentious *war-Alltag*.[52] The common man from the people had become a hero in the field, claiming his place upon returning to Germany after years of front deprivation. This psychic state was the basis for the stab-in-the-back myth and for nationalist sentiments.

Furthermore, contacts between Hitler and reactionary militaries went through Thule member and publisher Julius Lehmann, who had good contact with the highly conservative wing of the navy thanks to his naval publications. James and Suzanne Pool, who studied the financial background of Hitler's rise, believe that Hitler received funds for his political struggle through the navy, via the Thule Society and Lehmann. The reason for Hitler's military support would have been not only his völkisch-nationalist programme and his aversion to communism, but also his opposition to Bavarian separatism. In addition, the German fleet needed tax money from southern Germany to exist. Lehmann supported Hitler from ariosophical beliefs. His publishing house published many books on racial hygiene. The symbol of Lehmann's publishing house was a lion with the inscription *'Ich habs gewagt'* underneath, which would become the epitaph of Rudolf Hess.[53]

Bischoff and Berthold's Baltic experiences were important for other reasons. They provided Hitler with an important psychological experience so that he knew how to 'warm up' soldiers for the campaign to the east. Indeed, the Baltic interest did not stem only from völkische *Blut und Boden* sentiments. After the Red Army had directly invaded the Baltic states on 13 November 1918 and was at the gates of Latvian Narva after just one day, the Latvian authorities - who were not exactly pro-German - decided to strike a bargain with the German envoy to the Baltic region, August Winnig. On 29 December 1918, Winnig concluded a contract with them in which German volunteers for the Baltic cause could count on citizenship and a piece of land. This did not fall on deaf ears. It prompted the creation of a *Kurländische Ritterschaftskomitee*, and many discharged German soldiers saw it as an escape from their drab *Alltag*. Despite this opportunism of many of the volunteers, Bischoff and Berthold it to be a matter of honour. 'Vultures', Bischoff called the opportunistic volunteers for Baltenland.[54] As we shall see later, Hitler would warm up his *Ritterkreuzträger* with a new variation on the Prussian Knights' Courts of old.

Moreover, Hitler's experiences with the Freikorps taught him a second lesson. When the so-called Kapp-Putsch in Berlin came to nothing, Hitler - accompanied by Dietrich Eckart (Kapp was an avid reader of Eckart's *Auf gut deutsch*) - was still in Berlin (March 1920) just in time to meet a totally dejected and disillusioned Wolfgang Kapp, accompanied only by his daughter. The Generallandschaftsdirektor of East Prussia had tried to create a new government of 'order and discipline'. The Putsch had been brought down by treachery and lack of public cooperation. The Putsch had been put down on 17 March. Kapp had bought a plane and hired a pilot to escape to Sweden. Hitler leant that the military was an important factor, but that the people had to be the driving force behind any political movement. Kapp complained about the leaders of the reactionary Putsch. They thought only of their own interests and forgot the interests of the state.[55]

Furthermore, the conflict in the Baltic region paved the way for the belief that the Germans needed to operate militarily pre-emptively in the east. This debate unexpectedly became topical again some 10 years ago when a long article (later published in book form) by Victor Suvorov (Vladimir Rezun) was published in the Paris-based, Russian migrant magazine *Russkaia Mysl*. Suvorov, a former Soviet secret agent, claimed in the 1989 miracle year that Stalin had planned an attack on the West in the summer of 1941 and that Nazi Germany had just beat him to it. As evidence for his thesis, Suvorov argued, among other things, that the Soviet Union had established strong mountain army units on the western border, manned by mountain-experienced Caucasus troops, with the aim of a westward attack centred on the Romanian oil fields of Ploesti, indispensable to Germany. Besides this, Suvorov pointed to the huge number of airborne units (10 corps) Stalin had under arms, which were not useful for defensive warfare. In addition, according to Suvorov, the Soviet offensive plans were made clear by the starting positions of army, navy and air force, and Soviet marshals had special shock armies consisting of black (officially non-existent) divisions of Gulag prisoners.[56]

This thesis came just at a time when a stirring debate was going on in Germany about the *Einmaligkeit* of the Holocaust and the Nazi regime, or to what extent one could interpret Hitler-Germany as an 'ordinary' station in tragic, human history. Here it was mainly the theses of Nolte and Pipes, which we have covered before, that caused great consternation. Was the murder of the Armenians by the Turks comparable to the murder of the Jews? Was Stalin not a worse totalitarian ruler and murderer than Hitler? This rationale would eventually culminate in a monumentally thick study by Allan Bullock: *Hitler and Stalin, parallel lives*, where the emphasis should be on this subtitle.[57]

Suvorov's thesis was naturally embraced by those who wanted to show that Stalin was no better than Hitler and who believed that National Socialism should not be isolated from the rest of history by assigning this period an exceptionally dark status. Hillgruber, Bracher, Hoffmann, Messerschmidt, Broszat, Topitsch, Boog, Erickson and other leading (military) historians subsequently mingled into this debate. This cycle of discussion found its provisional climax in Werner Maser's *Der Wortbruch, Hitler, Stalin und der Zweite Weltkrieg*.[58] Elements of this discussion can also be found in the debate between David Irving and Martin Broszat. Irving in his monumental biography of Hitler[59] outlines the concept of the pre-emptive strike against the Soviet Union. Broszat believes there is an '*Über-Machiavellisierung*' and '*Rationalisierung*' of Hitler here.[60]

Until the search for documents in the 'free' East since 1989 is complete, all aspects of this discussion will not become fully understood. Perhaps even more important than the factual accuracy of Suvorov's thesis is the question of what was going on in the minds of the people and, above all, the military at the time. Given Hitler's remarks in *Mein Kampf*, his second book and his political will, we need not doubt his will to start a war against the Soviet Union. Nor need there be any doubt about Hitler's idea that Stalin approached world politics in such an aggressive manner. Hitler placed Stalin in his historical perception of the past, with Huns and Germanic people fighting for Lebensraum in Europe.

That Hitler himself flaunted the idea of preventive warfare is certain. It fits in with Hitler's view of inter-state relations too. What General Hermann Balck - certainly no friend of the Nazis - writes about this in his memoirs is interesting. At a meeting in Berlin, attended by generals von Schell, Buhle and Fromm, he learned that 'now that Britain had been driven from the European mainland, oil from Voorazia beckoned.' The 'Russian problem' remained, however, and Germany was forced to 'keep a large army in the east'. At that point, the generals believed, Germany was 'so much stronger than the Soviet Union' that it was 'no longer a serious match' for German forces. This partly explained the 'demonstrative friendliness' with which Russia accommodated supplies of raw materials to Germany and the pro-German tone in the press. However, Russia's true intentions were different. Russia 'made itself militarily strong', according to Schell, Buhle and Fromm, to 'attack Germany when the time was right'. They believed this would take place when Germany was ravaged by a crop failure or in conflict with the USA; that then, Russia would 'proceed by all means'. The conclusion the generals drew from this was to attack and destroy Russia as soon as possible. The Baltic states, the Ukraine and the Caucasus would have to come under German occupation, after which they could deal with the British in peace. The downside of attacking Russia would be that they would no longer get oil and food supplies. They had to put up with that for a short time.[61]

The underestimation of Soviet strength stemmed from the way relations between the two countries had developed after Hitler came to power in 1933. Initially, from 1925, there was fairly close German-Russian cooperation in the military and technical fields, with the Germans able to circumvent the rigid provisions of Versailles on Russian training grounds. Cooperation reached its peak between 1928 and 1932. When Hitler came to power in January 1933, there was initially still a positive attitude towards the Soviet Union. Most military officers, such as German military attaché Otto Hartmann, the *Chef der Heeresleitung* Kurt von Hammerstein-Equord and Generalleutnant Alfred von Vollard-Boeckelberg (who made one of the last military inspection tours of the Soviet Union) spoke highly of the Red Army's *Wehrkraft*, their technical progress and industrial rise. Germany did well to continue working closely together. The exact opposite happened. After 1933, the anti-communist rhetoric of the Nazis and the rise of the mythological worldview of Alfred Rosenberg and consorts caused relations to cool down. Knowledge about the

Soviet military was replaced by ignorance. In February 1936, the previously well-informed German military attaché complained that they were left with hundreds of questions. In addition, the propaganda machine drummed up anti-Sovietism and the drive for Lebensraum. The rumour circuit got underway. On the one hand, there were grisly omens, such as Major Lothar Schüttel's book *Luftkrieg über Deutschland*, which warned of how the heavily armed Soviet Union was gripping Germany and had secretly built Czechoslovakia into a Soviet aircraft carrier in the centre of Europe.[62] In *Achtung Panzer!*[63], tank expert Heinz Guderian warned of Soviet technological advances and the mobility of the Russian army. The Soviet Union would be capable of depth operations. On the other hand, there were purges in the Russian army in 1937 and large parts of the officer corps had been killed by Stalin. It was possible that the Red Army was strong on paper but weak in reality. Von Brauchitsch overconfidently reported to Hitler barely a year before the Soviet invasion that the Red Army had only 50 to 75 good divisions.[64]

Due to the polemical worldview of the Nazis, the time factor always weighed on security thinking. By 1914, 171 million Russians and 39 million Frenchmen had faced Germany, and those relations had only grown more skewed since then. American historian Steven E. Miller characterised this position of Germany in central Europe as one that 'made Moltke sweat and French revanchists laugh'. Germany drew its strength mainly from its economic development. In 1938, Germany supplied 12.7 per cent of the world's industrial output. France was by far the lesser with 4.4 per cent, Russia was a rising power with 9 per cent (7.6 per cent in 1880), the USA at a lonely height with 31.4 per cent. Thereby, Germany was the world's second steel producer (23.2 million tonnes of steel in 1938), but again the Soviet Union was the 'rising power' with 18 million tonnes in third place (vs 28.8 million tonnes). Such factors reinforced the sense of unease among military planners. Their dependence on raw materials also fuelled their disquiet.[65]

Besides völkisch sentiments and geopolitical analyses, there was also the 'Prussian factor', the Prussian borderland, the transition area from the German homeland to the *Deutschtum*, mostly represented by the knight's estates. This is significant because the German army still had very much noble blood even in World War II. Of the 160 senior officers known to the Army Staff, at least 20 were from these Prussian families. Seventeen Bülows, sixteen Arnims, thriteen Kleists, thirteen Oertzen, ten Bismarcken, ten Frankenbergen, nine Witzlebens and so on served in general or other senior officer posts in the army alone.[66] Erich Ludendorff was from 'German-Poland' as well, born on the Kruszewnia estate near Posen (Poznan).

On the knight's estates in Eastern Europe, nobility and peasants went to war together during the wheel time against 'the reds' who mostly caused unrest from outside. This reinforced the image of an 'evil plot' against völkisch Prussia, where rural idyll was paramount and traditional distrust of Slavic peoples was strongest. Not for nothing were the Prussian divisions on the Eastern Front among the most reliable of the German army. Of interest in this regard are the words of Fritz-Dietlof Graf von der Schulenburg:

'Ich spüre, dass ich mit grosser heisser Liebe mit Deutschland verwachsen bin, so stark, dass ich manchmal meine, ich spüre, wie es lebt und atmet, ich fühle seine Schmerzen und seine Not am eigenen Leibe.'

In lyrical-mystical fashion, von der Schulenburg described his fronter experiences in a military magazine: *'Eine lärmende, fröhliche Jagd... unsere Leute räucherten mit lauten Rufe und Lachen die verdutzten Russen aus'.*

At first glance Von der Schulenburg appears to be a staunch National Socialist, were it not for the fact that he belonged to the circle of officers around von Stauffenberg.[67]

The Prussian military had an interest in the Eastern Lebensraum primarily because they were Prussian and nationalistic. Their role was historically scarred, full of fear and hatred. Nobody had forgotten the days in August 1914 when throughout East Prussia the cry of fear sounded: the Cossacks were coming. In one of the letters to his wife, Generalfeldmarschall August von Mackensen (the Hussar general with his *Totenkopf* fur cap) describes how entire regions of the country emptied out in fear of the Russians. Fear reaped hatred, as shown in a poem by Alfred Kerrs:

'Hunde dringen in das Haus
Peitscht sie raus!
Rächtet Insterburg, Gumbinnen
Und vertobackt sie von hinnen...
Dürften uns nicht unterkriegen
Peitscht sie weg!
Peitscht sie weg![68]

In turn, the Slavs looked at the Prussians with suspicion. In 1926, Polish historian Stanislaw Slawski called Prussia the German bridgehead for the conquest of Eastern Europe.[69]

The nobility also engaged in self-examination. In 1926, Professor Hans Friedrich Karl Günther published the book *Adel und Rasse*, followed by *Führeradel durch Sippenpflege*, and the nobility itself also compiled the so-called iron book (*Eisernes Buch deutschen Adels deutscher Art, edda*), in which only noble families without Jewish blood were allowed to be included. Of course, the abbreviation does not form the word edda by accident; it is a reference to the Nordic element that many opportunistic nobles believed they saw in themselves. This self-examination was in part a reaction of the nobility, concentrated in the Deutsche Adelsgenossenschaft (DAG) of which Generalfeldmarschall von Hindenburg was honorary president, to the rise of National Socialism. On the other hand, anti-Semitism was of earlier origin.

A somewhat cynical example of this latent and overt anti-Semitism can be seen in the childhood years of none other than Hermann Göring. Indeed, young Hermann grew up with almost holy reverence for his godfather 'Pate Epenstein' (Hermann von Epenstein), an adventurous and wealthy man who had an affair with Göring's mother and won over young Hermann with his castles, armour and chamois hunting. When Göring entered boarding school in Ansbach, Franconia, the pupils were instructed by the teacher to write a patriotic essay. The students were, of course, supposed to write something about Wilhelm II, Bismarck or Frederick the Great. Hermann wrote his essay full of praise for Ritter von Epenstein. The next day, he was summoned to the rector's office, who informed Hermann that no papers were written in honour of Jews at his school. Göring protested that his godfather was Catholic, but according to the rector, this did not detract from his racial origin. Göring was sent away with the punishment of writing a hundred lines of punishment with the text: 'I am not allowed to write essays in honour of Jews.' In addition, Göring had to walk around the schoolyard with a sign on his neck reading 'My godfather is a Jew.' Göring resented this terribly. In the night, he crawled out of his bed and fled the boarding school. Before secretly catching the train to Neuhaus, towards his parental home, he cut the strings of musical instruments of the school orchestra. Göring was loyal to his heroes, as he would be to Hitler. This foreplay did not take place in the heyday of National Socialism; indeed, no one had ever heard of Hitler then, who himself was only a child at the time. It was only 1904.[70]

The DAG had existed since 1874 and represented above all the nobility east of the Elbe. This nobility, as well as the nobility in northern Germany, had the most to lose out of the 85,000 to 90,000 noble families Germany had.[71] In southern Germany and especially Bavaria, the German nobility had already lost most of its interests in the nineteenth century. In northern and, above all, eastern Germany, she clung to the remnants of a grand history. No wonder then that they were strongly anti-materialist, anti-individualist, anti-liberalist and anti-Semitic. Any change frightened them. They rejected the new industrial society, which was alienating itself from the rural idyll. The National Socialist idea dovetailed with the elitist idea that the nobility should be 'a closed circuit', marrying among themselves. Many völkische arguments that we saw with Darré and Rosenberg can therefore be found with the nobility. The young, propertyless nobility in particular, embraced Hitler's idea of Lebensraum. 'I do not need to explain the possibilities in the East,' mused Ewald von Kleist-Schmenzin as early as 1926, a few years after *Mein Kampf*.[72] Nor did the von Knobelsdorffs' descendants hesitate to openly ask for new estates in Eastern Europe as early as 1933. For them it was very simple, the future of much of the nobility depended on the success of the conquest of Lebensraum. In order to qualify for the newly divisible spoils, the lion's share of the nobility in Germany eventually gave in to the Aryan Paragraph the Nazis valued. In return, Hitler kept in check his most radical preachers against the 'Christian nobility'. It was one of Hitler's tactical manoeuvres. He needed the expertise of the noble lords, who, had been looking east of the Elbe for centuries and dreaming of large estates. The part that already owned estates was put on the block by the *Nationalsozialistische Führungsoffizier*, an internal magazine of the Wehrmacht: '*Farm, Kolchose oder Erbhof?* *Farm* painted a future like modernist, capitalist America, with no sense of rank and file, which was an abomination to the working-class Prussian nobility. Kolchoses represented the terrifying, equal-opportunity alternative in the East. 'Erbhof' stood for the old, familiar: '*Alle Schwankungen sind am Ende zu ertragen, alle Schicksalschläge zu überwinden, wenn ein gesundes Bauerntum vorhanden ist,*' Hitler mused in a speech in Berlin in April 1933. With the Prussian nobility thinking of their historical 'rights', Darré dreaming of his 'new nobility', Hitler divided and ruled.[73]

The legitimising influence of old distrust from the German-Polish borderland, on the edge of the *Deutschtum*, should not be underestimated. German-Polish relations were seriously disturbed in the years before World War II. We have already seen earlier in the book that the far (völkisch) right in Poland blamed the Germans and Jews for the Polish-Russian war in 1920. That was just the beginning of the antipathy that existed in Poland towards the Germans. When the Nazis came to power in 1933, Poles immediately feared a revision of Versailles would affect them too.[75] A Polish historian once took stock of what Poles thought of the German people's character. The Poles, he believed, thought the Germans were stupid, spineless, incorrigible, self-interested, harsh and unjust, cynical and arrogant, unreliable (even in alliances), miserly and materialistic, exploitative, rapacious, violent, nationalistic and revanchist, cowardly, treacherous, lying and hypocritical and endowed with an ample dose of faith in their own greatness. Researcher Frank Golzewski comes to this conclusion after studying Polish historiography and publications in the years 1918 and 1939. What is most interesting about his research is that there was one thing that annoyed the Poles the most by far; something for which they had even invented a separate word: *Zaborczosc*, the German people's trait of appropriating territories that did not belong to them. As positive traits of the German people, Golzewski found organisation, discipline and diligence. If we link these traits to the above traits, the Polish fear of *Zaborczosc* is not incomprehensible.[76]

Hatred of Germans, incidentally, was much older than the time frame covered by Golzewski's research. Over the centuries, we already find evidence of a strong anti-German mood among Poles in Polish literature, poetry and painting. This is expressed, among other things, by the frequent use of the word 'dog' for Germans, which is a gross insult in Poland. We see this as early as the thirteenth century when the Polish archbishop Jakob Swinka speaks of German dog heads. '*Co Niemiec, to pies*' (Every German is a dog). Jan Kochanowski called the Teutonic knights dogs in 1569. His example was followed by Jozef Szujski (1866), Adolf Dygasinski (1866), Jadwiga Luszczweska (1927) and Gustow Morcinek (1931), to name just a few authors. 'German dogs' also popped up in art, as with W. Brotanski painting: '*Psie Pole pod Wroclawem*' (The Dog Field of Breslau). Polish bishop Pawel Piasecki spoke of the 'German poison', against which Poles had to fight with all their might.

Polish antipathy did not only have geopolitical roots. Religion and Polish national pathos also played an important role. Poles saw themselves as a historical bulwark of Catholicism vis-à-vis the East, and believed in their own missionary mission. In this, Lutheran Germans were strongly distrusted and despised as infidels

> 'Is it true that Martin Luther was born a woman?
> No, a female wolf bore him from her rear
> Who raised him?
> Lucifer! His companion.
> What kind of person is he?
> He is the minister of hell.
> Or a god, which is what the Germans do not have

They only believe in Luther, the avenging
He was immediately exiled by Rome,
Then he invented a new church
He seduced women
A new order was his goal
Therefore, he had to flee from Rome to Germany
The pope wanted to castrate him
If Germans would not listen to Luther
Then they had clothes and food in winter
But the Schwab is stupid
He gives everything to Luther
And Luther collects the money
And buys wine for it at the pub'[77]

Tensions in the border country led to Polish repression of *Volksdeutschen*. Forced assimilation was not shunned in the process. This was particularly evident in naming: Else became Elzbieta, Eugen Eugeniusz, Albert Wojcieh, Nickolaus Mikolaj, Lorenz Wawrzyniak. Well-known historical figures became part of an ethnic debate: was it Nikolaus Kopernikus or Mikolaj Kopernik?

The Germans, for their part, expressed extremely negative and denigrating views on the Poles too. We have already seen in the previous chapter how Alfred Rosenberg acted against the Polish state. For many Germans, Poland was a 'monster from World War I', with no right to exist. Hitler called Poland the 'pet child of the Western democracies that did not belong at all to the cultural peoples'. The German clergy made their voices heard as well. Bishop Alois Hudal wrote that 'even if only two Germans lived in Poland that they were worth more than millions of Poles, because they were Germans after all'.[78] Moreover, politicians like Bismarck had made remarkable statements in the recent past. Regarding German-Polish relations, Bismarck constantly spoke of a struggle for 'being or not being'. In a private letter to his sister, he wrote without diplomatic ado: 'I understand their (Poland's) situation, but if we want existence then we can do nothing but exterminate them. A wolf cannot help being created by god the way he is, and yet people shoot him dead if they can.'[79]

In addition, there were great tensions between Germany and Poland due to the Polish corridor that separated part of German territory as well as the Volksdeutschen in Poland. Tensions had escalated shortly after World War I around the Annaberg in Oberschlesien. In May 1921, German Freikorps had stormed the mountain, which was in Polish hands. Initially they were successful, but eventually the Poles won the battle for the Annaberg. This renewed defeat soon reinforced the symbolism of the Battle of the Annaberg, which gained an almost mythical position in the völkisch movement. Kurd Eggers called the mountain *'Der Berg der Rebellen'* in 1935 and stressed that the German defeat had increased the emotional value of the Annaberg. The German psychologist Klaus Theweleit believes that the mountain stood for the *'dennoch-karacter'* of the völkisch thinkers, unwillingness to resign themselves to the facts and the course of history, the belief in the social engineering of the world, the triumph of the will, to paraphrase Leni Riefenstahl...[80]

The even-tempered German press reported atrocity upon atrocity against the Volksdeutschen. German propaganda reported that in all, no fewer than 58,000 Volksdeutschen had been killed by the Poles. In reality, the number was around 3850; nevertheless, one can conclude from this that the tension was around the corner. Incidentally, most of these Volksdeutschen were killed after the invasion on 1 September 1939.[81]

The victims of the massacres were photographed by the Germans and released in a shocking book, *Die Polnischen Greueltaten an den Volksdeutschen in Polen*. Most of the photos show the killings around the town of Bromberg. The ethnic violence was used by the Nazi authorities to legitimise their own barbaric policies towards Poles.[81a]

It was the era of overwrought nationalism, völkisch-emotional rhetoric, stereotyping and a dangerous belief in the malleability of the world. Eastern Europeans felt the undercurrent that lived in the German West. Polish intellectuals tried to debunk the German myth of the *Kulturträgertum*: 'The Germans are seen as magicians and that makes them 'mysterious, while in reality they possess only a higher technical culture". In contrast, Poles argued that the German cultural mission towards Poland and the East had 'always failed', that there was 'no unified German culture' and that Poland had 'acquired its own culture, outside German influences'.[82] The reality of cultures is that, of course, they constantly influence each other. There is an interesting anecdote referring to the 'duplicity' of mutual reproaches. When the city commander of Warsaw, General Rommel, had to capitulate, he pointed out to the German commander-in-chief of the Eighth Army, General Blaskowitz, that he had a Polish name, while he himself had a German name. In the tense *Alltag*, of course, there was little room for such *Vernunft*.[83]

On the other hand, there were also tensions between the nobility and the National Socialists. Richard Walther Darré's fundamental reforms in particular met with resistance. Darré did not so much see the nobility as the ones to take the lead in defending *Deutschtum* in the east, but the Nordic man, and above all the Nordic (soldier) peasant in general. The nobility had originally had a claim to be at the forefront of the nordic man, but cooperation with 'Christianity' had, in his view, perverted the old Germanic nobility. A 'new nobility' therefore had to emerge. As an example, Darré saw the Hungarian admiral without a fleet and *Reichsverweser* Miklos von Horthy. Horthy had not only successfully dealt with the bloody council republic of Bela Kun, but created a new nobility through his 'League of Heroes' (*Vitez*) as well. Successful war veterans had been rewarded in Hungary with a piece of land, the so-called hero or noble estate. These, according to Darré, were to lay the successful foundations for the new generations of Hungarians. The 'heroes' would set an example to society and youth through their impeccable lives, loyalty to the fatherland and through a large and pure posterity. By this *Blut und Boden* policy, Horthy had, in the eyes of the Nazis, definitively abandoned the 'nomadic path' of the Magyars and opted for the Germanic tradition. According to Darré, it was the best step against the danger of 'disruptive Tatar Marxism'.[84]

The 'left-revolutionary' element that had been very strong within the NSDAP until 1934 shimmered a little through this theory. The Nazis' antipathy to the old establishment also played a role. What the

Nazis had in common with the 'Junkers' was that they were convinced of their historical mission. Symbolic of the message the agrarian-ideologue Darré stood for was the poem *'Das sind wir!'* which he introduced in his book *Neuadel aus Blut und boden*, an elaboration of an earlier book:

Das sind wir!

Zu Helm und Schild geboren
Zu des Landes Schutz erkoren,
Dem König sein Offizier,
Treu unseren alten Sitten,
In unsrer Bauern Mitten,
Das sind wir!

Wir bauen unsre Felder,
Wir hegen unsre Wälder
Für Kind und Kindeskind.
Ihr spottet der Ahnen?! Die Hüter
Sind sie der einzigen Güter,
Die euch nicht käuflich sind.
Wir stehn mit starrem Nacken
In des Marktes Feilschen und Placken
In strenger Ritterschaft.
Wir wolln in stillem Walten
Dem Lande sein Bestes erhalten:
Deutsche Bauernkraft![85]

Things did not work out between the SS and the nobility either. The SS thirsted for elite status and the SS magazine *Schwarze Korps* did so by attacking the nobility, among other things. The von Stauffenberg attack therefore involved several senior officers from former Prussian soldier families, such as Erich von Witzleben, Karl Heinrich von Stülpnagel, Hans Karl Freiherr von Esebeck, Hennig von Tresckow, Fritz von den Lancken, Fritz von den Schulenburg, Graf Peter Yorck von Wartenburg and many others. Their commitment to von

Stauffenberg's side was not motivated by democratic ideals. Rather, they were fighting for their ancient traditions, their seven centuries-old knightly estates that defended *Deutschtum* on the edge of the East. Their concerns were justified. Hitler's fatal course meant the war was heading towards them. The advance of the Red Army, late 1944 - early 1945, would consign this age-old tradition to the history books once and for all.[86] On the other hand, they still saw a separate path for the nobility in history, even if the process of emancipation and democratisation continued. Friedrich Glum captured this aspiration of the nobility in the book *Das geheime Deutschland*, published in 1930. It was von Stauffenberg's last words before he died: 'Long live secret Germany!'[87]

Besides this völkische bridge, there was the German military success in World War I in Eastern Europe that still lived in the minds of German general staffs. While World War I in the west unfolded into horrific massacres at Verdun and on the Somme, the war in the east remained more fluid and went successfully for the central powers and Germany. When in the process the Russian Revolution broke out in 1917, Germany managed to penetrate deep into the Soviet Union and occupy Kiev, in the heart of Ukraine, for example. The great victories won in the east had to be largely abandoned under pressure from Versailles. However, a sense of supremacy over the east remained in the memory. This sense of supremacy was reinforced by the fact that entirely new states were emerging from the Habsburg legacy, such as Yugoslavia and Czechoslovakia. Their aspirations for autonomy were not yet firmly rooted in European history, and lifting this status was not a moral problem for the Nazis. Slavic mutual animosity, not least between Ukrainians and Russians, reinforced the image of a weak and chaotic East as well. Marshal Pilsudski's remarkable Polish victories at the gates of Minsk and at the Pripjet Marshes, strenghtened this.

The large area gains in the east could have been a military-strategic response to all sorts of deficits that Imperial Germany had felt in the agricultural and economic fields during World War I. The success of the British hunger blockade around Germany had created the idea among the military that Germany should strive for autarchy. This autarchy could not be achieved through maintaining the status quo.

Here, too, the lessons of Karl Haushofer, who believed that small states would 'languish', had come through.

Additionally, traditions within the German armed forces played an important binding element between this conservative elite and the new National Socialist rulers who were in control from 1933 onwards. In fact, the German army during the Weimar Republic and beyond was not much different from the army during the time of the empire. German officers regarded themselves as a social elite of rank and file, who watched over discipline and obedience and *zur Aufrechterhaltung der Manneszucht*. With so much vanity, there was little need to reach out and the stab-in-the-back myth was eagerly embraced.

This anti-Semitic and racial supremacy feeling became an important legitimising argument for 'Barbarossa' within the German armed forces. Before the war, high-ranking military officers, such as Admiral von Trotha, retired since 1920 but then politically active, invoked the fact that military interests lay above all with the völkische state, the German empire, making it clear that he had no love for the republic. When the National Socialists seized power, the racial aspect slid effortlessly under this. German historian Manfred Messerschmidt, who studied the attitudes of the military in the republic, concludes that the bulk of the officer corps could not identify with the Weimar republic. The republic was held responsible for Versailles' *Erfüllungspolitik*, which limited the army to 100,000 men. On the other hand, the wilhelminian structures in the army were still strong, and there was an elitist and anti-parliamentary leaning. In an existential crisis of the republic, the German armed forces intervened only where the 'state' was threatened, for example in the Kapp-Putsch. It was as von Seeckt put it: 'Today's society contradicts all my principles and political thinking.'

The attack on the Soviet Union was therefore more than an 'ordinary' conflict for many militaries. With the addition of the fight against Bolshevism, the war in the East had become a *Weltanschauungskrieg*, breaking down moral inhibitions and allowing the campaign for Lebensraum to take on its ideological and racial content. The shock reaction to the council republics in central and western Europe were, of course, also to blame.[88]

The jargon that had already made its appearance in the German armed forces with the stab-in-the-back myth came back to life during the campaign against the Soviet Union in particular. A senior officer like von Manstein, generally regarded as reasonably decent, spoke openly about how his soldiers should have an understanding of the *'harten Sühne am Judentum'* and against Jewish *'Untermenschen'*.

Besides the racial aspect, the element of discipline and obedience was an important weapon in the hands of National Socialism. Since National Socialist doctrine assumed an almost religious obedience, there was also a high degree of compatibility. Obedience within the German armed forces had already been held in high esteem since Frederick the Great, and on 5 May 1934, through an 'Erlass' by the Reich President, was reaffirmed and perfected throughout the war. Hitler's growing involvement and finally totalitarianism within the top of the German armed forces further strengthened this considerably. The element of obedience within the German army was tightly enforced throughout the Third Reich. During the war, for example, military lawyer Erich Schwinge believed that 50 to 90 per cent of deserters within the German army were 'psychologically inferior'.[89] Introducing the inferiority principle here, too, effectively created a World War II variant of the stab-in-the-back myth and traced military performance and success back to the issue of racial and hereditary descent and natural supremacy. It was, as we noted earlier in this book, a matter of reducing complex issues to very basic black-and-white propositions. A certain degree of comparison with the darkest days of communism comes to mind here. In the former Soviet Union, opponents of the regime were regularly declared 'mad', because from a Soviet perspective, you had to be mentally deranged if you did not want to embrace the communist 'workers paradise'. The same applied to the carefully constructed and cultivated idea of völkisch Germany. Anyone who was not in favour of it had to be very inferior and bad. As a result, the traditional enemy image of the German army - the given geopolitical reality - got competition from this fiction.

Despite the ideological sauce poured over 'Barbarossa' and the Third Reich, many tensions still occurred in the German army. This was logical since Operation 'Barbarossa' was the biggest campaign in human history and - in hindsight - the bloodiest. German historian Manfred Messcherschmidt speaks of a war of *'neuer Qualität'* here. A fine description of a hell on earth.[90] In doing so, we have already pointed out the compromising nature and the difficult military-technical course. Surely even the most convinced National Socialist must have doubted for a moment after an inferno like Stalingrad. Therefore, potential troublemakers within the German armed forces had to serve in the so-called *Sonderabteilungen* and *Bewährungs-einheiten*, the 500- and 999-units. These were specific units for the German army, which on the one hand had to be very strict and disciplined, but on the other hand could not waste a soldier because of the far-reaching goals it had set itself and had to carry out with few men. Roughly 10,000 'difficult' cases found their way to the *Feld-Sonderbataillonen* and, over time, 90.8 per cent were able to return to their regular unit. In the *Bewährungstruppe* 500, some 33,000 troops served with 6,000 personnel. These were the somewhat heavier cases, deployed in the focal points of the front. Due to the high losses these units suffered, over time they were seen as 'elite' rather than 'problem troops'. Typical of their deployment, for example, was an official military document that read: 'The Infanterie Bataillon z.b.V. 540 has held up fantastically, she is practically destroyed.' Finally, there were the *Bewährungstruppe* 999, made up of political opponents (30 per cent) and criminals (70 per cent), a total of 28,000 men strong. The first major 999 unit constituted the Afrika Division 999 strain, which was deployed in Tunisia and later on the Eastern Front between 28 March and 1 May 1943. Here, too, disciplinary measures generally helped reasonably well. Only among political offenders - often communists - did problems arise: 450 of them had to return to Germany.

Through the above special units, the German military leadership managed to provide a well-oiled machine for fighting on the Eastern Front. Despite this, it still ended up with three million military criminal cases with 370,000 'heavy sentences' handed out and 200,000 executed during the war. This resulted in a total of 50,000 death sentences - mostly for desertion - of which about 20,000 were carried out. This is the manpower of a very large infantry division.[91]

Knowing that only the army could be the crowbar that could give him Lebensraum, Hitler was prepared to accommodate the Reichswehr. He could only do this by halting the SA, the *Sturmabteilung* commanded by the adventurer and iron fighter Ernst Röhm.

That happened in June 1934. The facts on this are well known, so we can be brief. Over the years, the millions of members of the SA had increasingly become direct competition from the *Reichswehr* and *Stahlhelm*, the organisation for World War I veterans. The competition between them was so great that there were even deaths. The reason for this was that Röhm saw his SA as the core of the 'new army' of the 'new Germany' that was to emerge. Röhm leaned partly on what the literature calls the 'left wing' of the NSDAP. Armin Mohler refers to this as the 'Trotskyists' of National Socialism.[92] Key figures in this were brothers Gregor and Otto Strasser and, for a time, Joseph Goebbels. The Strassers came from a strict Catholic, Bavarian family. Gregor's role had grown considerably when Hitler was in prison at Landsberg am Lech after the failed 1923 Putsch. Gregor had then set himself up as the strongman of the NSDAP in northern Germany, where, with the help of Otto and Goebbels, he focused mainly on the NSDAP's word of 'Arbeiter'. Their rhetoric was strongly anti-capitalist, pro-labour with socialist undertones.

From the moment Hitler was back at large, he successfully fought the left wing. Goebbels was 'baited' by a promotion. He became Gauleiter of Berlin, a difficult but ambitious position that a grateful Goebbels gladly filled. He expressed this gratitude by diligently sawing away at the Strassers' chair legs from then on. In competition with the SA, the SS was founded, which was wholly and completely tied to Hitler. Gregor Strasser faced competition from Herman Göring, who threw his full weight as the front man of the right wing within the party. In July 1930, Otto Strasser called it quits and left the party.

This was the beginning of the end. After Hitler came to power, it became even more important to keep the 'left wing' in check in order to conduct politics. On 14 June, Hitler met Mussolini, who openly asked Hitler when he would finally rid himself of the 'undisciplined and anarchist elements' in his country. It was clear finger pointing at the SA. The Reichswehr had also made these noises, as had the big industrialists, like E. Kirdorf and A. Thyssen with whom Hitler was in contact. On 30 June, these tensions cumulated in the Night of the Long Knives and the power of Röhm and Strasser was broken.[93]

The Night of the Long Knives was a typical move by Hitler. He was a fanatic where his deepest ideals were concerned. Never would he compromise on the issue of Lebensraum or the race question. On the tactical terrain, however, he was unscrupulous, intuitive, demagogic, agile and unpredictable. The paramilitaries gave way to the real military, because only with them could he realise his dream of Lebensraum.[94]

Hitler's tactical manoeuvres, incidentally, had led him to choose the SA at the time. The more völkisch paramilitary Freikorps, while having his ideological sympathies, were a much more difficult instrument for conquering the streets of Germany than the SA. The völkisch paramilitaries were 'hampered' by regional targets.[95] Hitler needed a more 'general' instrument. When that instrument had done its job, Hitler once again opted for his völkisch targets. After a long period of hesitation what to do towards the SA, historian Max Gallo points to the (re)burial of Görings wife Karin as the moment when the right wing finally joined hands. The funeral of Görings wife Karin was a textbook example of Germanic/Nordic liturgy. Göring, who adored his wife, had staged the funeral very grandly, with a specially hired train bringing the coffin, a large horse-drawn procession, uniform pomp and, at the same time, a dedication of the Sonnewende festival. Gallo calls it a 'Shakespearean drama' with music by Wagner: *'Die Herrlichkeit der deutschen Erde umgibt dich nun für immer, und in dieser grossen Stille der Wälder wirst du den Widerhall des Dankes und des Grusses an dich hören und den Frieden Deutschlands.'* In the crypt around Karin's sarcophagus, the conspirators gathered. 'Röhm and the SA had been excluded from the mysterious world that had its roots in Germanic mythology,' Gallo writes. 'Here, in these woods, the SA had once again lost a battle. The Göring-Himmler connection was substantiated.'[96]

Karinhall, Göring's country house that his architects Tuch and Hetzelt had designed for him, bore all the völkisch characteristics of the landscape idyll. It was 'a Waldhof', writes Göring's biographer Mosley, 'worthy of a feudal ruler'.⁹⁷ Built of pine and oak beams, amid heath, forest and water, richly dotted with lilies, close to the border where eastern *Deutschtum* (north-eastern Prussia) began, it was the *Verkörperung* of völkisch myth. Opposite Karinhall, on the other side of the small lake Wuckersee, Karin's mausoleum had been erected. Göring had designed everything on his estate, right down to the furniture. Specially imported Canadian bison were to breed a primordial cow back on the heath and forest land on Schorfheide, two hours' drive northeast of Berlin. Göring owned his own *Rittergut*.

Finally, and unsurprisingly, the issue of Lebensraum meant a flourishing military career for many officers. In wartime, the army's interests and priorities were listened to, success could be achieved on the battlefield and *draufgängerische* officers could have careers. Hitler promised that the military too could share in the success of the Lebensraum expedition. This appealed to the völkische *Wehrbauer* of the past. Following the example of Horthy's League of Heroes and Walther Darré's 'new nobility', the German military would march east with 'sword and plough'. Successful, brave and obedient soldiers would be rewarded with a piece of land and, depending on their performance and prestige, even entire knightly estates.

The army naturally followed these promises and their implementation closely. The *Wehrmacht-Fürsorge-Gesetz* of 1938 embraced the land option as a concession to soldiers who were wounded in battle and could no longer fight. Instead of professional placement, the German state could give them land. This involved huge numbers of people. Already in the first year of the war, 18,344 people qualified for the 1938 law. In the following years, 43,202 and 76,077 men were added.⁹⁸ The army thereupon soon established a special department (bw Sied) that would oversee the future distribution. It is not unimportant to note that this post was assigned to the *Bevollmächtigte der Wehrmacht für Siedlungsfragen* Karl von Borhaupts. Borhaupts, like Rosenberg, von Scheubner-Richter and Theodor Fritsch, was a *Baltendeutscher*, descended from a merchant family. In World War I, he had guided the return of Russian-Germans. Now a reverse movement had become possible. In the event of a victory over the Soviet Union, Borhaupt faced an enormous task. In order to contain pressure from the military side, the outward distribution of land was slowed down somewhat. In reality, a considerable battle was already underway between the army and Himmler's SS over the spoils.

The Reichsführer-ss Heinrich Himmler was inundated with requests for pieces of land. The old nobility did not hesitate to make requests either, such as Erbgrossherzog von Oldenbourg, who asked for estates for his six sons. Himmler held this off, saying 'that he was not very fond of the old nobility'. In Himmler's eyes, of course, Darré's new nobility consisted above all of the bravest soldiers of his Waffen-ss, who were politically educated, had to prove their eliteness on the battlefield and, above all, were of 'Aryan descent'. Officers of the army, which was in league with the SS, also sought support from Himmler. For instance, Generalmajor Johann-Joachim Stever, the commander of the 4. armoured division during the campaign against France, reported to Himmler asking for an estate and 'people's political cooperation'. The OKH saw this as disloyal to its own organisation and demoted Stever to commander of an infantry division.[99]

Despite all the grand plans, very little came of the whole *Siedlungspolitik*. The lack of victory over the Soviet Union was, of course, to blame. The Soviet area remained unsettled. Poland was turned into a huge concentration and labour camp and served as a shelter for Volksdeutschen from central and eastern Europe. Indeed, as we have seen, the Third Reich's Lebensraum policy went far beyond merely conquering enemy territory. The conquered territory was völkisch redeveloped, which was preceded by a phase of cultural and social destruction, mass murder and forced labour. The Third Reich never got beyond the phase of destruction due to the developments on the battlefield.

In doing so, the army needed every soldier and few could truly become 'soldier farmers'. The organisation overseeing distribution, the *Hauptreuhandstelle Ost* led by Hermann Göring, had 130,000 Polish holdings to distribute in 1940. Of these companies, 100,000 were deemed too 'small' to survive at all. Of the remaining 30, 000 holdings, 90 per cent were allocated to 'Volksdeutschen' and 3,000 were reserved for the Wehrmacht.[100]

As things got worse at the front, the German propaganda machine did appeal more and more to the 'great promise' of Lebensraum politics. Helmut Dietlof Reiche's poem *'Toter Feind'* included the following:

'Du musstest sterben, damit wir leben, und unsere Zukunft ist dein Verderben, denn meine Jungen werden erben, was niemand dir einst gegeben. Dein Tod gibt Land für Deutschlands Söhne und Raum für deutscher Bauern Treck, aufblüht unser Volk zu herrlicher Schöne, unsrer Jugend Trommlen dumpfes Gedröhne geht über die sterbenden Völker hinweg.[101]

It is remarkable how undisguised German propaganda brought out these policies. In this respect, the focus around the crimes and abuses concerning Nazi Germany has always been concentrated on Jewish politics. In fact, the Lebensraum concept differed little from that. In the plan 'darken or exterminate' Poland, 'exterminate' Polish culture, the Polish state and the Polish elite was given top priority. Entirely in line with Hitler's ideas that the country belonged to those who could conquer it, Poland was immediately chopped to pieces. Without going into details about daily politics, a brief 'glimpse' into German occupation politics is in order here. The German-occupied part of Poland, about half of its pre-war territory with 23 million inhabitants, was chopped into two large pieces. The western part was added to the German Reich and named the 'incorporated eastern territories'. The eastern half was given the name 'General-Gouvernement'. The German minority in the country was immediately mobilised and over 100,000 men were assigned to the *Volksdeutscher Selbstschutz*. Heinrich Jaenecke rightly notes that a kind of 'Polish reserve' was created, without any independence. The western part was not part of Prussia but divided into three *Gauen* (Danzig, West Prussia and Warthegau) In these areas, German policy was as follows: the elite were to be rounded up and transferred to concentration camps. In effect, this amounted to a murder order. To this elite the Nazis included teachers, clergy, the nobility, officers. The 'primitive' Poles would serve as workers for the Germans, but were no longer allowed to live in the Gauen and had to be deported to the General Government. In turn, the Jews were gathered in the ghettos in the big cities, where they could be better seen. In an order to the *Einsatzgruppen*, ss-Gruppenführer Reinhard Heydrich, Chief of the *Reichssicherheitshauptamt*, described on 21 September 1939 that the Pole was to remain 'a perpetually itinerant worker and that his permanent residence was to be in the vicinity of Kraków'.[102] Anyone who glances at the map knows that this was near the chimneys of Auschwitz.

The actions of the *Einsatzgruppen* were so gruesome that for many Volksdeutschen, who had not had an easy time under the Poles anyway, it was no longer bearable. 'Is it really the Führer's will to exterminate the entire Polish population?' wrote Lily Jungblut, owner of an estate in the Hohensalza district, to Hermann Göring.[103] The deportation of Poles from the 'added territories' gave way to the many thousands of Volksdeutschen coming from Eastern Europe, mostly from those territories that had been given away to Moscow as a result of German-Russian agreements on the eve of World War II. In total, as many as six million hectares of farmland were expropriated for this purpose. Every Pole was allowed to take one suitcase with him on his deportation, 200 zlotty and, of his jewellery, only the wedding ring. In addition, the population of Poland was subjected to a 'racial survey'. The so-called German people's list was used to find out which Poles had 'German' blood running through their veins. There were four qualifications: the Volksdeutschen (divided into two groups) were given the same rights as Reich Germans; group three, the doubtful persons (1.6 million people), were given a 'provisional citizenship' and the remainder, the bulk who were stamped 'Polish' and thus at the mercy of the slave regime. The inspection was carried out by Himmler who was 'Reich Commissioner for the Strengthening of the German People's Nationality'. Group three consisted mainly of the Polish folk tribe of the Kassoeben, living in the Polish corridor, many of whom had to serve in the German Wehrmacht.

The remaining 6 million Poles were completely disenfranchised and gagged. Their church and education had been taken away from them, and their homes, property and land as well. Polish schools were closed, theatres and cinemas closed; they were allowed to shop in certain shops only at certain hours. Food rations and incomes were determined by the Germans. Poland's total business capital had been confiscated. A salute ordinance had been issued; every German officer had to be greeted with the Hitler salute. Demonstrating anti-German affiliation was punishable by death. Jaenecke rightly called this a 'rubber band article' by which any unwanted Polish worker could be executed, which was done in abundance. In 1942, in the annexed territories alone, 63,000 Poles were convicted, 930 executed (three executions a day) and 45,000 Poles imprisoned in concentration camps.

Things looked a little better for the 16 million Poles in the General-Gouvernement. Here a trace of a Polish society still remained, and could still be paid with Polish zlottys. Hans Frank, the German commander over the General-Gouvernement, apologised about this: 'We cannot end the struggle by this, that we give sixteen million Poles a shot in the neck. If the Polacks do not keep the trains running, who should do it?'[104] The purpose of all this was clear. Hitler endorsed it again in May 1940:

'For the non-German population there should be no higher schooling than the fourth grade of primary school. The aim of the education should be simple arithmetic to 500, writing one's name and learning the commandment, that it is God's will to obey the German. Reading I did not find necessary… This population will be at our disposal as a working-class people with no culture of their own and, in the absence of their own culture, will have the task, under the strict guidance of the Germans, of cooperating in the eternal cultural deeds and constructions of the German people.'[105]

Of course, by no means all German servicemen and officers who came into contact with developments in eastern and central Europe agreed with the terrible state of affairs. 'It is so terrible that one cannot be happy for a second when staying in this city,' wrote Lieutenant Colonel Helmuth Stieff to his wife from Warsaw. 'One is here not as victor but as guilty.'¹⁰⁶ Yet the fixation of the German military seems to have been mainly on survival, on the obedience principle, the primacy of politics, being a 'nur-Soldat', on one's own career, the völkisch-mythological dream of the *Deutschtum*, the belief in one's own supremacy, or being a National Socialist. Of course, the Nazis also tried to make it 'easy' for them to live with the consequences of the *Weltanschauungskrieg*. In a *Weisung of 16-09-1941*, for instance, Keitel explained that the *Kommissarbefehl* (the execution of Russian political commissars) was a necessary evil. After executing these Jewish-Bolshevik elements in Russia, the 'real', national Russia would re-emerge and the conflict would turn into a 'normal war' between two neighbouring countries.¹⁰⁷

One or more of these legitimations embraced the German soldiers who took up land in the added Polish areas, where the effects of the German *Blut und Boden policy* had gone furthest. A total of at least 1357 *Militär-Siedler* were admitted to the area. Among them were resounding names, such as the tank genius and fellow Blitzkrieg designer Heinz Guderian, who had so insisted on a knight's court in the Warthegau that he had quarreled with Gauleiters Albert Froster and Arthur Greiser. The famous Erich von Manstein was among the owners of a knight's court in the plundered and völkisch redeveloped Warthegau, as was the Danish Waffen-ss volunteer ss-Obersturmbahnführer Freiherr von Schalburg (Freikorps 'Danmark') and the Generaloberst der Waffen-ss Daluege.

Had the campaign against Russia been a success, it could not have been ruled out that, for example, the *Ritterkreuzträger* - a high decoration - would have been authorised to obtain a knighthood. Some did not want to wait for the outcome of the war, such as *Fallschirm* general Ramcke, who wrote to Himmler that he did expect a knighthood after obtaining the *'Eichenlaub zum Ritterkreuz'*.¹⁰⁸

This prepared the Third Reich's armed forces for Hitler's Lebensraum expedition. Looking back, it is shocking to see how straightforward Hitler set the course for war - although he stated otherwise in interviews and took tactical side roads. If we only look at the year 1933 from the moment Hitler ruled through the *'Verordnung des Reichspräsidenten zum Schutz von Volk und Staat'* of 28 February

1933, one day after the Reichstag fire, we see a series of measures heading towards war: 16 March: the Reichswehr is expanded to 200,000 troops, 25 March: creation of *Luftsportverbande* (dlv) as a secret forerunner of the Luftwaffe, 6 May: creation of the so-called *Risiko-Luftwaffe*, 1 July: speech by Reichswehrminister von Blomberg on need for armament; 15 August: establishment of Antikomitern; 24 August: termination of German-Russian military cooperation; 1 September 1933: establishment of the Luftwaffe, 14 November: exit from the League of Nations, 18 October: Hitler calls Germany the '*Volk ohne Raum*' in interview with Western press, 24 October: Hitler warns of the Bolshevik danger at the Berlin Sports Palace.[109]

Russian historian Lew Besymensky's observation that the attack on the Soviet Union was the subject of debate earlier than the first concretely worked out military plans are therefore quite correct.[110] Although Hitler often spoke openly about the danger of Bolshevism, the really concrete plans are of a relatively late nature. Generally, 31 July 1940 is seen as the date when Hitler finally shifted course eastwards. Before then, detailed plans were premature. With the invasion of Poland, Germany had brought the war of France and Britain upon itself, and this war was fought first. Now that the war against Britain '*an sich gewonnen war*', Hitler told officers of the OKW, army, air force and navy, and Operation Seelöwe (invasion Britain) were off the table, the time was ripe for war in the east. Britain, according to Hitler, was counting on support from the Soviet Union and the US. If the former nation fell away, the latter would no longer be willing to engage in battle. After the fall of the Soviet Union, Nazi Germany would be 'lord of Europe and the Balkans'. In line with his ideas, Hitler used Russia's '*Vernichtung der Lebenskraft*' when describing the aim of the attack on the Soviet Union. The German attack was planned for spring 1941 and worked out in a series of *Führerweisungen*.

It is important to recall here earlier unofficial documents regarding Hitler's plans for conquest. The most important document is the so-called Hossbach Protocol of 10 November 1937. In the presence of Defence Minister Generalfeldmarschall von Blomberg, Army

Commander-in-Chief Freiherr von Fritsch, Navy Commander Admiral Raeder, Foreign Minister Konstantin Freiherr von Neurath as well as Göring and Colonel Hossbach, Hitler spoke candidly about his plans in the Reichskanzlei. The meeting took place on 5 November and Hitler delivered a speech in which all his hobbyhorses featured: his fear of overpopulation, the German lack of raw materials and food, the need to conquer Lebensraum, his fear of Bolshevism and the race issue. This was concretised with a timetable. On 10 November, in his office in the Ministry of Defence, Hossbach made a record of the discussion that is considered reliable by the bulk of historians. Indeed, on examination of the protocol, there is little reason to believe that Hossbach - who later became embattled with Hitler because of von Blomberg's and von Fritsch's resignations - fabricated it. Nor do the thoughts propagated by Hitler in the protocol give any reason to do so. They fit into Hitler's many writings: *Mein Kampf*, his secret second book and his 1945 political will. As document ps-386, it was used in the Nuremberg trial. After the war, the authenticity of the Hossbach protocol was once again demonstrated by Bradley F. Smith in 1994 in the *Zeitschrift für Geschichtswissenschaft*.[111]

'Ich habe einem sehr hohen Vertreter der Kirche gelegentlich einmal gesagt: Eure Zeit ist vorbei, jetzt kommt an Euch genau das heran, was Ihr uns getan habt; die 2000 Jahre sind herum, die Ihr an der Sonne und wir im Schatten gelebt haben. Jetzt kommt die Zeit, in den wir in der Sonne leben und Ihr im Schatten.'

Heinrich Himmler (1937)

Vision

Gottesdienst. Das Eingangslied ist verklungen. Der Pfarrer steht am Altar und beginnt:
'Nichtarier werden gebeten, die Kirche zu verlassen!'
Nobody rührt sich.
'Nichtarier werden gebeten, die Kirche zu verlassen!'
Wieder bleibt alles still.
'Nichtarier werden gebeten, die Kirche zu verlassen!'
Da steigt Christus vom Kreuze des Altars herab und verlässt die Kirche.'

(Evangelischer Ruf, 14 October 1933)

Chapter 5

Swastika replaces cross

Battle of dogmas - Ernst Niekisch and the demons of the Third Reich - bachelor Hitler - Rosenberg and the index of banned books - The authencity of primordial Christianity - *Artgeist* and *Artseele* - The nation between myth and utopia - The Conservative Revolution and Nationalism as *Ersatzreligie* - *Die Geächteten* - *Deutscher Gottglauben* - Religious experience of the SS - Being versus thinking - Paul Hausser, Felix Steiner and the new crusaders - *Der neue Gott* - Otto Rahn and the quest for the grail - Cathars - Wolfhounds - Von Stuck - Gaius Cassius - Barbarossa and the eagle's nest - Goldhagen, Luther and the continuity thesis - Church fear of communism - Hochhuth and postwar criticism - Hudal, cic, Barbie and Draganovic - Murder of Polish priests

In recent literature and articles, it seems to have become customary to mention the church and the Vatican in the same breath as the crimes of the Third Reich. Recently, the Vatican itself has reached out and discussed their role in the second world war within the Christian community.[1] Such candour is obviously conducive to putting the demons of the past behind us. On the other hand, it should also not derail into Goldhagen-like situations where the blame is evenly distributed among entire populations and even peoples.[2] If we look at anti-Semitism, for example, we can indeed observe religious anti-Semitism[3], but it is not right to equate that with the term elimination anti-Semitism used by Goldhagen.[4]

A common ideology between church and Nazism is lacking. Indeed, Nazism and Christianity were two mutually exclusive dogmas that, had the Third Reich existed longer, would eventually have come into full confrontation with each other. That said, the guardians of Christianity and the Nazis made pacts and partial pacts, sometimes shared common fears and antipathies, and the church's recent expressions of regret for anti-Judaism are appropriate.

The main similarity between National Socialism and Christianity is the fact that the Nazis, too, made ample use of (pseudo-)religious arguments and techniques and, especially where the völkische, ariosophical undercurrent of the brown movement was concerned, the 'faith content' was amply represented. The major distinction, however, is that Nazism espoused a completely different faith from Christianity but nevertheless managed to link Christian symbolism to racial politics and the pursuit of Lebensraum.

This primordial soup of uses, abuses, fears and sentiments is perhaps best uncovered as a first inventory through the Prussian Bolshevik Ernst Niekisch. In his book *Das Reich der niederen Dämonen*, he made an inventory of the main differences of Nazism and Christianity. The Nazis, Niekisch opined, placed *Herrenmensch* versus *Untermensch*; the *Volksmann* versus the inferior; the Nordic 'nobility' versus the Eastern bastard; Aryans versus impure of race; the bourgeois man of honour versus the Jewish impostor; youth versus the elderly; frontline soldiers versus deserters; soldier versus civilian; the Prussian versus the Jacobin; the hero versus the coward; the *Tatmensch* versus the doubter; the hard fist versus liberalism; harshness versus humanism; blood versus spirit; instinct versus education; the plattenland versus the city; property versus dispossession; *abendländische* culture versus Asian 'non-culture'; common good versus selfishness; pagan versus Christian; the anti-romantic rebel versus the infallible pope.[5]

Interestingly, there is a comparison list from the National Socialist camp. In this list, published in the weekly *Blitz* of 10 January 1937, the Nazis try to indicate the distinction between Christianity and their own ideology: yes to life versus no to life; self-consciousness versus guilt; pride versus courage; bodily care versus bodily chastisement; an inquisitive will versus blind faith; confession towards race and people versus reverence for the concept of humanity; earthly commitment versus absolute precedence for the religious; sacrificial readiness for the popular community versus sacrificial readiness to God; vigorous commitment to workplace versus complete submission to church dogma; self-responsibility versus dependence on God's grace; readiness for battle versus peace at any cost; energetic defence of evil versus toleration of evil; veneration of blood and soil versus denial of blood and soil; full commitment to people, land and family versus church interests above all other interests; rejection of enemy Jewry versus recognition of Jews as God's chosen people; religious freedom versus religious compulsion; joy of life versus flight from life, believing in the social engineering of one's own life versus believing in original sin.[6]

From this inventory, it is clear that the differences were particularly stark. In some respects, they were even opposites. Not for nothing did Reichsführer-ss Heinrich Himmler speak of his ss as of a *'Gegenorden'* and called Christianity 'the worst plague that had ever befallen Germany'.[7]

This antipathy towards Christianity can be traced back to the spiritual roots of Nazism in which it focused on the *ausserchristlichen, arteigenen, weltanschaulichen Grundlagen*.[8] Troubled church fathers already pointed to Hitler's *Mein Kampf*, in which Christianity played only a very modest role. The cleric Ingbert Naab believed that many Christians wrongly assumed that Hitler was doing Christianity a service. With this, Naab confirms the successful operation of German

propaganda and the gullibility of German Christians, because the practice was indeed different. In *Mein Kampf,* Hitler made it clear that he was to have little to do with Jewish influence on Christianity. In the process, Hitler showed himself to be a proponent of the theory of evolution, which was not appreciated either. Church leaders therefore mockingly spoke of the 'bachelor' Hitler, who showed his true colours in supporting anticlerical leaders such as Alfred Rosenberg.[9]
Der Mythus des 20. Jahrhunderts by Nazi ideologue Alfred Rosenberg was on the index of banned books. Since the book was published by the NSDAP publishing house, several church fathers pointed out that Adolf Hitler himself was the publisher of the book. According to critical Christians, Rosenberg's ideology was Hitler's secret ideology and allowed the Baltic German to bellyache for him. What stung them above all was that Rosenberg, *'der Gottesleugner'*, created a dichotomy within German Christians. On the one hand, Rosenberg spoke of the positive Christians, by which he meant those Christians who believed in the mission of the Nordic race and the blood bond. On the other hand, he outlined the negative Christians who stuck to old church dogmas. To the church fathers, this was inadmissible. Equally inadmissible was the way Rosenberg doubted the monotheistic basic principle of Christianity. In his Germanic polytheism, the church saw the work of the devil. It was therefore judged that Alfred Rosenberg was a man without religion. His defence of having children out of wedlock - for the glory of the expanding Nordic race - was also seen as an outright attack on the Christian heritage.[10]

In fact, the entire ariosophical and radically völkische roots of National Socialism were difficult for Christianity. The question at stake was the question of the authenticity of *Urchristentum*. Brown activists saw it as their task to transform *Urchristentum* back into what it had originally been: the Germanic/Nordic or Aryan view of life. In doing so, they wanted to get rid of the Christian (read Jewish) elements of the philosophy of life that had been 'imposed' on them since Christianisation. How seriously this battle was fought becomes clear when we consider the flood of literature on the subject. To get some grip on these publications, we could distinguish them into the following works:

- Germanic mythology (historical, philosophical, religious, educational and poetic);
- Edda translations and stories;
- folk beliefs and legends;
- Germanic customs;
- critical and polemical writings;
- history of religion;
- church history.[11]

In fact, at the outset, these elements provide a complete alternative to the society of the Christian Occident and that is how they were presented. I write in onset, because there were strong differences among themselves in the brown camp.

The Nazis struggled, as it were, with two of their inspirations: Nietzsche and Wagner. According to the writer Ernst Jünger, the two were linked like weathermen.[12] Nietzsche believed that recognition of Christianity and Christian values also implied recognition of Judaism. Nietzsche rejected both beliefs and opted for a position as antichrist and the new *Übermensch*. For Wagner, though, Christianity was a viable option although he gave it his own (ariosophical) interpretation. All this led to profound debates and huge series of battle writings and pamphlets.

The alternative provided by the right wing in the *Kulturkampf* with the Christian heritage had many variations. The stakes were always the same: the *Artgeist* and the *Artseele*:

'Bedenke, dass ein Gott
In deinem Leibe wohnt.
Und vor Entweihung
Sei der Tempel stets verschont.'[13]

On the how and why of the temple, the battle went from the national left to the national right. The right-nationals were a motley and big bunch of all sorts, by no means all Nazis, but nationalistic enough to ignore the biblical Ten Commandments. I am thinking here of the circle around Ernst von Salomon, who killed Walther Rathenau because he was a 'Jewish danger and country traitor-Bolshevik'. Or the heroic rationalism of Ernst Jünger, who wanted nothing to do with Erich Marie Remarque›s interpretation of World War I or Ernst Friedrich›s *Krieg dem Kriege*[14] and described the *Soldatentum* with pseudo-religious admiration. The *Alldeutschs* who dreamed of Germany's mission in the world also mixed their religious feelings with their desire to change the geopolitical status quo. Religious 'supremacy' here served as an argument for Lebensraum.[15]

A practically religious worship of the German spirit, state and people preceded this. *Die Nation* hovered between myth and utopia, drawing on political romanticism. At the end of the eighteenth century, Georg Friedrich von Hardenberg, under the pseudonym Novalis, was already articulating this thought: *'Das Volk ist eine Idee, wir sollen ein Volk werden.'*[16] There was a boundless belief in the social engineering of the world, the social engineering of the German empire. The historian Richard Herzinger sees in this bigotry with the *deutsche Geist* a rebuff to the universalism of Rome and the French Revolution.[17] Von Hardenberg placed these two opposites directly opposite each other in his thesis: Christianity or Europe Remarkable again here that the geographical demarcation of the *Kulturkampf* is actually missing and covers all of Europe and not just the German-speaking area. [18]

The origins of this huge nationalism, as we have already seen, came from the Napoleonic occupation of the German-speaking regions of Europe. The way völkische writers like Johann Gottlieb Fichte, Ernst Moritz Arndt and Heinrich von Kleist reported on this led straight into the *Reichsmythos*. The state and the people got their mythological scope in comparisons with *Die Hermannschlacht* and in references to the mythical German *Urvolk*, and the necessity of the German 'peoples' war' against Napoleon. The *Trivialmodern* stood in opposition to Langbehns' *Rembrandtdeutsche*.[19] In his *Die Zeitgenossen*, Moeller van den Bruck wrote as early as 1906 about the *'junge Völker'* of Nordic origin, who would supplant the soulless Western spirit with the new German spirit. A process he dubbed *Das Dritte Reich* in 1923, the year of the Hitler-Ludendorff-Putsch in Munich.[20] A new war, World War I, ensured that the pre-existing pompous over-identification with being German once again got wind of the fact that nationalism could become an *Ersatz religion*. After the horrors on the battlefields, the *neuen Nationalists* of the Conservative Revolution believed that humanism and Western rationalism had been done away with once and for all. The soldiers returning from the front had seen life in its true essence and considered themselves insiders. In this regard, Ernst Jünger pointed to war as a dynamic of life. Civilian life, Ernst von Salomon believed in *Die Geächteten* (1930), merely levelled out. All (pseudo-)religious hyper-nationalist sentiments coalesced around the myth of empire. '*Wir waren Krank an Deutschland*,' wrote Ernst von Salomon.[21]

Explicitly anti-Christian were those forces that believed they knew the cosmic secrets. In the chapter 'Reich and Romanticism', we have already dealt in detail with the ideas of Theosophy, the ariosofie around List, Lanz von Liebenfels and their influence on the ariosophical nuclei in Munich (Sebottendorff/Eckart/Ludendorff) and Bayreuth (H.St. Chamberlain and Wagner). Their main similarity was their antipathy to Christianity, besides that there were some other major differences. Chamberlain, Wagner, Eckart and Wiligut, for instance, drew above all on Western *Urgeschichte*. The ariosophists tended more towards a reinterpretation of Eastern philosophy. Others, like the Ludendorffs, tried to bring about a reorientation of the *deutscher Gottglaube*. To join the Ludendorff club, a written declaration that one had left the Christian church was required. Characteristic of all the variants was that they were very vital movements, action- and deed-oriented. Mathilde Ludendorff described Christianity as contrary to the German *Wesensart*. In her view, all the stories about Jesus, the *Welterlöser*, were taken from ancient Indian literature that had been written down partly four thousand years, and partly three hundred years before the Bible. The Bible was the work of the 'Jewish gospel writers' and contrary to the German *Wesensart*. By contrast, ariosophical and völkische 'religion' was based on the *Things an sich*, the *Wesen der Erscheinung*. Nature is not god, but understanding nature is the only way to know god.[22]

As we have already seen, the Nazi leadership publicly distanced itself from the most radical forms of the völkische-ariosophical antichrist. Nevertheless, initial steps had been taken towards the new *post-Kulturkampf* world. To gain some insight into the religious feelings of the NS leadership, it is interesting to take a closer look at the religious life of the Reichsführer-ss Himmler, as the personification of the 'new man'.

Himmler fit seamlessly into the tradition of nationalism as an *Ersatz religion*. However, where the conservative revolution limited itself to nationalism, the Nazis and the SS added racialism. There was a revolutionisation of the conservative revolution. From heroising the war, as with Ernst Jünger and Ernst von Salomon, the struggle became an end in itself. All this was accompanied by a tremendous dynamism, the *In-Bewegung-Sein*. *Hurra-Patriotism* was replaced by the iron-fisted *Einzelnkämpfer*, conscious of race and task. Oswald Spengler had already insisted: *'Politik im höchsten Sinne ist Leben, und Leben ist Politik,'* and Heinrich Himmler was eminently intent on heeding this.[23]

Himmler was convinced of the existence of a god, who had named the SS *'der Uralte'* and *'der Altvader',* and he believed that this God had sent Hitler to earth to save 'Germanism' in the world and lead the fight against the East. Hitler was a 'Light Spirit' of rare magnitude. These words by Himmler, spoken before the officer corps of the *Leibstandarte Adolf Hitler* (The First Division of the Waffen-ss, also Hitler's bodyguard) on 7 September 1940, were significant because Himmler saw Hitler 'as sent by God', and that the campaign to the east was a 'divine mission'. This pattern of thinking is consistent with Rosenberg's view in *Der Mythus* of the historical mission of 'Atlantic man' to the east, as would have been done at the beginning of our civilisation by the descendants of Atlantis. In this role, Himmler saw the *Schutzstaffel*, the SS, as 'predestined'.

Himmler believed in reincarnation. He thought he himself was the reincarnation of Heinrich dem Löwen (1129-1195). Life, Himmler believed, was not lived in one lifetime. All good and bad experiences and deeds were included in the karma of the new life. In Himmler's eyes, this was the correct Germanic interpretation of life: to know that what you do will be what you will be judged on. Through one's own strength, life could have its meaning. It was Himmler's reckoning with original sin. Additionally, he believed in astrology, although this was partly a stopgap, as many occult scholars had been put behind bars by the SS, but as the chances of war turned, Himmler increasingly tried to get support from this side too. Rudolf Hess and Karl Haushofer are known to have been strongly inspired by astrology. Wilhelm Th.H. Wulf became Himmler's court astrologer and had to resist the astrological propaganda offensive unleashed on Germany by the British through the Hungarian De Whole.[24]

Victory over original sin was an important element in the SS's faith. The SS's belt buckle read *'Meine Ehre Heisst Treue'*, while the more bourgeois Wehrmacht had to make do with *'Gott mit uns'*. With the SS, Hitler thus seemed to be above God. Reckoning with original sin made room for the *Tatmensch*, nordic, fearless, who was not bothered by individualistic, intellectual musings, but rolled up his sleeves and wanted to be judged only on his actions. Such a view of life, coupled with the idyllic, industrious countryside versus the perverted and 'jaded' city, was reflected in the SS. We recall the romantic murals on the Wewelsburg, where Wiligut mused about a bastion against the 'new Huns': the Bolsheviks. For Wiligut, it was an ancient battle, against an equally ancient enemy. This was also true for Dietrich Eckart. In *Der Bolschewismus von Moses bis Lenin*, a diatribe with Adolf Hitler, this thought was already mooted. Literally from Moses to Lenin, in his view, the same enemy is being fought against: the race war and the struggle for blood and soil.[25]

Overcoming original sin created good officials and soldiers with whom one could conquer Lebensraum. Moreover, Himmler tried to convey this thought to the armed branch of his organisation, the Waffen-ss, which initially operated under the name *ss-Verfügungstruppe*. The Waffen-ss was drilled according to new military insights under the leadership of generals Felix Steiner and Paul Hausser, who shaped the concept of the shock trooper. In their view, the new type of soldier of the future had to be agile, lest a battle could become bogged down in the bloody trench warfare of 1914-1918. The *Einzelkämpfer* of the Waffen-ss had to set an example to that end. The best Nordic human material available across Europe had to be brought together for this purpose. The 5.SS armoured division *Wiking* became the example of what Steiner and Hausser envisaged with their new troops. A rotating sunnad (a swastika with rounded legs) symbolised the decisiveness of this new division, which soon, following the example of distant ancestors, went to war to conquer Russia. Other units had heroic names as well, such as *Hohenstaufen*, *Frundsberg*, *Totenkopf* (within which the unit served *Thule*), *Prinz Eugen* and *Götz von Berlichingen* and *Maria Theresa*. Furthermore, Hitler seemed to see death on the battlefield as a kind of crowning achievement of a Nordic life. About the Waffen-ss, his elite, he said that 'the losses could not be great enough', only in this way could an elite also be elite. Eternal struggle would keep a people and race strong. After World War I, Hitler once said that 'the best had died'. He repeated these words almost verbatim in 1945, with doom looming: 'The best have died anyway'.[26]

The troops of the Waffen-ss appealed to the rural, völkisch element. Felix Steiner wrote after the war that the *'Freiwillige'* of the Waffen-ss came mainly from the agricultural part of Germany. They got the complement to their men (in peacetime) mainly from the countryside and from small towns in Schleswig-Holstein, Lower Saxony, Franconia and from the Saar. Almost every third farmer's son served in the Waffen-ss. In the 'materialistic age', Steiner believed, they were a 'rare shining example' for German youth: 'It was a soldier phenomenon borne of idealism'. Such sentiments were fostered by Richard Walther Darré as well, who above all advocated *'Körpererziehung'* of rural youth. His monthly magazine *Odal* (entirely fitting his image of new nobility) paid almost monthly attention to 'weather sports' for German rural youth.[27]

The elite feeling of the Waffen-ss was based on the fact that they believed they were the select few of their race. This entailed a 'natural supremacy' that was proven in battle. This battle of the Waffen-ss would take place above all on the Eastern Front where, from a National Socialist point of view, Jewish Bolshevism ruled. Not for nothing were volunteers recruited for the Waffen-ss from Europe under the banner of the *crusade* against Bolshevism, and Himmler spoke of the ss in general (and not just the Waffen-ss) as an *'anti-*

bolschewistische Kampforganisation'.[28] The use of the word crusade of course refers to the earlier crusades to Palestine, and especially to the conversion field trips of the German knightly orders, the Teutons, to the East.

The pseudo-religious and mythical feelings that many of the volunteers felt is reflected in their field letters:

'We are the sons of a people,' wrote a Danish volunteer, 'who have conquered the seas since the days of the Vikings. We are the sons of a people who want to realise again the heritage of the North Race within themselves, to win for themselves the place to which they are entitled among the Germanic peoples.'[29]

'There is now no time for anything but for one thing, which is to prove the superiority of our race. Proving that it is we who are entitled to life and, through our life force, also to the ruling position'.[30]

Although the transformation from Christianity to paganism could not happen overnight, it was visible in all sorts of signs that it was actually taking on great proportions: 'I do not want to be guilty of blasphemy,' mused ss-Obergruppenführer Schulz from Pommern, 'but who is greater, Christ or Hitler? At his death, Christ had only 12 followers, Hitler has as many as 70 million followers behind him.'

It was this kind of claim that expressed the (pseudo-)religious feeling of the Nazis, created an Ersatzreligion. It was with horror that the Christian church saw old prayers before and after meals being replaced by new ones addressed to *der neue Gott*.

'Führer, mein Führer, von Gott mir gegeben,
beschütz und erhalte noch lange mein Leben!
Hast Deutschland gerettet aus tiefster Not,
Dir danke ich heute mein täglich Brot.
Bleib lang noch bei mir, verlass mich nicht,
Führer, mein Führer, mein Glaube, mein Licht!

To be followed after dinner by:

'Dank sei Dir für diese Speise,
Beschützer der Jugend, Beschützer der Greise!
Hast Sorgen, ich weiss es, doch kümmert's Dich nicht,
ich bin bei Dir bei Nacht und bei Licht.
Leg ruhig Dein Haupt in meinen Schoss,
bist sicher, mein Führer, denn Du bist gross.

Heil, mein Führer.'[31]

The competition that Ersatzreligie - Bracher speaks of *'politische Religion'*[32] - provided from National Socialism caused outright clashes between Christianity and Nazi ideology. In much post-war literature, this struggle has been portrayed somewhat too mildly. It is not true that Pope Pius xii only warned about repressive Nazi politics in his encyclical *Mit brennender Sorge* (14 March 1937). In the same year, for example, he warned again about the terrible dangers of the Nazi regime on 19 May, 9 June, 16 June, in September, October and December.[33] Where people did not *attack* the Nazis, they sometimes chose another tactic of ignoring them. For example, when Hitler visited Rome in spring 1938, the *L'Ossorvatore Romano*, the Vatican newspaper, refused to utter a word about it.[34]

The church had reason to be concerned. Church governance was under threat, church directives were censored, the church ousted from the educational field. Catholic education had been curbed, apostle work had become difficult and church youth organisations had received Nazi competition from *Jungvolk* and *Hitlerjugend*. Therefore, the conclusion was that work was being done to 'destroy the Catholic Church and Christianity in general'. The main culprits pointed to the government, Gestapo and SD, the party and, above all, the new ministry, the Rosenberg ministry, the *Reichskulturkammer*, the *Reichspressekammer* and the *Reichsschrifttumskammer*.[35]

No wonder part of the clergy saw in National Socialism the devil, absolute evil. A telling example for the church of the *Wotanskult* in the Third Reich was the support a young, unknown historian received from the highest echelons of the NSDAP and SS: Otto Rahn, author of the book *Kreuzzug gegen den Gral*. Rahn placed himself in the spotlight because of his hunger for knowledge of the Gnosis. Himmler and Rosenberg subsequently decided to sponsor the young man. In the summer of 1931, only 27 years old, Rahn spent three months in the Neolithic beauty of the Pyrenees. Rahn had come there to discover nothing less than the holy grail. The holy grail captured the imagination of völkische thinkers. For instance, Hermann Pohl, with Theodor Fritsch co-founder of the Germans-Orden (a forerunner of the Thule Society), had founded an organisation called *Germans-Orden Walvater vom Heiligen Gral*, and Lanz von Liebenfels' ONT was based on the grail legend too, as was Wiligut's interpretation of Wewelsburg as the grail castle. Rahn was convinced that the holy grail had last been in the possession of the Cathars, a small group of apostates who, after long sieges by papal troops, eventually ended up burned at the stake and wiped out of the history books. In the Pyrenees, around the white castle ruins of Montségur, Rahn hoped to unravel the riddle and uncover the past. Rosenberg and Himmler believed that Rahn could be right and that Montségur could be a corruption of Montsalvat (Mount of Salvation) and would indeed be the last refuge of the grail. The mystery was never solved because, as we already saw in chapter three, Rahn never came to Montségur a third time but was killed on a 'mountain hike' around Kufstein.

There has been earlier speculation about whether Rahn was homosexual and this contributed to his 'murder'. Jean-Michel Angebert and Lewis A.M. Sumberg, two French investigators, came up with another surprising hypothesis. Rahn is said to have committed suicide near Mount Kufstein by ingesting poison. The reason for his suicide would have been his homosexuality. His orientation did not fit the völkische, idyllic worldview of the Nazis, nor did it match the worldview of the Cathars he so admired, who chose death by fire to remain true to their faith. Where the Arians stood for the 'pure people', the Cathars knew their *perfecti*, the perfect man through ascetic priests. Rahn would not have been able to bear that burden anymore and followed his Cathar example in a desperate suicide.[36]

This interest in Gnostic *Urgeschichte* smelled a little too much of occultism, black rituals and devilry, according to the church. Contemporaries signalled that the devil in Goethe's *Faust* first manifested himself in the form of a dog, a black poodle. In modern Satanism, the dog would stand for the antithesis of God. This could be deduced from a play on words: when one mirrors the word God in the English language, the word *dog* appears. For many biblical scholars, dogs stood for evil: the dog was historically the symbol of shameless sexuality; Polish Satan worshipers still drank steaming dog's blood; in ancient Egypt, the dog was considered the lord of the graveyard; the Gnostic god Osiris had returned from the underworld as a Wolf and the goddess Isis rode on dogs. For gnostics, on the other hand, dogs were often bringers of light, which was true of coyotes and wolves as well. Anti-occultists pointed out that Hitler had used the name Herr Wolf early in his political career, which was said to be a sign of Hitler's devil-worship. A very fierce anti-Nazi book by Colonel T.H. Minshall characterised the German as 'wolfish' with a 'wolf discipline'.[37]

Psychologist Robert G.L. Waite has elaborated on this, noting that Hitler frequently used the term wolf. So, early in his political career he chose the pseudonym Herr Wolf and his favourite dog was the German shepherd (in German *Wolfshunde*). He named one of its pups Wolf. His headquarters in France was called *Wolfsschlucht*, his headquarters in the Ukraine *Werwolf* and in East Prussia *Wolfsschanze*. He called his SS 'my pack of wolves'. About his SA, he said they 'ran like wolves'. In 1922, he himself wrote an article on his political rise, stating 'a wolf was now born'. The Volkswagen factory was named Wolfsburg.[38] The origin of Hitler's fondness for Wolf lies in his own first name, which he believed was derived from the old German *Athalwolf* (*Athal* = noble, *Wolfa* = wolf) which became 'noble wolf'. It may be telling how far Hitler was apparently guided by such ancient wisdoms and legends. A painting by Franz von Stuck may have been of influence as well (1863-1928), *Die Wilde Jagd*, in which a horseman - who bore an astonishing resemblance to Hitler (moustache and lock of hair) - surrounded by wolves rides all smashing through the night. With red cape, as we could so often witness at the parades in Nuremberg, the painted person sits on horseback. Von Stuck mainly painted canvases with erotic, mythological motifs. '*Mein erstes Oelgemälde 1889*' is written in the corner of *Die Wilde Jagd*. It is the year of Adolf Hitler's birth. Hitler called von Stuck, along with Wagner, his greatest inspiration. Von Stuck's paintings, such as *Sinnligkeit, Verfolgung, Das Laster*, are almost all set in mystical, mythological territory. Von Stuck was a pupil of Wilhelm Lindenschmit and Ferdinand Löfftz and one of the founders of the Munich School. How should we interpret these facts? Did Hitler copy his appearance from von Stuck's painting? We know from old photographs that Hitler, for example at the time of World War I, looked different. Heinz Linge, Hitler's long-time adjutant, does not seem to have known about the resemblance to von Stuck's wolf-rider. In his memoirs, he speculates whether Hitler sometimes imitated Napoleon's lok.[39]

In my opinion, the history surrounding von Stuck and the wolves are all part of the undercurrent of National Socialism, in which feeling versus reason, 'being' versus 'thinking', had been taken to the extreme. In this Wagnerian opera, Hitler had given himself the lead role, as a lone but ruthless wolf. This brings us into even more speculative territory, touched on by the writer Trevor Ravenscroft, around the spear of Gaius Cassius (Longinus). This spear, according to tradition, had been thrust between Jesus' fourth and fifth ribs as he hung on the cross. Since then, a myth hung around the spear and it was said to be the key to world doom. According to Ravenscroft, as many as 43 leaders have since made use - for better and worse - of 'the power' of the spear, which had come into contact with Jesus' blood. According to Ravenscroft, the mystique surrounding the spear had appeal to Nietzsche and Wagner, who viewed the spear together in Vienna, and to the young Hitler. According to Ravenscroft, Hitler was captivated by the spear, although its political role had been played out since Otto the Great (Napoleon claimed the spear after Austerlitz, but one managed to hide it successfully). Hitler is said to have discovered the spear in his poor Viennese years and researched its entire history. What particularly inspired Hitler was the fact that two of his great examples, Friedrich Barbarossa (1152-1190) and Friedrich II Hohenstaufen (1212-1250) had made use of the spear. Barbarossa's Teutonic campaign to the east in particular captured Hitler's imagination. Barbarossa restored the Roman Empire without legions, conquered Italy, stormed the Vatican and had himself made emperor by the Pope with the spear. According to Ravenscroft, Hitler believed that the spear had a great historical mission in store for him. On one of his frequent visits to the spear, he had an 'epiphany' in which part of his future became clear. Himmler and the scientific bureau of the SS were set to work by Hitler after 1933 to unravel the riddle of Longinus' spear.[40]

Although there are demonstrable errors in Ravenscroft's book,[41] the underlying idea of predestination and life missions fits the pseudo-religious image of the Third Reich. In fact, the Nazis were still searching. To Felix Kersten, Heinrich Himmler, admitted that *'Alles noch im Fluss war'*. National Socialism was one big pseudo-religious experiment, building on a (supposed) historical legacy, wanting to build on Aryan lineage myths, just as the French had their Gallo-Frankish lineage myth, the Spaniards their Gothic, the Russians their Byzantine, the Serbs Kosovo, the Greeks their Trojan War, the Portuguese Lusiadas and Vasco da Gama, the Scandinavians their Vikings, the Swiss Wilhelm Tell, the Romanians their Daco-Romanian myth and the Hungarians their initiatory crown. The German nation was young; the national epic was a bit thin with *Das Nibelungenlied*. Surrounding countries teased them with the image of the 'noble savages', provoking emotional reactions:

'Barbarians sei's!
Sie nennen uns Barbaren.
Sie sollen fühlen der Barbaren Kraft![42]

In fact, the 'experiment' drew on three main sources, which we have already mentioned in the chapter Reich and Romanticism: Vienna, Munich and Bayreuth; the Viennese ariosophists, the Munich Germanic orders and the Thule Society and the Bayreutsche, Wagnerian years. In addition, endless side roads were taken, drawing and robbing from other worldviews, from Cathars to theosophists, anthroposophists, ariosophists, Edda, Vedda, Riga-vedda, Buddha, Visudi-Magga and the Oera Linda chronicle. The final interpretation of many things had not yet been done. For that, one simply possessed too little knowledge about pre-Christian, Germanic culture and too little research had been done. One had begun to write this new chapter. But even better than the new *Tatmensch* could write, he could fight. With the launch of the fatal operation 'Barbarossa' for Lebensraum, the *Tatmensch* destroyed research before it had even begun properly.

Not everyone, including within the SS, took this gnostic interest of part of the Nazi leadership equally seriously. Cosmic interest was not given to everyone. There is no evidence, for instance, that Hitler was interested in astrology, unlike Lanz von Liebenfels, Sebottendorff and Haushofer. The Ludendorffs were interested in number symbolism and alchemy although they vehemently opposed the Rosicrucians who shared this interest. The Dutch editor-in-chief of the magazine *Storm-ss*, believed that Mathilde Ludendorff was 'crackpot' and described the Oera *Linden book* as a fascinating story, but a forgery. Dutch völkische researcher F.J. Los, on the other hand, took this Frisian primal interpretation of world history extremely seriously. Swinging between eastern and western primordial wisdom about earliest history and the cosmos, the spiritual roots of National Socialism tried to crystallise. The short existence of the Third Reich prevented the *Kulturkampf* in its full consequence and the sedimentation of its final thought.[43]

What did unite the different interpretations was their antipathy to 'luciferian' Bolshevism, in which matter took precedence over spirit, the fear of change, urbanisation, industrialisation, emancipatory processes, the disappearance of the scenic idyll, the failure of pure Germany. Within this primordial soup of discontent, alongside all the differences, lay the common ground between church and Nazis.

Fritz Stern once said that the German path to dictatorship was long, winding and much trodden. Stern thereby points to the fact that Germans believe in the transition from the First (the medieval) Reich, into the Second (Bismarck) and Third (Hitler) Reichs. In a sense, Germans are thus themselves at the cradle of the rationale, the continuity theory, of the controversial Daniel J. Goldhagen. In this, the First Reich could count on warm sympathy and nostalgia, both on the part of the church and Christianity and the Nazis. For the church it was *'Das Heilige Römische Reich deutscher Nation'*, for the

Nazis it was a life-and-death struggle around *Deutschtum*. The greatest hero for both in that period was none other than Friedrich Barbarossa, emperor, crusader errant knight and soldier, champion for God and *Deutschtum*. Barbarossa became a legend passed on to Germans generation after generation. According to tradition, Friedrich Barbarossa had never died, was still sitting at the foot of an old oak tree (often symbolic of Germany) or at a large wooden table in a cave. Yet one day, when his beard had grown all the way around the table and Germany would need him most, the great leader would shake off the sleep of centuries and establish a magnificent, all-powerful empire. According to some, Barbarossa's resting place was in the Harz, according to others - including Hitler - in the Bavarian Alps; one whispered near Berchtesgaden. Was it a coincidence that Hitler built his Berghof, the eagle's nest, there? That, like his fondness for wolves and von Stuck's *Wilde Jagd*, it was a coincidence? Probably not.[44]

Besides Barbarossa, the man of the Reformation, Martin Luther, attracted warm interest from both camps as well. According to Heinrich Heine, Luther was 'the most German German there was'. Luther, contrary to Goldhagen's claims, was not really the spiritual ancestor of the Nazis, though he did do them two favours: Luther emphasised obedience of the people (whom he saw as Satan) to their leaders (*Staatsfrömmigkeit*) and, on the other hand, he harboured a religious hatred of the Jews. In one of his writings, he openly advocated burning their houses and taking away their possessions. In Luther's eyes, the Jews were 'pear-bakers' (a synonym for lazy) and parasites who exploited the Germans and who should be chased out of Germany 'like mad dogs'. Anti-Semites like Theodor Fritsch, List, Lanz von Liebenfels and Wagner quoted from this part of Luther's work to their heart's content. Hitler too praised Luther's insights. Robert G.L. Waite thus calls it a painful twist of history that *Reichskristallnacht* (on which synagogues and shops belonging to Jews went up in flames) took place on the night of 9-10 November 1938, Luther's birthday.[45]

When Hitler came to power in 1933, a different Easter message than usual sounded from many a pulpit. The evangelical church in Prussia stressed that the *Wende* was a message from God, that God wanted them to be Germans and that 'their national character is

God-given'. Christianity and *Deutschtum* had gone hand in hand for a thousand years, which is why the church wanted to serve the state faithfully even in 1933.⁴⁶

Nor did church leaders understand exactly what National Socialism was heading for from the outset; what the undercurrent of the movement was and how far removed it was from Christian thought. As Bracher said, the history of Hitler is the history of his underestimation

Hitler and the Nazis were given the benefit of the doubt more than once, even from their fiercest Christian opponents. The best example is Cardinal Faulhaber, the man Rosenberg criticised. When the Reichstag went up in flames in February 1933 and the Nazis used this as an opportunity to arrest and murder opponents en masse, Faulhaber believed the Nazis should take even harsher measures. He advised the Pope to stay out of this matter so as not to inhibit the Nazis. A conversation with Vice-Chancellor von Papen, of which notes have been preserved, also shows that Faulhaber fully endorsed his view of the whole thing, which corresponded to Görings open accusation against the communists. Faulhaber and von Papen believed in a plot against Germany, a plot against the 'Christian Evening Land', as they called it, caused by what Ludendorff and Rosenberg referred to as the überstaatliche powers: Jews, communists and socialists. Faulhaber and von Papen discussed the possibilities of an economic boycott against Russia, which was seen as the great evil. Negative coverage of the repressive Nazi measures after the fire was dismissed as the work of the international Jewish media.⁴⁷

The church's feelings towards the red menace were clearly expressed in a poem from the 1930s:

'Nicht hoffen mehr nach alter Sitte
dass dir ein Wunderstern erscheint,
dich führend zu des Heilands Hütte.
So ist die Sage nicht gemeint.
Schau auf, ein Stern in hellem Scheine,
der Sozialismus, winkt dir zu,
und jene Hütte ist die deine,
*und der Erlösser, der bisst du.'*⁴⁸

On 10 March 1933, Faulhaber visited Pope Pius xii. Notes of this conversation have been preserved as well. From these it is clear that both gave Hitler the benefit of the doubt. The pope told Faulhaber that 'Hitler pleased him because he was the first statesman who had attacked Bolshevism on political grounds'.[49] From the Church's side, then, there was a certain 'state raison d'etre', with the Vatican seeing in the Nazis an ally against communism, the Russian revolution, the council republics, the Reichstag fire, the Spanish civil war and disturbances in Hungary, Romania and Poland. As a good tactician, Hitler naturally played these cards too. Shortly after taking power, meeting with a number of leading clergymen was a high priority. In Berlin, he received Bishop W. Berning (Osnabrück), Prelate P. Steinmann (Berlin) and H. Kapler of the German-Evangelical Church Association (deck). At this, Hitler, a notorious liar in tactical politics, stressed that the German state was unthinkable without a Christian basis. Rosenberg, he reassured the gentlemen, could not count on his support. *Der Mythus* is not a political party book, Hitler believed, and Rosenberg would have written it only in a personal capacity. It told the clergy that he did not consider his racial politics more important than the religion issue. Indeed, he could easily argue that, because the race issue was his 'religion'. Hitler then played the card of 'eerily new' modernism, liberalism with uncontrollable freedoms and, of course, 'fire-breathing' communism, referring to Spain, Poland and Romania. The church, Hitler believed, was no longer the right instrument to reverse this danger; for that, the NSDAP was needed. It was the same argument Hitler used against monarchists asking him to restore the Hohenzollern throne. Finally, Hitler believed that the Third Reich could not do without unquestioning and faithful soldiers, because those are good soldiers and there were 'dark clouds' looming in the east. The ingredient of religious, *abendländische* soldiers versus Jewish-Bolshevik Russians is already here in the bud. For its part, the church blew its match, stressing to Hitler that church authorities were not to be fought, but to be involved in his struggle against Marxism. Looking back, Bishop Berning thought he had spoken to a serious statesman. Hitler's history is the history of his underestimation.[50]

In his *Zeit der Ideologien,* German historian Karl Dietrich Bracher also reflected on the role of the church in the age of totalitarian rulers. The church did not rely on ideology or state form, but was still guided by the principle of the old church institutions. On the one hand, a certain ambivalence was visible, Bracher believed, as the church tilted towards the national-conservative camp in the political arena. As an important reason for this, Bracher brings up not only communism, but the other new movement, liberalism, as well, and advancing science that was seen as threatening and atheistic.[51] On the other hand, there was resistance from within the church to new secular religious movements from which National Socialism had drawn too. These movements, such as Lanz von Liebenfels' ONT, were incidentally also restricted by the National Socialists, although they were indebted to them. However, Hitler was generally not very appreciative of his teachers, except for Eckart and von Scheubner-Richter.

Martin Greiffenhagen, in his *Das Dilemma des Konservatismus in Deutschland,* further explores the Church's interest in conservatism as such. One of the church's great fears of liberalism - with which the Weimar Republic was partly identified - was the fact that egalitarianism was abhorred. The church wanted to cling to old institutions, belief in divine providence and the fallibility of man. Or as Swiss historian Walter Schubart once put it: 'The heroic man does not regard the world as a gift (like the messianic man) but as his loot which he may furnish according to his own judgements. Heroism is his sense of life,' Schubart opined, but 'tragedy is his end,' he added from his own Christian experience. After all, the spoils could not be taken to the afterlife. According to Greiffenhagen, the church was particularly afraid of the autocratic rule of liberalism. Conservatism, of which the NSDAP was a part, was seen as a counterweight to the enlightenment, the French Revolution and rationalism. Furthermore, conservatism was the driving force behind traditionalism, for which the church had a certain mythical, völkische, German-medieval picture in mind.[52]

The fight against the *Überstaatlichen* was an old battle for Christianity. Socialism, the latest danger on the horizon, had been banned by the Pope in the 1891 encyclical *Rerum Novarum*. Remarkably, liberalism also received a swipe at it and the church - like the National Socialists - felt it had to take a 'third way'. Whereas the Nazis opted for the *Führer state*, the church opted for the denominational organisation of society. Marxism was banned because it was 'incorrect, impractical, unethical, unnatural and anti-religious'. Feminism was an abomination to the church as well. The völkische, romantic picture à la Darré was then rather given the benefit of the doubt.

There are other sources that confirm the fact that the Vatican considered Bolshevism a much greater danger than National Socialism. The papal envoy Pacelli kept an eye on politics in Germany. He reported on the advance of the National Socialists that he considered it less threatening than the rise of the Communist Party. Historians Denzler and Fabricius further state that the Vatican considered pacifism and disarmament in Europe very dangerous. Pacifism taken too far could make Europe an easy prey for non-European powers. Obviously, this pointed to the Soviet Union. Pacifism was in itself a fine aspiration, but unrealistic. Wars were of all times.[53]

Consequently, when World War II broke out, many church leaders joined the national camp. Typical of this attitude, for example, was the speech made by the Reichsbundsführer of the clerical association (he represented 16,000 men):

'*Grossdeutschland ruft zum Dienst! Es ruft jedermann, alt und jung, Mann und Weib - es ruft auch uns... Es ist kampf. Im Kampf verstummt jeder Missklang im eigenen Lager.... Gott segne uns in dieser Verbundenheit des Glaubens zu Dienst und Kampf für unser deutsches Volk und Vaterland!*'[54]

Just as there was common ground between many of the German generals and the Nazis, so too the Nazis and the church had shared interests in some areas. The resulting international and especially German debate culminated in 1963 when Rolf Hochhuth's *Der Stellvertreter*[56] was published. In this drama, Hochhuth criticised the role of the Vatican in no uncertain terms. The result was a very large public discussion initiated by Fritz J. Raddatz in *Summa iniuria, oder Durfte der Papst schweigen?* When the editors closed the 'letterbox', more than three thousand written responses had already been inventoried. Again, the continuity thesis immediately resurfaced. According to some, the pope should have already condemned the inhabitants of ancient Rome for their anti-Semitism. In addition, it was interesting to see what time documents showed. The *New York Times*, for example, heavily criticised Pius xii on a number of occasions. Herbert L. Matthew wrote on 5 July 1944 - the negative turnaround against Germany had long been visible - 'that the Pope's only concern seemed to be communism'.[57] There were also other, smaller signals, from which one could detect a friendly attitude towards fascism. For instance, the pope regularly spoke very positively about the Spanish dictator Franco, deviating from the alphabetical order in his New Year's message to bring Spain somewhat to the fore. Moreover, important clerics made overtly pro-German statements, such as the Protestant bishop Dibelius, who openly said in Nolte-like fashion that 'the Jews had started an action against Germany'. Similarly, some clerics were not free of völkische sentiment. It was shocking to see that at the papal nuncio in Lisbon, the flag hung at half-mast when it was announced on 3 May 1945 that Adolf Hitler had committed suicide. Another shocking example is Bishop Dr Alois Hudal who wrote a book whose title clearly referred to the work of Chamberlain and Rosenberg: *Die Grundlagen des Nationalsozialismus,* and the many dozens of examples given by Friedrich Heer in his work of collaboration of the (Austrian) church. On the other hand, new material has surfaced very recently showing that Pius xi. worked on several versions of an 'anti-antisemitic' encyclical just before his death that unfortunately disappeared into the Vatican archives after his death until it was resurfaced by historians Georges Passelecq and Bernard Suchecky. This encyclical condemned Nazi *'Endlösungs-antisemitism'*, but was characterised by Christian primal antisemitism. This is probably why it was never brought up as an alibi.[58]

After the war, the shocking fact came to light that many clergy in central and eastern Europe, who had colluded more than their western counterparts and even sometimes actively participated directly or indirectly in massacres, sought safe haven in the West. German historian Ernst Klee investigated these facts and in the process discovered a sinister collaboration between the US military intelligence cic (Counter Intelligence Corps) and the clergy. Through the so-called 'monastery route' and false papers from the cic, clergymen, as well as war criminals such as Klaus Barbie (nicknamed the 'Butcher of Lyon'), Adolf Eichmann (responsible for the deportations) and Walter Rauff (driving gas vans) managed to escape. Senior clerics from central and eastern Europe sometimes even played double roles after the war. Because of their knowledge of the region, they cooperated with the cic and passed on this information to their spiritual authorities as well. We saw an example of this with Croatian professor and theologian Krunoslav Draganovic, who was held responsible for the deportation of tens of thousands of Jews and Serbs but found shelter in the Vatican.[59] These are serious facts that were amplified and magnified by post-war left-wing researchers and publishers.[60] This leads to a somewhat distorted picture. Perhaps Hitler explained the relationship with the church best: 'A German state without a Christian basis was inconceivable,' Hitler declared on 26 April 1933. He must have thought 'not yet conceivable', but of course, as a good strategist, he kept that to himself.[61]

In the eyes of the Vatican, Hitler possibly lived up to his image as anti-Christ the most in Poland. Nowhere did he rail against the Church as he did there. The reason was logical. The church was the cornerstone of Polish society, the clergy was the basis of Polish existence and resistance. By simply exterminating or imprisoning the priests, any possible resistance was nipped in the bud. For instance, in Gau Danzig-West Prussia alone, 214 priests were shot in the first two weeks of the German occupation. In total, over 2,500 Polish clergy fell victim to German terror. Some of the priests were replaced by German priests who had volunteered for this vacuum in the *Seelensorge*. In Wartheland in 1941, only 30 of the 431 churches were still open.[62]

However, despite such angry feelings back and forth, church and Nazism saw eye to eye on a number of issues. The church had laid the foundation for religious life in Germany, and the legacy of the German Middle Ages was also cherished by the Nazis. Not for nothing was medieval Nuremberg the venue for the Reich Party Days every year. More important is the fact that the Christians and the Nazis shared the same fears: those of atheistic communism and of competing Jewry. The most reactionary forces went one step further, namely that it was of the same cloth.

'Erwartet nichts von dem Bolschewismus!
Er bringt den Arbeiter die Freiheit nicht!....
'Der Bolschewismus ist jüdischer Betrug!'

Anton Drexler in 'Mein politisches Erwachen (1919)

'Es ist das Zeichen einer wahren Demokratie, dass sie in Zeiten der Todes-gefahr ihren Diktator findet. Auch England und Frankreich taten das. Wenn Deutschland anders handelt in der heutigen Lebensgefahr, wird es kaum wieder hochkommen.
Es muss gehandelt werden, nicht verhandelt werden.'

Hugo Stinnes, major industrialist (23 January 1920)

What do those letters on German cars mean? Dutch people ask. And they immediately find the answer:

W.H.   *We Pick Up*
W.L.   *We Lend*
W.M.   *We Kill*
H.K.P. *Hitler gets the plague!*

Know-you-who?
A collection of wartime folk humour.
Publisher d.a.v.i.d. Amsterdam

Chapter 6

Grosswirtschaftsraum Europa: The realm of unlimited possibilities

The meaning of the Hitler salute - The US war potential - Baku oil - Soviet production figures - *Lehrtruppen* in Romania - Ploesti fields - Danube, the river of the future - Soviet armament - Resource ratio 1:100 - Economic goals and *Führerweisungen* - Berlin-Baghdad - Finland, Romania, Hungary and operation 'Barbarossa' - The patchwork of the Caucasus - Von Pannwitz and Vlassov - Ploesti and *Frühlingserwachen* - Ribbentrop and *Lebensräume* - Görings four-year plans - The autarky idea - *'Herr Reaktion'* - Hitler and the big industrialists - *Unterschiedliche Intentionen* - Crisis - Practice of a Grosswirtschaftsraum - Divide and rule - Bureaucrats vs Goebbels, Speer, Funk and Ley - Arbeitsstab Russland - Kriwoj Rog and Nikopol - Blast furnaces and coal mines - The soot-blackened miners of the Donets coal basin - Involvement of German heavy industry - Red Army's 1943 summer offensive - Scorched earth again - The boned-out East, slavery, famine, holocaust

Up until now, we have dwelt extensively on the mental and spiritual thinking that led to the tortuous path to 'Barbarossa'. Yet it was not only irrational thoughts that played a role in conceiving, legitimising and executing the plan to conquer Lebensraum. Conquest also served an economic purpose and was therefore a matter of geopolitical and geo-economic importance. In the words of Mackinder, the conquest of European *Kernraum* would create a *Grosswirtschaftsraum* for Germany.

What did the Nazis expect to find in Central and Eastern Europe for their *Grosswirtschaftsraum*? We take a look at the inventory Nazi Germany drew up for the soon-to-be-distributed estate. Additionally, I want to consider the role of big industrialists in the campaign for Lebensraum and to what extent the idea of *Grosswirtschaftsraum* was realised in practice.

The question of the role of big business particularly excited Marxist historians. This sentiment was depicted in a photo compilation by John Heartfield of Hitler titled *'Der Sinn des Hitlergrußes'*, which showed Hitler with his hand folded backwards, the characteristic pose of the Führer salute, with which he responded to the outstretched arms of the Hitler salute. It was a salute that Hitler could always make with a certain nonchalance, while his followers had to extend the whole arm. The picture showed a pile of banknotes being placed in the backward-folded hand by big business. Now the meaning of the Hitler salute was suddenly 'clear'.

What this was meant to make clear speaks for itself. Hitler would be the plaything of big business. This thesis also fitted flawlessly with communist doctrine, which, after all, assumed that capitalism would automatically degenerate into fascism. However, Hitler was no plaything of big business any more than he was of the military, monarchists or Christians. He did cooperate with them, however, where they could support his worldview, where they fitted into his strategic concept. No doubt both sides will have thought they could influence and guide each other in doing so. Hitler's history is the history of his underestimation.

Raw materials and food were the key elements Germany was looking for in its quest for Lebensraum from the geo-economic perspective. Let us recall the economic figures mentioned earlier. Germany produced 12,7 per cent of the world's industrial output in 1938. With this, it had more than passed its arch-rival France, at 4,4 per cent, and economically reduced it to a nation of the second order. On the other hand, France could traditionally count on Britain, and possibly, as in 1917, the USA, in the event of imbalances on the continent. It has often been argued that Nazi Germany underestimated the USA. This is partly true, if we recall Hitler's almost careless declaration of war to the USA the moment the German attack was stranded in front of Moscow. On the other hand, there is also good evidence that Nazi Germany had indeed mapped out the huge potential of the USA and took it into account.

General Thomas, *Chief of the Wehrwirtschaftsamtes*, had sent Warlimont, then a major, to the USA for a year before the war to research the war potential of the Americans. Warlimont came to some interesting conclusions:

– the USA were barely capable of providing a large army at that time;
– the conversion from peace to war would take about one year;
– then the USA would produce more war gear within one to one and a half years than all other states in the world put together.[1]

The advice of the level-headed General Thomas was therefore to keep the US out of the war with Germany and make them a 'major supplier' to Germany. History would decide otherwise.

Besides the 'threat' of the democratic-capitalist states in the west, Germany faced the emerging geo-economic bloc in the east: the Soviet Union. With an economic output of 9 per cent, the Soviet Union was the world's third industrial power.[2] Not only was that a giant leap forward given the tsarist backwardness of the 19th century, it was a huge threat to Germany as well, given that the Soviet Union's industrial efforts largely benefited its defence.

A striking example of the explosive expansion of the Soviet economy in a very crucial geo-economic field was the expansion of the oil industry, a commodity that Nazi Germany sorely lacked. The scale that this process had assumed was particularly evident in the old Tatar village of Baku.

Baku, located on the southern coast of the Apsheron Peninsula in a semi-circular bay, had quickly become the heart of Russian petroleum extraction. The city's history was entirely linked to the discovery of black gold. Baku was the oil capital and the connecting centre to Astrakhan, Emba and Krasnowodosk. Seven to eight thousand drilling rigs pumped up as much as 60,000 tonnes of crude oil per day. Thousands of kilometres of pipeline then carried the fuel inland to the rapidly emerging Russian industry, which was running at war strength day and night. Baku was, in a way, the Achilles' heel of the Russian economy. Twenty years before, it had been an insignificant Tatar village, but Soviet leaders saw the importance of oil for their four-year plans and the ideological struggle that would soon engulf Europe. As a result of these policies, Baku's population grew stormily. In 1880, the city had 20,000 inhabitants; by 1926, it had reached 400,000. That was only the first phase. Between 1926 and 1938, the population doubled again to a whopping 800,000. After Moscow and Leningrad, this had made Baku the third city of the Soviet Union. The Volga, mythical as the Rhine and important as the Rhine artery, ensured that oil flowed from Baku to Russia's northern industrial centres. It was one of the main reasons why Hitler always looked so obsessively on the map at Stalingrad on the Volga, the reason why he sacrificed his 6th von Paulus army for it. In a speech on 8 November 1942 at the Löwenbräukeller in Munich, Hitler stressed the strategic importance of Stalingrad. Its importance was none other than an economic one, Hitler argued. After all, Stalingrad was a *gigantic Umschlagplatz* for manganese ore, and nine million tonnes of oil (as much as total German production) flowed across the Volga to Soviet industrial regions. Thereby, Stalingrad was at the junction of the Caucasus, Kuban and Ukraine.[3]

The Soviet Union possessed all the raw materials necessary for a modern economy. One possessed coal, iron ore and petroleum. Coal amounted to no less than 26,4 per cent of the world supply, iron was at least 8,4 per cent of the world supply. Manganese ore (necessary for steel production) was massively mined in Ukraine and Georgia. More than 8 per cent of the world's copper supply was in the Soviet Union. Oil was in Ukraine and the Caucasus. Some Soviet production figures from 1940:

iron: 15 million tonnes
steel: 18,3 million tonnes
coal: 166 million tonnes
oil: 31 million tonnes (fuel total 118 million tonnes)[4]

The commodity that obsessed Hitler was oil. Even before Operation Barbarossa, he had sent *Lehrtruppen* to Romania to ensure that the Romanian dictator Ion Antonescu would properly look after German oil interests in Romania. The Ploesti fields, which employed as many as 25,000 people, were an important strategic 'asset' for the Germans. In addition, Romania's refining capacity was of great geo-economic importance. With its 28 refineries, Romania was among the world's leading countries in this field. 80 per cent of these refineries were in the vicinity of the oil town of Ploesti. Romanian oil accounted for almost 40 per cent of Romania's total exports in 1937 and a significant part of it went to Nazi Germany. In 1939, German off-take of oil accounted for 30.8 per cent of Romanian oil exports. When war broke out, almost all production came to serve the German war economy. As much as 22 per cent of all train shipments in Romania were used to transport the black gold westward. Much of the transport was also via waterways. Yet Romanian oil production was not comparable to that of the Soviet Union. Bucharest's total oil production was between 6,5 and 8 million tonnes annually. Nevertheless, Ploesti's fields were among the best protected areas within Nazi Germany's sphere of influence. Nowhere was more anti-aircraft artillery deployed than at Ploesti, which American bombers had to pay for when they dared to brave the huge Flak batteries. Security of the area was commanded by the energetic ss-Brigadeführer Hoffmeyer, who relied more on his (popular) German and Ukrainian volunteers than on his

Romanian allies, who were often mockingly called 'our gypsies', and ran off at every air alert.⁵

Ploesti's oil would have to stand in the shadow of the new fields Hitler hoped to capture. German interest here was above all in the fields in the Ukraine and, more importantly, the fields in the Caucasus and oil transport via the Volga. In an early geo-economic study *Oil and War*, E.M. Friedwald points out that in 1941 the Soviet Union's fields were estimated to be larger than those of the USA. When the book was published just before 'Barbarossa', new fields had just been discovered in the Volga and Ural regions in 1941. The Grozny and Maikop fields alone covered 15 per cent of total Soviet oil production.⁶

In his table talks, Hitler liked to muse on the economic role of rivers, which were given an important role in geopolitical and geo-economic terms in Haushofer's vision (*Paralellschaltung*). If Germany assumed its 'natural size', the Danube would be the river of the future, over which treasures would flow from east to west. 'If I were in America,' Hitler mused in his table talk on 13 October 1941, 'I would not be afraid. It would be enough to build a gigantic, autarkic economy. With their area of 9,5 million square kilometres, the problem would be solved in five years.'

For his 'solution', Hitler then turned to the East:

'The river of the future is the Danube. We will be able to connect it to the Dnieper and Don through the Black Sea. The oil and grain will flow to us... add to this the canal from the Danube to the Oder and we will have an economic circuit of unprecedented magnitude. Europe will gain influence, by itself alone. Europe, and no longer America, will become the land of unlimited opportunity... There can be no country with a greater degree of autarchy than Europe will have. Where can one find an area that can supply iron better than Ukrainian iron? Where can more nickel, coal, manganese and molybdenum be found?... Currently, only a quarter of the Earth's surface is still available to humanity. For this quarter, everyone is fighting. And this is all contained in the natural course of events - because it is about overcoming the fittest.' ⁷

In part, this was already happening with oil from Ploesti, just as Hitler wanted to do with oil from Ukraine and the Caucasus.

Germany felt its dependence on outside raw materials to a great extent. In 1937, Germany sourced its fuel from several countries, including the US, Romania, Mexico, the Soviet Union, Venezuela and Peru, despite all attempts to achieve autarky. The main oil states on the eve of World War II were the US (60 per cent of world production), Romania (3.5 per cent), Russia (12 per cent) Venezuela (10 per cent) and Iran (about 5 per cent).[8]

The Soviet Union thus represented a major spoil for resource-poor Nazi Germany. Unfortunately, the Soviet Union's resource wealth also made it a geopolitical and geoeconomic threat, given the unimaginable arms industry it had set up. British military expert B. Liddell Hart, in his *Europe in Arms* published in 1938, warned of Moscow's build-up of 'mighty tank units' and the growing number of recruits coming under arms. By June 1941, the Soviet Union had nine million soldiers (only 2.3 million actively available in November 1941 after terrible losses), equipped with relatively good small arms. A number of extensive tank production programmes had come into operation, of which (from heavy to light) the types kw1, kw2, t-34, t-26, bt, t-50, t-38, t-40 were the best known. Even before the war, production amounted to several thousand tanks on an annual basis, rising to 30,000 tanks produced per year during the war. According to a communication from Stalin to Hopkins, Russian tank production in 1941 was as high as 24,000. Monthly production would have been 1500. This was a huge production when one considers that German tank production in 1941 was 5,200, while in 1940 it had not exceeded 2,200 on an annual basis. The same applied to the air force. While the Tsars had only five hundred obsolete French-type Caudron and Nieuport aircraft at their disposal, the Red Army had at least 18,000 aircraft in June 1941 (German intelligence had expected six thousand) and still produced some seven to eight hundred aircraft per month in 1939, rising to 40,000 on an annual basis during the war. German annualised production of military aircraft was 8070 in 1940 and 9540 in 1941.[9]

Through his dictatorial proxies, Stalin had prepared the Soviet Union for the showdown with the capitalist and fascist West. To this end, the Soviet Union had made great sacrifices. In 1928, Stalin had still expressed extremely negative views on the Soviet Union's level of production, which he described as 'half barbaric' compared to Western Europe and the USA. Stalin's geopolitical mind assumed that the Soviet Union had to modernise at lightning speed, because if the country's strength grew, resistance from abroad would increase. Some of Stalin's associates realised early on what this would mean for the country. 'Stalin will let nothing stop him, he will kill us, he will strangle us,' Bukharin mused with anticipation. Stalin had set two goals. The country was to be industrialised and agriculture collectivised. Bukharin advocated a gradual path, but Stalin was in a hurry. By 1928, 14 per cent of Ukrainian peasant families had been incorporated into a Kolchoz; in the North Caucasus, the figure was 19 per cent. This was a reasonable short-term success, but Stalin was dissatisfied. There was, especially in Ukraine, an increasing number of attacks on proponents of collectivisation, and in the process the pace was too slow for him. In the *Pravda*, Stalin proclaimed that 1929 would be the year of the great turnaround and that collectivisation would be completed by 1930. Under a wave of terror and famine, the number of collectivised peasant families increased leaps and bounds. By 1934, over 70 per cent of peasant families were included in Kolchoz alliance.[10]

As a result of this forced new agricultural policy, millions lost their lives. Commenting on these gruesome figures, Stalin biographer Isaac Deutscher said that no one, Hitler included, had inflicted such severe damage on socialism as Stalin.[11] Historians Nolte, Pipes and Conquest calculated the total number of victims of Bolshevism, including (deliberate) famine at many millions of deaths.[12]

Stalin's industrial plan was unimaginably ambitious as well. The focus here was heavy industry. It was, to quote Stalin, 'the line of steel' to be followed, not 'the line of textiles' as he mockingly called the consumer goods industry. Just how (over)ambitious the plans were was shown, for example, by the claims of the Soviet economist Sabsovich, who wanted the Soviet Union to have surpassed the US in the industrial field by 1936. It did not succeed, of course, but nevertheless, progress was enormous. Annual industrial growth was calculated by the official Soviet authorities at 19,2 per cent. This was an overstatement but still indicated robust growth. Large steel centres sprang up in the Urals (Magnitogorsk) and the Ukraine. Dams were built, canals and railways constructed, oil fields mined and coal basins uncovered. New cities sprang up, 1,500 large new factories saw the light of day. Production figures rose; for instance, coal production went from 35,5 million tonnes (1928) to 64,4 million tonnes in 1932. The period of forced build-up was followed by a period of consolidation between 1934 and 1939. Major purges took place among the armed forces and among critical politicians. Seventeen of the 26 members of the politburo that Lenin had last been in contact with were deported, murdered or forced to commit suicide.[13]

The economic and especially industrial contribution that the German economy had to make to the Lebensraum conquest was, above all, to supply the necessary war potential. From 1933, Hitler could deliberately start building his grand plan of operation 'Barbarossa'. Consequently, German defence spending went up by leaps and bounds. In 1932, only 4 per cent of German state spending was on defence, in 1933 this rose to 30 per cent, 50 per cent in 1935 and 58 per cent in 1938/ 1939, which was 18,4 billion Reichmarks. The military spending of neighbouring countries was watched with suspicion too. The efforts of France and Russia were particularly important. In the extreme, France could muster some 3,448.000 trained troops; another one million colonial troops could be added. Together with Russia and Poland (and these were not even all of Germany's opponents), Hitler found himself facing 16 million trained soldiers. The task Germany set itself was almost insane. Especially if we consider that the balance of forces regarding strategic resources was even more imbalanced. Regarding the ratio of fuel between the Allies and Nazi Germany, we have to think of 1:100 in favour of the Allies. Furthermore, in line with General Thomas' warnings about the (especially American) war potential, German war production minister Albert Speer could already conclude in the summer of 1944 that the war was 'production-wise lost'. Nazi Germany could therefore only come to such a plan if they truly believed in their own black-and-white proposition: world power or downfall. The conquest of raw materials was a necessity to become a world power.[14]

Therefore, 'Barbarossa' was a grab, a surprise attack on the resources of the east. At the height of the territorial conquest to the east, the Germans possessed 65 per cent of Soviet coal capacity, 68 per cent of their crude iron capacity, 58 per cent of their steel supply, 60 per cent of their aluminium production, 38 per cent of their crop and 84 per cent sugar. Had this been consolidated, and had the German occupiers taken advantage of the initial ignorant sympathy of the population in the areas they occupied, Hitler's autarchic Germany, as the basis for Darré's völkische peasant soldier state, would have been well underway. Between June and November 1941, the total output of the Soviet economy sank by as much as 50 per cent. Steel production, important for warfare, had fallen by as much as two-thirds; the ball-bearing industry was running at only 5 per cent.[15] Only thanks to a successful evacuation of large parts of the Soviet economy and success on the battlefield - which simultaneously demonstrated the effectiveness of the planned economy in the early years - did Soviet production soon recover. The Urals flourished as an economic region.

From late 1940, three *Führerweisungen* went out in preparation for Operation 'Barbarossa'. These documents give a clear insight into the fact that economic goals were a particularly important facet of the conquest programme. On 18 December 1940, *Führerweisung 21* (nine copies only existed of this document) appeared, announcing the destruction of the Soviet Union openly and on paper for the first time. *Führerweisung 32* (11 June 1941, also nine copies) went even a step further and dealt with the steps to be taken after the successful conclusion of 'Barbarossa'; followed by *Führerweisung 32a* on 14 July 1941 (Operation 'Barbarossa' had already begun), which anticipated the first successes of the campaign. Besides the order for the rapid destruction of Soviet forces, emphasis in these *Führerweisungen* was on economic-strategic, geopolitical goals. The main geo-economic goals that Hitler's military apparatus had to achieve for the winter of 1941-1942 were:

- conquest of Crimea so that the Romanian oil fields (Ploesti) were safe from the Russian bombers stationed in Crimea;
- the conquest of the industrial area on the Donets (Donets coal basin);
- cutting off Russian oil shipments from the Caucasus (across the Volga via Stalingrad) and capturing oil fields in the Caucasus;
- the encirclement of Leningrad and union with the Finns.[16]

In *Führerweisung 32,* there was already further speculation about what was to happen after victory. First of all, Germany would be military master of the continent. The *Kernraum* Europa, to speak with Mackinder, would be German. This would have further power-political consequences as well. For example, Spain could now be definitively forced to deal with Gibraltar, the British position at the 'gateway' to the Mediterranean. The Mediterranean front and North Africa could be given greater priority. Economic exploitation of Eastern Europe was to be set in motion immediately, and an army of 60 divisions and an air fleet was to ensure order. Additionally, and here Hitler allows himself to look into the map, a motorised expeditionary force should be deployed that would push on through the Trans-Caucasus into Iraq. For Hitler, the oil fields of Baku were not enough. Baghdad-Berlin, and who knows, Bombay, were the almost mythical goals Hitler had set himself. The land bridge between east and west, the route once taken by Rosenberg's Atlantic man.[17] Initially, however, Hitler would be satisfied with the line: Archangel-Astrakhan. Shortly after the successful launch of 'Barbarossa', Hitler was so convinced that these days too would soon come, that preparations were already being made to downsize the army as well. In particular, the production of tanks and anti-tank guns would then no longer be given top priority. Hitler would soon have to revise his *Weisung 32a* when victory failed at the gates of Moscow.

Even in later military-strategic decisions, Hitler allowed economic factors to weigh heavily. In the summer field march of 1941, the start of operation 'Barbarossa', economic goals, as we saw, were very important. Less than other commanders in the past, Hitler was obsessed with Moscow but had his sights set on resource areas too.

We saw the priority Hitler gave to Crimea, as a threatening area of operations for actions towards the important Romanian oil fields. Furthermore, Hitler had initially hesitated about the allies he would allow to participate in the campaign. He feared they would claim territories for themselves, while Hitler did not want to share his Lebensraum with anyone. Only the Finns and the Romanians he trusted from the start. Both countries had good territorial reasons to hate the Russians. Finland had lost large parts of Karelia at the Peace of Moscow on 12 March 1940 after a very bloody Soviet attack on Finland. Romania should have agreed to Molotov's ultimatum on 26 June 1940, regarding Bessarabia and northern Bukowina, which fell to the Soviet Union. The Romanians, who also had to deal with angry Hungarians in the west who were reclaiming Transylvania from the Lesser Entente, sought backing in Berlin, whereupon King Carol II and Marshal Antonescu welcomed the German military mission of General Kurt von Tippelskirch. This meant that Hitler had given the Romanians and Finns a place in the conquest from the start.

For geo-economic reasons, Hitler was more cautious with Horthy's Hungary. Hitler - wrongly, according to Swiss/Hungarian historian Peter Gosztony - feared Hungary's territorial demands in Galicia. The reason why Hitler feared these territorial demands above all was the fact that that very area, near Drohobycz, contained valuable oil fields. Thereby, there was a general distrust of one's own allies. 'We cannot trust our allies,' Goebbels noted in his diary in the summer of 1943. 'Our best allies', he further opined, 'are the Romanians, followed by the Italians'. As 'worst allies', Goebbels named the Hungarians, of whom only some officers would be trustworthy: '*Der ungarische Staat ist ganz jüdisch durchsetzt.*' Despite Hitler's request to Horthy to crack down on this, he had only partially succeeded.[18]

Moreover, the summer field trip of 1942 was dominated by economic, strategic objectives. On 28 May 1942 (*Führerweisung 41*), the German army broke through the Soviet positions around Bjelgorod and Kursk and on 22 July 1942 launched the attack on the city of Rostov, at the gateway to the Caucasus. On 24 July, German soldiers were able to bathe in the Don for the first time. From there, the German army pushed further east, with the German 6th Army heading for Stalingrad and the other units descending the Caucasus, hunting for Soviet oil treasures. The campaign in the Caucasus again showed what opportunities lay ahead for the German conquerors in that area. In the Ukraine, the Germans had mostly been brought in as liberators. Still, after the regular troops, the *Einsatzgruppen* appeared, immediately executing anything that was 'German-hostile' or passed for that, and staging mass executions of Jews. And then there was industry, which was only interested in production figures and treated the Slavic population as if they were slaves, just like the Poles before. The peasant population was deprived of their crops. The Caucasus, this patchwork of peoples and nations, offered the Germans many opportunities as well. From the beginning of time, these peoples had been striving for autonomy. Moscow had not given them this; Stalin had bitterly fought, persecuted and deported them. Proud cavalry peoples like the Cossacks, important under the tsars but now misunderstood, were not unwelcome to German troops, and Reinhard Gehlen, head of German intelligence, saw an important opportunity here. The Islamic peoples from the heart of the Caucasus helped the Germans conquer the Russian oil fields, served in the so-called *Ostlegionen* - or *Landseigenen Verbände* - in German uniform but with a shield with Islamic shrines on it on the upper arm. Many units were formed, the most famous being the xv. Kosakenkavalleriekorps commanded by von Pannwitz was and the Vlassov Army (ROA), consisting of (White) Russian and Ukrainian volunteers. Despite the fact that more than one million Soviet citizens signed up for German military service (in his Vlassov monograph, the historian Hoffmann even speaks of possibly two million Soviet citizens in German service), they were never used efficiently. Racial doctrine stood in the way of this. Ariosophical thought had calcified the veins of the Nazi bureaucracy. Anyone who thinks back to the German conquest of Grozny, so much easier than Yeltsin in our days, and the Chechen-German cooperation in capturing the oil fields near the city, realises what a once-in-a-lifetime opportunity the Third Reich let slip here. How flexible Hitler had been in his early years and tactical operations, so rigid and cramped was he now working towards his final goal.[19]

In the summer of 1944, Hitler's strategic agenda was largely determined by the disastrous developments in Romania, which meant that the advance of the Red Army and a sudden change of course by the Romanians endangered the Ploesti oil fields, which were so important to Germany. As the war progressed, Hitler became increasingly obstinate in his economic-strategic views, to the point of absurdity. This led him to move the Third Reich's last reserves (Sepp Dietrich's 6. (ss) Pz. Army), after the Ardennes offensive went awry in late 1944, all the way to Hungary. This was aimed at pre-emptively protecting the small oil fields south of Lake Balaton and recapturing the Ploesti oil fields in a major spring offensive (operation 'Frühlingserwachen'). The German military wondered in amazement whether all those troops were not needed to protect German territory and the Weichsel and later the Oder front. Unfortunately, Hitler believed 'that his generals knew nothing about economics'. Guderian noted that 'oil was capitalised for Hitler'. Budapest was sacrificed as a *Festung* and more soldiers died on Lake Balaton than at the battle of Berlin.[20]

The main spoils of the Soviet *Grosswirtschaftsraum* to be created lay in different places. Between Kazan and Kiev lay the Soviet Union's famous black soil layer (chernozem soil), a rich agricultural area that had earned Ukraine the nickname 'granary of Europe'. Around the Donets Basin were Ukraine's rich mining and industrial areas, where Germany could get its coal and steel from. Southeast of that beckoned the oil fields of the Caucasus and, finally, the large industrial areas around the major cities: Leningrad, Kiev and Moscow, which incidentally interested him the least.[21]

Hitler's generals, as Dr Ten Kate's study, among others, shows, were generally fairly enthusiastic about the upcoming operation and about German chances. On the question of whether all the objectives would be achieved, however, they were somewhat sceptical, although this was only whispered. Perhaps Archangel-Astrakhan was a very distant goal, and the Caucasus expedition for the first year not yet possible. Surely, when the Murmansk-Leningrad-Moscow-Rostov line was reached, the plea had to be decided.[22]

The German plans are remarkable from a purely rational point of view because until the time of Operation Barbarossa, German-Russian relations were of great benefit to both sides. Germany obtained large quantities of raw materials from the Soviet Union - delivered punctually - and the Soviet Union received half- and whole-manufactured goods in return. Given Germany's supremacy over much of central Europe, one could argue that the *Grosswirtschaftsraum* already existed. German foreign minister Joachim von Ribbentrop had tried unsuccessfully to convince Hitler that a Greater Germany could coexist with a communist Russia. The three-power pact (Germany, Italy, Japan) could be extended to a four-power pact (with the Soviet Union). Japan would be eager to do so, given its expansionism southwards. The *Lebensräume*, one now began to speak in plural, would 'touch' but not 'overlap'. Hitler wanted none of this and stuck to his course. The Soviets' geopolitical interest, made clear on a visit to Berlin by Soviet foreign minister Molotov, confirmed Hitler's views that a conflict with the Soviet Union was inevitable. A day before *Führerweisung 21,* Hitler told Alfred Jodl that the European continental problem would be solved at once if the Soviet Union was defeated. In doing so, he stressed that the war was in a hurry. Not only had Britain stood firm during the *Battle of Brittain*, but the USA was still lurking in the background.[23]

The creation of the *Grosswirtschaftsraum* could only take place if the German home front showed closed ranks. The mass of the German people and large numbers of the military proved strongly susceptible to the Nazis' völkische, idealistic narrative. It was of utmost importance for Hitler to win industry to his plans as well. Or as he himself described it several times: domestic politics is nothing more than preparing the country for its foreign political tasks. In Hitler's case: persecution of Jews and the conquest of Lebensraum.

To exert sufficient control over the economy here, Hitler (like Stalin) could fall back on four-year plans. These four-year plans were characterised by three facets:

- Germany was a highly industrialised society;
- the Nazi politicians controlled economic processes like a commando industry;
- production remained largely based on private funding.[24]

As a result, as in the religious question, Nazism had found a 'third way', between capitalism and communism.

The whole autarchic endeavour already had the characteristics of the third way in it. In fact, the pursuit of autarchy was an idea that stemmed from the eighteenth century, coupled with mercantilism. In the nineteenth century, the facet of national sovereignty slid over this. The state as an autarchic unit, just as it had to be a völkische, political, linguistic, historical and ethnic unit, was considered a fine commodity. Of course, not everyone was equally enamoured with the autarchy idea and voices were raised in favour of a more open window to the world. These capitalist and Western-oriented tendencies were stifled in the firestorm of 1914-1918, that catastrophic war that acted as a huge, sucking engine for völkische thinking, anti-Semitism, irredentism, frustration and economic malaise.

After November 1918, the dream of the open window to the world was over. As we have seen, all kinds of colonial societies did dream and muse about the usefulness of overseas territories. However, irrational elements like honour and recognition played as big a role in this as economic desires. The *Diktat* of Versailles made Germany passionately autarchic, which best fitted the myth of the scenic idyll so cherished by the völkische thinkers.

Not surprisingly, the initiatives Hitler took after 1933 were all aimed at creating a strong starting position of the German economy for the coming Lebensraum conquest. In 1936, the first year of the first four-year plan, Hitler drafted a 'Denkschrift' in August, which he presented at the Party Day in Nuremberg. The speech was full of the typical Nazi interpretation of a country's economic forces. The whole thing was drawn into the social Darwinist perspective. Once again, Hitler stressed the importance of Lebensraum for Germany regarding raw materials and food supplies. It made immediately clear where this was to be sought; 'among the Marxists and the Jews', a finger pointing to the Soviet Union. And just as Germany was preparing for this power politically (anti-commitment pact with Italy and Japan), and militarily (expanding the old 100,000-man army), there had to be an economic programme for this. That Hitler attached great importance to the autarchy idea may be seen from his following comment in the 'Denkschrift': *'Selbstversorgung ohne Rücksicht auf die Kosten.'*[25]

The first four-year plan was placed in the hands of Hitler's confidant Hermann Göring, who was named prime minister of the four-year plan in this position. Göring was supported in his tasks by a committee consisting of Defence Minister Blomberg, Finance Minister von Krosigk, Economy Minister Schacht, Agriculture Minister Darré and Prussian Finance Minister Popitz. The essence of the four-year plans was getting the German war industry ready and manufacturing synthetic raw materials, above all fuel.

The choice of Göring was, above all, a political one. Not only was Göring one of Hitler's confidants, he was also, as we saw earlier in the book, the representative of the right wing of the party. In this case, not the völkische wing, which Hitler supported but at the same time kept more and more in the background, but the 'bourgeois reactionary' wing. Just as the military was afraid of the left-revolutionary wing of the NSDAP, of the Strasser brothers and the undisciplined SA of Ernst Röhm, the petty and big industrialists were naturally wary of the left wing. An open battle had ensued between Göring and the left wing, in which the Strassers lost out. Göring could further boast of a hard confrontation with the SA in the past. The Reichswehr general Werner von Blomberg had had the SA's phone tapped and had uncovered shocking data about the revolutionary attitude of Röhm and his allies, as well as their dislike of Göring as the reactionary front man of the NSDAP. In conversations with sa-Gruppenführer Karl Ernst, Röhm's man in Berlin who had to face Goebbels, Göring was routinely addressed as 'that swine' or *'Herr Reaktion'*. Full of enthusiasm, they spoke of 'the day when this friend of the big industrialists would be eliminated and the true aims of the National Socialist revolution would be realised'. Karl Ernst regretted that Göring had waived an offered SA bodyguard, 'because that would have made it easier one day to beat the boar's brains out.'²⁶ Just as Hitler needed the army over the SA, Hitler needed industry over the lumpenproletariat of the brown shirts. This does not mean that Hitler did not share the völkische and partly 'red ideals' of the left NSDAP wing, they were of no use to him to achieve his main goals, race war and the conquest of Lebensraum, for the time being. Hitler met workers' demands only insofar as he was electorally obliged to do so. It was the immense political talent of the Gauleiter of Greater Berlin, Goebbels, to balance that just fine in the turbulent capital all these years. He colluded with strikes and riots so as not to alienate the workers from the Nazis. On the other hand, he lunged at big business, which also had to stay 'on board'.²⁷

So industry could rest easy with Göring at the helm. He posed no threat to industry, although, as we saw above, his industrial government existed more on paper than in practice. Göring had become an economic dictator. Of course, one man could never regulate as much as needed to be regulated, and the result was a competence struggle in his organisation. The four-year plans set themselves big goals. For instance, fuel production was to rise by 475 per cent; oil production (planned at 5,3 million tonnes in 1940) was to rise to 13,8 million tonnes in 1942-3. However, the war and the dramatic course of the fighting in the east sent the plans into disarray.²⁸

The economic powers and the NSDAP were to some extent each other's natural allies. Hitler's relationship with reactionary military, Freikorps, (Prussian) nobility and common interest in Christianity were all elements that the economic powers in Germany were not dismissive of. They constituted a safeguard against the spectre of communism that rang through Europe. From the beginning, Hitler, the DAP and the NSDAP tried to put the industrialists at ease. In the first directives of the DAP, Hitler already spoke of the need to spare big business as a bread provider and work provider. The workers and the DAP only had to fight against usurers.²⁹ There was no doubt about who these usurers were. Drexler, in his 1919 brochure *Mein politisches Erwachen* (the booklet that helped persuade Hitler to join the DAP), believed that the effortless profits were 'Jewish profits' and posed a danger to German workers. It is also notable that Drexler in his pamphlet continued on the völkische road, turning away from big capital in general and advocating 'the productive bourgeoisie', while Hitler would soon distance himself more from such jargon, so as not to offend the big capitalists.[30] Here the tactician came around the corner again. In practice, Hitler experienced reality, at least in part, as Drexler saw it too. This can be seen in a 1922 *Denkschrift* by Hitler. In it, he writes that the healing of the German people requires not the healing of the economy but the healing of the German people's institution. No less than 40 per cent of the total German population, Hitler believed, 'adhered to international Marxism'.[31]

In practice, Hitler focused his economic policy not on Drexler's brochures but largely on the advice of veteran warrior Gottfried Feder. Feder, an anti-Semite, warned about the danger of Jews in trade, industry and banking, but on the other hand, he emphasised from a very early stage, which was reflected in *Mein Kampf*, the need for private property. In doing so, Feder partly preached to his own parish. Born in 1883 in Würzburg, Feder studied architecture in Munich, where he graduated in 1905. After briefly working for a concrete firm, he became independent in 1908 and collaborated on major construction projects in Eastern Europe, especially in Bulgaria. Influenced by World War I, Fuer's political sentiment won out over his business instinct and he became a confidante of Dietrich Eckart and introduced Mathilde von Kemnitz to Ludendorff. Feder took part in the Hitler-Putsch and had to go into hiding in Czechoslovakia for some time. When the skies cleared again, he put his economic knowledge, topped with a völkische sauce, to work for the NSDAP. For Feder, the most important criterion for owning private property was that one had 'worked for it'. Here, too, we find an overwrought, völkische, überstaatliche view of the economy, with apparently large groups (Jews) withdrawing money from the economy without working for it. We see this in the 19th century as well, where, for example, Bernhard Förster (Elisabeth Nietzsche's husband) submitted tens of thousands of signatures to Bismarck demanding that Jews were no longer allowed to participate in stock trading.[32]

Fencing the (Jewish) Bolshevik danger had from the start proved an effective weapon to free up funds from industrialists for the reactionary political camp. A good example of this, and in some ways a precursor to the DAP, was Dr Eduard Stadtler's anti-Bolshevik League. Stadtler addressed 50 of Germany's leading industrialists at a rousing meeting in January 1919, including the 'Ruhr king' Hugo Stinnes, owner of the Deutsch-Luxemburgischen Bergwerk -und Hütten ag; Carl Friedrich von Siemens of Siemensen Halke ag/Flick-Gruppe; Ernst Borsig, chairman of the employers' association; and Albert Vögler, general manager of the Vereinigte Stahl-werke. Stadtler gave a powerful speech on the dangers of communism. When he had finished, an ominous silence fell, which was broken by Hugo Stinnes. He called on the leading industrialists to support the anti-Bolshevik League by 'buying' an 'insurance premium' against Bolshevism. The figure of 500 million marks was soon mentioned. If people were not willing to pay that, Stinnes said, the industry was not worth calling itself 'German industry'. That same day, the sum was together, flowing on to Freikorps and other reactionary groups and parties. Stinnes was both an industrialist and a patriot, and from him came a famous quote from the Kapp-Putsch era, which he supported: *'Es ist das Zeichen einer Wahren Demokratie, dass sie in Zeiten der Todesgefahr ihren Diktator findet'*.[33]

That dictator was Hitler. Stinnes also soon recognised this and supported the NSDAP financially, although it should be noted that big business generally supported conservative parties rather than the reactionary NSDAP. Financial help was given to Hitler through the Reichswehr too, which could count on support from the anti-Bolshevik League, as well as through the fame of some of Hitler's closest associates. A key pivot here was again Erich Ludendorff.[34] Ludendorff was of great value as a symbol figure of reactionary Germany, and steel magnate Frits Thyssen - who would become one of Hitler's best-known financial backers thanks to his memoirs - travelled to Munich just before the 1923 Bierhalle-Putsch. Munich in those days, Thyssen also saw, was becoming the centre of reactionary Germany. He encountered Ludendorff and Hitler who asked him for financial support for 'a military expedition'. Thyssen - Ludendorff and Hitler tried to 'play him off' a bit - heard that Stinnes had 'already paid' and promptly pledged 100,000 goldmark. Characteristic of the still-present distrust of the Nazi nouveau riche, he did not give this money to the Balten-German treasurer and Rosenberg confidant von Scheubner- Richter, but to Ludendorff personally.[35] Thyssen partially saw through the Nazi strategy. He got a strong impression that Hitler was primarily a pragmatist, a tactician, who had brought together people with different antipathies to the system of the time. Among the conspirators, Thyssen detected Gustav Ritter von Kahr as an emissary of Crown Prince Rupprecht, who wanted to reclaim the throne of the Wittelsbucher dynasty after the Putsch.

Thyssen saw this entirely correctly. Beyond the pact the lords had made, at play within the NS camp was Darré's newly noble ideas, which were at odds with the interests of existing dynasties. *'Unterschiedliche Intentionen,'* Thyssen noted dryly.[36] Such continuing contradictions in the reactionary camp contradict an 'overly tight catapulting' of Hitler, as we discussed earlier.[37] The Kahr-Hitler alliance was one of a fundamental nature: namely, that it hated *Erfüllungspolitik* and the republic.

Furthermore, a resurgence of Germany from the shadow of Versailles benefited German industry and trade. Hitler's anti-communism was enthusiastically welcomed too. This was evident when from 1926 Hitler began to pay more and more attention to big business, where power beckoned in the distance. In February 1926, Hitler was given one of the first major firing tests in this area. He spoke before a large group of big industrialists from the *Hamburger Nationalklubs von 1919*. Hitler successfully brought out his showpiece. First he pointed out the danger and his dislike of Marxism, and then the creeping danger it posed to Germany: one-third of the German population was apolitical Hitler believed. Another third were international (often communist or social-democratic in orientation) leaving only a third in the national camp. The German state could only become healthy again if, like a tuberculosis patient, it first overcame its disease (the communist danger). What was interesting in this speech was that Hitler stressed that the destruction of Marxism had been his party's goal from the start.[38] Hitler spoke the truth: he had perverted the destruction of Marxism into racial doctrine and the conquest of Lebensraum. One did not exist without the other. Not all industrialists will have understood this when they applauded Hitler. They only remembered the 20,000 soldiers' and workers' councils that had sprung up like mushrooms in November 1918 and the anarchy it brought.[39]

The 1928 global crisis was grist for the Nazis' mill. Unemployment in Germany ran into many millions and the GDP index (1928=100) fell to 72 by 1932. As an indicator of economic malaise, it is worth pausing to consider a few other numbers. Coal consumption, typical of the state of the industry, fell from 163,440.000 tonnes to 104,740.000 tonnes. In iron production, the decline was even more dramatic, from 13,239.000 tonnes to 3,932.000 tonnes between 1928 and 1932. Steel production fell from 16,019.000 to 5,621.000 tonnes during the same period.[40]

It takes little imagination to conclude that German industrialists were panicking. It does seem typically German that they too reduced the matter to a very profound essence. In a 1929 *Denkschrift* of the *Reichsverband* for German Industry, blackly titled *Aufstieg oder Niedergang,* the darkest scenario was outlined. In it, the government was given a fair shake. Parliament would not be up to the task. There had to be a tight government, strong and direct. Politics - and this is interesting - did not have to shy away from using emergency ordinances. That was exactly the tactic Hitler would adopt when in February 1933, barely in power, the Reichstag dubiously went up in flames. Through emergency ordinances, Hitler drew power to himself, never to return it. The industrialists made an error of judgement... Another *Denkschrift* by the *Reichsverband* chaired by Carl Duisberg entitled *'Revision des Youngplans'* followed in 1931. This contained some remarkable sentences of a political nature: Germany could only be a bulwark against Bolshevism if it was economically strong.[41] Duisberg openly strove for a *Grosswirtschaftsraum* under German hegemony and advocated a major industrial bloc from 'Bordeaux to Odessa'.[42] In addition to groups of industrialists, Hitler also approached individual industrialists with influence, such as Emil Kirdorf (Gelsenkirchener Bergwerks ag), through a 'secret brochure',

Der Weg zum Wiederaufbau, in which the big industrialist was reassured about the 'revolutionary character' of the movement and the efforts against communism of the NSDAP.[43]

What became of the Grosswirtschaftsraum plans in the Lebensraum to be conquered? There were a number of reasons why the whole plan was ultimately unsuccessful. Firstly, of course, because final victory on the Eastern Front failed to materialise. Secondly, because Hitler declared war on the USA in December 1941, which considerably accelerated the collapse of the Third Reich. And then there were administrative and bureaucratic reasons as well as the madness of German racial policy that contributed to the fiasco. The German idyll of the völkische Lebensraum story would be plunged into a rock-hard power struggle between various agencies and the blood of the local population.

The aim here is not to give a description of the day-to-day practice of *Grosswirtschaftspolitik*. What is most important here are the patterns the policy followed and what they meant for the functioning of the *Grosswirtschaftsraum*.

The real expansion of the Lebensraum plan would, of course, only have taken place after Operation 'Barbarossa' was successfully concluded. After initial great successes, eliminating millions of Russian soldiers, the attack eventually foundered at the gates of Moscow in the resistance of the Red Army and the onset of winter. The *Grosswirtschaftsraum* would thus have to be built up under continuing war conditions. This only increased the pressure on German planners, as resource-poor Germany had entered the war with alarmingly small supplies of strategic raw materials (fuel for 4,5 to 6 months). It was therefore necessary to tackle the production and exploitation of the occupied territories energetically. In practice, most of the effort would take place in Ukraine, the area that had been in German hands the longest.

In doing so, the Third Reich encountered all sorts of problems that it largely owed to itself. Governing in the newly conquered country was very impractically arranged. Hitler again showed his tactical prowess here, by having as many as four organisations operating side by side:

- the army, through the Wirtschaftstab Ost;
- Heinrich Himmler's SS;
- the *Reichsministerium für die besetzten Ostgebiete*, headed by Alfred Rosenberg, which was in charge of *allgemeine Verwaltung*;
- Hermann Göring's four-year plan apparatus.

Such a complicated and overlapping division of labour was further complicated by all sorts of personal discord between the main performers. The somewhat isolated position of Alfred Rosenberg has already been explained in the chapter on völkische thinkers. Rosenberg was placed somewhat in the suspect corner as a 'Balten German' and his sensitivity to the fate of minorities in Central and Eastern Europe was harshly played off by his competitors as 'racial weakness'. Hans Adolf Jacobsen called Rosenberg one of the few idealists in the foreign policy field. Partly influenced by his second mentor (Dietrich Eckart was his first) Max Erwin von Scheubner-Richter, Rosenberg advocated a restoration of Central and Eastern Europe in a more classical sense. Rosenberg did not oppose 'slavedom' but communism. He therefore supported the idea of a Berlin-Kiev axis against Moscow. However, in the racial vision of Nazi Germany, this was not a viable option. The army was the odd one out. The emergence of the *Wirtschaftsstab Ost* was a remarkable feature. This gave the German military far-reaching political power and made it partly responsible for many abuses without having much experience in the political field.

There was much ambition and lack of experience in the SS. Himmler had largely missed out on the spoils in Poland and was now lurching towards Soviet industry and above all the arms industry. However, within a short time, the bureaucratic Himmler managed to create no less than three SS institutions that worked *alongside, with*, but also often *against* each other: the *Reichssicherheitshauptamt* (Heydrich), the *Wirtschaftsverwaltungshauptamt* (Oswald Pohl) and the *Reichskommissariat für die Festigung deutschen Volkstum* (Ulrich Greifelt). And then there was Göring, the morphine-addicted air marshal, who was increasingly gripped by his personal problems which hampered his important duties.

This organisational and administrative chaos fortunately had some inhibiting effect on the implementation of the terrible plans that soon came to the table. It is not possible to cover all the ideas and *Denkschriften* of this period in detail here, but a brief look at the consequences of the *Generalplan Ost*, which was rewritten and elaborated several times, shows the enormous impact on the population of the occupied territories. The plan was the brainchild of real scientists, such as agronomist Konrad Meyer, affiliated to the University of Göttingen. Meyer made a stormy career after, through the *Reichsstelle für Raumordnung (which* fell under Hitler's supervision and was headed by Hanns Kerrl), where he focused on the spatial planning of occupied territories in Eastern Europe. Detailed knowledge for these guidelines was drawn from university departments and the result was a Blut und Bodenwetenschap. According to the various reports, between 46 and 51 million Slavs were to be deported, which was later revised to 31 million. The 'vacant' places were to be filled by about 10 million Aryan newcomers. What is striking and shocking is the fact that the planners already took into account even those population groups yet to be exterminated that were 'in the way' of the Nazis. For example, Meyer conveniently assumed that less than 10 per cent of the original population would remain around the Leningrad city area.[44]

All these grotesque plans and institutions competed with each other. The only clarity in such administrative chaos lay in the 'Führer' orders. Yet, that too became increasingly difficult the longer the war went on. First of all, Hitler was completely obsessed with the military course of the conflict, tended to lock himself up more and more in his military headquarters, and the threshold to come to him became ever higher. Second, a circle of bureaucrats had sprung up around him who contributed diligently to this. These bureaucrats were above all Hitler's secretary Martin Bormann, Chef OKW Wilhelm Keitel, Hans-Heinrich Lammers (*Chef der Reichskanzlei*) and Fritz Sauckel (*Generalbevollmächtigter für den Arbeitseinsatz*). Due to their privileged position around Hitler, they benefited from an unclear position of power in the field and all power at the top. From the 'field', there were often only modest attempts to change the existing course. The pseudo-religious image that existed around Hitler did not make it easy to confront him with the 'truth'. On the other hand, his subordinates were simply too cowardly to communicate their clear opinion to him. We know from the many military memoirs on World War II that there were only a handful of generals who dared to openly tell Hitler where things stood. In the political arena, it was little different. At the end of 1942, a small club around propaganda (Minister Joseph Goebbels, Minister for War Production Albert Speer, Economy Minister Walter Funk and leader of the *Deutscher Arbeitsfront* Robert Ley) tried to break up the bureaucratic blockade of Bormann and consorts, hoping to achieve a better and more effective mobilisation of German forces. Initially, they got Hermann Göring on board in their plot against the bureaucrats. However, when it came down to it, Göring did not dare, sank into apathy and Himmler whispered to Speer to keep a low profile from now on. Himmler had sided with the bureaucrats. In his recollections of this power struggle, which dragged on until May 1943, Speer described this time as the 'detuned keyboard of mutual relations'.[45]

In addition, it was much more difficult than expected to exploit the resources of Eastern Europe. As we have already seen, the exploitation of Poland was most advanced. In particular, the new administrative structures. Danzig-Westpreussen and Wartheland, the two new *Reichsgaue* in western Poland had been added to the German empire. Areas around Kattowitz and Zichenau had been added to Silesia and East Prussia, respectively. The rest fell under the *Generalgouvernement*, headed by Hans Frank. For the newly conquered territories after 1941, the following was planned: the Baltic States were to be merged into the so-called *Reichskommissariat Ostland* (with the four *Generalkommissariats* Estonia, Lettland, Litauen and Weissruthenien). Most important would be the *Reichskommissariat Ukraine* as a supplier of food and raw materials. Then there would be the *Moscow Reichskommissariat*, consisting of the rump state of Russia without Baltic states and Ukraine, running to the Urals and the industrial regions of Magnitogorsk and Chelyabinsk. 'Caucasia' was also to become a *Reichskommissariat*; a staff of a thousand had already been drafted for this administrative monster that would never see the light of day. Special status would be given to the important oil regions. The area along the Volga and Baku, Hitler declared on 16 July 1941, would be declared a *deutsches Reichsgebiet*. The 'Öl ag', a half private company (I.G. Farben) and half state-owned company would take charge of exploiting the oil areas. Nazi Germany had already given the 'Öl ag' a 99-year mandate. Crimea was destined to be a key strategic point to protect Ukraine and the Black Sea.[46]

Besides the economic exploitation of these territories, there was a major population policy programme in the pipeline as well. Crimea, Hitler stated on 16 July 1941, was to be freed from 'foreign peoples' and inhabited by German settlers. The intention was to make the peninsula a *Reichsgebiet*. Even the name of the area was to be changed, from Crimea to Gothenland. The cities of Simferopol and Sebastopol were to be changed to Gothenburg and Theodorichhafen. In this, Hitler embraced the plan of the Gauleiter of Vienna, Alfred Frauenfeld, who proposed moving the Südtiroler (who lived under Italy) en masse to Crimea, to settle this dispute between Berlin and Rome once and for all. The Tyroleans, Hitler and Frauenfeld believed, were ideally suited to life in Crimea because of similar climatic conditions. Thereby, Crimea would be optimally connected to the hinterland of the empire through the Danube.[47]

In the longer term, Ukraine would have to go too. Over the course of twenty years, Hitler reported in the summer of 1942, Ukraine was to be completely colonised by Germans. As the main settlement areas for the Germans, Hitler designated the main roads in a west-east and north-south direction. In practice, this would amount to the lines Krakow-Lemberg-Schitomir-Kiev, Leningrad-Kiev, Schitomir-Winitza-Odessa. At the junctions, 'fulcrum-like settlements' were to be built, consisting of 15,000 to 20,000 inhabitants around which were to be entirely German agricultural areas.[48]

The wild plans to divide and use the spoils were not uncontroversial. Hitler's word was law, as in the case of Crimea and Ukraine. Yet, his final decisions were preceded by several ideas that competed side by side for recognition. For instance, Rosenberg hoped to establish a more or less autonomous Ukraine that could exist closely allied to the

Third Reich. He wanted to raise the historical consciousness of Ukrainians and allow them a university in Kiev. Secretly, Rosenberg dreamt of the Berlin-Kiev axis as the weapon against Moscow. The Reichskommissar Erich Koch thought otherwise. No doubt he shared Rosenberg's anti-Semitism but his hatred of Slavic peoples was hardly less. Koch literally spoke of the Ukraine as an *'Aussbeutungsobjekt'* and referred to *Mein Kampf* which qualified the 'slave nation' as an 'inferior race'. 'The aim of our work,' Koch told a meeting in Rovno in 1942, 'must be that the Ukrainians work for us, not for themselves'.[49] It was typical of Hitler's divide-and-conquer tactics that he allowed Koch a free hand (through Bormann), while Koch was officially under Rosenberg's jurisdiction. Indeed, Koch acted according to Hitler's views, who after all demonstrated time and again that 'state-building' in the occupied territories was out of the question. *'Der Weg zur Selbstverwaltung führt zur Selbständigkeit,'* he believed. Even villages were not allowed to have contact among themselves, let alone administrative contact. In short, Ukraine should become a new *Ostmark*. There were also differences of opinion regarding the Baltic states. Rosenberg was moderately positive about the Balts and not unwilling to leave them some form of self-government. However, the Reichsführer-ss believed, on the basis of his 'racial knowledge', that only the Latvians would be suitable for assimilation to the Third Reich. Hitler eventually decided that the entire Baltic region should become *Reichsgebiet*. It is interesting to note that this vision of Himmler manifested itself in the formation of Baltic Waffen-ss divisions. Although Estonian (and later Latvian) Waffen-ss divisions existed and operated on the northern front, divisions of Lithuanian origin were absent.[50]

Very little came of the *Siedlungspolitik*. People tried to distribute loot that was only on loan. As a result of the acts of war, the wild plans did not get off the ground. The new, German *Siedlungen* could be counted on two hands. Those of the SS were all around Himmler's headquarters, like lonely islets in a Slavic sea. Where the Germans had longer opportunities, as in Poland, the terrible *Alltag* became more than apparent. One day, Hans Frank believed with foresight, 'the Weichseldal will be as German as the Rhine Valley'. To achieve this, a ruthless *Germanisierungspolitik* was necessary, involving assimilation, slavery, deportation and murder. In all seriousness, Frank suggested deporting the 'superfluous Poles' to Siberia. In the same vein, Hitler expressed his views on the people of Crimea, who should just go and live somewhere else in the Soviet Union, because there was 'enough land'.[51]

The ultimate lack of success in expanding the *Grosswirtschaftsraum* had not been due to the preparations. Göring, who at times regained his old energy from his pilot days, had started very ambitiously and energetically. To gain an accurate understanding of the scale of the work ahead of him, he had called on the *Wehrwirtschafts und Rüstungsamt* of the OKW, headed by General Thomas. Under the cover name 'Oldenburg', his *Arbeitsstab Russland* had then immediately embarked on an accurate inventory. According to Thomas, a short time later his department had 'fantastic material' on the table.

With this data in their pockets, Göring's German officials marched directly behind the German forces into the Soviet Union. One of these economic experts was Pleiger, an industry manager and general director of the *Reichswerke ag für Erzbergbau und Eisenhütten* and Dr Schlotterer of the *Reichswirtschaftsministerium*. Both men, armed with Thomas' report, rushed to the high-grade iron and manganese mines of Kriwoj Rog - according to Russian historian Telpuchiowski, the most important industrial area in Ukraine and Nikopol.[52] Great was the shock when experts closely examined these areas, which fell into German hands barely two months after 'Barbarossa' (in mid-August 1941). The destruction wrought by the Red Army in its burnt-earth tactics was colossal. In addition, it was remarkable that the Soviet authorities had managed to evacuate most of the heavy equipment - even equipment weighing around 100 tonnes - in time. At the Kriwoj Rog blast furnaces, which were normally powered by at least two thousand electric motors, barely fifty engines were left. The mine shafts were in bad shape too. The fifty shafts had been blown up or flooded to such an extent that only a handful could be reopened. In doing so, the German authorities had hoped to make use of local workers, but it soon emerged that 70 per cent of the trained personnel had migrated east with the Red Army. 80 per cent of all available workers in the Kriwoj Rog area were totally unskilled and did not work hard enough by German standards.

There was little else left but to bring materials and people from Germany to Ukraine, concluded damage experts Dr Ende and Dr Lillig for Herman Göring. And there was enormous haste with the job. Germany had imported no less than 65,000 tonnes of manganese ore from the Soviet Union in 1940 and ordered and received another 75,000 tonnes in 1941 until the invasion, out of a total import of 116,00 tonnes. Rebuilding Nikopol was therefore of great importance.[53]

The reconstruction was placed in the hands of the 'Bergbau-bataillon mot.26', among others, but these experts encountered major problems. They needed power to operate but the Red Army had decommissioned the main power station, the one at Saporoschje. There was a hole (180 metres wide) in the dam and its repair would take until spring 1943. The only possibility of getting power (among other things to pump out the mine shafts) could be provided by a small coal-fired power plant near Kress. However, there, too, German engineers faced enormous problems. The coal would have to be brought in from the Donets basin, but the railway lines were full of military transports. Additionally, many coal mines had been blown up or flooded, so coal was an extremely scarce commodity and could only be fired very sparingly. The largest coal reserves within the Donets coal basin were found in Stalino. But here, too, the conquerors came out cold. The mines had been carefully blown up, the industry evacuated. Specialists calculated that only 10 to 20 per cent of pre-war coal production could be extracted in the foreseeable future. The only windfall for the Germans was that in the city of Mariupol, they got their hands on almost everything whole. To the German side's delight, the major steel works were intact and there were large stocks of coal (90,000 tonnes) in the city. Still, this was actually little more than a drop in the ocean if we consider that the German occupation authorities in the region consumed at least 1,000 tonnes per day.[54]

In practice, the daily production of the Germans was barely 5-10 per cent of the pre-war daily production of the Soviets. And this despite the fact that the Germans had employed as many as 24,000 Russian workers in the coal basin from January 1942. It was an extremely sad, bleak reality unfolding in Ukraine. The unclear chain of command, the inability of the Nazis and their arrogant policy towards the Russians made cooperation a hellish task. The Russians were malnourished, uneducated, humiliated and had to withstand snow and storms. It became too much for some of the German officials. There was too little food, spare parts were late. For instance, there were far too few typewriters, there was no paper, not enough drawing materials; all daily consumables for the mining engineers. Workers' working conditions were degrading. Work boots took six months to arrive. There were periods when soap was not available to miners for four months. Coal-black workers populated the scenic idyll of the Third Reich. Transporting spare parts and supplies was an agony without end. Due to overcrowding on the railway lines, as well as attacks by partisans, the 130-km journey between Stalino and the coal basin took no less than 24 hours. A journey to Mariupol (250 km) took 36 hours. People therefore mainly relied on panjew cars for transport. Horse food had to be brought over a distance of 100 km or more. To keep horses and people alive, the German authorities proceeded to swap coal for food with Ukrainian farmers. 'We lack everything,' complained a German official in a report to his Berlin authorities, 'how can we work like this?'[55]

There was only some improvement as time passed. More and more specialists, including German industry, had arrived in the east. Virtually the entire German heavy industry was now represented in the Ukraine and deployed its know-how. For example, Hoerder blast furnaces from Dortmund had taken charge of the Stalino and Rykowo blast furnaces; Hoesch ag was involved in work at Krowoj Rog; Klöckner Werke ag at the Mariupol blast furnaces; and Krupp ag at the Asow steelworks in Mariupol, the Kramatorsk machine plants and the Taganrog blast furnaces. Of great importance was the fact that from the summer of 1943, energy supplies via Saporoschje were restored. Successes achieved then can be seen in coal productions. In January 1943, German engineers set a new record of 455,000 tonnes. In March, this record was already broken again with a monthly production of 455,600 tonnes, to culminate in the absolute record of 487,000 tonnes in July. These tonnages were badly needed and quickly forgiven. 277,000 tonnes were used directly by industry, the army needed 111,000 tonnes and 99,000 tonnes went to the railways.[56]

However, the success of the embattled Grosswirtschaftsraum came too late. In July and August 1943, the Red Army, after a successful defence of Stalingrad and a recapture field march through the Caucasus and Kuban, pushed on to Ukraine. 'The Donets must be preserved at all costs,' Hitler ordered to German Minister of War Albert Speer in mid-August 1943. Yet Speer was an architect and manager of the war industry; he had no knowledge of military affairs. So the loss of the coal basin did not allow itself to be stopped in this way. On 3 August, the Germans began evacuating the city of Kharkov, one of Ukraine's most important cities. On 20 August, the Germans were forced to blow up 70 per cent of the city's businesses as the Red Army was anxiously approaching. On 22 August, the last German soldiers left the city. This effectively began the dismantling of the entire 'German' industry east of the Dnieper.

The Red Army entered a destroyed country. On 31 August, the German authorities had ordered the economic destruction of all the area east of Mariupol-Makejewka-Slawjanks. On 1 August, Stalino was in the line of fire when Red Army planes bombed the city. Evacuation from Taganrog took place on 14 August. On 2 September, the blast furnaces at Makejewka were blown up, the next day at Kramatorsk, the following day at Konstantinowka and on the 8th at Mariupol. Coal production for the benefit of the German war industry came to a complete halt on 3 September 1943.[57]

Speer called what followed the era of the illusionists. Göring partly denied the bad situation. Speer called him a bankrupt who wanted to deceive himself until the last moment in order to escape stifling reality in this way. The bureaucrats only gained power. Given they acted as yes-men to Hitler, they could do little wrong. Heinrich Himmler, the head of the SS, was appointed interior minister on 20 August 1943. This gave the völkische ideologues increasingly free rein in the economic sphere and in German society. Bormann, meanwhile, was drawing the Gauleiters closer to him. In early November, the Red Army threatened the resources of Nikopol for the first time. Hitler was diabolical and swore his generals not to give an inch. Indeed, they had to go on the offense because without the manganese, Hitler argued, Speers' production would be completely flat in three months. The war would be lost. General Kurt Zeitler called Speer with his hands in his hair. The latter was able to reassure him by reporting that fortunately there was still a supply for 11 months. That was the entire gain of the dream to Lebensraum. This supply could not hold Nikopol, which was captured on 8 February in a joint operation by the 4th Ukrainian and 3rd Ukrainian fronts of Generals Tolbuchin and Malinovsky. On 23 February, Kriwoj Rog fell. Speer took sad stock of Germany's reserves on strategic resources. It was notable that he did not include supplies from the Balkans, Turkey, Nikopol, Finland and northern Norway. In his view, these were already lost, just as the entire war was lost for production reasons before it had even begun properly.[58]

General Thomas had predicted that it would take the USA a year and a half to raise their army. This time had passed since December 1941. The final collapse of the Third Reich was drawing near. The *Festung* Europa that Hitler wanted to build was on fire in the east and threatened in the west from Italy and soon from the Normandy coast. In the process, the *Festung* possessed no roof and Allied bombers set fire to the German (synthetic oil) industry.

The exploitation of Soviet agriculture was not much better. We can let the numbers speak for themselves in this regard. Despite a tough policy towards the local peasantry, the occupation army had to be 'supplemented' from Germany. Thus, the learned shortage was 14 per cent flour, 32 per cent meat, 50 per cent fat and 60 per cent sugar. The fact that the German army, like German industry for that matter, started running its own farms under its own management did little to change this. In fact, there was a great similarity between the spoils in 1941-1942 and that in the mid-1917-1918 period, when much of Ukraine was occupied by German forces. During that period, the German occupation authorities had managed to get their hands on 1,249.950 tonnes of food. As much as 710,000 tonnes, even then, was eaten by the occupying forces and thus did not benefit the homeland. An annual report of the *Wirtschaftsstab Ost reports* loot of 1,030.000 tonnes of grain, 47,200 tonnes of fat, 213,500 tonnes of meat. Again, the most primary objective of the Lebensraum policy was not achieved. Only the first objective, feeding the hungry mouths of the German army, could only be partially achieved. Again, transport problems, opposing agencies and (passive) resistance from the population due to an arrogant occupation policy were the main factors negatively affecting the process for the Germans.[59]

With a German victory, things would not have looked any better for the native population. An important document of the Economic Staff *Ost, Gruppe Landwirtschaft*, dated 23 May 1941, makes it clear that the Germans had come to the conclusion that, above all, the southern regions of the Soviet Union, the Ukraine and the Caucasus were rich agricultural areas due to their good soil, where there was basically a food surplus. By contrast, the forested north, Leningrad and Moscow, were areas with too low a food production that had to be 'supplemented' from the south. From the German point of view, this policy would be ended. The southern surpluses, and even much more than that, would be utilised entirely for the benefit of Germany; the north would be allowed to largely die out. It is known of Leningrad that Hitler had spoken out against its survival. The order to destroy this city was one of the evidence documents against the Nazis at the Nuremberg trial. The southern areas that were to be fed were mainly the important industrial areas.[60]

The boned east was left behind. Twice it had been burned: on the retreat of the Red Army and on the retreat of the Wehrmacht. Not only had the country's economic infrastructure been completely ruined, but völkische racial politics had also taken its toll. Poland and the Soviet Union were the areas where most Jews lived. From December 1941, systematic efforts were being made to exterminate them. At the bottom of the Soviet Union alone - small borders for 1939 - between 700,000 and 750,000 Soviet Jews were murdered, according to Raul Hilberg. *Yad Vashem* published a figure of 1,000.000 to

1,100.000 dead in 1989. If we add the Soviet-annexed Polish territories, we end up with over a million more victims.[61] In the centre of the *Grosswirtschaftsraum*, the Donets coal basin and the area around Nikopol, the bloody handiwork was done by *Einsatzgruppe C* that reached the town of Nikopol in September 1942.[62] The Jews lived largely (85 per cent) in the cities that were relatively easy for the Germans to control. They had been handed over to terror. The *Einsatzgruppe D* went into action in the Caucasus. Soldiers and engineers, politicians and executioners had collectively entered the field for the phantom of Lebensraum.

Besides the Jewish population, there were the other Soviet citizens who were hardly better off. German historian Rolf-Dieter Müller gives a shocking example of this from the mouths of generals involved in the administration of the occupied territory. They were not inferior in racial fanaticism to the most stubborn Nazis. The generals involved in the exploitation of the country joined in talking about 'superfluous eaters' (Leningrad) and the fact that 'superfluous population' of the Donets coal basin should be imprisoned in concentration camps. In the Ukraine, a general of the staff the *Wirtschaftsstab* Ost posed the following question to the other occupation authorities as they went over the future of the area: 'If we shoot all the Jews, let the prisoners of war die, let most of the city's population starve to death and also starve a large proportion of the peasants by taking their crops, who is to implement our economic plans?' To emphasise his proper 'Aryan disposition', he added that he was not asking this question out of sentiment but out of 'mere economic interest'.[63]

The concerns of the *Wirtschaftsstab* Ost all came true in practice. Jews were killed by the *Einsatzgruppen*, prisoners starved to death by the millions behind the barbed wire. The Slav population was left to starve or put to work in the industry that was to make the German empire a nation of unlimited possibilities.[64]

What remained of the *Grosswirtschaftsraum* was soon not much bigger than the *Reich* itself. Only under the energetic leadership of Albert Speer did Germany manage to experience another notable economic boom. In 1942, war production rose by 55 per cent and by the end of 1944, 3,5 times more weapons were produced than in 1941. This was only possible by squeezing all those countries in the grip of the Nazis and employing as many as 7 million forced labourers in German industry. In the SS camps, Jews worked on the assembly lines of the 150 firms of the *ss-Wirtschafts und Verwaltungshauptamt*.[65] All this would only delay the defeat and had nothing more to do with the idyll, the myth of once...

'Wir erhoben unsere Gläser und sagten mit leiser Stimme: 'Auf die Zerstörung der Feinde!'
'Auf die Wiedererhebung Deutschlands!'
'Auf Adolf Hitler, den Weltführer!'
'Ich fühlte, wie sich meine Augen mit Tränen füllten, als ich diese Worte von mir gab und in meinem Sinn die glückliche Zeit erinnerte, in der ich darauf wartete, dass die deutschen Armeen bei Stalingrad durchbrechen und über das hochgelegene Asien in Indien einmarschieren würden, den alten Eroberungsweg entlang, die ganze arische Welt vereinigt.'

Savitri Devi Mukherji in 'Gold im Schmeltziegel. Erlebnisse im Nachkriegsdeutschland', 1953, translated from Indian.

'Der Nationalsozialismus ist kein Zufall, nicht die Erfindung einzelner Männer, keineswegs ein radikaler Umschwung, sondern seit langem im deutschen Wesen und seiner Entwicklung vorbereitet. Er gehört hinein in das Strombett deutscher Geschichte und wurzelt in seiner Vergangenheit.'

Bishop Alois Hudal in Die Grundlagen des Nationalsozialismus (1937)

'The drumbeat of the SS - Two slow, three fast beats - echoed continuously throughout the city yesterday.
It's three o'clock in the morning: I was awakened by the nearby drumming and now I can still hear it in the distance, Now I know what it is. It is the great tam-tam of the tribe, being stirred. Even our sleep must be switched on and in the subconscious the lurid rythme must continue.'

Denis de Rougemont, in 'A year in the Third Reich'

Chapter 7

Journey to the underworld

Hitler's history is the history of his underestimation. This is shown by the fact that historians and contemporaries mostly did not want to make Orpheus' descent into the underworld to penetrate to spiritual roots of National Socialism. The result is still visible: one-dimensional studies and conclusions like those of Nolte and Goldhagen. The consequences are profound. Historians often still find themselves at a questionable distance from their subjects. The relatively late recognition of Raul Hilberg's work on the Holocaust is a good example. Recognition that the race war and the conquest of Lebensraum were the linchpin of Hitler's foreign policy (the only political field that Hitler really cared about) had to wait until Eberhard Jäckel's *Hitler's Weltanschauung* and several other books that did not appear until after Hilberg. While books on the Holocaust now fill libraries, the gap around the issue of Lebensraum is still visible.

I would therefore like to see this study mainly as a first *Grundlage Arbeit*. In doing so, I wanted to chart the spiritual roots of the Lebensraum concept. Since no historical gap on such a large subject could ever be closed in a book before, I realise that this is a first inventory. In doing so, I have tried to avoid the one-dimensional nature of someone like Goldhagen. Where he goes full throttle and effortlessly knits together a chain of cause and effect, the painted facts show that reality can rather be portrayed as a stepping-stone idea. The question of the origin and legitimisation of the Lebensraum concept is a big puzzle with many pieces and small steps. These pieces were very different in nature and origin, even sometimes opposites, nevertheless they all formed a step in Orpheus' descent into the underworld of National Socialism.

In summary, the views, thoughts and mystifications that led to the emergence of the destructive Lebensraum philosophy can be reduced to roughly seven factors:

- the idealistic, romantic factor;
- the mythological factor;
- the racial factor;
- the scientific factor;
- the economic factor;
- the military factor;
- the religious factor.

The idealistic, romantic factor is deeply immersed in Germany's genesis. Being young nation, Germany struggled with a self-image defined by extremes: a völkische glorifying self-image, in which the newly emerging Germany was depicted by Paul de Lagarde and Julius Langbehn as a romantic, scenic idyll surrounded by a strange, modernist, enemy world. The awakening superpower was demanding of itself and full of irrational expectations. An almost pseudo-religious hyper-nationalist overidentification with being German was the order of the day. '*Das Volk ist eine Idee. Wir sollen ein Volk werden,*' mused Georg Friedrich von Hardenberg, alias Novalis. Wagner's aesthetic man was here to flourish as a thinker in the cloud forests in a rapidly liberalising world (West) and, on the other hand, hemmed in by eternal Russia. Germany's great ambitions were expressed in its colonial ambitions, represented in the *Alldeutscheverband* and the *Reichskolonialbund* of Alfred Hugenberg, Alfred Leher and Ernst Hase. Propelled by the conservative revolution, the vestibule of Lebensraum philosophy was formed here. Before long, the president of the *Reichskolonialbund*, General Ritter Franz von Epp, would present himself as a 'political soldier of Adolf Hitler', a term normally used only for the Waffen-ss.

The idealists were convinced that they were merely protecting their country's interests, as any other European patriot would do for his country. In doing so, they eagerly referred to the spirit of Fichte, von Kleist, Treitschke and others. August Winnig transformed from left-wing politician to conservative protector of the *Deutschtum* in the East when he saw how the Weimar republic was no longer safeguarding German interests and revolution, anarchy and pan-Slavism were building up on the empire's borders. Fencing economic figures, military statistics and a demographic apocalypse, they campaigned for Germany's place under the sun. From these ambitions and the *Mut der Ahnungslosen,* 'Volldampf' Wilhelm II developed his fateful policy that would eventually deliver a defeated Germany to the provisions of Versailles.

The 'dictate' of Versailles, in turn, allowed all sorts of mythological, mystical and sentimental thoughts and reasoning to translate into political reality. The invisible victory of the Allies on the western front, coupled with the attitude of stubborn military reactionaries who did not want to know about defeat, as well as uprisings at home, placed a veil of mystification around German defeat and the future prospects of the empire. This culminated in a widely held belief in the fate and destiny of the Aryan German, who had been removed from her true *Deutschtum* and German (*Arteigene*) religious experience by evil forces - Jews, Bolsheviks, Freemasons, Rosicrucians and even the Christian Church. Such mystifications existed in many degrees. The origins of the Aryan myth, as we saw, went back to Blavatsky and Theosophy. The belief in original races was perverted into ariosophy in Viennese radical circles around Jörg Lanz von Liebenfels and Guido List, and through detours found access to völkische and ariosophische circles in Munich, where it was built into an effective political force in Rudolf von Sebottendorff's Thule Society and would eventually recruit Hitler as an orator. Besides this Thule Society, mystification was also carried by reactionary military men, the most famous of whom was Erich Ludendorff, who, together with his wife Dr Mathilde von Kemnitz, through their Volkswarte-Verlag and Tannenbergerbund, argued for a return to the völkisch-mystical roots of being German and warned against *überstaatliche* powers, which included Freemasons and Jesuits in addition to Jews and Bolsheviks.

The most important exponent of the radical rendition of völkische thought was the Balten German and Nazi philosopher Alfred Rosenberg. The latter went so far in his mystifications around the Aryan thought that he declared the Indian-Germanic link that underpinned it to be primordial Germanic missionary power in an eastern direction. By this reasoning, the Lebensraum in the East had actually always belonged to Aryan (German) man. Many völkische-ariosophical works muse on the Berlin-Baghdad-Bombay land link as a connecting road within a vast empire, from the Obersalzberg to the maharajas of India. These conceptions translated for Hitler into the belief that Russia had always been led by an Aryan (tsarist) upper class over the centuries and that it had only very recently - through the 'Jewish-Bolshevik revolution' of 1917 - fallen by the wayside. Hitler therefore wanted to intervene and bring order. Ariosophical incitements that legitimised this thinking were to be found among older precursors of the National Socialists as well, such as Housten Stewart Chamberlain and Richard Wagner.

The only teacher Hitler ever recognised, Dietrich Eckart, came from the circles around the mystical Thule Society that relied heavily on perverted theosophy. In a bizarre but relatively unknown book, *Der Bolschewismus von Moses bis Lenin*, Eckart interviewed Hitler about his view of the world. This made it crystal clear that Hitler was much more ariosophically inclined than many biographers would have us believe.

The racial factor runs like a thread through the mystical narrative. It is important to reiterate here that Hitler and many Nazis were convinced that Bolshevism and Judaism were identical. From this came the accusation that 'true socialism' - namely of a national nature - had been betrayed by the Jews. This sheds light on a forgotten theme of the Third Reich, the attraction and common interest in socialism of both National Socialism and Communism. Despite their enormous hatred of Bolsheviks, the Nazis imitated many of their techniques and rhetoric. It is well known that an ardent Nazi like Joseph Goebbels had strong leftist sympathies well into the 1920s. In addition, recent research material has made it clear that Hitler's role during the Munich council republic was anything but uniformly on the reactionary side. Indeed, the Führer appears to have been adorned with the red armband.

The hatred of the Jews, who played a prominent role within the council republics emerging everywhere in Europe, was only becoming more intense. To this underexposed theme, I wanted to pay some extra attention, partly on the basis of remarkable new literature, such as that by the Jewish-Russian writer Sonja Margolina. This made it clear that the Jewish myth of Bolshevism had an explicable background. For many Jews, like the French Revolution at the time, the communist revolution was an opportunity for emancipation. The flight to the front that followed was in part compromising, placing Jews in an iron tongs of repression on the one hand and historically unprecedented positions of power on the other. Not least, conceptions of 'Jewish Russia' were carried into Germany through the migrants, the best known of whom were Alfred Rosenberg and von Scheubner-Richter, and these conceptions, including through the *Protocols of the Wise Men of Zion*, poisoned the German mind.

Besides anti-Semitism, there was the Germanic-Slavic conflict. As we have already seen, the Nazis believed that Russia's original upper class was not Slavic but Germanic and had been replaced by Jews since the revolution. In addition, an extremely tense atmosphere prevailed especially in the German borderland. Besides racial factors, strong religious feelings played a role in this as well. Catholic Poles harboured fears of the Lutheran Germans on their western border. The Germans, on the other hand, tirelessly supported their Volksdeutsche brethren in the east and defined their interests in highly threatening dimensions.

This brings us directly to the scientific factor. Geopoliticologists like Karl Haushofer, inspired by Mackinder and Kjellén, provided the intellectual fuel for expansive ambitions. Haushofer, who already knew Hitler when he wrote *Mein Kampf* in 1923, inspired the Nazis with his geopolitical thinking. The terms Lebensraum and *Heim ins Reich* flowed from his pen. He taught Rudolf Hess, Hitler's deputy, and was no stranger to mystical, ariosophical organisations like the Thule Society either, which helped shape Hitler's ariosophical views and were at the cradle of his political career.

For economists, the need to obtain Lebensraum, as described by Karl Haushofer, was mainly about a *Grosswirtschaftsraum* for Germany. The hunger blockade (between 600,000 and 800,000 casualties) from World War I had made it clear to Germans that maintaining the status quo would be a dangerous situation. The east offered space and resources. The *Führerweisungen* that accompanied the launch of

Operation 'Barbarossa' were heavily influenced by the economic interests of the Third Reich. Hitler saw himself as an economic strategist and complained that his generals had no understanding whatsoever of economics. The German bureaucratic apparatus worked out the plans for the *Arbeitsstab Russland*, which wanted to mine the Donets coal basin and use the blast furnaces of Nikopol and oil from the Caucasus for Hitler's *Festung Europa*. Even in the earliest days, the conservative big industrialists belonged to the right-wing camp of politics. Through strategic political policy, in which Hitler controlled the most radical exponents of ariarchy and the left wing of the NSDAP, Hitler managed to avoid a split with them and secure their support at key moments.

The military, as a reactionary force, had been involved in Hitler's rise from the start. We have pointed to Erich Ludendorff, the World War I general who was willing to march with the unknown corporal to the Feldherrhalle in 1923. In addition, the reactionary military bloc in Bavaria was quick to recognise in Hitler the great orator who could prevent Germany from falling into the hands of communists or fragmenting into separate states, which would be disastrous for the expensive armed forces. Hitler's relationship with the army was always somewhat problematic. He distrusted the 'blue-blooded' generals, but on the other hand was realistic enough to recognise that without their support he would never be able to realise his Lebensraum ideal. Towards them, he curbed the most radical elements of the brown movement. He successfully managed to appeal to the Prussian element within the German armed forces who were sensitive to the oath of allegiance to politics and the turbulent times in the Prussian borderland, where Polish and German Freikorps were fighting each other to the death. Furthermore, Hitler did not shy away from cracking down on the army if necessary. No less than 50,000 death sentences were carried out by the field courts, almost half of which were carried out. The Waffen-ss, the *Weltanschauungs-soldiers* of National Socialism, grew into an army of some 38 divisions and became a rival to the regular army. So here again, Hitler applied divide-and-conquer tactics. Yet he managed to reward his generals and share in the gains. Following the example of the Hungarian Reich Regent von Horthy,

Hitler too wanted to give brave soldiers who had acquired the *Ritterkreuz* a knightly estate in the East. Important generals, such as Heinz Guderian, already received them during the war.

Running through all this was the religious issue: Germany, the Occident, as medieval Christianity versus distant Byzantium with its slavedom, which in the eyes of many Germans nevertheless had something inferior. Documents show that the Pope to some extent justified the Nazis' policy because of his enormous fear of communism. Examples abound of fanatical clerics who embraced the Ariosophical version of Christianity: *'Grossdeutschland ruft zum Dienst!'* On the other hand, even here the love in its deepest essence was not sincere and in reality the interests of Christianity and the Nazis were at very odds. The Nazis' interest in the occult; the lineage myths in which Jesus was considered an Aryan; the belief in reincarnation, of the Reichsführer-ss Heinrich Himmler; Karl Maria Willigut's maddening runic wisdom and the ruthless murder of Catholic priests in Poland, are examples.

It is my belief that Christianity was on the list of opponents of the regime too. However, it never got around to dealing with this opponent. History determined otherwise. Nevertheless, the Nazis were able to cleverly borrow from Christianity and, for example, put Luther in support of *Deutschtum*. Whole and half religious sentiments played through the other elements. In *Der Bolschewismus von Moses bis Lenin*, Hitler already indicates in his conversation with Dietrich Eckart that they saw a common thread in history, in which Christianity had already been infiltrated by the Jews at an early stage. Since then the *Weltanschauungskrieg*, the *Kulturkampf* as Alfred Rosenberg called it, had been raging, and this battle was to be decided in the twentieth century. Two aspects were needed for this decision: the inevitable race war had to be won and for that Germany needed its Lebensraum, to be able to mould the world in Hitler's image as an autarchic ordering power.

The various factors have been presented separately above, but it should be clear that they had all sorts of interrelationships, and many a contradiction could also be found in the grab bag of argument and sentiment. On the one hand, Nazi Germany invoked its medieval

Christian traditions; on the other, it warned against the false prophecies of Christianity and the importance of *Deutschchristentum*. Whereas the West was accused of creepy modernism and itself advocated the scenic idyll, the East patted itself on the back as urban planners and bringers of culture. Mutual relations further reinforced the grabbing effect. For instance, Hitler protected the ideas of his sorcerer's apprentice Rosenberg on the one hand, only to hand him over rock-hard to the whims of his political opponents like Himmler, von Ribbentrop and Goebbels on the other. In practical politics, too, many plans backfired due to built-in contradictions. Although the aim was to create a *Grosswirtschaftsraum* for Germany in the east, the unimaginable repression, racial politics, anti-Semitism and the famines created deprived them of necessary labour. Even the scientific thinkers were inconsistent. Karl Haushofer was initially a mainly water-inspired geopolitical thinker. Only after it became clear to him that Hitler's interest was in a *Kontinental empire rather than* overseas colonies did he focus his theories more on the *Kernraum* Europa. As for the myth of the Jewish Bolshevik, he preferred sentiment to insight. Was it strange that after a long period of repression, the Jews made their escape to internationalist communism, which freed them from nationalist sentiments? Incidentally, contradictory developments were visible within the Jewish community as well. There were Jews who pioneered German conservatism, and certainly not all Jews fled into communism. The liberalism that had taken hold of the West since the French Revolution also provided a home for displaced Jews. In addition, a Jewish nationalist movement also developed with Zionism. Such issues were largely ignored.

A great mixture, a primordial soup of all the factors that formed the breeding ground for the aggressive supremacist idea behind the Lebensraum thought processes was already visible in 1920s Bavaria. The spiritual roots, the creative exponents of what was to degenerate into the destructive campaign to the east, showed their crystallised reality there in all sorts of cross-relationships. It was the political forecourt for the road to power, the home ground of reactionary and frustrated soldiers; loyalty pacts were made there, revanchism preached; wounded pride was there, fear of the council republic, fear of German separatism, the wishful thinking of the great strong Germany, the idyllic rural myth, the Aryan idea, sectarian thinking and the stab-in-the-back myth as the driving engine behind whole and half-truths. This is where the *deutscher Gottglaube* was introduced, this is where Gottfried Feder and Karl Haushofer gave their racial and geopolitical lectures; this is where iron-fighters Ludendorff, Röhm, Dietl and many others were child's play; from here the Kapp-Putsch was planned, the Baltic campaign demanded and closely followed, the Ludendorff-Hitler-Putsch catapulted. Balten-Germans and völkische forces reached out to each other here. Here, the trench aristocrats presented themselves, purified at the front they saw themselves as the 'knowers' and spoke openly about their role in the coming Third Reich.

This colliding effect in Munich, where the interplay of different forces becomes so clearly visible, has so far remained too much out of focus because historians have too often been guided by the image the Nazis themselves presented of this era. Early masters, such as the key figure Gottfried Feder, were sidelined and did not stimulate any scholars to research in depth. Eckart died before the heyday of the Third Reich. Erich Ludendorff, who in some respects was even more radical than the Nazis, was hushed up even at the time of the Third Reich although his Munich home can be labelled without exaggeration as Germany's first 'Braunen Haus'. Within these walls, Hitler became socially acceptable and the Reichsführer-ss Heinrich Himmler and the later Auschwitz commander Höss reached out to each other for the first time. This made the deadliest friendship in history a reality. Here was the first impetus of the pact between the reactionary military and the young Hitler. Despite this, there is hardly any literature on the role Ludendorff played in the building-up period of National Socialism, and where it does exist, it is unblinkingly mentioned that Ludendorff hardly influenced Hitler's career and thinking. It is similar to the way many contemporary historians report on Alfred Rosenberg, drawing on the arguments of his enemies. Today, we know that there were direct contacts between Hitler's spy service for Captain Mayr and Ludendorff, just as there were with the secret Thule Society. Within these groups was the basic idea that *überstateliche* powers, Jews, Freemasons and Bolsheviks, were influencing the course of history to the detriment of Germany. Their main cradle was in Moscow, from where Jewish-Bolshevism threatened the European homeland like an ever-lengthening shadow.

Other völkische-ariosophical inspirers like von Sebottendorff, Lanz von Liebenfels and List were gagged. The 'dark enigma' surrounding Hitler had thus been created. This made Hitler seem rootless, a direct emissary of 'cosmic forces', just as he preferred to have himself presented by propaganda minister Goebbels: single-minded and unapproachable. The creation of this myth was largely Hitler's achievement. He wrested power politics away from his masters and schools of learning although - partly secretly - he remained true to the core of Ariosophical thought. This is best evidenced by the key points of his Weltanschauung: race war and the conquest of Lebensraum in the East; two macabre goals that served each other.

When the *grosse Rausch* was over, the world was left violated and unable to understand. It was as if Nazism had struck the earth like a thunderclap and disappeared just as suddenly. In the rebuilt German cities, Bismarckstrasse appeared next to Adenauerrstrasse. Hitler's era had been expertly carved out of history. The mystification of the *Hitler era* persisted. Where words and explanations were lacking, a sonnet offered clarification, found on the disembodied and murdered body of Albrecht Haushofer, the son of the inventor of the term Lebensraum, Professor Karl Haushofer:

RATTENZUG

Ein Heer von grauen Ratten frisst im Land.
Sie nähern sich dem Strom in wildem Drägen.
Voraus ein Pfeifer, der mit irren Klängen
Zu wunderlichen Zuckungen sie bannt.

So liessen sie die Speicher volle Getreide -
Was zögern wollte, wurde mitgerissen,
Was widerstebte, blindlings totgebissen -
So zogen sie zum Strom, der Flur zuleide...
Sie wittern in dem Brausen Blut und Fleisch,

Verlockender und wilder wird der Klang -
Sie Stürtzen schon hinab den übergang -

Ein schriller Pfiff - ein gellendes gekreisch:
Der irre Laut ersäuft im Stromgebraus...
Die Ratten treiben tot ins Meer hinaus...

Thank you

To conclude, I would like to thank a number of people. First of all, Martin Ros, who through his constant enthusiasm, encouragement and readership gave me stimulus and useful advice many times during the long period of writing. Professor Bart Tromp referred me to a number of important studies and provided valuable comments on the text. Thus, it became clear to me that geopolitics is undergoing a certain 'revival' again and that Haushofer, the inventor of the term Lebensraum, although hardly ever quoted literally, is 'present' again in the background of many a study. Thanks also to those who contributed ideas on specific areas, such as Jünger specialist Jan Ipema, historian Marcel Reijmerink and Russia expert Michiel Klinkhamer. Furthermore, much gratitude to Wim Meulenkamp who pointed out the contradictory attitude of the Nazis towards the völkische movement and in particular its 'folkloric' character. As the Third Reich took shape, this side was increasingly pushed aside by 'modern' Germany, which perverted its technical achievements into an extermination apparatus. We saw a similar development with Hitler, who silenced his former teachers and focused entirely on the Führer state. Further important was Henk Pors's commentary, especially on developments in the 1920s. In doing so, he allowed me to draw liberally from his library. I am indebted to Jan Willem de Groot, a specialist in the field of the Aryan gnosis, who advised me and gave me access to literature that was very difficult to trace. His personal library in this field is unique. My thanks go further to M.K. and H. van G. with whom I had long conversations about specific discoveries and problems that arose on the trail. A thank you to Peter and Hanneke as well. During conversations with them on Friday nights, my thoughts were able to streamline.

I also want to mention a number of people who helped me very practically. First of all, Jet van Swieten and Henny van Mil, who focused with care on text and photos. Karin ten Kate carefully went through the text again for final corrections, for which I am grateful. I also enjoyed the very energetic support of Mr Geert Bovenhuis of bookstore-antiquarian Bagage in Utrecht, who diligently and successfully searched for all kinds of literature from which I could draw. Finally, my thanks to Ester and my family for their understanding, patience and support.

Soesterberg, May 1999

Notes

Chapter 1

LEBENSRAUM: THE CONTINENTAL EMPIRE OF ADOLF HITLER

1) Raymond Poidevin, *Die unruhige Grossmacht. Deutschland und die Welt im 20. Jahrhunderts.* (1985)
2) Eberhard Jäckel, *Das deutsche Jahrhundert.* (1996)
3) Alfred Kruck, *Geschichte des alldeutschen Verbandes* 1890-1939. (1954) pp 13-17./*Reichskolonialbund, Kreisverband Aachen Stadt, Deutschland deine Kolonien!* (1937) pp 5-30./Paul M.Kennedy, *The Rise of the Anglo-German Antagonism 1860-1914.* chapter 10 (London 1980)/Christian Graf von Krockow, *Bismarck, eine Biographie* (1997) chapter 18.
4) Christian Graf von Krockow, *Unser Kaiser. Glanz und Sturtz der Monarchie.* (1996) p 36.
5) These goals are still a point of debate, see, among others: Fritz Fischer, *Griff nach der Weltmacht. Die Kriegszielpolitik des kaiserlichen Deutschland 1914/18.* (1961)/Ernst W.Graf Lynar (Hg.), *Deutsche Kriegsziele 1914-1918.* (1964)/ Manfred Funke, *Mass und Anmassung. Wie kam es zur Katastrophe des Ersten Weltkrieges?* Rheinische Merkur (17-10-1997).
6) For a good overview of the Bismarck-1933 period see:Raymond Poidevin/ Hans Fenske, *Ungeduldige Zuschauer.* Die Deutschen und die europäische Expansion 1815-1880 in: Wolfgang Reinhard (Hg.), *Imperialistische Kontinuität und nationale Ungeduld im 19. Jahrhundert.* (1991) pp 87-123.
7) Used here: Raul Hilberg, *Die Vernichtung der europäischen Juden* [1961] (1991).
8) Martin Broszat, Holocaust und die Geschichtswissenschaft in: *Schriftenreihe der Vierteljahrshefte für Zeitgeschichte* (1979) pp 285-298.
9) *War Documentation 40-'45.* Sixth yearbook of the National Institute for War Documentation. Dick van Galen Last, *Vijftig jaar geschiedsschrijving over de Tweede Wereldoorlog* (1995) pp 176-238.

10) Michael Ruck, *Bibliographie zum Nationalsozialismus.* (1995)/Helen Kehr, *The Nazi Era, 1919-1945* (1982).
11) Fritz Fischer, *Hitler war kein Betriebsunfall.* (Munich 1992).
12) Norman Rich, *Hitler's War Aims. Ideology, the Nazi State and the Course of Expansion.* [1975] (1992).
13) Jochen Thiess, *Hitler's 'Endziele': Zielloser Aktionismus, Kontinentalimperium oder Weltherrschaft?* in: Bracher/Funke/Jacobsen (Hg.), *Nationalsozialistische Diktatur 1933-1945. Eine Bilanz.* Schriftenreihe der Bundeszentrale für politische Bildung Band 192 (Bonn 1983).
14) Walter C. Langer, *The Mind of Adolf Hitler, the Secret Wartime Report* (1972)/ Dr Otto Strasser, incidentally, made further striking predictions about the future of Nazi Germany in *Kommt es zum krieg?*, a brochure against the Hitler regime published in Prague in 1937.
15) John Toland, *Hitler, het einde van een mythe* (1980) pp 415-442.
16) Wiegand's book, *Hitler Foresees His End* (1939) has since faded into the background. Nevertheless, the book still finds mention here and there. See, among others, Gerhard Schreiber, *Hitler Interpretationen 1923-1983* (1984) p 107.
17) Marcel van Hamersveld, Vreemde vrijspraak in showproces. *De Volkskrant* 9-9-1995. Review of Stephen Koch's book *Double Lives-Stalin, Willy Münzenberg and the Seduction of the Intellectuals.*
18) *Das Braune Netz,*(1935)/Albert Schreiner, *Hitler treibt zum Krieg* [Paris 1935]. Here used republication from Pahl-Rugenstein Verlag (Frankfurt am Main 1979).
19) *Das Braune Netz*, pp 5, 6.
20) *Das Braune Netz*, p 68.
21) Sebastian Haffner, Germany Jekyll&Hyde. 1939 - *Deutschland von innen betrachtet.* [1940] (Berlin 1996)/See also: Elke Schubert, *Ein Krieg gegen die Liebenden.* Jekyll&Hyde-Sebastian Haffner's Bericht über Deutschland im Jahre 1939. in: *Süddeutschen Zeitung* no. 280. 4-12-1996.
22) Frank H. Simonds, *Can Europe keep the peace?* (London 1932).
23) Fritz Sternberg, *Hoe lang kan Hitler oorlog voeren? Het lot van Duitsland in de volgende oorlog*(1939).
24) Eberhard Jäckel, *Hitler's Weltanschauung. Entwurf einer Herrschaft* [1969] (1983).
25) Walter Hofer, *The Unleashing of World War II* (1965)
26) Hermann Rauschning, *De nihilitische revolutie. Schijn er werkelijkheid in het Derde rijk* (1939).
27) Jäckel, pp 11-18.
28) Jäckel, pp 24-28.
29) John Lukacs, *Hitler, Geschichte und Geschichtsschreibung* (1997).
30) John Lukacs, p 243.

31) Jäckel p. 13/Christian Zentner, *Adolf Hitlers Mein Kampf. Eine kommentierte Auswahl* [1974] (1994)/Werner Maser, *Hitlers Mein Kampf* [1967](1998).
32) Gerhard Schreiber, *Hitler Interpretationen* pp 29, 30.
33) A.J.P. Taylor, *Europe, grandeur and decline* (1967) Taylor's dissenting view of Hitler and his foreign policy is best expressed in his *The Origins of the Second World War*, (London 1961).
34) M. Horthy, *Ein Leben für Ungarn* (1953).
35) Robert G.L. Waite, *Adolf Hitler als psychopaat* (1978) pp 34, 35/Jäckel p 127.
36) Waite, *Adolf Hitler* p 49.
37) Waite, *Adolf Hitler* p 91.
38) Adolf Hitler, *Mein Kampf* p 141.
39) *Mein Kampf* chapter 14 Band ii/Here it becomes clear that Nazi Germany followed a completely different 'Kriegsziel' policy than the empire. While the empire, on the one hand, was trapped in template-like military plans (Schlieffen), politics constantly reacted to changing situations and the first real programme did not emerge until September 1914 when the Battle of the Marne was in full swing. Political objectives were adjusted accordingly. Hitler defined his plans from the outset. For the war aims in imperial Germany, see, among others, Ernst W. Graf Lynar, *Deutsche Kriegsziele* 1914-1918 (1964), which deals extensively with the discussion around Fritz Fischer's *Griff nach der Weltmacht. Die Kriegszielpolitik des kaiserlichen Deutschland 1914/18* (1961). For the military-political relationship at the time of World War I see also: Martin Kitchen, Civil-Military Relations in Germany In: R.J.Q. Adams, *The Great War, 1914-18. Essays on the Military, Political and Social History of The First World War.* (1990) pp 39-68.
40) *Mein Kampf* pp 144-151.
41) *Mein Kampf* pp 154, 155.
42) *Quellen und Darstellungen zur Zeitgeschichte Band 7*, Gerhar L. Wein-berg, Hitlers Zweite Buch. Ein Dokument aus dem Jahr 1928 (1961).
43) Joachim von Ribbentrop, *Zwischen London und Moskou. Erinnerungen und letzte Aufzeichnungen. Aus dem Nachlass herausgegeben von Annelies von Ribbentrop.* (1953) p 43.
44) Gerhard L. Weinberg, *Hitlers Zweite Buch.* pp 80-84.
45) For a summary elaboration this policy see: Hans Adolf Jacobsen, *Nationalsozialistische Aussenpolitik 1933-1938* (1968) pp 391-445.
46) Waite, *Adolf Hitler* pp 94, 95.
47) James Joll, *Europe since 1870* (1973) pp 87-89.
48) The anecdote about the tsarina is taken from Friedrich Heer, *Gottes erste Liebe. 2000 Jahre Judentum und Christentum. Genesis des Österreichischen Katholiken Adolf Hitler.* (1968) (1976) p 371.
49) Lothar Gruchmann, Nationalsozialistische Grossraumordnung. Die Kon-

struktion einer 'deutschen Monroe-Doktrin'. In: *Schriftenreihe der Vierteljahrshefte für Zeitgeschichte* No 4, p 11.
50) Lothar Gruchmann, *Nationalsozialistische Grossraumordnung.* p 11.
51) Lothar Gruchmann, *Nationalsozialistische Grossraumordnung.* p 12.
52) On the historical interpretation of the term Reich see: Waldemar Besson (Hg.), *Das Fischer Lexikon Geschichte.* [1961] (1973) pp 303-308.
53) On the ability of peoples to reinterpret the past see Eric J. Hobsbawm, *Nationen und Nationalismus,* - after E. Renan, *Ou'est ce que c'est une nation?* (1882) - p 7. On current quest for national identity see: Gertjan Dijkink, 'Een nieuwe Europese deling? Duitsland en Rusland op zoek naar nationale identiteit'. *Internationale Spectator* June 1995.
54) Quoted from Bracher, *Wendezeiten der Geschichte.* p 203.
55) Andreas Hillgruber, Die Endlösung und das deutsche Ostimperium als Kernstück des Rassenideologischen Programms des Nationalsozialismus. In: *Vierteljahrsheft für Zeitgeschichte 1. Heft* (1973) pp 133-153.
56) Richard Walther Darré, Das Bauertum als Lebensquell der Nordische Rasse (1929)/*Schriftenreihe des Reichsausschusses für Volksgesundheitsdienst* Heft 13 Richard Walther Darré, *Blut und Boden. Eine Grundgedanke des Nationalsozialismus.*/Richard Walther Darré, *Nieuwe adel uit bloed en bodem* (1942) For an overview on the role Spengler and the relations between völkischen and Jungkonservativen see Jan Ipema, *In dienst van Leviathan. Ernst Jünger, tijd en werk 1895-1932* (1997) chapter 7/Over Hans Friedrich Karl Günther and his influence on Darré and a reference to the work of Otto Ammon - *Die natürliche Auslese bei Menschen* (1893) - and Georges Vacher de Lapouge, - L'Aryen, son role social (1899) - see Elvira Weisenburger, Hans Friedrich Karl Günther, *Professor für Rassenkunde,* In: Michael Kissener/Joachim Scholtyseck (hg.), *Die Führer der Provinz. NS-Biographien aus Baden und Württemberg. Karlsruher Beiträge zur Geschichte des Nationalsozialismus Band 2* (1997) pp 161-199.
57) Theodor Fritsch, *Handbuch der Judenfrage.* Faksimile-Dokumentation zur Morphologie und Geschichte des Nationalsozialismus 15. Reihe Band 1. [1933] (1991).
58) References to the important role of German urban planners in the East can be found in a large number of period documents. For example at: A. Schürmann, Festigung deutschen Volkstums in den eingegliederten Ostgebieten. in: Reich, *Volksordnung, Lebensraum. vi. Band* (1943).
59) On the Madagascar plan of Polish politicians see: Hans Jansen, het Madagascar plan. De voorgenomen deportatie van europese joden naar Madagascar (1996). On anti-Semitism in Hungary see: Perry Pierik, *Hongarije 1944-1945, de vergeten tragedie* (1995).
60) Corliss Lamont, *The Peoples of the Soviet Union* [1944] (1946) pp 82, 83/ On the 'Austromarxism' of Hitler's youth see: Gerhard Botz/ Ivar Oxaal/Michael

Pollak (hg.), *Eine zerstörte Kultur. Jüdisches Leben und Antisemitsmus in Wien seit dem 19. Jahrhunderts.* (1990) p 7.
61) Sonja Margolina, das Ende der Lügen. Russland und die Juden im 20. Jahrhunderts (1992) Selective quoting and thereby inadvertently leading the reader on the wrong track has happened to Margolina in: Georg Franz-Willing, *Weltherrschaft durch Umerziehung?* (1994)
62) Margolina p 33).
63) R.N. Coudenhove-Kalergi, *Judenhass von Heute.* (1935) p 16.
64) Margolina page 37.
65) Margolina pp 38, 39.
66) Margolina page 45.
67) Corliss Lamont pp 88, 89.
68) Margolina page 48/Perry Pierik, Joden in Rusland slachtoffer en dader. in: Utrechts Nieuwsblad 3-7-1992.
69) Margolina p 51.
70) The Protocols were introduced and translated into Germany by Nazi ideologue Alfred Rosenberg. This was done under the title: Alfred Rosenberg, *Die Protokolle der Weisen von Zion und die jüdische Weltpolitik* (1920). For a standard work on origins of the Protocols, see e.g. Norman Cohn, *Warrant for Genocide*, used here: *Die Protokolle der weissen von Zion. Der Mythus von der jüdischen Weltverschwörung.* (1969) See further also: Coudenhove-Kalegri, *Judenhass von Heute* pp 51-67/Bruno Naarden, The Protocols of the Elders of Zion, in: Z.R. Dittrich/B.Naarden/H.Renner, *Knoeien met het verleden* pp 111-126 Coudenhove-Kalegri and Naarden point out that the creator of the Protocols committed plagiarism and had borrowed texts from: *Dialogue aux Enfers entre Montesequieu et Machiavel (Dialogue in Hell between Montesequieu and Machiavelli* by Maurice Joly).
71) Pipes, *Russia under the Bolshevik Regime,* 98-103/Corliss Lamont p 85.
72) F.J. Los, *Rusland tussen Azië en Europa. Een geschiedkundige bijdrage tot de kennis van het bolsjewisme.*(Amsterdam 1943) chapter 16. The quote from Hitler can be found on page 369.
73) Der Nationalsozialistische Führungsoffizier, Farm, Kolchoze oder Erbhof? Schulungsthema Nr.11 Führungsunterlagen Folge 3, Nur für den Gebrauch innerhalb der Wehrmacht. (1944).
74) Hudal, *Die Grundlagen des Nationalsozialismus* (1937) pp 85, 86, 92
75) M. Alberton, *Birobidschan, die Judenrepublik* (Leipzig, Wien 1932).
76) Marvriks Vulfsons, Das Lettische Nationalgefühl und die Juden. In: *Zeitschrift für Geschichtswissenschaft* (1995).
77) Sven Hedin, *Duitschland en de wereldvrede* (1937) pp 268-279
78) Emil Franzel, *Das Reich der Braunen Jakobiner p* 24/Martin Hobeck, Der jüdische Anteil an der deutschen Geschichte pp 7-42 in: Alfred Gerstl/Ger-

hard Löwenthal/Marcel Prawy, *Juden und Deutsche: Vergangenheit und Zukunft* (1994) p 20.
79) Norman Cohn, *Warrant for Genocide*, used here: *Die Protokolle der weissen von Zion. Der Mythus von der jüdischen Weltverschwörung.* (1969).
80) Norman Cohn, *Die Protokolle*, Chapter 1: Die Ursprünge des Mythos pp 27-50/Daniel Jonah Goldhagen, *Hitlers gewillige beulen* (1996)/The volume of conspiracy books took on astronomical proportions. By 1923, the year of the Hitler-Ludendorff-Putsch, 40,000 publications about the how and why of Freemasonry were already known. Increasingly, these included the various scenarios of conspiracies attributed to Jews. An overview of the various conspiracy ideas can be distilled from Dr F. Wichtl, *Weltfreimaurerei, Weltrevolution, Weltrepublik. Eine Untersuchung über Ursprung und Endziele des Weltkrieges.* This book was published by the völkische publisher J.F. Lehmann and reached more than ten printings in a short time. An overview of all the accusations to which Jews were exposed can be found in Julius H.Schoeps/Joachim Schloer, *Antisemitismus, Vorurteile und Mythen.* (1995) The authors listed 24 prejudices. Remarkably, many angry conspiracy theories contradicted each other. For instance, an Austrian writing reported that mainly Protestant Germans were behind Freemasonry practices in their country, with the aim of detaching Catholic Vienna from Rome. And that while the German Kaiser, figurehead of Protestantism, was actually strongly anti-Masonic, to the point of obsession. See: Annuarius Osseg, *Der Hammer der Freimaurerei am Kaiserthrone der Habsburger.* (Amberg 1875). On the Kaiser's attitude towards the Freemasons, see e.g. Perry Pierik/Henk Pors, *De verlaten monarch* (typescript)/Thomas A. Kohut, *Wilhelm II and the Germans. A Study in Leadership.* (New York/Oxford 1991) Most recently, another study by Robert G.L. Waite, *Kaiser and Führer, A Comprarative Study of Personality and Politics* (1998) comparing Hitler's and the Kaiser's dislike of the freemasons. Above all, see Chapter 2, Weltanschauungen.
81) Coudenhove-Kalegri p 12/Der 'durchleuchtete' Paneuropa-Graf in: *Am heiligen Quell deutscher Kraft. Ludendorffs halbmonatschrift Folge 10* 11-08-1939. pp 429,430./Ger Harmsen, *Federalism in the service of American war mongers in Politics and Culture* (1950) p 167.
82) Pipes, *Russia* p 258).
83) Gunnar Heinsohn, *Warum Auschwitz? Hitlers Plan und die Ratlosigkeit der Nachwelt,* (1995) pp 213-215.
84) Emil Franzel pp 24, 32.
85) Robert Conquest, *The Great Terror. A Reassessment*/Robert Conquest, *The Harvest of Sorrow. Soviet Collectivisation and the* Terror-Famine/Marcel van Hamersveld/Michiel Klinkhamer, *Messianisme zonder mededogen. Het communisme, zijn daders en zijn slachtoffers* (1998).

86) K.I. Albrecht, *Der verratene Sozialismus. Zehn Jahre als hoher Staatsbeamter in der Sowjetunion.* (1941).
87) David Irving, *Goebbels, Macht und Magie* (Kiel 1997). From Irving's biography, Goebbels does not seem to have been so convinced of Nazism on the ideological plane and distanced himself from his more 'red thinking', but seems to have been influenced mainly by Hitler's personality. Opportunism also played a role in Goebbels' 'far-rightness' over the years. In addition, it is clear from the biography how deep the gulf was regularly between the SA from the 'red Berlin' and the völkische 'home base' in Munich, for example, and how both camps were plotting against each other.
88) Gunnar Heinsohn, *Warum Auschwitz?* pp 112-128.
89) Raul Hilberg, *Die Vernichtung der europäischen Juden* [1961] (1991)
90) Arno J. Mayer, *Why did Heavens not darken?*
91) See debate Broszat-Browning in response to Irving's thesis in the *Vierteljahrsheft für Zeitgeschichte*: Christopher R. Browning, *Zur Genesis der Endlösung. Eine Antwort an Martin Broszat.* In: *Vierteljahrsheft für Zeitgeschichte 2. Heft* (1981) Browning's most important work on the holocaust is *Ordinary Men*, published in Dutch under the title *doodgewone mannen* (1993). David Irving's theory of the holocaust, like Nolte's view, is under constant 'construction'. The revisionist nature of his theses seems to have waned somewhat since the mid-1990s, possibly under heavy international pressure - which he reports on the internet in the so-called 'Actions Reports'. In an interview with Ron Casey (Canada) in July 1995, Irving opined that the Holocaust had claimed at least four million victims. The discussion around Nolte has meanwhile resumed after publication of his book *Historische Existenz. Zwischen Anfang und Ende der Geschichte?* which was published by Piper-Verlag and immediately met with critical reactions. See, among others, Micha Brumlik, Eine Apologie des Antisemitismus. Ernst Noltes jüngstes Buch in: *Neue Zürcher Zeitung* 6-10-1998.
92) Daniel Gerson, Der Jude als Bolschewist. Die Wiederbelebung eines Stereotyps. In: *Wolfgang Benz (Hg.), Antisemitismus in Deutschland. Zur Aktualität eines Vorurteils.* (1995) pp 157-180. The fear of revival of old stereotypes is not entirely imaginary. On this, see for example the rising anti-Semitism in Eastern Europe in Theodore Friedgut, *Antisemitism and Its Opponents in the Russian Press: From Perestroika until the present* (1994)/Leon Volovici, *Antsemitism in Post-Communist Eastern Europe: A Marginal or Central Issue?* (1994).
93) We find one of the most important proofs of this in the work of Hungarian historian Dr Albert Váry, who calculated that of the 45 Council Commissioners of the Bela Kun era, 31 were Jewish. Of Kun's hard core of 10 collaborators, eight had a Jewish ethnic background. Albert Váry, *A Vörös uralom áldozatai magyarszágon* (1993) p 172.

94) Richard Pipes, (ed.) *The Unknown Lenin. From the Secret Archive.* (1996).
95) Richard Pipes, *The Unknown Lenin.* p 10.
96) Arkady Vaksberg, *Stalin against the Jews.* (1984) chapters 1 and 2/The 1882 Solymosi case suddenly became topical again in 1934 when the diaries of investigating judge Dr Josef Bary and Hungarian Minister of Justice Theodor Pauler showed that they took ritual murder seriously. The heavily anti-Semitic *Weltdienst* published a special theme issue around the case. In: Weltdienst no.I./13 1-6-1934.
97) Sebastian Haffner, *Het duivelspact. De Duits-Russische betrekkingen van de Eerste tot de Tweede wereldoorlog.* Chapter 1 pp 7-22 and Sebastian Haffner, *Die sieben Todsünden des Deutschen Reiches im Ersten Weltkrieg,* chapter 5.
98) Frank Golczewski, *Das Deutschlandbild der Polen 1918-1939.* Eine Untersuchung der Historiographie und der Publizistik. Geschichteliche Studien zu Politik und Gesellschaft. (1974) pp 276, 278, 279, 281.
99) A clear proof of this is the fact that the crimes committed by the Germans against the Jews in World War II were systematically stripped of their Jewish facet by the communist authorities. The Babi Yar murders were 'not a murder of Jews, but a murder of Soviet citizens'. In a ravine near Babi Yar, near Kiev, the German 'Einsatzgruppen' murdered tens of thousands of Jews. See: Arno J. Mayer, *Why Did The Heavens Not Darken? The Final Solution in History.* p 268. Margolina discusses the lie of Babi Yar on pages 87-93. On the 'double role' of Jews in Central Europe see also Tibor Kovács in *Het drama Hongarije.* He draws the 'victim-perpetrator' parallel to the postwar era: 'It is obvious that the Russians initially trusted only the Jews'. p 22.
100) On appropriation by others of the suffering of Auschwitz see Marcel Reijmerink, Auschwitz is van de joden, niet van de Polen. In: *Algemeen Dagblad* 26-1-1995.
101) Gunnar Heinsohn, p 120.
102) Hans Herzfeld, *Die Weimarer Republik* (1966) pp 14, 15.
103) Allgemeine Richtlinien für die politische und wirtschaftliche Verwaltung der besetzten Ostgebiete in: *Schriftenreihe der Vierteljahrshefte für Zeitgeschichte Heft 1* (1977), pp 257-261.
104) Allgemeine Richtlinien, pp 257-261.
105) Allgemeine Richtlinien, pp 257-261/For the Finnish-Russian war see, among others, Allan Landstroem, *Krieg unter der Mitternachtssonne. Finnlands Freiheitskampf 1939-1945* (1989) (1996)/For the operation of the Soviet army against the Kwangtung army see, among others, Marschall Schukow, *Erinnerungen und Gedanken.* (Stuttgart 1969)/ *The Oxford Companion to the Second World War* estimates Soviet losses at at least 200,000 men (p 375), other sources, such as Khrushchev, speak of much greater losses. see: *Chrus-*

chtschow erinnert sich. *Die authentische Memoiren*. (1970) (1991) p 148 et seq. Khrushchev, in his memoirs, shares the view that the Red Army's weak performance against Finland strengthened the Germans' belief that Operation 'Barbarossa' would be a success.

106) On this bloody collaboration see, among others: B.F. Sabrin (ed.), *Alliance for Murder. The Nazi-Ukrain Nationalist Partnership in Genocide* (1991). Shocking examples can also be found in: Christopher Browning, *Deathly Men* (1993)/Wolfgang Benz (hg.), *Dimension des* Völkermords/Ernst Klee/Willi Dressen (hg.), *'Gott mit uns', Der deutsche Vernichtungskrieg im Osten 1939-1945*. (1991).

107) See reports xxx.corps, 11 army (02.08.1941), report of the Armeeoberkommando 6 August 1941 and many others, including in: Ernst Klee/Willi Dressen (Hg.), 'Gott mit uns', pp 101-116: *'Juden die Hauptträger des Bolschewismus'*.

108) Walter Hofer, *De ontketening van de Tweede Wereldoorlog*, (Utrecht 1965) cited in: Karl Bracher, *Wendezeiten der Geschichte*, p 203.

109) Daniel Jonah Goldhagen, Hitler's Willing Executioners, used here: Hitlers gewillige beulen (1996).

110) Such discussions will always persist. Recently, for instance, a pamphlet by Michal Bodemanns was published, again presenting a very different sound from Goldhagen. In his view, the Holocaust idea is literally 'dead-remembered' and misused for all kinds of political purposes. Instead, the Germans burden themselves with guilt in order to 'get out from under the guilt'. This is in contrast to Goldhagen who does not consider the 'Vergangenheitsbewältigung' sufficient. See: Alphons Silbermann, Erinnern heisst vergessen. Michal Bodemann's Pamphlet gegen die Vergangenheitsbewältigung in the *Frankfurter Allgemeine Zeitung* 09-07-1996. On the Goldhagen debate, see also, among others, Johannes Heil/Rainer Erb, *Geschichtswissenschaft und Oeffentlichkeit. Der Streit um Daniel J.Goldhagen*. (1998).

Chapter 2

THE SCHREIBTISCH CONQUERORS

1) Hans Grimm, *Volk ohne Raum* (1932)/For the life of Konrad Meyer see Mechtild Rössler/Sabine Schleiermacher (hg.), *Der Generalplan Ost. Hauptlinien der nationalsozialistischen Planungs- und Vernichtungspolitik*. (1993) pp 8, 9.

2) Hans-Adolf Jacobsen, *Karl Haushofer, Leben und Werk. Band I Lebensweg*

1869-1946 und ausgewählte Texte zur Geopolitik. (1979) p 777/Grimm's enormous tome received positive reviews from the National Socialists. Despite this, Grimm never became a member of the NSDAP, much to the annoyance of the Nazis who, however, did not act against him because of his status. After the war, a debate raged about how wrong Grimm had been. Hans Sarkowicz called him an anti-Semite but believed that he had not been an advocate of the Holocaust. The very German-critic Erich Kuby believed that Grimm was among the 'vilest' the German 'Ungeist' had produced. Others saw in Grimm's work more general sentiments that had nothing to do with the Nazis. Thereby, Grimm did not receive any cultural or literary prizes during the Third Reich. Grimm made an unsuccessful attempt to re-establish himself as an author after World War II. He died in 1959. For the life of Grimm and his relations to the Third Reich see: Hans Sarkowicz, Zwischen Sympathie und Apologie: Der Schriftsteller Hans Grimm und sein Verhältnis zum Nationalsozialismus in: Karl Corino, *Intellektuelle in Bann des Nationalsozialismus.* pp 120-135 (1980).

3) G. Bakker, *Duitse geopolitiek 1919-1945.* pp 2, 3, 129, 130/Karl Haushofer et al, *Bausteine zur Geopolitik* (1928)/Kruck, *Geschichte des Alldeutschen Verbandes 1890-1939.* p 33.

4) Karl Haushofer, *Weltmeere und Weltmächte* [1937] (1941)

5) Friedrich Paul Heller/Anton Maegerle, *Thule. Vom völkischen Okkultismus bis zur Neuen Rechten.*(1995)pp 42-48/H.A. Jacobsen Band I p 4/Bakker, German Geopolitics p 2/Trevor Ravenscroft, *The Spear of Destiny* [1973] (1995) chapter *19/Das braune Netz,* pp 33-39 (1931)/Rudolf Jordan, *Erlebt und Erlitten* (1971) p 213./Lately, a multitude of articles and essays of a highly speculative nature have appeared on the internet outlining Haushofer as the 'evil magician'. See, among others, Servando Gonzáles, *The Swastika and the Nazis.*

6) Gustavo Corni/Horst Gies, *Brot, Butter, Kanonen. Die Ernährungswirtschaft in Deutschland unter der Diktatur Hitlers.* (Berlin 1997) pp 400-402/Hermann Reichsle, *Kann man Deutschland verhungern?* (Berlin 1940) p 33.

7) Bakker p 39/Wolfgang Schwanitz (Hg.), *Jenseits der Legenden. Araber, Juden, Deutsche* (1994) p 97. A Dutch period paper that writes very positively, even admiringly about Rudolf Kjellén is J.G. Loohuis, *Mensch en mogendheid, een probleem van alle tijden* (1944).

8) Joachim Petersen, *Hitlers Polar-Eisenbahnpläne 1940 bis 1945 in Nordnorwegen* (1992). Even today, Iraq and Baghdad still play a role as strategic trump cards. Vladimir Zhirinovsky called Iraq Moscow's most important forward post in the Middle East. Russia's far-reaching diplomatic meddling to prevent the Gulf War confirms that he is not the only one who thinks so in the Kremlin.

9) George Mikes, *Any Souvenirs? A Native Returns to Central Europe and a Second Expulsion* (1972).

10) Hugh Seton-Watson, What is Europe. Where is Europe? From Mystique to Politique in: George Schöpflin (ed), *In Search of Central Europe* (1989).
11) Hans-Peter Burmeister, Möglichkeitssinn und Wertezerfall - Mitteleuropa als deutsche Frage In: *Amsterdam Studies in Cultural Identity volume 3/Hans Ester/ Hans Hecker/Erika Poettgens* (Hg.), Deutschland, aber wo liegt es? *Deutschland und Mitteleuropa. Analysen und Historischen Dokumente.*/Karl Schlögel points to the 'arrogance' embedded in the word Central Europe: 'Das Wort Miteleuropa lässt sich kaum ohne ein gewisses Pathos aussprechen, vielleicht ist es sogar Arrogant, indem es anderen einen Platz an der Peripherie zuweist'. In: *Amsterdam Studies in Cultural Identity* quoted from: Karl Schlössel, *Die Mitte liegt ostwärts* p 11/Hans Ester, *Mitteleuropa und Deutschland*. Einführung in die Problematik, In: Amsterdam Studies *in Cultural Identity* pp 3-12. Others believed that this conceptualisation was a necessary evil to provide a certain counterbalance to the influential West (and East). To some extent, the discussion on Central Europe still continues. For very specific explanations, see, for example, Akos Nagy, *A Cultural and Historical Review of Central Europe* (1995).
12) Hans Hecker, 'Mitteleuropa' aus historischer Sicht. pp 25-55 in: *Amsterdam Studies in Cultural Identity* p 26.
13) Hans Ester, p6.
14) Bakker, pp 40-45, 72-78.
15) Macintyre, *Vergeten vaderland. Op zoek naar het fascistisch paradijs van Elisabeth Nietzsche* (1994).
16) Haushofer, *Weltmeere und Weltmächte.* (1941).
17) On this, see e.g. John M. Steiner, Über das Glaubensbekenntnis der SS, in: *Schriftenreihe der Bundeszentrale für politische Bildung Band 192*, Bracher/Funke/Jacobsen (Hg.), *Nationalsozialistische Diktatur 1933-1945. Eine Bilanz* (Bonn 1983) pp 206-223)/Self-purification by violence took extreme forms with Hitler. About his political soldiers, the Waffen-ss, he once said that, as far as he was concerned, 'the losses could not be great enough', G.H. Stein, *Geschichte der Waffen-ss* [1966] (1978)/The historian Sebastian Haffner, in his Hitler biography, goes so far as to attribute Hitler's self-purification to the extent of a deliberate and intended self-destruction of Germany. Haffner allows this moment to begin in December 1941, when Hitler, after failing in the battle for Moscow, declared war on the USA and set the holocaust in motion. Others see the 'Nero order' in 1945 - the deliberate destruction of Germany - as the start of this process.
18) Rudolf Kjellén/Karl Haushofer, *Die Grossmächte vor und nach dem Weltkriege.* (1930).
19) Rudolf Kjellén, *Der Staat als Lebensform.* (1917).
20) Karl Haushofer, *Der Kontinentalblock.* (1941).
21) H.A .Jacobsen *Band i* p 278.

22) Karl Haushofer, *Weltmeere und Weltmächte* (1941)/It was a wild time in terms of plans relating to space and technology. Another typical example of this zeitgeist is found in H. Soergel, *Atlantropa* (Munich 1932), which sought a political and economic synthesis between large parts of Western and Eastern Europe as well as the Middle East and North Africa.
23) Ernst Hanfstaengl, Zwischen Weissen und Braunem Haus. *Erinnerungen eines politischen Aussenseiters.* (1970) p 93.
24) Irving, Hess. *The Missing Years 1941-1945* (1987) pp 22, 23. Haushofer's eight visits to the prison are recorded in the prison register.
25) John Toland, Adolf Hitler pp 207, 213.
26) H.A. Jacobsen, Karl Haushofer, *Leben und Werk Band II Ausgewählter Schriftwechsel 1917-1946* (1979) pp 568, 569.
27) H.A. Jacobsen Band II pp 568, 569.
28) Werner Maser, *Hitler, legende, mythe, werkelijkheid* p 240/From various quarters during the time of the Third Reich, Hitler was praised for his knowledge of *Vom Kriege*. The German general von Metzsch wrote in 1937: 'Germany has two great sons: Clausewitz and Hitler.' See: Metzsch, Clausewitz Katechismus (1937)/Norbert Krüger examined Clausewitz's real impact on Hitler in the *Wehrwissenschaftliche Rundschau* in 1968 and concluded that there was no real study. In Hitler's private library was a short summary of *Vom Kriege*. Clausewitz does not appear in Hitler's table talk or *Mein Kampf*. See: Norbert Krüger, *Adolf Hitler's Clausewitzkenntnis, Wehrwissenschaftliche Rundschau no.18* (1968)
29) H.A. Jacobsen *Band ii* p 569.
30) H.A. Jacobsen *Band ii* p 412/Bakker p 4. Harsh criticism of Haushofer also came from *Reader's Digest* which, in a special issue, scrutinised Haushofer's Munich geopolitical institute and its '1,000 staff' (in reality about 80 staff). The magazine concluded in 1941 that Haushofer's institute had 'whispered' Hitler's ideas. In March 1941, an article appeared in the *Atlantic Monthly* with the telling title 'paving the way for Hitler' in which Haushofer and bestseller Hans Grimm were mentioned in the same breath. These noises were also heard in German media from time to time. *Die Neue Weltbühne* wrote in 1940 that Hitler was 'following Haushofer's programme'.
31) Baker, p 5.
32) Irving, *Hess* p 32.
33) H.A.Jacobsen, *Band i*, pp 35, 36.
34) H.A.Jacobsen, *Band i*, pp 41-42.
35) L.P. Lochner, (Ed.), *The Goebbels Diaries 1942-1943*. (1948) p 85.
36) H.A.Jacobsen *Band* i, pp 414, 427.
37) W. von Goldenbach/H.R. Minow, *Deutschtum erwache. Aus dem Innenleben des staatlichen Pangermanismus* (1994) pp 41, 45-47.

38) Prof Dr P.Geyl, German and Italian figures. (1969) pp 50-56.
39) H.A. Jacobsen, *Band i* page ix/Brzezinski was the first Pole in a hundred years to be in such an important position that he could take revenge on the Soviets, Utrecht-based Americanist Dr Maarten van Rossem opined in his *Amerika, het land van de begrensde mogelijkheden*. This position of power and Brzezinski's geopolitical obsession led to dangerous secret military adventures on many continents.
40) H.A.Jacobsen, Band I p IX./A current standard work on the subject of geopolitics is *Political Geography, World-Economy, Nation-State and Locality* by Peter J. Taylor. [1985] (1996).
41) A.E. Zucker, *Deutschlands vergessene Freiheit. Eine Anthologie deutscher freiheitlicher Schriften von Luther bis zur Gegenwart* (1948) p 296.
42) Dr Henry Picker, *Hitlers Tischgespräche im Führerhauptquartier* pp 113, 245.
43) Raymond Aron, Frieden und Krieg p 230.
44) Martin Ros, *Jakhalzen van het Derde Rijk. Ondergang van de collabo's 1944-1945* (1995) pp 205-245.
45) Perry Pierik, *Hongarije 1944-1945, de vergeten tragedie* pp 247, 248/Viktor Reimann, *Goebbels* (1971) pp 303-305/Sepp Dietrich, the commander of the 6.ss Armoured Army was deeply offended and ignored it. Goebbels too joined in the adulation of Frederick the Great. 'We must be like Frederick the Great' he mused, 'and behave accordingly'. In the final days of the Third Reich, the propaganda minister drew hope from the fact that the Prussian hacking legend had time and again managed to extricate himself from hopeless geopolitical situations. With eagerness, he read what the Scot Thomas Carlyle, a Germany adept, had written about Frederick the Great. Carlyle, who called himself an 'auroch from the Teutonic forests' created a spirited cult of heroes around the Prussian monarch and called Frederick the Great a bearer of world-historical duties. Carlyle belonged in the ranks of boundless British admirers of Germany, as did Houston Stewart Chamberlain, who dwelt on Wagner and Goethe and predicted a great future for the German people. Goebbels had also studied the Punic Wars between Rome and Carthage, hoping for fruitful lessons.
46) Kurt Pastenaci, *From Jutland to Byzantium* (1943) pp 87, 88.
47) Raymond Aron, *Frieden und Krieg*, p 234.
48) Raymond Aron, *Frieden und Krieg*, p 234.
49) *Das Braune Netz*, p 12.
50) Wolfgang Sofsky, *Der Ordnung des Terrors. Das Konzentrationslager* (1993).
51) In this, see already Langer's secret OSS report on Hitler in Chapter 1.
52) William L. Shirer, *The Rise and Fall of the Third Reich. A History of Nazi Germany*. [1959] (1973) pp 1091, 1092.

Chapter 3

REICH AND ROMANCE

1) Christoph Prignitz, *Vaterlandsliebe und Freiheit. Deutscher Patriotismus von 1750 bis 1850* p 96/Andreas Molau, *Das politische Vermächtnis der* Romantik/ Andrzej Madela, *Volk ohne Raum*, Übergangsmomente von Volks in völkische Literatur in: Wir selbst, Zeitschrift für nationale Identität. Heimat, identität braucht Raum und Geschichte. Territorialer Imperativ oder Traum vom grenzenlosen Geisterreich. 1/1990).
2) A. Labrie, *Het verlangen naar zuiverheid. Een essay over Duitsland* (1994) p 27.
3) Wolfram Steinbeck, *Johann Gottlieb Fichte, Weltanschauung. Sein kampf um die Freiheit in einer Auswahl aus seinen Schriften* (1941).
4) Paul Nolte in '*1900: Das Ende des 19. und Beginn des 20. Jahrhunderts in sozialgeschichtlicher Perspektive points* to Georg Simmel's study: *Die Grossstädte und das Geistesleben* (1903) in: *Geschichte in Wissenschaft und Unterricht* (5-6-1996).
5) Hans Ulrich Thamer, *Verführung und Gewalt, Deutschland 1933-1945. Die Deutschen und Ihre Nation*. Leon Poliakov, *De arische mythe* [1971] (1977)
6) For an introduction to völkische thought, see George L. Mosse, *The Crisis of German Ideology. Intellectual Origins of the Third Reich*. London 1964 pp 13-126/Ea survey of völkische literature can be found in Uwe-K. Ketelsen, *völkisch-nationale und nationalsozialistische Literatur in Deutschland 1890-1945. Sammlung Metzler Band 142* (1976)/For detailed information on Julius Langbehn see Benedikt Momme Nissen, *Der Rembrandtdeutsche, Julius Langbehn*. (1937). Here used pp 14, 19, 71, 76, 137, 139, 179. It is notable that Langbehn also sought his 'organic paradise' outside German territory -as the reference to Rembrandt also indicates- and in his search for the 'supreme purity' attributed an important role to the Frisians (see also the völkische onderzoeker Los). His anti-Semitism was directed above all against the Ostjuden and less against the older (Portuguese) Jews already present in Germany for some time.
7) Alfred Rosenberg, *Der Mythus des 20. Jahrhunderts. Eine Wertung der seelisch-geistigen Gestaltenkämpfe unserer Zeit* [1930] (1936), introduction/That Rosenberg was the main spokesman of the radical völkisch/ariosophical camp is emphasised by G. van den Burg in *Het Nationaal Socialisme* (1940) p 70 in which Rosenberg is called the 'geistige Generalstabschef' der NSDAP.
8) Walter Laqueur, *Weimar, die Kultur der Republik* [1974] (1976) p 116.
9) J. de Kadt, *De gang der geschiedenis, De stem* (1939) quoted from: *De deftigheid in het gedrang. Een keuze uit zijn verspreide geschriften*. (1991) p 158.

10) Wilhelm Reich, *Die Massen-psychologie des Faschismus* [1933] (1977).
11) Altsächsicher Bardenchor, in: *Odal, Monatschrift für Blut und Boden*, Ostermond 1935, p 779.
12) AO-series *Geboeid door verdwenen landen*. No. 2472 18-6-1973. The name Thule could possibly derive from Thilensel or Thyland, as the Shetland Islands are sometimes called. It is also possible that Thule stands for Turf Island. The latest research indicates that Thule would have been located in central Norway.
13) Rosenberg, *Der Mythus* pp 23-27.
14) Herbert von Hintzenstern, *H.St.Chamberlain. Darstellung des Urchristentums.* (1941) p 65.
15) Dr Georg Traue, *Aryan Gott-Zertrümmerung. Wider falsche Propheten im neuen Deutschland* (1934) pp 108-109.
16) Dr Henry Picker, *Hitlers Tischgespräche* [1976] (1983) p 80.
17) Poliakov, pp 92-94.
18) Rosenberg, *Der Mythus* p 28.
19) Hans Joachim Störing, *Geschiedenis van de filosofie. Deel-1* (1971) pp 28-35.
20) Rosenberg, *Der Mythus* p 30
21) On the swastika and its history see Malcolm Quinn, *The Swastika. Constructing the Symbol* (1994)/Wilhelm Scheuermann, *Woher kommt das Hakenkreuz*. (1933). In the origin and spread of the swastika, Kaiser Wilhelm II also took great interest. During his archaeological research in Greece after World War I, he carefully investigated the appearance of the swastika on the island of Corfu. For this, see, among other things, notes in the museum of the Royal Military Police in Buren: *Über den Ursprung des Sonnensymbols* (Ostern 1925) and written response by Freiherr von Duhn 22 March 1925. These notes can be found in the collection of Marius Cornelis van Houten, the military police officer responsible for Kaiser Wilhelm II's security during his stay at Doorn. For background information in this see H. Pors, *Marius Cornelis van Houten. Marechaussee par excellence*. Museum brochure no. *4* (1994).
22) See chapter 'Die magische Weltauffassung' in *Alfred Rosenberg, An die Dunkelmänner unserer Zeit. Eine Antwort auf die Angriffe gegen den 'Mythus des 20. Jahrhunderts'* (1935) pp 50-55.
23) Rosenberg, *Der Mythus* preface 3. Auflage.
24) Rosenberg, *Der Mythus* pp 641, 642.
25) Georg Lukács, *Von Nietzsche zu Hitler* [1962] (1966) p 217/For Georg Schott's statement see: dr G.van den Burg, *Het Nationaal-Socialisme* (1940) p 68.
26) H.St. Chamberlain, *Die Grundlagen des xix. Jahrhunderts i. Band ii. Band.* [1894] (1932).
27) Chamberlain, see main chapter 'Der Eintritt der Juden in die abendländischen Geschichte' *Band 1* pp 353-504.
28) R.N. Coudenhove-Kalergi, *Judenhass von Heute*. (1935) p 11.

29) Chamberlain, *Die Grundlagen/Günter Hartung, Goethe und die Juden* in: *Weimarer Beiträge*. Zeitschrift für Literaturwissenschaft Aesthetik und Kulturwissenschaften no.1 (1994) pp 398-416.
30) Hermann Kurzke/Stephan Stachorski (Hg.), *Thomas Mann Essays. Band 5: Deutschland und die Deutschen 1938-1945*. Cited from: *Zu Wagners Verteidigung* [1939] (1996) p 75/About the relationship Wilhelm II and Chamberlain see Hans Rall, *Wilhelm II. Eine Biogaphie* (1995) pp 239-241.
31) A. Labrie, *Het verlangen naar zuiverheid* pp 25-26.
32) Berndt W. Wesseling, (Hg.) *Bayreuth im Dritten Reich. Richards Wagner's politische Erben. Eine Dokumentation*. (1983) 86-90, 95, 105, 107/Heinz Linge, *In the footsteps of the Führer* (1985) p 62. For further information on Dinter and Kühn see Geoffrey G. Field, *Evangelist of Race. The Germanic Vision of Houston Stewart Chamberlain* (1981) pp 400-405/Artur Dinter, *Die Sünde wider das Blut*. (1919) afterword/Theodor Fritsch, *Handbuch der Judenfrage* [1933] (1991) p 541/For opposition by contemporaries to Dinter see Dr Hermann L.Strack, *Jüdische Geheimgesetze?* (Berlin 1925) pp 26-32.
33) S. Kuusisto, Alfred Rosenberg in *der nationalsozialistischen Aussenpolitik 1933-1939 Studia Historica 15* pp 79, 80/Not only the Nazis made use of Ropps knowledge of German and British politics. Even MI6, the British intelligence service, used Ropp's German connection to learn more about the build-up of the German armed forces, above all that of the air force. For a detailed account of this see: F.W. Winterbotham, *De nazi connectie. Belevenissen van een meesterspion in Hitler-Duitsland*. [1978] (1979).
34) Von Neurath eventually lost his job because of his cautious opposition to the Nazis. For the life history of Konstantin Freiherr von Neurath, see Frank Raberg, *Konstantin Freiherr von Neurath, Aussenminister des Deutschen Reiches* (1932-1938) in Michael Kissener/Joachim Scholtyseck (hg.), *Die Führer der Provinz. ns-Biographien aus Baden und Württemberg. Karlsruher Beiträge zur Geschichte des Nationalsozialismus Band 2* (1997) pp 503-538. We find another example of these struggles in Rudolf Rahn's memoirs, *Ruheloses Leben. Aufzeichnungen und Erinnerungen* (1949).
35) For full title details, see bibliography at the back of the book.
36) Werner Maser, *Hitler, legende, mythe, werkelijkheid* [1973] (1975) p 182.
37) Kuusisto, pp 28, 29/For the international dissemination of the protocols, see Norman Cohn, chapter 11.
38) Elke Suhr, *Carl von Ossietzky. Pazifist, Republikaner und Widerstandskämpfer* [1988] (1989) p 226.
39) David Irving, *Goebbels, Macht und Magie* (1996) p 197.
40) Werner Maser, *Hitler, legende, mythe, werkelijkheid* pp 208, 209.
41) William Carr, *Hitler a Study in Personality and Politics*. (1978) p 127

42) Bruno Naarden, *The Mirror of the Barbarians. Socialist Europe and revolutionary Russia 1848-1923* (1986) pp 7-9, 22, 23.
43) Werner Maser, *Hitler* pp 208, 209.
44) Richard Pipes, *The Unknown Lenin.*
45) Kuusisto p 13/Andreas Molau, Alfred Rosenberg, *Der Ideologe des Nationalsozialismus. Eine politische Biografie* (1993) pp 62, 63/J.&S. Pool, *Who financed Hitler? The Secret Funding of Hitler's Rise to Power 1919-1933* [1978] (1979) pp 54-56/Ernst Nolte, *Der Europäische Bürgerkrieg 1917-1945* p 114/Erich Ludendorff, *Auf dem Weg zur Feldherrnhalle. Lebenserinnerungen an die Zeit des 9-11-1923 mit Dokumenten in 5 Anlagen* (1937).
46) Thomas Urban, Schreiben und Spitzeln. Die Russische Emigranten in Deutschland, 1918 bis 1941 in *Süddeutsche Zeitung* 3-4-1996.
47) Trevor Ravenscroft, *The Spear of Destiny* [1973] (1995) p 91.
48) Robert G.L.Waite and note 56. It is interesting to note that Waite sees Eckart as one of the most important intellectuals of southern Germany but that he believes that one should not exaggerate his influence on Hitler.
49) Ernst Hanfstaengl, *Zwischen weissem und braunem Haus. Erinnerungen eines politischen Aussenseiters.* (1970) p 50.
50) Heinrich Hoffmann, *Hitler, wie ich Ihn sah* (1974) p 20.
51) Wilhelm Grün, *Dietrich Eckart als Publizist.* (1939) pp 7, 8.
52) John Toland, *Adolf Hitler* p 92, 93/James/Suzanne Pool, *Wie financierde Hitler?* (1979) p 25.
53) Andreas Molau, p 62/Trevor Ravenscroft, *The Spear of Destiny* pp 103, 105.
54) Toland, pp 92, 93, 98, 114-123.
55) Dietrich Eckart, *Bolshevism from Moses to Lenin.* (1924).
56) Eckart, pages 2-24/Waite page 135 Waite believes that the booklet has little to do with Bolshevism. Here, Waite misses the continuity idea which portrays 'Jewish Bolshevism' as an eternal hereditary enemy, as the title of the pamphlet also indicates.
57) Eckart, pp 22-24.
58) H.P. Blavatsky, *The Secret Doctrine* (1888).
59) Opitz, p 42.
60) Thule pp 48, 49, 173/Hans-Günter Richardi, *Hitler und seine Hintermänner. Neue Fakten zur Frühgeschichte der NSDAP* p 38/Opitz, p 43/Harry Count Kessler, *Walther Rathenau.*(1939)pp 376-393/Walther Rathenau, *Von Kommenden Dingen.*(1917)/- *Der Kaiser, Eine Betrachtung,* (Berlin 1919)/Jan Ipema, *In the service of Leviathan. Ernst Jünger, tijd en werk 1895-1932.* (1997) pp 88-90/Kessler mentions the number of 300 political murders, Ipema 350./ Recently, another thorough study of the attack on Rathenau appeared: Martin Sabrow, *Die verdrängte Verschwörung. Der Rathenau-Mord und die deutsche Gegenrevolution.* (1999).

61) Jacob Slavenburg, *H.P.Blavatsky, de theosofie en de meesters* p 13.
62) René Zwaap, *De keizer van Atlantis*. In: *De Groene Amsterdammer*, 26-4-1995.
63) H.P. Blavatsky, *De geheime leer. De synthese van wetenschap, religie en filosofie.* Two volumes [1888] (1988)/H.P. Blavatsky, *Isis entschleiert. Ein Meisterschlüssel zu den Geheimnissen alter und neuer Wissenschaft und Theologie.* Two volumes [1877].
64) Jacob Slavenburg, H.P. Blavatsky. *De theosofie en de meesters* (1991).
65) R. Zwaap, *De keizer van Atlantis/Theosofische perspectieven*, Ronden & rassen. Onze goddelijke afkomst en bestemming. Freely adapted from Getrude W. van Pelt. (1986)/G. de Purucker, *Occulte woordentolk. Het handboek van oosterse en theosofische termen* (1981).
66) Leon Poliakov, pp 18, 110.
67) L. Lewin, *Wenen, de wereldhoofdstad van het vergeten, herdenkt Theodor Herzl.* NRC-Handelsblad 13-04-1996.
68) Wilfried Daim, *Der Mann der Hitler die Ideen gab. Jörg Lanz von Liebenfels*, introduction to the 1985 edition of the book.
69) Wilfried Daim, *Der Mann der Hitler die Ideen gab. Jörg Lanz von Liebenfels* [1985] (1994).
70) R. Zwaap, *De keizer van Atlantis*/For a brief table of contents of the various Ostara issues see: Friedrich Heer, *Der Glaube des Adolf Hitler. Anatomie einer politischen Religiosität* (1968) pp 49, 709-718/Daim, pp 313-330. A total inventory as well as a short but reliable biography of Lanz von Liebenfels can be found in Ekkehard Hieronimus, *Lanz von Liebenfels, eine Bibliographie/ Toppenstedter Reihe no 11.*
71) Ekkehard Hieronimus, *Lanz von Liebenfels, eine Bibliographie. Toppenstedter Reihe no 11.*
72) Daim (1985) p 210.
73) For Lanz von Liebenfels' place in 'German biology' see: Anna Bäumer, *ns-Biologie. Edition Universitas* (1990).
74) See the Dutch-language edition of the 1925 Queenshal lectures in London by Dr Annie Besant, president of the Theosophical movement: *De wereldproblemen van dezen tijd.*
75) Poliakov, p 113/The (re)introduction of Ostara, incidentally, went back much further than Lanz von Liebenfels or Rosenberg. It was Philipp Clüver (1580-1622) who rediscovered the ancient Germanic gods when studying Scandinavian chronicles. Born in Gdansk, Clüver was studying at the time in Leiden, the intellectual heart of northern Europe, where he would later teach. His passion for Ostara, Wodan and Freya caused an upsurge in interest in the contents of the ancient chronicles that theosophists, anthroposophists and ariosophists picked up on.
76) George L. Mosse, *Intellectual Origins of the Third Reich.* (1966) p 14.

77) Heller/Maegerle, *Thule* pp 30-33/Emil Franzel, p 29.
78) Toland, p 102.
79) Toland, pp 103, 104.
80) Daim, pp 20, 21, 137/Rudolf J. Mund, *Jörg Lanz von Liebenfels und der Neue templer Orden. Die Esoterik des Christentums,* (1976) p 13/Charles Bracelen Flood, *Hitler the Path to Power* (1989) p 237. According to Amsterdam-based ariosophy scholar Jan Willem de Groot, Mund was the last leader of the ont.
81) Goodrick-Clark, *The Occult Roots of Nazism. Secret Aryan Cults and Their Influence on Nazi Ideology. The Ariosophists of Austria and Germany, 1890-1935* [1985] (1992) p 195/Helga Grebing, *Der Nationalsozialismus. Ursprung und Wesen.* [1959] (1964) pp 24, 25.
82) William Carr, *Hitler, a Study in Personality and Politics* (1978) p 119/See also Gideon Hausner, *Die Vernichtung der Juden. Das grösste Verbrechen der Geschichte.* (1979) 'Hitler wurde [...] stark beinflusst von den Rassenlehren eines seltsamen religiösen Sektieres namens Lanz von Liebenfels, dessen Zeitschrift Ostara er hingebungsvoll sammelte und gierig verschlang.' p 17.
83) Daim pp 137-139.
84) Toland p 98.
85) Adolf Eichmann, *Ich Adolf Eichman* p 138/Carr, pp 74, 75./For a detailed account of the Madagascar Plan and a chronology of the genesis of the idea see: Hans Jansen, Het Madagascarplan. The proposed deportation of European Jews to Madagascar. (1996).
86) Claudia Steur, *Theodor Dannecker. Ein Funktionär der Endlösung* (1997).
87) On the various cross-references see Daim pp 183-184./On plagiarism see: Ekkehard Hieronimus, p 16.
88) The text of the bdc-Personalakte 16 May 1937 is printed in Karl Hüser, *Wewelsburg 1933-1945 Kult und Terrorstätte der SS Eine Dokumentation* (1982) pp 202-204/In a television documentary, Himmler's former adjutant Wolf reports that the name Weisthor is derived from two terms. 'Thor' from the Germanic god, while 'weis' indicates that Wiligut was from a 'changeling' family. It is noteworthy in this that after World War I, the 'Jungkonservativen' too considered themselves 'knowing' through all the front experiences, as if they had penetrated to the cosmic secrets through the violence of war. This enlarged self-awareness was also sometimes referred to by the phrase trench aristocracy. See: Heinrich Himmler's Burg. *Die Wewelsburg. Das weltanschauliche Zentrum der ss.*/For an overview of Wirth's wild theories see: *Europäische Urrelgion und die Externsteine.*
89) Goodrick-Clark pp 177-191/Richard Breitman, *Der Architekt der Endlösung. Himmler und die Vernichtung der europäischen Juden.* [1991] (1996) pp 193, 194.
90) Karl Hüser, *Wewelsburg* pp 9-61,/Wulff E. Brebeck, *Das Historische Museum*

des Hochstifts Paderborn. Geschichte, Ausbau, Konzeption. Kreismuseum Wewelsburg. (1996)/Struckmeier, H-J., Föderverein Kreis-museum Wewelsburg e.v. Sonderdruck aus 'die Warte'-Summer 1996/Over the obligatory Hun literature see: Richard Breitman, *Der Architekt der Endlösung* p 56.
91) Goodrick-Clarck, pp 177-191.
92) Goodrick-Clarck, pp 184-185.
93) Westfälische Landeszeitung, printed in Hüser, Wewelsburg.
94) Richard Breitman, *Der Architekt der Endlösung* pp 98, 99.

Chapter 4

THE ESTABLISHMENT AND THE NEW ORDER

1) Kurt Tucholsky, *Drei Minuten Gehör* p 237
2) On the problems of German armed forces within the European constellation of power see: Herbert Rosinski, *Die Deutsche Armee, Vom Triumph zur Niederlage.*
3) Arnulf Baring, *Unser neuer Grössenwahn. Deutschland zwischen Ost und West.* Stuttgart 1988 pp 30, 31.
4) Michael Salewski, *Zur deutschen Sicherheitspolitik in der Spätzeit der Weimarer Republik Vierteljahrsheft für Zeitgeschichte 2.* (1974) Heft pp 121-147.
5) A.J.P. Taylor, *Hoe oorlogen beginnen* (1980) p 130/Boog et al, *Der Angriff auf die Sowjetunion* p 8.
6) Percy Ernst Schramm, *Hitler als militärischer Führer. Erkenntnisse und Erfahrungen aus dem Kriegstagebuch des Oberkommandos der Wehrmacht.* p 188.
7) Erich von Manstein, *Verlorene Siege.* (1964).
8) Hans Speidel, *Invasion 1944. Der letzte Chef des Generalstabes Von Feldmarschall Rommel über die Invasion und das Schicksal seines Oberbefehlshabers.* [1949] 1974) p 18/The example of 8 July 1941 is from: Wolfgang Benz, *Judenvernichtung aus Notwehr? Die Legenden um Theodore N. Kaufman. Schriftenreihe der Vierteljahrshefte für Zeitgeschichte (*1981).
9) John Keegan, *Von Rundstedt* [1974] (1979) p 6/Erich Jansen in: 'Ein genialer' Feldherr ohne Krieg. Vor 150 jahre wurde Graf Alfred von Schlieffen geboren.
10) 'Seeckts Maxime ist der unpolitische Soldat' in: Fritz Birnstiel, *Generaloberst Hans von Seeckt 1866-1936.*
11) Sebastian Haffner, *Kanttekeningen bij Hitler* p 61.
12) Blumentritt's memories of the battle of Moscow are beautifully described in the book *The Fatal Decisions*, a collection of war memories with a foreword

by Siegfried Westphal (London 1956)/Christopher Browning, *Deathly Men*, p 2.
13) Friessner, *Verratene Schlachten.*
14) For organisation, origins and deployment of the Waffen-ss, see George H. Stein, *Geschichte der Waffen-ss* and Bernd Wegner, *Hitlers politische Soldaten.*
15) For a detailed technical account of the origins of the Schlieffen plan see: Eugen Bircher and Walter Bode, *Schlieffen, Mann und Idee.* Zurich 1937.
16) Christian Graf von Krockow, *Von deutschen Mythen.* [1995] (1997) pp 29-44/See also Klaus von See, *Barbar, Germane, Arier. Die Suche nach der Identität der Deutschen.* (1994).
17) August Winnig, *Das Reich als Republik 1918-1928.* (1928)/Winnig, *Europa, Gedanken eines Deutschen* (1938) p 49/For Winnig's thoughts on the workers, hovering between communism and patriotism see: *Vom Proletariat zum Arbeitertum*[1930] (1940)/ Francesco Nitti, *Der Niedergang Europas. Die Wege zum Wieder-aufbau.* (1922) pp 53, 54.
18) Theo Schwarzmüller, *Zwischen Kaiser und Führer. Generalfeldmarschall August von Mackensen.* [1995] (1996)/Robert B. Asprey, *The German High Command at War. Hindenburg and Ludendorff and the First World War.* [1991] (London 1993)/For a 'new' image of Ludendorff, see: Wolfgang Venohr, *Ludendorff, Legende und Wirklichkeit.* (1993).
19) Arthur Rosenberg, *Entstehung der Weimarer Republik* (1961) p 101.
20) Wolfgang Foerster, *Der Feldherr Ludendorff im Unglück. Eine Studie über seine seelische Haltung in der Endphase des ersten Weltkriegs*
21) Wilhelm Breucker, *Die Tragik Ludendorffs. Eine kritische Studie auf Grund persönlicher Erinnerungen an den General und seine Zeit.* (1953) p 68/Ravenscroft claims that this conversation is said to have taken place with General McClean, a 'Freemason of high rank' p 304, 305/N still, incidentally, the dagger-throwing legend is the subject of debate in some circles. See, for example, Gerhard Müller, *Dolchstoss oder Dolchstoss-Legende?* November 1918. (Stuttgart 1978).
22) Breucker, p 68.
23) Asprey, p 470.
24) Emil Franzel, *Das Reich der braunen Jakobiner,* p 53.
25) Werner Beumelburg, *Sperrfeuer um Deutschland* (1929)/Beumelburg, *Deutschland in Ketten* (1931)/For cross swords between Beumelburg and Mann and Zweig see: Rolf Geissler, *Dekadenz und Heroismus. Zeitroman und völkisch-nationalsozialistische Literaturkritik.* in: Schriftenreihe der Vierteljahrshefte für Zeitgeschichte number 9 chapter 5 pp 104-119. (Stuttgart 1964).
26) Ernst Röhm, *Geschichte eines Hochverräters,* (1934) p 112.
27) Breucker, p 70/Ludendorff reports on Beumelburg at various times in his journal *Am heiligen Quell deutscher Kraft.*

28) Breucker, p 107.
29) Gottfried Feder, *Der Deutsche Staat auf nationaler und sozialer Grundlage.*/ The Himmler-Höss encounter is mentioned in Richard Breitman, *Der Architekt der Endlösung. Himmler und die Vernichtung der europäischen Juden.* [1991] (1996) p 249/The comment on Wolfgang Kapp is found at Flood, *Hitler,* p 107.
30) Röhm, p 305.
31) On the religion debate of the Ludendorffs and Karl Pieper see: *Ludendorff und die heilige Schrift. Antwort auf die Schrift 'Das grosse Entsetzen - Die Bibel nicht Gottes Wort'* - by Dr Karl Pieper, theology professor in Paderborn, published by the Erzb. Ordinariat Munich in an edition of at least 125,000 copies.
32) Erich Ludendorff, *Auf dem Weg zur Feldherrnhalle* p 37/ In a political pamphlet from the summer of 1923, Ludendorff highlighted the necessity of the anti-Semitic aspect of the völkisch movement. He saw Marxism as an offshoot of Jewish revolutionary plans.
33) German Nording, *Geheimnisse vom Rosenkreuz. Heft 1 des Ldf. Schriftenbezuges.* (1938).
34) Breucker 108-111, (auto)biographical material on Mathilde Ludendorff can be found e.g. in *Mathilde Ludendorff, ihr Werk und Wirken.* (1937)/Alfred Stoss, *Ludendorff der ewige Recke* (1936)/Karl Tschuppik, *Ludendorff. Die Tragödie des Fachmanns* (1935), last chapter. The quote is on page 424. Franz Uhle-Wettler, *Erich Ludendorff in seiner Zeit, Soldat-Stratege, Revolutionär. Eine Neubewertung* page 405 et seq. Further information from Mathilde Ludendorff's six-volume memoirs: *Statt Heiligenschein oder Ehrenzeichen mein Leben* of which used here are parts 2 *Durch Forschen und Schicksal zum Sinn des Lebens* (Munich 1936) and 3: *Erkenntnis - Erlösung* (1980 reissue). On her ideas and political influence see: *Mathilde Ludendorff, Hinter den Kulissen des Bismarckreiches.* (1931)/Relation Von *Kemnitz-Ostara* see: Friedrich Heer, *Der Glaube des Adolf Hitler, anatomie einer politischen religiosität* (1968) p 166 and *Die Dritte Konfession? Materialsammlung über die nordisch-religiösen Bewegungen (*1934). On the post-war (meant here is World War II) role of Mathilde von Kemnitz Ludendorff see: Jens Mecklenburg (Hg.) *Handbuch deutscher Rechts Extremismus.* (1996), pp 374-376/Over Feder's influence on Röhm See: Ernst Röhm, *Geschichte eines Hochverräters* p 123/For the text of Hitler's eulogy See: *Mensch und Mass, drängende Lebensfragen in neuer Sicht, Folge 24* 23-12-1997. p 1122, Hans Kopp, *Erinnerung.*
35) Ernst Röhm p 115/Over the role of Karl Mayr see further: Hellmuth Auerbach, *Hitlers politische Lehrjahre und die Münchener Gesellschaft 1919-1923* Schriftenreihe der Vierteljahrshefte für Zeitgeschichte (1977) Heft 1, pp 1-45.
36) James & Suzanne Pool, p 42.

37) Bernd Steger, *Der Hitlerprozess und Bayerns Verhältniss zum Reich 1923/24*. Schriftenreihe der Vierteljahrshefte für Zeitgeschichte (1977) pp 441-466.
38) Emil Carlebach, *Hitler war kein Betriebsunfall. Hinter den Kulissen der Weimarer Republik: die programmierte Diktatur*. [1993] (1996)/Fritz Fischer, *Hitler war kein Betriebsunfall. Aufsätze*. (1992) Fischer advocates the continuity thesis in his book, as well as in his *Griff nach der Weltmacht Die Kriegszielpolitik des kaiserlichen Deutschland 1914/1918* (1961)/Reinhard Opitz, *Faschismus und Neofaschismus*. (1996)/Manfred Weissbecker/Kurt Pätzold, *Adolf Hitler*. (1995) pp 48-55.
39) Sebastian Haffner, *Germany: Jekyll & Hyde. 1939-Deutschland von innen betrachtet* (1996) pp 38, 39.
40) Charles Bracelen Flood, *The Path to Power* (1989) chapter 1.
41) H.B. Gisevius, *Adolf Hitler*, pp 95, 96.
42) Richardi, Blz 49-52/Wolfram Meyer zu Uptrup, *Wann wurde Hitler zum Antisemiten?* Zeitschrift für Geschichtswissenschaft Heft 7 (1995)/Charles Bracelen Flood, *Hitler, The Path to Power*, p 3.
43) Ulrike Hörster Philipps, *Wer war Hitler wirklich? Grosskapital und Faschismus 1918-1945* Dokumente p 33.
44) Wolfram Meyer zu Uptrup, p 690/Hans-Günter Richardi, *Hitler und seine Hintermänner. Neue Fakten zur Frühgeschichte der NSDAP.* (1991).
45) Trevor Ravenscroft, p 102.
46) Hans-Günter Richardi, *Hitler und seine Hintermänner. Neue Fakten zur Frühgeschichte der NSDAP,* pp 200-212.
47) Otto Gritschneder, *Das dümmste Gericht. In Namen des bayerischen Volkes: Wie dem Terroristen Hitler 1924 zu Bewährungsfrist verholfen wurde*. in: *Süddeutschen Zeitung* No 211 13/14-9-1997. The documentation Gruchmann and Weber are working on is: *Der Hitler-Prozess 1924*.
48) For the numbers of 'Volksdeutschen' in Europe see: Hans-Adolf Jacobsen, *Nationalsozialistische Aussenpolitik 1933-1938*. p 161.
49) G. Tschocke, *Der Feldzug im Baltikum 1919 als Ausgang östlicher Sieldung*. p 15.
50) For a detailed description of the battle in the Baltic region see: Bernhard Sauer, *Vom Mythos eines ewigen Soldatentums Der Feldzug deutscher Freikorps im Baltikum im Jahre 1919* in: Zeitschrift für Geschichtswissenschaft Heft 7 (1995)/An atmospheric account of the horrors of this war can also be reviewed in the DDR publication Alexander Stenbock-Fermor, *Der Rote Graf. Baltischer Aristokrat, Weissgardist, Bergarbeiter, Widerstandskämpfer, Schriftsteller* (1973)./A detailed military overview can be found in Günther Bardéij, *Die Eiserne Division 1919-1920 in the DsJb*./Albert Leo Schlageter became a symbolic figure of the Baltikum fighters. This was partly due to his sabotage actions in the Allied-occupied Ruhr region, which he paid for with

death by execution by the French on 26 May 1923. For the (otherwise highly coloured) life of Schlageter and his actions in the Baltic region see: Wolfram Mallebrein, Albert Leo Schlageter. Eine deutscher Freiheitskämpfer. (1990).

51) Robert G.L.Waite, *Vanguard of Nazism. The Free Corps Movement in Postwar Germany 1918-1923*. [1952](1969) pp 285-296
52) Röhm, p 307
53) Hans-Günter Richardi, *Hitler und seine Hintermänner,* pp 133-139/James and Suzanne Pool, *Who financed Hitler? The Secret Funding of Hitler's Rise to Power 1919-1933* pp 37, 38/For the life history of J.F. Lehmann see: Verleger J.F. Lehmann, *Ein Leben im Kampf für Deutschland*. (1935). Among the authors brought by Lehmann were many 'race specialists': K. Abel, Ludwig Ferdinand Clauss, Walther Darré, R. Eichaenauer, Dieter Gerhart, J.A. Gobineau, E. Haag, Fritz Kern, Paul de Lagarde, G. Paul, Hermann Meyer, Wolf Meyer-Erlach, Otto Sigfrid Reuter, Georg Schott, B. Schultz, Max Wundt.
54) Richardi, pp 138, 139.
55) Richardi, p 144/Erwin Könnemann, *Kapps Vorbereitungen auf einen Prozess, der nie stattfand. Dokumente aus seinem Nachlass* Zeitschrift für Geschichtswissenschaft Heft 7 (1995) pp 698-735.
56) Viktor Suvorov, *Der Eisbrecher. Hitler in Stalins Kalkül* (1989).
57) Allan Bullock, *Hitler and Stalin. Parallel lives* (London 1991).
58) Werner Maser, *der Wortbruch. Hitler, Stalin und der Zweite Weltkrieg* (Munich 1994). For the Suvorov debate, see, among others, Gabriel Gorodetsky, *Stalin und Hitlers Angriff auf die Sowjetunion. Eine Auseinandersetzung mit der Legende vom deutschen Präventivschlag*. Schriftenreihe der Vierteljahrshefte für Zeitgeschichte 1985/Gerd R. Überschar, *Das Unternehmen 'Barbarossa' gegen die Sowjet-Union-ein Präventivkrieg?* Zur Wiederbelebung der alten Rechtfertigungsversuche des deutschen Überfalls auf die UdSSR 1941, in: Brigitte Bailer-Galanda/Wolfgang Benz/Wolfgang Neugebauer (Hg.), Die Auschwitzleugner (1996).
59) David Irving, *Hitler's War*, New York (1990).
60) Martin Broszat, *Hitler und die Genesis der Endlösung. Aus Anlass der Thesen von David Irving*. Schriftenreihe der Vierteljahrshefte für Zeitgeschichte. (1977) pp 739-775).
61) Bradley, D. (Hg.), *Soldatenschicksale des 20. Jahrhunderts. Volume 1*, Hermann Balck, *Ordnung im Chaos. Erinnerungen 1893-1948*. (Osnabrück 1981). pp 333, 334 Balck was not a National Socialist and from that point of view had no reason for this account of the facts. For Balck's political positioning during World War II see: Perry Pierik, *Hongarije 1944-1945, de vergeten tragedie*, chapters: 'Prelude 'Konrad' and 'Frühlingserwachen', Hitlers voorjaarsoffensief'.

62) Hans-Erich Volkmann (Hg.), *Das Russlandbild im Dritten Reich* (1994) pp 125-163.
63) Heinz Guderian, *Achtung Panzer! The Devolpment of Armoured Forces , their Tactics and Operational Potential.* (1937) (1995)
64) Volkmann, pp 125-163.
65) For figures on economic developments at the beginning of the 20th century in Europe see: Steven E. Miller, *Military Strategy and the Origins of the First World War. An International Security Reader.* (1984) pp 8, 9, 10, 16.
66) Walter Görlitz, *Die Junker, Adel und Bauer im deutschen Osten. Geschichtliche Bilanz von 7. jahrhunderten.* (1964). p 404.
67) Karl-Heinz Janssen, *Preusse, Nationalist und Hochverräter* in: Die Zeit Nr 15-6 April 1990.
68) Theo Schwarzmüller, *Zwischen Kaiser und Führer. Generalfeldmarschall August von Mackensen.* (1996) p 48.
69) Frank Golczewski, *Das Deutschlandbild der Polen 1918-39 Eine Untersuchung der Historiographie und der Publizistik Geschichtliche Studien zu Politik und Gesellschaft.* p 46.
70) Leonard Mosley, *Hermann Göring, Portrait of a Reich Marshal,* pp 8, 9. For the work of Hans Friedrich Karl Günther, see Elvira Weisenburger In: Michael Kissener/Joachim Scholtyseck (hg.), *Die Führer der Provinz.* ns-Biographien aus Baden und Württemberg. Karlsruher Beiträge zur Geschichte des Nationalsozialismus Band 2 (1997) pp 161-199.
71) George H. Kleine, *Adelgenossenschaft und Nationalsozialismus* in Schriftenreihe der Vierteljahrshefte für Zeitgeschichte 1. heft 1976 pp 100-143.
72) Georg H. Kleine, p 135.
73) Nationalsozialistischer Führungsstab der Wehrmacht (Hg.), *Der Nationalsozialistische Führungsoffizier, Farm, Kolchose oder Erbhof?* Schulungsthema Nr.11 Führungsunterlagen Folge 3. Nur für Gebrauch innerhalb der Wehrmacht. (1944).
75) On German-Polish relations in the pre-war years, see: Marian Wojciechowski, *Die Polnisch-Deutschen Beziehungen 1933-1938.*
76) Frank Golczewski, *Das Deutschlandbild der Polen 1918-1939* pp 64-102.
77) Else Loeser, *The Image of the Germans in Polish Literature/See* also examples in: Franz Wagner/Fritz Vosberg, *Polenspiegel. Die Aktivitäten der Polen in Deutschland nach ihren eigenen Zeugnissen.* [1908] (1988).
78) Hudal, pp 89, 90.
79) Hans Rothfels, *Bismarck, der Osten und das Reich.* (1960) p 75
80) Klaus Theweleit, *Männer Phantasien. Band 1 Frauen, Fluten, Körper, Geschichte.* [1977] (1980) p 251.
81) Heinrich Jaenecke, *Polen, kleine geschiedenis van een opstandige natie* pp 74-76, 87/The 'official Goebbels statistic' gives the figure of 60,000 victims.

See Walter Dirks in *Frankfurter Hefte, Zeitschrift für Kultur und Politik.* Heft 6 June 1951 pp 445, 446 in a review of Gerhard Ludwig's book *Massamord im Weltgeschehen* (1951).

81a) Die Polnischen Greueltaten an den Volksdeutschen in Polen. Im Auftrage des auswärtigen amtes auf Grund urkundlichen Beweismaterials zusammengestellt, bearbeitet und herausgegeben (1940).

82) Frank Golczewski, *Das Deutschlandbild der Polen 1918-1939*, pp 102, 103.

83) Heinrich Jaenecke, p 84.

84) Richard Walther Darré, *Neuadel aus Blut und Boden*, pp 54-59.

85) Richard Walther Darré, *Neuadel aus Blut und Boden*, p 10.

86) Walter Görlitz, *Die Junker, Adel und Bauer im deutschen Osten* pp 373-376).

87) Friedrich Glum, *Das geheime Deutschland. Die Aristokratie der demokratische Gesinnung* (Berlin 1930).

88) For relation crusade against Bolshevism and decay moral inhibitions see: Manfred Messcherschmidt in the introduction to Boog/Förster/Hoffmann et al, *Der Angriff auf die Sowjetunion.* pp 13-23/For a biography of Admiral von Trotha see B. von Bargen (hg.), *Admiral von Trotha. Persönliches, Briefe, Reden und Aufzeichnungen 1920-1937.* (1938).

89) Manfred Messcherschmidt, *Zur Aufrechterhaltung der Manneszucht.* in: Norbert Haase/Gerhard Paul (Hersg.), *Die andere Soldaten, Wehrkraftzersetzung, Gehorsamsverweigerung und Fahnenflucht im Zweiten Weltkrieg* p 35.

90) Manfred Messcherschmidt, *Der Krieg im Osten, Ursachen und Charakter des Krieges gegen die Sowjetunion.* in: Reinhard Kühnl/Ulrike Hörster-Philipps (hg.), *Hitlers Krieg? Zur Kontroverse um Ursachen und Charakter des Zweiten Weltkrieges.* Köln 1989) pp 109-125).

91) On militia justice see Norbert Haase/Gerhard Paul (hg.), *Die andere Soldaten. Wehrkraftzersetzung, Gehorsamsverweigerung und Fahnenflucht im Zweiten Weltkrieg* and Manfred Messerschmidt, Der 'Zersetzer' und Denunziant in Wolfram Wett (Hersg.), *Der Krieg des kleinen Mannes. Eine Militärgeschichte von Unten.* pp 55-279/EA gripping description of an execution is found in *Paris diary 1941-1943* (private domain no.123) by Ernst Jünger (1979) pp 28, 29.

92) Armin Mohler, *Die konservative Revolution in Deutschland 1918-1932. Grundriss ihrer Weltanschauungen.* (1950).

93) Ernst Niekisch makes this very explicit in his *Das Reich der niederen Dämonen* (1953) p 262.

94) On the Night of the Long Knives and its background see, among others, Charles Bloch, *Die sa und die Krise des ns-Regimes* 1934. On the role of Strasser see, among others, Günter Bartsch, *Otto Strasser, Zwischen drie Stühlen.* On Hitler's methods, and tension between strategic aims and tactical moves see: Joachim Leuschner, *Volk und Raum zum Stil der Nationalsozialistischen Aussenpolitik* pp 57-77.

95) Bloch, p 14
96) Max Gallo, *Der Schwarze Freitag der sa. Die Vernichtung des revolitionären Flügels der nsdap durch Hitlers SS im Juni 1934.* [1970] (Munich 1977) pp 155-161. For further details and some impressive photographs surrounding this funeral see: David Irving, *Göring a Biography.*
97) Leonrad Mosley, *Herman Göring, Portrait of a Reich Marshal* pp 204, 205.
98) Rolf-Dieter Müller, *Hitlers Ostkrieg und die deutsche Siedlungspolitik.* p 27.
99) Rolf-Dieter Müller, p 29.
100) Rolf-Dieter Müller, p 28.
101) Rolf Dieter Müller, p 33.
102) Heinrich Jaenecke p 88/For the 'Volksdeutsche Selbstschutz' see Christian Jansen/Arno Weckbecker, Der 'Volksdeutsche Selbstschutz' in Poland 1939/40 in: Schriftenreihe der Vierteljahrshefte für Zeitgeschichte. Band 64 (1992).
103) Jaenecke, p 88.
104) Jaenecke p 91/For an inventory of Nazi crimes against Poland see Czeslaw Pilichowski, *Es gibt keine Verjährung.* (1980) He puts the total Polish losses in World War II at 6,028.000 people, or 19.3 per cent of World War II victims. About 5.4 million of them were civilians. (p12).
105) Jaenecke, p 92.
106) Jaenecke, p 85.
107) Helmut Krausnick, *Kommisarbefehl und 'Gerichtbarkeitserlass Barbarossa in neuer Sicht.* Vierteljahrsheft für Zeitgeschichte pp 682-738 (1977) p 684/the role of the Wehrmacht in the East is still under discussion: see the spring 1997 debate on the Wehrmacht's crimes during operation 'Barbarossa' in, among others, *Der Spiegel*: 'Rudolf Augstein, Anschlag auf die Ehre des deutschen Soldaten?' (11/1997)/Theo Sommer, 'Nur Hinsehen macht frei. Münchener Lektionen: Die Rolle der Wehrmacht lässt sich nicht beschönigen.' Die Zeit 28-02-1997.
108) Rolf-Dieter Müller, pp 34, 35.
109) Hans-Adolf Jacobsen, *Nationalsozialistische Aussenpolitik 1933-1938* pp 766-781.
110) Lew Besymenski, *Sonderakte 'Barbarossa'. Dokumente, Darstellung, Deutung* (1968).
111) Friedrich Hossbach, *Zwischen Wehrmacht und Hitler 1934-1938* (Hannover 1949) pp 207-220/Bradley F.Smith, *Die Überlieferung der Hossbach-Niederschrift im Lichte neuer Quellen* in: Zeitschrift für Geschichtswissenschaft 1994.

Chapter 5

SWASTIKA REPLACES CROSS

1) Salomon Bouwman, Vaticaan aanvaardt nu 'schuld voor jodenvervolging'. (NRC-handelsblad 25.05.1994)/Vaticaan wil boete doen in kwestie van jodenvervolging (Trouw,25-5-1994)/Gernot Facius, Auschwitz: Deutsche Bischöfe bekennen Mitschuld (Die Welt25-1-1995)/Deutsche Bischöfe: Mitschuld an Auschwitz (Süddeutsche Zeitung 25-1-1995)/Janny Groen, R.K.-kerk erkent schuld aan jodenvervolging (de Volkskrant 21-10-1995)/ Paus erkent antisemitisme in katholieke kerk. (Algemeen Dagblad 1-11-1997)/ Marc Leijendekker, Paus bereidt 'mea culpa' jegens jodendom voor (NRC-Handelsblad 31-10-1997)/Marc Leijendekker, Rome: 'Antisemitisme is een belediging van God' (NRC-Handelsblad 3-11-1997)/ Wilfred Scholten, Simonis kan beter zwijgen over Pius XII (Utrechts Nieuwsblad 20-11-1997)/Robert A. Graham, S.J., How to Manufacture a Legend: The Controversy over the Alleged Silence of Pope XII in World War II. (1998)/Robert A. Graham, Pius XII and the holocaust/Pius XII's Defense of Jews and Others: 1944-45 (1998)/ Jan van der Putten/Theo Koelé, Kerk prijst rol Pius XII tijdens Shoah. (de Volkskrant 17-3-1998)/Eelco van der Linden, Vaticaan maakt joden excuses voor haat en rol in de oorlog. (Utrechts Nieuwsblad 16-1-1998).
2) J.M. Bik, Harvard-professor stelt Duitsers lastige vragen (NRC-handelsblad 17-4-1996/CoWelgraven, Volle zalen en felle kritiek bij 'tournee' van Goldhagen (Trouw 7-9-1996).
3) See in this, for example, Hans Jansen, *Christelijke theologie na Auschwitz. Twee Nieuwtestamentische wortels van het antisemitisme* a1: Diagnosis and therapy in writings of Jews and Christians parts 1 and 2 (1985).
4) Daniel Jonah Goldhagen, *Hitlers gewillige beulen.* Chapter 3.
5) For a complete overview of the comparison list see: Ernst Niekisch, *Das Reich der niederen Dämonen* p 269.
6) 'Blitz' 10 Januar 1937: In: Johann Neuhäusler, *Kreuz und Hakenkreuz. Der Kampf des Nationalsozialismus gegen die katholische Kirche und der kirchliche Widerstand. Erster Teil* (1946) pp 256, 257.
7) Bernd Wegner, *Hitler's Politische Soldaten. Die Waffen-ss 1933-1945* [1982] (1997) p 51.
8) Bernd Wegener, chapter 2.
9) *Prophetien wider das Dritte Reich.* Aus den Schriften des dr. Fritz Gerlich und des Paters Ingbert Naab O.F.M. Cap. Gesammelt von dr. Johannes Steiner. (reissue 1946) pp 20, 33, 36, 42.
10) Prophetien wider das Dritte Reich pp 19-44.

11) For a review of such literature see: Emil Hulbricht, *Buchweiser für das völkisch-religiöse Schriftum und dessen Grenzgebiete. Toppenstedter Reihe, Sammlung bibliographischer Hilfsmittel zur Erforschung der Konservativen Revolution und des Nationalsozialismus nr. 5* [1934] (1983).
12) Ernst Jünger, *Paris diary 1941-1943*. [1979] (1986).
13) Friedrich Rückert quoted in H.R.Flurschütz, *Das ewige Erbe der Deutschen. Deutsch-Nordischer Glaube* (1933) p 25.
14) Ernst Friedrichs', *Krieg dem Kriege* [1924] (1980) is one of the greatest anti-war books of all time with the dedication: Den Schlachtendenkern, den Schlachtenlenkern, den Kriegsbegeisterten aller Länder ist dies Buch freundlichst gewidmet.
15) For the 'Alldeutschen', see the first chapter.
16) Quotation taken from Novalis, *Fragmente und Studien. Vermischte Bemerkungen 1797-98* quoted from Richard Herzinger, 'Der Sieg der Deutschheit über die Erde', 'Die Nation zwischen Mythos und Utopie im Denken der politischen Romantik, der Konservativen Revolution und der neuen Rechten in: Michale Kessler/Wolfgang Graf Vitzthum/Jürgen Wertheimer (Hg.), *Neonationalismus, Neokonservatismus. Sondierungen und Analysen. Stauffenburg Diskussion, Studien zur Inter und Multikultur Band 6* (1997) p 23/Novalis is also the progenitor of a later famous ss saying: 'Wenn alle untreu werden, so bleib' ich doch treu', quoted from Dr W.J. Aalders, *Groote Mystieken, Novalis.* (1914) p 37.
17) Richard Herzinger, 'Der Sieg der Deutschheit über die Erde' p 23. The French historian Joseph Rovan sees in the rejection of the French Revolution by the Germans an attempt to upgrade the German late Middle Ages. Joseph Rovan, *Geschichte der Deutschen. Von ihren Ursprungen bis Heute.* [1994] (1997).
18) See previous comments on German Urgeschichte and Frühgeschichte.
19) For Langbehn's role in the völkische movement, see chapter 3.
20) Richard Herzinger, 'Der Sieg der Deutschheit über die Erde' pp 23-44/ See also Jan Ipema, *In dienst van Leviathan*, p 122 on the concept of the Dritte Reich, and chapter 9 on the relationship conservative revolution and the Nazis.
21) Richard Herzinger, pp 23-44.
22) For the sake of completeness, it should be noted that Lanz von Liebenfels biographer Rudolf J. Mund emphasises not so much the ariosopher's anti-Christian stance but, above all, his similarities with Christianity. According to Mund, Lanz von Liebenfels, at least in his own experience, always remained closely associated with the monastic period at Heiligenkreuz to which he joined in July 1893, only to leave the order again after 20 months. Liebenfels did so with the blessing of the clergy. There was no breach or quarrel/Ideology/programme and the (pseudo-)religious work of the Ludendorffs is still brought out by the publishing house Verlag Hohe Warte in Pähl in which a series of religious-philosophical works such as the *Triumpf des Unsterblich-*

keitswillens, Schöpfungsgeschichte, Des Mensches Seele, Selbstschöpfung, Der Seele Wirken und Gestalten, Die Volksseele und ihre Machtgestalter, Das Gottlied der Völker, das Hohe Lied der göttlichen Wahlkraft, In den Gefilden der Gottoffenbarungen, Das Jenseitsgut der Menschenseele, Aus der Gottererkenntnis meiner Werke, Von der Moral des Lebens, Induziertes Irresein durch Okkultlehren, Erlösung von Jesu Christo, Ist Gotterkenntnis möglich? Within the *Tannenbergerbund* and the Volkswarte publishing house, other authors were also active in the (pseudo-)religious field. Today, we find the ideas of the Ludendorffs in the journal 'Mensch und Mass'.

23) Bernd Wegner, *Hitler's Politische Soldaten* pp 29-42.
24) John M. Steiner, *Über das Glaubensbekenntnis der SS*, in Bracher/Funke/Jacobsen (Hg.), Nationalsozialistische Dikatur. Eine Bilanz. Schriftenreihe der Bundeszentrale für politische Bildung Band 192 pp 206, 207/Over the astrology of Hess/Haushofer see, among others, Haushofer's correspondences, compiled by H.A. Jacobsen. In the book's appendix is a handmade astrological sketch of Haushofer made by himself. For the reminiscences of Himmler's court astrologer see: Wilhelm Th.H. Wulf, *Tierkreis und Hakenkreuz. Als Astrologe an Himmlers Hof.* The British waged an astrological war against the Germans through forged copies of the astrologer's journal *Zenit*. Through backdating, it seemed that the British predicted correctly each time that German U-boats would sink, for example.
25) See chapter 3.
26) The Oxford Companion of the Second World War assumes a Waffen-ss casualty rate of between 20 and 25 per cent. More than four hundred Waffen-ss officers received the Ritterkreuz. I.C.B. Dear (Ed.), *The Oxford Companion to the Second World War*, p 1046/George H.Stein, *Geschichte der Waffen-ss* pp 8-12/John Keegan, *Waffen-ss the Asphalt Soldiers*, pp 39-57/Felix Steiner, *Von Clausewitz bis Bulganin. Erkenntnisse und Lehre einer Wehrepoche* (1956) pp 132,134/Bernd Wegner, Chapter 2/Paul Hausser, *Soldaten wie andere Auch. Der Weg der Waffen-ss, Erster Teil* [1966] (1988).
27) Richard Walther Darré, *Odal, Monatschrift für Blut und Boden, Wir und die Leibesübungen* pp 710-728/Bernd Wegner, Chapter 2
28) Himmler's statement about the anti-Bolshevik Kampforganisation dates from 1937. Bernd Wegner p 38.
29) Germaansch ontwaken. Brieven van Germaansche vrijwilligers (1942) p 9.
30) Germaansch ontwaken, p 9.
31) Neuhäusler, p 251.
32) Karl Dieter Bracher, *Zeit der Ideologen. Eine Geschichte politischen Denkens im 20. Jahrhunderts.* (1982).
33) Neuhäusler, p 12.
34) Neuhäusler, p 14.

35) Neuhäusler, pp 15-17/Walter Hagen writes in *Die geheime Front*, a study published shortly after World War II, that the SD was fully engaged in infiltrating reliable HJ-ers into the church apparatus so that it could be dismantled from within. Hitler personally put a stop to this.
36) Jean-Michel Angebert, *The Occult and The Third Reich*, pp 10-15/On the role of the Cathars in medieval history, see a.o. H.P.H. Jansen, *Geschiedenis van de Middeleeuwen* pp 268, 269.
37) Josef Dvorak, *Satanismus, Schwarze Rituelen, Teufelswahn und Exorzismus. Geschichte und Gegenwart.* pp 88-93/Colonel T.H. Minshall, *Duitslands wil totwereldoverheersing. Geschiedkundige en filosofische verklaring* (1939) Minshall draws on sociological research (W. Trotter) that classifies humanity into three types of 'gregarious animals': 1) the socialised 2) the protection-seeking and 3) the attacking or wolfish. According to Minshall, the German people were a typical 'wolf-like people', having been under the spell of this destructive trait since the days of ancient Rome, where Germanic barbarians plundered Italy. This racial view of Minshall does not seem to fully convince the author himself. On page 76 of his books, he suddenly believes that 'Germans are incomprehensible', all sociological classifications apparently notwithstanding. Incidentally, Minshall speaks of Britain in terms of 'sheep characteristics' pages 66-69, 76.
38) Robert G.L. Waite, *Adolf Hitler als psychopaat*, p 45/ John Toland makes the connection once: 'He (Hitler) named this peaceful shelter Wolfsschlucht, after his own nickname from the early days of the party p 656.
39) Waite/Heinz Linge, *In het voetspoor van de Führer. Onthullingen van Hitlers privé-adjudant.* (Utrecht 1985) p 64/Hans-Adolf Jacobsen, *Der Zweite Weltkrieg. Grundzüge der Politik und Strategie in Dokumenten* pp 211-212, Lagebesprechung 12-12-1942/Hans Wolfgang Singer (Hg.), *Allgemeines Künstler-Lexicon. Leben und Werke der berühmtesten Künstler.* (1898) p 360/Jane Turner (Ed.), *The Dictionary of Art. Vol.29* (1996) pp 845-847.
40) Trevor Ravenscroft, *The Spear of Destiny. The Occult Power behind the Spear which pierced the Side of Christ... and how Hitler inverted the Force in a bid to Conquer the World.* [1973] (1995).
41) Harsh criticism of Ravenscroft came above all from the anthroposophical side, given that anthroposophist Walter Johannes Stein is attributed a guru-like role by the author in Ravenscroft's book. In an article and review in Flensburger Hefte, Anthroposophie im Gespräch (1991), Heft 32 Anthroposophen und National Sozialismus, Christoph Lindenberg and Arfst Wagner take a stand against Ravenscroft's theses pointing out that many data contain errors. Peter Orzechowski also criticises Ravenscroft in *Schwarze Magie-Braune Macht*. In the chapter the old order and new order, I referred earlier to a difference in names between Ravenscroft and a contemporary of Ludendorff, in which

Ravenscroft claimed to be a Freemason of high rank. In that case, too, Ravenscroft seems to have been careless with his sources.

42) On descent myths see Leon Poliakov in previous text as well as Klaus von See, *Barbar, Germane Arier*. p 189 The quote is from Karl Alexander von Gleichen-Russwurm. (von See p 189) Gustav Freitag undertook an attempt to write a new national epic for Germany in his six-volume work *Die Ahnen*. (von See p 286)
43) For Los on the Oera Linden book, see, among others, Wim Zaal, *De verlakkers, literaire vervalsingen en mystificaties*. (1991) Chapter 7.
44) Waite, pp 262, 263.
45) Waite, pp 264, 265.
46) Salemink/Van Dijk, *Omdat het slechts om politiek gaat. De machtsovername door de nazi's in 1933 als keerpunt van het politieke christendom* p 10.
47) Salemink/Van Dijk, p 111.
48) Volkmar Herntrich, p 26.
49) Salemink/Van Dijk, p 112.
50) Salemink/Van Dijk, pp 118, 119, 133/Klemens-August Recker, *Wem wollt ihr glauben? Bischof Berning im Dritten Reich*. (1998) pp 58, 59.
51) Karl Dieter Bracher, *Zeit der Ideologen*, p 46.
52) Martin Greiffenhagen, *Das Dilemma des Konservatismus in Deutschland*. (1986)/Walter Schubart, *Europa und die Seele des Ostens* (1938).
53) Georg Denzler/Volker Febricius, *Die Kirchen im Dritten Reich, Christen und Nazis Hand in Hand?* p 164.
54) Denzler/Fabricius, p 173.
55) Erich Goldhagen, *Weltanschauung und Endlösung. Zum Antisemitsmus der nationalsozialistischen Führungsschicht*. In: Schriftenreihe der Vierteljahrshefte für Zeitgeschichte (1976) pp 379-405.
56) Rolf Hochhuth, *Der Stellvertreter* (1963).
57) Summa Iniuria, p 13.
58) Summa Iniuria, p. 10/Bishop Dr Hudal, *Die Grundlagen des Nationalsozialismus* (Leipzig/Wien 1937)/Hansjakob Stehle, *Endloses Versteckspiel: Erstmals publiziert: die vom Vatikan geheimgehaltene Enzyklika gegen Antisemitismus und Judenverfolgung*. Die Zeit no.39 19 September (1997)/In his two standard works, *Gottes Erste Liebe* (1967) and *Der Glaube des Adolf Hitler* (1968), the Austro-Marxist Friedrich Heer emphasises Hitler's Catholic background time and again.
59) Ernst Klee, *Passierscheine und falsche Pässe/Pierik, Hongarije 1944-1945, de vergeten tragedie*, p 95.
60) See, for example, Vladimir Dedijer, *Jasenovac- das Jugoslawische Auschwitz und der Vatikan*. This book contains a long list of Croatian clerics who were decorated by the Ustascha-state for their loyal services.

61) Summa Iniuria, p 13.
62) Jaenecken, p 89/a partial list of names of the murdered clergy can be found in: *The Nazi Kultur in Poland* by a number of anonymous authors (1945) On German atrocities in Poland see also: Erich Kuby, *Als Polen deutsch war* (1936)/ On the arrival of German priests in Poland see Stefan Samerski, *Priester im annektierten Polen. Die Seelsorge deutscher Geistlicher in den an an das Deutsche Reich angeschlossenen polnischen Gebieten 1939-1945.* (1997).

Chapter 6

GROSSWIRTSCHAFTSRAUM EUROPA: THE REALM OF UNLIMITED POSSIBILITIES

1) H.A. Jacobsen 1939-1945, *Der Zweite Weltkrieg in Chronik und Dokumenten* p 398.
2) O.E.Paul/W.Claussen, *Grossdeutschland und die Welt. Ein Wirtschafts abc in Zahlen.* (1938) pp 63, 83, 155, 157, 293, 441, 442.
3) Anton Hantschel, *Baku, ein Kampf um Bohrtürme* pp 7, 8/Hans-Adolf Jacobsen, *Der Zweite Weltkrieg. Grundzüge der Politik und Strategie in Dokumenten*, pp 209-210.
4) Ploetz, *Geschichte des Zweiten Weltkrieges 2. teil Die Kriegsmittel* p 64.
5) On Romanian oil production see: *The Royal Institute of International Affairs, South-Eastern Europe, a Political and Economic Survey*, pp 128, 129 and E.M. Friedwald, *Oil and War.* (London 1941) chapter 5/For the protection of Romanian oil areas see: Perry Pierik, *Hongarije 1944-1945, de vergeten tragedie,* chapter 'de brandende olie van Ploesti' pp 31-54/For the air raids on Ploesti see: J. Dungan/C. Stewart, *Ploesti, The spectacular Ground-Air Battle of 1st August 1943.*
6) E.M. Friedwald, *Oil and War* (1941) pp 22, 23.
7) *Hitlers Tafelgesprekken* pp 39, 40.
8) Otto Ernst Paul/Wilhelm Claussen, *Grossdeutschland und die Welt. Ein Wirtschafts-abc in Zahlen.* (1938)
9) Ploetz, pp 442, 443, 448, 453, 470/Ten Kate p 48/For Soviet arms productions see also: S.A. Tyushkevich, *The Soviet Armed Forces. A History of their Organizational Development. A Soviet View.* (1978) and Heinz Abraham, 1941-1945, *Grosser Vaterländischer Krieg der Sowjetunion* (1985). For Lidell Hart's remarks, see *Europe Mobilises* (1938) pp 34, 35.
10) Alec Nove, *Stalinism and After. The Road to Gorbachev*, pp 44, 45.
11) Isaac Deutscher, *Stalin, eine politische Biographie.* [1966] (1990)

12) Ernst Nolte, *Der Europäische Bürgerkrieg* 1917-1945, *Nationalsozialismus und Bolschewismus* pages 115/Richard Pipes, *The Unknown Lenin/Robert* Conquest, *The Great Terror/Robert* Conquest, *The Harvest of Sorrow*, in this one above all the chapter 'The Death Roll' pages 299-307/See also Marcel van Hamersveld/ Michiel Klinkhamer, *Messianism without compassion. Communism, its supporters and its victims.* (1998).
13) Alcc Nove, *Stalinism and After.* [1975] (1989) chapter 1/Volkmann, pp 357-385.
14) Albert Speer, *Der Sklavenstaat. Meine Auseinandersetzungen mit der ss* blz [1981] (1984) 63-80.
15) Ploetz, *Geschichte des Zweiten Weltkrieges 2.teil Die Kriegsmittel* p 65.
16) H.R. Trevor-Roper (Ed.), *Hitler's War directives 1939-1945.* [1964] (1966)/ Werner Maser, *Hitler*, pp 400, 401.
17) On the attack on Iraq see: Trevor-Roper, *Hitler's War directives* p 132.
18) Peter Gosztony, *Hitler Fremde Heere. Das Schicksal der nichtdeutschen Armeen im Ostfeldzug* p 80/Hans-Adolf Jacobsen, pp 197, 198/Diary entry Goebbels 08-05-1943.
19) For Ostlegions and Vlassovleger see: Joachim Hoffmann, *Einzelschriften zur militärischen Geschichte des Zweiten Weltkrieges 19, Die Ostlegionen 1941-1943* /1976] (1981)/Einzelschriften zur militärischen Geschichte des Zweiten Weltkrieges 35, Kaukasien 1942/ 1943 (1991)/Die Geschichte der Wlassow Armee [1984] (1986)/For the war in the Caucasus see o.a.o. Wilhelm Tieke, *Der Kaukasus und das Öl, der Deutsch-Russische Kampf im Kaukasien 1942/43* (1970)/For Reinhard Gehlen's attitude towards these units see E.H. Cookridge, *Gehlen. Spy of the Century.* (1971)
20) Perry Pierik, *Hongarije 1944-1945, de vergeten tragedie* (1995).
21) Ten Kate, *De aanval op de Sovjet-Unie* pp 65, 66.
22) Ten Kate p 87.
23) Boog/Förster et al. *Der Angriff auf die Sowjetunion* pages 58, 59
24) Dieter Petzina, *Autarkiepolitik im Dritten Reich. Der nationalsozialistische Vierjahresplan.* In: Schriftenreihe der Vierteljahrshefte für Zeitgeschichte. p 11.
25) Petzina, p 49.
26) Mosley, p 213.
27) Victor Reimann, *Goebbels* chapter 2, see also Heinrich Fraenkel/Roger Manvell, *Doktor Goebbels. Het leven en de dood van een verderfelijk genie*, chapter 4.
28) Petzina, pp 57, 58, 125.
29) Hörster-Philipps p 28.
30) Hörster-Philipps p 29.
31) Hörster-Phillipps p 35.
32) John Macintyre, *Vergeten land* p 109/Hörster-Phillipps p 34, 35/Völkische Beobachter 30 July 1933: portrait Feder/Gottfried Feder, *Der Deutsche Staat auf nationaler und sozialer Grundlage. Nationalsozialistische Bibliothek Heft 35* (1932).

33) Hörster-Philipps pp 39, 40, 44.
34) See chapter 4.
35) Fritz Thyssen, *Ik financierde Hitler. Verbijsterende onthullingen door den Duitschen Grootindustrieel.* (1957)/Hörster-Philipps pp 56, 57.
36) Hörster-Philipps pp 57, 58.
37) See chapter 4.
38) Hörster-Philipps, p 60.
39) Walter Görlitz mentions the figure of 20,000 in his November 1918. *Bericht über die deutsche Revolution* (1968) p 193.
40) Hörster-Philipps, p 73.
41) Hörster-Philipps, p 140.
42) Reinhard Opitz, *Faschismus und Neofaschismus* p 80.
43) Hörster-Philipps, pp 144-146.
44) Hans-Adolf Jacobsen, *Nationalsozialistische Aussenpolitik 1933-1938* p 51/For the SS plans concerning Eastern Europe see Rössler/Schleiermacher, *Der Generalplan Ost*, pp 13, 68, 69.
45) Albert Speer, *Der Sklavenstaat,* chapter 4.
46) Lothar Gruchmann, *Nationalsozialistische Grossraumordnung* p 102.
47) Lothar Gruchmann, pp 93-109.
48) Lothar Gruchmann, p 101.
49) Lothar Gruchmann, p 100/Hans-Adolf Jacobsen, *Nationalsozialistische Aussenpolitik 1933-1938,* p 51.
50) Lothar Gruchmann pp 100, 101/*The Oxford Companion of the Second World War* pp 1047, 1048.
51) Lothar Gruchmann, p 96.
52) B.S.Telpuchowski, *Die Sowjetische Geschichte des Grossen Vaterländischen Krieges 1941-1945,* p 339.
53) A detailed account of German efforts with regard to heavy industry in the Donets coal basin see: Matthias Riedel, *Bergbau und Eisenhüttenindustrie in der Ukraine unter deutscher Besatzung (1941-1944).* In: Vierteljahshefte für Zeitgeschichte (1973) pp 245-284.
54) Riedel, pp 250-255.
55) Riedel, pp 257-265.
56) Riedel, p 273.
57) Riedel, p 276.
58) Albert Speer, Memories p 82.
59) Boog/Förster/Klink et al, *Der Angriff auf die Sowjetunion* pp 1202-1209.
60) Das deutsche Kapital im zweiten Anlauf auf die 'Neuordnung Europas' p 47.
61) Wolfgang Benz, *Dimension des Völkermords,* p 558 For a comparison number on the number of Jewish victims in Soviet Union, see Benz p 16.
62) Benz, p 517.

63) Rolf-Dieter Müller, *Hitlers Ostkrieg und die deutsche Siedlungspolitik* p 43.
64) Bernd Bonwetsch took stock of the fate of Soviet prisoners of war and concluded that 46 per cent of Soviet soldiers who entered German captivity died. About 37 per cent of German POWs died in Soviet captivity. This according to German sources. Soviet estimates are slightly lower. Bernd Bonwetsch, *Die Sowjetischen Kriegsgefangenen zwischen Stalin und Hitler* in: Zeitschrift für Geschichtswissenschaft Heft 1 (1993) pp 135-143.
65) For figures on war production see: Avraham Barkai, *Das Wirtschaftssystem des Nationalsozialismus* pp 217-226.

Literature*

I Books

Aalders, W.J., *Groote mystieken. Novalis* (Baarn 1914)
Abraham, H., *1941-1945, Grosser Vaterländischer Krieg der Sowjet Union* (Berlin 1985)
Adams, R.J.Q., *The Great War, 1914-18. Essays on the Military, Political and Social History of The First World War* (London 1990)
Alberton, M., *Birobidschan, die Judenrepublik* (Leipzig/Wien 1932)
Albrecht, K.I., *Der verratene Sozialismus. Zehn Jahre als hoher Staats beamter in der Sowjetunion* (Berlin/Leipzig 1941)
Allgemeine Richtlinien für die politische und wirtschaftliche Verwaltung der besetzten Ostgebiete. In: *Schriftenreihe der Vierteljahrshefte für Zeitgeschichte,* Heft 1 (1977)
Angebert, J.M., *Hitler et la tradition cathare* (Used here: *The occult and the Third Reich. The Mystical Origins of Nazism and the Search for the Holy Grail* [1971] (1975)
Aron, R., *Paix et guerre entre les nations* (Used here: *Frieden und Krieg. Eine Theorie der Staatenwelt*) [1962] (Frankfurt am Main 1986)
Asprey, R.B., *The German High Command at War. Hindenburg and Ludendorff and the First World War* [1991] (London 1993)
Auerbach, H., *Hitlers politische Lehrjahre und die Münchener Gesellschaft 1919-1923* in: *Schriftenreihe der Vierteljahrshefte für Zeitgeschichte,* Heft 1, pp. 1-45 (1977)
Bakker, Dr. G., Duitse geopolitiek 1919-1945. Een imperialistische ideologie (Assen 1967)
Bargen, B. von (Hg.), *Admiral von Trotha. Persönliches, Briefe, Reden und Aufzeichnungen 1920-1937* (Berlin 1938)
Baring, A., *Unser neuer Grössenwahn Deutschland zwischen Ost und West* (Stuttgart 1988)
Barkai, A., *Das Wirtschaftssystem des Nationalsozialismus. Ideology, Theory, Politik 1933-1945* [1977] (Frankfurt am Main 1988).
Barnouw, D., *Weimar Intellectuals and the Threat of Modernity* (1988)
Bartsch, G., *Zwischen drei Stühlen. Otto Strasser. Eine Biografie* (Koblenz 1990)

Bäumer, A., *NS-Biologie*. Edition Universitas. (Stuttgart 1990)
Benz, W., *Judenvernichtung aus Notwehr? Die Legenden um Theodore N. Kaufman*. in: *Schriftenreihe der Vierteljahrshefte für Zeitgeschichte. 2. Heft* (1981)
Benz, W. (Hg.), *Dimension des Völkermords. Die Zahl der jüdischen Opfer des Nationalsozialismus*. [1991] (Munich 1996)
Benz, W. (Hg.), *Antisemitismus in Deutschland. Zur Aktualität eines Vorurteils*. (Munich 1995)
Besson, W. (Hg.), *Das Fischer Lexikon Geschichte*. [1961] (1973)
Best, W./Klopfer, G./Stuckart, W. (Hg.), *Reich, Volksordnung, Lebensraum. VI. Band. Zeitschrift für völkische Verfassung und Verwaltung*. (1943)
Besymenski, L., *Sonderakte 'Barbarossa'. Dokumente, Darstellung, Deutung*. (Stuttgart 1968)
Beumelburg, W., *Sperrfeuer um Deutschland*. (Oldenbourg 1929)
Beumelburg, W., *Deutschland in Ketten*. (Oldenbourg 1931)
Bircher, E./Bode, W., *Schlieffen. Mann und Idee*. (Zurich 1937)
Blavatsky, H.P., *De geheime leer. De synthese van wetenschap, religie en filosofie*. [1888] (1988)
Bloch, C., *Die sa und die Krise des ns-Regimes 1934*. (Frankfurt am Main 1970).
Bonwetsch, B., *Die Sowjetischen Kriegsgefangenen zwischen Stalin und Hitler* in: *Zeitschrift für Geschichtswissenschaft Heft 1* (Heidelberg/Berlin 1993)
Boog, H./Förster, J./Hoffmann, J. et al, *Der Anfriff auf die Sowjetunion*. [1983] (Frankfurt am Main 1991)
Botz, G./Oxaal, I./Pollak, M., (Hg.), *Eine zerstörte Kultur. Jüdisches Leben und Antisemitsmus in Wien seit dem 19. Jahrhunderts*. (1990)
Bouhler, P., (Hg.), *Der grossdeutsche Freiheitskampf, II. Band. Reden Adolf Hitlers von 10 März 1940 bis 16 märz 1941*. (1942)
Boveri, M., *Der Verrat im XX. Jahrhunderts, für und gegen die Nation. Das unsichtbare Geschehen*. (Hamburg 1956)
Boyer, J.W., *Political Radicalism in Late Imperial Vienna. Origins of the Christian Social Movement 1848-1897*. (Chicago 1981)
Bracher, K.D., *Die deutsche Diktatur: Entstehung, Struktur, Folgen des Nationalsozialismus*. (Used here: *The German Dictatorship. The Origins, Structure and Effects of National Socialism*. [1969] (New York 1970)
Bracher, K.D., *Zeit der Ideologen. Eine Geschichte politischen Denkens im 20. Jahrhunderts*. (Stuttgart 1982)
Bracher, K.D., *Wendezeiten der Geschichte. Historico-politische Essays 1987-1992*. [1992] (Stuttgart 1995)
Bradley, D. (Hg.), *Soldatenschicksale des 20. Jahrhunderts. Band 1, Hermann Balck, Ordnung im Chaos. Erinnerungen 1893-1948*. (Osnabrück 1981)
Breitter, G., *Die Rote Armee im 2. Weltkrieg. Eine bibliographie. Schriften der Bibliothek für Zeitgeschichte. Band 24*. (Koblenz 1984)

Breucker, W., *Die Tragik Ludendorffs. Eine kritische Studie auf Grund persönlicher Erinnerungen an den General und seine Zeit.* (Stohllhalm 1953)
Broszat, M., *Hitler und die Genesis der Endlösung. Aus Anlass der Thesen von David Irving.* in: Schriftenreihe der Vierteljahrshefte für Zeitgeschichte. (1977)
Broszat, M., *'holocaust' und die Geschichtswissenschaft.* in: Schriftenreihe der Vierteljahrshefte für Zeitgeschichte. (1979)
Browning, C.R., *Ordinary men.* (Used here: *Ordinary men*) (Amsterdam 1993)
Browning, C.R., *Zur Genesis der Endlösung. Eine Antwort an Martin Broszat.* in: Schriftenreihe der Vierteljahrshefte für Zeitgeschichte 2. Heft. (1981)
Buchheim, C., *Die besetzten Länder im Dienste der deutschen Kriegswirtschaft während des Zweiten Weltkriegs. Ein Bericht der Forschungsstelle für Wehrwirtschaft.* in: Schriftenreihe der Vierteljahrshefte für Zeitgeschichte. (1986)
Bullock, A., *Hitler and Stalin. Parallel lives.* (London 1991)
Burg, G.van den, *Het nationaal-socialisme.* (Rotterdam 1940)
Burmeister, H.P., *Möglichkeitssinn und Wertezerfall - Mitteleuropa als deutsche Frage* in: *Amsterdam Studies in Cultural Identity volume 3*, Hans Ester/Hans Hecker/Erika Poettgens (Hg.), *Deutschland, aber wo liegt es? Deutschland und Mitteleuropa. Analysen und Historischen Dokumente.* (Amsterdam 1993)
Carlebach, E., *Hitler war kein Betriebsunfall. Hinter den Kulissen der Weimarer Republik: die programmierte Diktatur.* [1993] (Bonn 1996)
Carpentier, H., *Het leven van J.R.R.Tolkien* (Utrecht 1983).
Carr, W., *Hitler, a Study in Personality and Politics.* (London 1978)
Chamberlain, H.St., *Die Grundlagen des XIX. Jahrhunderts. Band I. Band II.* (Munich 1932)
Chruschtschow. N., *Chruschtschow erinnert sich. Die authentische Memoiren.* [1970] (1991)
Cohn, N., *Die Protokolle der Weissen von Zion. Der Mythos von der jüdischen Weltverschwörung.* (Köln/Berlin 1969)
Conquest, R., *The Harvest of Sorrow. Soviet Collectivisation and the Terror-Famine.* [1968] (New York/Oxford 1986)
Conquest, R., *The Great Terror. A Reassessment.* [1990] (London 1994)
Cookridge, E.H., *Gehlen. Spy of the Century.* (London 1971)
Corino, K., *Intellektuelle in Bann des Nationalsozialismus.* (Hamburg 1980)
Corni, G./Gies, H., *Brot, Butter, Kanonen. Die Ernährungswirtschaft in Deutschland unter der Diktatur Hitlers.* (Berlin 1997)
Coudenhove-Kalegri, R., *Judenhass von Heute.* (Wien/Zürich 1935)
Daim, W., *Der Mann der Hitler die Ideen gab. Von den religiösen Verirrungen eines Sektierers zum Rassenwahn des Diktators.* (Munich 1958)
Darré, R.W., *Blut und Boden. Eine Grundgedanke des Nationalsozialismus. Schriftenreihe des Reichsausschusses für Volksgesundheitsdienst Heft 13.* (Berlin 1936)
Darré, R.W., *Das Bauertum als Lebensquell der Nordische Rasse.* [1929] (Munich 1942)

Darré, R.W., *Neuadel aus Blut und Bodem*. (Used here: *Nieuwe adel uit bloed en bodem*) [1942] (Den Haag 1943)

Dear, I.C.B.,(Ed.), *Oxford Companion of the Second World War* (Oxford/New York 1995)

Denzler, G./Febricius, V., *Die Kirchen im Dritten Reich, Christen und Nazis Hand in Hand? Band 1 Darstellung*. [1984] (Frankfurt am Main 1985)

Deutscher, I., *Stalin, eine politische Biographie*. [1966] (Berlin 1990) *Deutschland deine Kolonien! Unsere Kolonialarbeit 1937*. Reichskolonialbund, Kreisverband Aachen-Land. (1937)

Dickhuth-Harrach, G. von (Hg.), *Im Felde unbesiegt. Der Weltkrieg in 28 Einzeldarstellungen*./Dickhuth-Harrach,G.von (Hg.), *Im Felde unbesiegt 2 Der Weltkrieg in 24 Einzeldarstellungen*. (Munich 1921)

Diner, D., *'Grundbuch des Planeten'. Zur Geopolitik Karl Haushofers*. in: *Schriftenreihe der Vierteljahrshefte für Zeitgeschichte. Heft 1* (1984).

Dinter, A., *Die Sünde wider das Blut*. (Leipzig 1919)

Dittrich, A.R./Naarden, B.,/Renner, H., *Tampering with the past. Thirteen famous cases of history falsification. From the Piltdown man to the diaries of Adolf Hitler*. (Utrecht 1984)

Dvorak, J., *Satanismus, Schwarze Rituelen, Teufelswahn und Exorzismus. Geschichte und Gegenwart*. [1989] (1991)

Eckart, D., *Der Bolschewismus von Moses bis Lenin. Zweigespräch zwischen Adolf Hitler und mir*. (1924) (used here: *Bolshevism from Moses to Lenin*)

Eichmann, A. *Ich Adolf Eichmann. Ein historischer Zeugenbericht*. [1980] (Leoni am Starnbergersee 1981)

Erfurth, W., *Die Geschichte des deutschen Generalstabes von 1918 bis 1945*. (Göttingen 1957)

Ericksen, R.P., *Theologians under Hitler*. [1985] (1986)

Evang. Pressverband für Deutschland, *Die 'Dritte Konfession?'. Materialsammlung über die nordisch-religiösen Bewegungen*. (Berlin 1943)

Feder, G., *Der deutsche Staat auf nationaler und sozialer Grundlage. Neue Wege in Staat, Finanz und Wirtschaft. Nationalsozialistische Bibliothek/Heft 35* (Munich 1932).

Field, G.G., *Evangelist of Race. The Germanic Vision of Houston Stewart Chamberlain*. (New York 1981)

Fischer, F., *Griff nach der Weltmacht. Die Kriegszielpolitik des kaiserlichen Deutschland 1914/18*. (Düsseldorf 1961)

Fischer, F., *Hitler war kein Betriebsunfall*. (Munich 1992)

Fleischhauer, I., *'Unternehmen Barbarossa' und die Zwangssiedlung der deutschen in der UdSSR*. in: *Schriftenreihe der Vierteljahrshefte für Zeitgeschichte 1.Heft*. (1981).

Flensburger Hefte, Anthroposophie im Gespräch, Anthroposophen und National-Sozialismus. Heft 32. (1991)

Flood, C.B., *Hitler. The Path to Power.* (Boston 1989)
Flurschütz, H.R., *Das ewige Erbe der Deutschen. Deutsch-Nordischer Glaube* (Berlin 1933).
Foerster, W., *Der Feldherr Ludendorff im Unglück. Eine Studie über seine seelische Haltung in der Endphase des Ersten Weltkriegs* (Wiesbaden 1952)
Fraenkel, H/Manvell, R., *Doctor Goebbels. His Life and Death.* Used here: *Doktor Goebbels. Het leven en de dood van een verderfelijk genie.* (Amsterdam 1960)
Franzel, E., *Das Reich der braunen Jakobiner.* (Munich 1964)
Friedgut, T., *Antisemitism and Its Opponents in the Russian Press: From Perestroika until the present* (Jerusalem 1994)
Friedrich, E., *Krieg dem Kriege.* [1924] (1980)
Friedwald, E.M., *Oil and War.* (London 1941)
Fritsch, T., *Handbuch der Judenfrage. Die wichtigsten Tatsachen zur Beurteilung des jüdischen Volkes. Faksimile-Dokumentation zur Morphologie und Geschichte des Nationalsozialismus. 15. Reihe-Band 1.* [1933] (1991)
Gallo, M., *Der Schwarze Freitag der SA. Die Vernichtung des revolutionären Flügels der NSDAP durch Hitlers SS im Juni 1934.* [1970] (Wien/Munich 1977)
Geissler, R., *Dekadenz und Heroismus. Zeitroman und völkisch-nationalsozialistische Literaturkritik.* in: *Schriftenreihe der Vierteljahrshefte für Zeitgeschichte Nummer 9* (Stuttgart 1964)
Germaansch ontwaken. Brieven van germaansche vrijwilligers. (Amsterdam 1942).
Gerstl, A./Löwenthal, G./Prawy, M., *Juden und Deutsche: Vergangenheit und Zukunft* (Graz 1994).
Geyer, D., *Ostpolitik und Geschichtsbewusstsein in Deutschland.* in: *Vierteljahshefte für Zeitgeschichte Heft 2.* (1986)
Geyl, Prof. Dr. P., *Duitse en Italiaanse figuren.* (Amsterdam, Antwerp 1969).
Gisevius, H.B., *Adolf Hitler.* [1963] (1973)
Glum, F., *Das geheime Deutschland. Die Aristokratie der demokratische Gesinnung* (Berlin 1930).
Golczewski, F., *Das Deutschlandbild der Polen 1918-1939. Eine Untersuchung der Historiographie und der Publizistik. Geschichtliche Studien zu Politik und Gesellschaft.Band 7* (Düsseldorf 1974)
Goldendach, W. von/Minow, H.R., *'Deutschtum erwache!'. Aus dem Innenleben des Staatlichen Pangermanismus.* (Berlin 1994)
Goldhagen, E., *Weltanschauung und Endlösung. Zum Antisemitsmus der National-al-sozialistischen Führungsschicht. Schriftenreihe der Vierteljahrshefte für Zeitgeschichte.* (1976) pp. 379-405
Goldhagen, D.J., *Hitler's Willing Executioners.* (Used here: *Hitlers gewillige beulen)* [1996] (1997)
Goodrick-Clarke, N., *The Occult Roots of Nazism. The Ariosophist of Austria and Germany 1980-1935.* (Northamptonshire 1985)

Gordon, S., *Hitler, Germans and the 'Jewish Question'.* (1984).
Görlitz, W., *Die Junker. Adel und Bauer im deutschen Osten. Geschichtliche Bilanz von 7 Jahrhunderten.* (1964)
Görlitz, W., *November 1918. Bericht über die deutsche Revolution.* (Hamburg 1968)
Gorodetsky, G., *Stalin und Hitlers Angriff auf die Sowjetunion. Eine Auseinandersetzung mit der Legende vom deutschen Präventivschlag.* in: *Schriftenreihe der Vierteljahrshefte für Zeitgeschichte* (1985)
Gosztony, P., *Hitler's Fremde Heere. Das Schicksal der nichtdeutschen Armeen im Ostfeldzug.* (Düsseldorf 1976)
Grebing, H., *Der Nationalsozialismus. Ursprung und Wesen.* [1959] (Munich/Wien 1964)
Greiffenhagen, M., *Das Dilemma des Konservatismus in Deutschland.* (Frankfurt am Main 1986)
Grimm, H., *Volk ohne Raum. Ungekürzte Ausgabe in einem Band.* (Munich 1932).
Gruchmann, L., *Nationalsozialistische Grossraumordnung. Die Konstruktion einer 'deutschen Monroe-Doktrin'. Schriftenreihe der Vierteljahrshafte für Zeitgeschichte. No. 4* (Stuttgart 1962)
Grün, W., *Dietrich Eckart as Publizist.* (Munich 1941)
Guderian, H., *Achtung Panzer!* [1937] (1992)
Haase, N/Paul, G., (Hg.), *Die andere Soldaten. Wehrkraftzersetzung, Gehorsamsverweigerung und Fahnenflucht im Zweiten Weltkrieg.* (Frankfurt am Main 1995)
Haffner, S., *Die sieben Todsünden des deutschen Reiches im Ersten Weltkrieg.* [1964] (1981)
Haffner, S., *Kanttekeningen bij Hitler.* (Amsterdam 1978)
Haffner, S., *1918/19. Eine deutsche Revolution.* (1979)
Haffner, S., *Der Teufelspakt: die deutsch-russischen Beziehungen von Ersten zum Zweiten Weltkrieg.* (Used here: *Het duivelspact. De Duits-Russische betrekkingen van de eerste tot de tweede wereldoorlog).* [1988] (1989)
Haffner, S., *Germany: Jekyll & Hyde. 1939-Deutschland von innen betrachtet.* [1940] (Berlin 1996)
Hagen, W., *Die geheime Front. Organisationen, Personen und Aktionen des deutschen Geheimdienstes* (Stuttgart 1949).
Hamann, B., *Hitlers Wien. Lehrjahre eines Diktators.* (Munich 1996)
Hamersveld, M.van/Klinkhamer, M., *Messianisme zonder mededogen. Het communisme, zijn aanhangers en zijn slachtoffers.* (Nieuwegein 1998)
Hanfstaengl, E., *Zwischen Weissem und Braunem Haus. Erinnerungen eines politischen Aussenseiters.* (Munich 1970)
Hantschel, A., *Baku. Messianisme zonder mededogen. Het communisme, zijn aanhangers en zijn slachtoffers.* (Amsterdam 1943)
Hartung, G., *Goethe und die Juden* in: *Weimarer Beiträge. Zeitschrift für Literaturwissenschaft Aesthetik und Kulturwissenschaften no.1* pp. 398-416 (1994)

Hartog, L.J., *Hoe ontstond de jodenmoord? Hitler, Amerika en de Endlösung.* (Den Haag 1994)

Hausner, G., *Die Vernichtung der Juden. Dass grösste Verbrechen der Geschichte.* (Munich 1979)

Hausser, P., *Soldaten wie andere auch. Der Weg der Waffen-SS.* [1966] (Osnabrück 1988)

Haushofer, K./Oberst, E.,/Lautensach, H., et al. (Hg.), *Bausteine zur Geopolitik.* (Berlin 1928)

Haushofer, K.,(Hg.), *Die Grossmächte vor und nach dem Weltkriege. Zweiundzwanzigste Auflage der Grossmächte Rudolf Kjelléns.* (Leipzig, Berlin 1930)

Haushofer, K., *Der Kontinentalblock. Kriegschriften der Reichstudentenführung.* (Munich 1941)

Haushofer, K., *Weltmeere und Weltmächte.* [1937] (Berlin 1941)

Hecker, H., *'Mitteleuropa' aus historischer Sicht.* in: *Amsterdam Studies in Cultural Identity* part 3 *Deutschland, aber wo liegt es? Deutschland und Mitteleuropa. Analysen und Historischen Dokumente.* (Amsterdam 1993)

Hedin, S., *Duitschland en de wereldvrede (Den Haag 1937).*

Heer, F., *Der Glaube des Adolf Hitlers. Anatomie einer politischen Relogiosität.* (Munich 1968)

Heer, F., *Gottes Erste Liebe. 2000 Jahre Judentum und Christentum. Genesis des Österreichischen Katholiken Adolf Hitler.* [1967] (1968)

Heiber, H., *Adolf Hitler. Biografie.* (Utrecht 1968)

Heil, J.,/Erb, R., *Geschichtswissenschaft und Öffentlichkeit. Der Streit um Daniel J. Goldhagen.* (Frankfurt am Main 1998)

Heinsohn, G., *Warum Auschwitz? Hitlers Plan und die Ratlosigkeit der Nachwelt.* (Reinbek bei Hamburg 1995)

Heller, F.P./Maegerle, A., *Thule. Vom völkischen Okkultismus bis zur Neuen Rights.* (Stuttgart 1995)

Herntrich, V., *Neu-Heidentum und Christenglaube* (Gütersloh 1935).

Herzfeld, H., *Die Weimarer Republik. In: Deutsche Geschichte. Ereignisse und Probleme, herausgegeben von Walther Hubatsch.* (1966)

Hieronimus, E., *Lanz von Liebenfels. Eine Bibliographie. Toppenstedter Reihe 11.*

Hilberg, R., *Die Vernichtung der europäischen Juden* (3 volumes) [1961] (Frankfurt am Main 1993)

Hildebrand, K., *Das vergangene Reich. Deutsche Aussenpolitik von Bismarck bis Hitler.* (Stuttgart 1995)

Hillgruber, A., *Die Endlösung und das deutsche Ostimperium als Kernstück des rasidiologischen Programms des Nationalsozialismus. Schriftenreihe der Vierteljahrshefte für Zeitgeschichte (*1973 1. Heft/Januar)

Hintzenstern, H. von, *H.St.Chamberlain's Darstellung des Urchristentums. Studien zur deutscher Theologie und Frömmigkeit Band 6* (Weimar 1941)

Hitler, A., *Mein Kampf. Zwei Bände in einem Band. Ungekürzte Ausgabe.* [1924] (Munich 1943)
Hobsbawm, E.J., *Nationen und Nationalismus. Mythos und Realität seit 1780.* [1990] (Stuttgart 1996)
Hofer, Prof Dr W. (Hg.), *Der Nationalsozialismus. Dokumente 1933-1945.* [1957] (1982)
Hofer, Prof Dr W., *Die Entfesselung des Zweiten Weltkrieges (*Used here: *De ontketening van de Tweede Wereldoorlog)* (1965)
Hofer, W., *Die Vorgeschichte des Zweiten Weltkrieges. Legende und Wirklichkeit.* (Zurich 1963)
Hoffmann, J., *Einzelschriften zur militärischen Geschichte des Zweiten Weltkrieges 19, Die Ostlegionen 1941-1943* [1976] (Freiburg 1981)
Hoffmann, J., *Einzelschriften zur militärischen Geschichte des Zweiten Weltkrieges. 35, Caucasia 1942/1943 Das deutsche Heer und die Orientvölker der Sovjet-Union* (Freiburg 1991)
Hoffmann, J., *Einzelschriften zur militärischen Geschichte des Zweiten Weltkrieges Die Geschichte der Wlassow-Armee.* [1984] (Freiburg 1986)
Hoffmann, H., *Hitler wie ich ihn sah. Aufzeichnungen seines Leibfotografen.* (Munich 1974)
Horrabin, J.F./Gregroy, J.S., *Sovjet-Unie. Bodemgesteldheid, bevolking, industrie en productie.* (Amsterdam 1946)
Hörster-Philipps, U., *Wer war Hitler wirklich? Grosskapital und Faschismus 1918-1945. Dokumente.* (Cologne 1978)
Hossbach, F., *Zwischen Wehrmacht und Hitler 1934-1938* (Hanover 1949)
Hubricht, E., *Buchweiser für das völkisch-religiöse Schriftum und dessen Grenzgebiete. Toppenstedter Reihe. Sammlung bibliographischer Hilfsmittel zur Erforschung der Konservativen Revolution und des Nationalsozialismus. Band 5.* [1934] (Toppenstedt 1983)
Hudal, A., *Die Grundlagen des Nationalsozialismus.* (Leipzig/Wien 1937)
Hüser, K., *Wewelsburg 1933-1945. Kult und Terrorstätte der SS.* (Paderborn 1982)
Institut für Marxismus-Leninismus beim ZK der SED (Hg.), *Die Grosse Oktoberrevolution und die Entstehung einer revolutionären Krise in Deutschland.* (Berlin 1978)
Ipema, J., *Ipema, J., In dienst van Leviathan. Ernst Jünger. Tijd en werk. 1895-1932* (Nieuwegein 1997)
Irving, D., *Hess. The missing Years 1941-1945.* (London 1987)
Irving, D., *Hitler's War.* (New York 1990)
Irving, D., *Göring, a biography.* [1989] (New York 1990)
Irving, D., *Goebbels, Macht und Magie.* (Kiel 1997)
Jäckel,E., *Hitler's Weltanschauung.* [1981] (1983)
Jäckel,E., *Das deutsche Jahrhundert. Eine historische Bilanz.* (Stuttgart 1996)

Jacobsen, H.A., *1939-1945. Der Zweite Weltkrieg in Chronik und Dokumenten.* (Darmstadt 1959)

Jacobsen, H.A., *Der Zweite Weltkrieg. Grundzüge der Politik und Strategie in Dokumenten* (Frankfurt am Main 1965).

Jacobsen, H.A., *Nationalsozialistische Aussenpolitik 1933-1938.* (Frankfurt am Main/Berlin 1968)

Jacobsen, H.A., *Karl Haushofer, Leben und Werk Band I Lebensweg 1869-1946 und ausgewählte Texte zur Geopolitik.* (Boppard am Rhein 1979)

Jacobsen, H.A., *Karl Haushofer, Leben und Werk Band II Ausgewählter Schriftwechsel 1917-1946* (Boppard am Rhein 1979)

Jaenecke, H., *Poland, Träumer, Helden, Opfer.* (Used here: *Polen, kleine geschiedenis van een opstandige natie).* [1981] (1982)

Jansen, C./Weckbecker, A., *Der 'Volksdeutsche Selbstschutz' in Poland 1939/40* in: *Schriftenreihe der Vierteljahrshefte für Zeitgeschichte. Band 64* (1992)

Jansen, H.,Christelijke theologie na Auschwitz. Twee Nieuwtestamentische wortels van het antisemitisme. a1: Diagnose en therapie in geschriften van joden en christenen Band 1 en 2.(Den Haag 1985)

Jansen, H., Het Madagascar plan. De voorgenomen deportatie van europese joden naar Madagascar. (Den Haag 1996)

Joll, J., Europe since 1870. An international history. [1973] (1987).

Jong, L. de, De Duitse vijfde colonne in de Tweede Wereldoorlog. [1953] (Amsterdam 1977)

Jordan, K., Barbarossa. (Den Haag 1963).

Jordan, R., *Erlebt und Erlitten. Weg eines Gauleiters von München bis Moskou.* (Leoni am Starnbergersee 1971).

Jünger, E., *Das erste Pariser Tagebuch/Kaukasische Aufzeichnungen.* Used here: Parijs dagboek 1941-1943. Privé domein nr.123 [1979] (Amsterdam 1986)

Kadt, J. de., *De deftigheid in het gedrang. Een keuze uit zijn verspreide geschriften.* (Amsterdam 1981).

Keegan, J., *Waffen-SS, The Asphalt Soldiers.* (London 1970)

Keegan, J., *Von Rundstedt.* [1974] (1977).

Keegan, J., *A History of Warfare* (Used here: *Die Kultur des Krieges.*) [1993]. (Berlin 1995)

Kehr, H., *The Nazi Era, 1919-1945* (London 1982)

Kessler, M.,/Vitzthum,W.Graf.,/Wertheimer, J. (Hg.), *Neonationalismus. Neokonservatismus. Sondierungen und Analysen. Stauffenburg Discussion Band 6* (Tübingen 1997).

Kessler, H., *Walther Rathenau* (Arnhem 1939).

Ketelsen, U-K., *Völkisch-nationale und nationalsozialistische Literatur in Deutschland 1890-1945.* Sammlung Metzler Band 142 (Stuttgart 1976).

Kissener, M./Scholtyseck, J. (Hg.), *Die Führer der Provinz. NS-Biographien aus*

Baden und Württemberg. Karlsruher Beiträge zur Geschichte des Nationalsozialismus Band 2 (1997).
Kjellén,R., *Der Staat als Lebensform.* (Leipzig 1917).
Klee, E., *Persielscheine und falsche Pässe. Wie die Kirchen den Nazis halfen.* (Frankfurt am Main 1991)
Klee, E., *'Die sa Jesu Christi'. Die Kirche im Banne Hitlers.* (Frankfurt am Main 1989)
Klee, E./Dressen,W. (Hg.), *'Gott mit uns'. Der deutsche Vernichtungskrieg im Osten 1939-1945.* (Frankfurt am Main 1989)
Kleine, G.H., *Adelgenossenschaft und Nationalsozialismus* in *Schriftenreihe der Vierteljahrshefte für Zeitgeschichte 1. heft 1976.*
Kohut, T.H., *Wilhelm II and the Germans. A Study in Leadership.* (New York/Oxford 1991)
Könnemann, E., *Kapp's Vorbereitungen auf einen Prozess, der nie stattfand. Dokumente aus seinem Nachlass.* in: *Zeitschrift für Geschichtswissenschaft.* Heft 7 (1995)
Kovacs, T., *Het drama Hongarije.* (Utrecht 1957)
Krausnick, H., *Kommisarbefehl und 'Gerichtbarkeitserlass' Barbarossa in neuer Sicht.* in: *Vierteljahrsheft für Zeitgeschichte.* (1977)
Krockow, Graf C. von, *'Unser Kaiser. Glanz und Sturtz der Monarchie'.* [1993] (Munich 1996)
Krockow, Graf C. von, *Von deutschen Mythen.* [1995] (Stuttgart 1997).
Krockow, Graf C. von, *Bismarck. Eine Biographie (*Stuttgart 1997).
Kroll, F-L., *Geschichte und Politik im Weltbild Hitlers.* in: *Vierteljahsheft für Zeitgeschichte 1.Heft.* (1996).
Kruck, A., *Geschichte des alldeutschen Verbandes 1890-1939.* (Wiesbaden 1954).
Kuby, E., *Als Polen deutsch war (*Munich 1986).
Kurzke, H/Stachorski, S. (Hg.), *Thomas Mann Essays. Band 5: Deutschland und die Deutschen 1938-1945.* (Frankfurt am Main 1996)
Kuusisto, S., *Alfred Rosenberg in der nationalsozialistischen Aussenpolitik 1933-1939. Studia Historica 15.* (Helsinki 1984)
Labrie, A., *Het verlangen naar zuiverheid. Een essay over Duitsland.* (1994).
Lamont, C., *The Peoples of the Soviet Union.* [1944] (New York 1946).
Landstroem, A., *Krieg unter der Mitternachtssonne. Finnlands Freiheitskampf. 1939-1945.* (1989) (1996)
Langer, W.C., *The Mind of Adolf Hitler. The Secret Wartime Report.* (New York 1972)
Laqueur, W., *Russia and Germany. A Century of Conflict.* (London 1965).
Laqueur, W., *Weimar a cultural history 1918-1933.* (Used here: *Weimar. Die Kultur der Republik.* [1974] (Munich 1976).
Lehmann, M. (Hg.), *Verleger J.F. Lehmann. Ein Leben im Kampf für Deutschland. Lebenslauf und Briefe.* (Munich 1935)

Leuschner, J., *Volk und Raum. Zum Stil der Nationalsozialistischen Aussenpolitik.* (Göttingen 1958).

Liddel Hart, B., *Europe in Arms.* Used here: Europa mobiliseert (Amsterdam 1938)

Linge, H., *In het voetspoor van de Führer. Onthullingen van Hitlers privé-adjudant.* (Utrecht 1985)

Lochner, L.P. (Ed.), *The Goebbels Diaries 1942-1943.* (New York 1948)

Loeser, E., *The Image of the Germans in Polish Literature.* (?)

Loohuis, J.G., *Mensch en Mogendheid. Een probleem van alle tijden. (Leiden 1944)*

Los, F.J., *Rusland tussen Azië en Europa. Een geschiedkundige bijdrage tot de kennis van het bolsjewisme. (Amsterdam 1943)*

Luckács, G., *Von Nietzsche zu Hitler oder der Irrationalismus und die deutsche Politik.* [1962] (1966)

Lukács, G., *Die Zerstörung der Vernunft Band-I. Irrationalismus zwischen den Revolutionen.* [1953] (1973)

Lukacs, J., *The Hitler of History.* (used here: *Hitler, Geschichte und Geschichtsschreibung.* [1997] (Munich 1997)

Ludendorff, E., *Mathilde Ludendorff, ihr Werk und Wirken.* (Munich 1937)

Ludendorff, E., *Auf dem Weg zur Feldherrnhalle. Lebenserinnerungen an die Zeit des 9-11-1923 mit Dokumenten in 5 Anlagen.* (Munich 1937)

Ludendorff, E./Ludendorff von Kemnitz, M., *Das Geheimnis der Jesuitenmacht und ihr Ende.* (1929)

Ludendorff von Kemnitz,M., *Hinter den Kulissen des Bismarckreiches.* (Munich 1931)

Ludendorff von Kemnitz, M., *Deutscher Gottglaube* (Munich 1934).

Ludendorff von Kemnitz, M., *Durch Forschen und Schicksal zum Sinn des Lebens. II. Teil von: Statt Heiligenschein oder Ehrenzeichen. Mein Leben.* (Munich 1936)

Ludendorff von Kemnitz, M., *Erkenntnis-Erlösung. iii. Teil von: Statt Heiligenschein oder Ehrenzeichen. Mein Leben.* (reissue 1980)

Ludendorff von Kemnitz, M., *Der Seele, Ursprung und Wesen teil 1: Schöpfung Geschichte.* [1923] (1937)

Ludendorff, *Studie eines Revolutionärs* (Pähl 1985)

Lynar, E.W. Graf (Hg.), *Deutsche Kriegsziele 1914-1918.* (Berlin 1964)

Macintyre, B., *Vergeten vaderland. Op zoek naar het fascistisch paradijs van Elisabeth Nietzsche.* [1993] (Amsterdam 1994)

Malia, M., *The Soviet Tragedy. A History of Socialism in Russia, 1917-1991.* (New York 1994)

Mallebrein, W., *Albert Leo Schlageter. Ein deutscher Freiheitskämpfer.* (Oldendorf 1993)

Manstein, E. von, *Verlorene Siege.* (Frankfurt am Main 1964)

Manvell, R./Fraenkel,H., *Hess. A Biography.* (London 1971)

Margolina, S., *Das Ende der Lügen. Die Russland und die Juden im 20. Jahrhunderts.* (Berlin 1993)

Martin,W., *Die fernen Söhne. Deutsche Wanderung und Siedlung in aller Welt.* (Hamburg 1944)

Maser, W., *Die Frühgeschichte der nsdap. Hitlers Weg bis 1924.* (Frankfurt am Main/ Bonn 1965)

Maser, W., *Hitler's Mein Kampf.* [1969] (1998)

Maser, W., *Adolf Hitler, Legend, Mythos, Wirklichkeit.* (Used here: *Hitler. Legende, mythe, werkelijkheid.* [1973] (Amsterdam 1985)

Maser, W., *Der Wortbruch. Hitler, Stalin und der Zweite Weltkrieg.* (Munich 1994)

Mayer, A.J., *Why did the heavens not darken? The Final Solution in History.* [1988] (New York 1990)

Mecklenburg, J. (Hg.), *Handbuch deutscher Rechts Extremismus* (Berlin 1996)

Meclewski, E., *'Ostforschung' im Dienste des Dranges nach Osten.* (1963)

Messcherschmidt, M., *Der Krieg im Osten, Ursachen und Charakter des Krieges gegen die Sowjetunion.* in: Reinhard Kühnl/Ulrike Hörster-Philipps (Hg.), *Hitlers Krieg? Zur Kontroverse um Ursachen und Charakter des Zweiten Weltkrieges.* (Cologne 1989)

Metzsch. von, *Clausewitz Katechismus.* (1937)

Meyer zu Uptrup, W., *Wann wurde Hitler zum Antisemit?* in: *Zeitschrift für Geschichtswissenschaft Heft 7* (1995)

Michal, W., *Deutschland und der nächste Krieg.* (Berlin 1995)

Mikes, G., *Any Souvenirs? A native returns to Central Europe and a second expulsion.* (Boston 1972)

Miller, S.E., *Military Strategy and the Origins of the First World War. An International Security Reader.* (1984)

Minshall, T.H., *Duitsland's wil tot wereldoverheersing. Geschiedkundige en filosofische verklaring.* Also appeared under the name of: *Wat te doen met Duitschland?* (Den Haag 1939)

Mohler, A., *Die konservative Revolution in Deutschland 1918-1932. Grundriss ihrer Weltanschauungen.* (Stuttgart 1950)

Molau, A., *Alfred Rosenberg. Der Ideologe des Nationalsozialismus. Eine politische Biography.* (Koblenz 1993)

Mosley, L., *The Reich Marschall-A Biography of Hermann Göring.* (Used here: *Göring, Portret van een Rijksmaarschalk* [1974] (1979)

Mosse, G.L., *The Crisis of German Ideology. Intellectual Origins of the Third Reich.* [1964] (London 1966)

Mosse, G.L., *Nazism. A Historical and Comparative Analysis of National Socialism. An interview with Michael A. Ledeen.* [1977] (New Brunswick 1978)

Mukherji, S.D., *Gold im Schmelziegel. Erlebnisse im Nachkriegsdeutschland.* in: *Kritik die Stimme des Volkes.* no.60 [1952] (1982)

Müller, G., *Dolchstoss oder Dolchstoss-Legende? November 1918.* (Stuttgart 1978)

Müller, R.D., *Hitler's Ostkrieg und die deutsche Siedlungspolitik.* (Frankfurt am Main 1991).

Mund, R.J., *Jörg Lanz von Liebenfels und der Neue Templer Orden. Die Esoterik des Christentums.* (Stuttgart 1976)

Naarden, B., *De spiegel der Barbaren. Socialistisch Europa en revolutionair Rusland (1848-1923).* (Amsterdam 1986)

Nagy, A., *A Cultural and Historical Review of Central Europe.* (Melbourne 1995)

Nationalsozialistischer Führungsstab der Wehrmacht (Hg.), *Der Nationalsozialis-tische Führungsoffizier, Farm, Kolchose oder Erbhof? Schulungsthema Nr.11 Führungsunterlagen Folge 3. Nur für Gebrauch innerhalb der Wehrmacht.* (1944).

The Nazi Kultur in Poland. Written in Warsaw under the German Occupation and Published for the Polish Ministry of Information by his Majesty's Stationery Office. (London 1945)

Neuhäusler, J., *Kreuz und Hakenkreuz. Der Kampf des Nationalsozialismus gegen die katholische Kirche und der kirchliche Widerstand. Erster Teil* (Munich 1946)

Niekisch, E., *Das Reich der niederen Dämonen.* (Hamburg 1953)

Nipperdey, T./Doering-Manteuffel, A./Thamer, H-U. (Hg), *Weltbrüderkrieg der Ideologists. Antworten an Ernst Nolte. Festschrift zum 70.Geburtstag.* (Berlin 1993).

Nissen, B.M., *Der Rembrandtdeutsche, Julius Langbehn.* (Freiburg 1937)

Nitti, F., *Der Niedergang Europas. Die Wege zum Wiederaufbau.* (1922)

Nolte, E., *Der Europäische Bürgerkrieg 1917-1945. Nationalsozialismus und Bolschewismus.* (Berlin 1987)

Nording, G., *Geheimnisse vom Rosenkreuz.* (Munich 1938)

Nove, A., *Stalinism and after. The Road to Gorbachev.* [1975] (1989)

Opitz, R., *Faschismus und Neofaschismus.* (Bonn 1996).

Osseg, A., *Der Hammer der Freimaurerei am Kaiserthrone der Habsburger.* (Amberg 1875)

Pastenaci, K., *Die beide Weltmächte.* Used here: *Van Jutland tot Byzantium. De 500 jarige strijd der Germanen tegen Rome* (Zwolle 1943).

Pätzold, K./Weissbecker, M., *Adolf Hitler.* (Leipzig 1995)

Paul, O.E.,/Claussen, W., *Grossdeutschland und die Welt. Ein Wirtschafts -ABC in Zahlen.* (Berlin 1938)

Pauley, B.F., *Hitler and the Forgotten Nazis. A History of Austrian National Socialism.* (1981)

Petzina, D., *Autarkiepolitik im Dritten Reich. Der nationalsozialistische Vierjahresplan.* in: *Schriftenreihe der Vierteljahreshefte für Zeitgeschichte.* (Stuttgart 1968).

Picker, Dr H., *Hitlers Tischgespräche im Führerhauptquartier. Hitler, wie er wirklich war. Volständig überarbeitete und erweiterte Neuausgabe.* [1976] (1977). Used here: Hitlers tafelgesprekken, het echte dagboek van Adolf Hitler (Amsterdam 1983).

Pieper, K., *Ludendorff und die heilige Schrift. Antwort auf die Schrift 'Das grosse Entsetzen - Die Bibel nicht Gottes Wort'.* (Munich)

Pierik, P., *Van Leningrad tot Berlijn. Nederlandse vrijwilligers in dienst van de Duitse Waffen-SS 1941-1945.* (Nieuwegein 1995)
Pierik. P., *Hongarije 1944-1945. De vergeten tragedie. De laatste Duitse offensieven van de Tweede Wereldoorlog. De ondergang van de laatste joodse gemeenschap van Europa.* (Nieuwegein 1995)
Pilichowski, C., *Es gibt keine Verjährung.* (Warszawa 1980)
Piotrowska, S., *Hans Franks Tagebuch* (Warsaw 1963)
Pipes, R., *Russia under Bolshevik regime.* (New York 1993)
Pipes, R., *The Unknown Lenin. From the Secret Archive.* (London 1996)
Ploetz (Hg.), Bearbeitet von Dr. Percy Ernst Schramm/Dr. O.H. Stange/Dr. Andreas Hillgruber *Geschichte des Zweiten Weltkrieges 1939-1945 1. Teil: Die militärischen und politischen Ereignisse. 2. Teil: Die Kriegsmittel.* (Würzburg 1960).
Poidevin, R., *L'Allemagne et le monde au xxe siecle.* (Used here: *Die unruhige Grossmacht. Deutschland und die Welt im 20. Jahrhundert.* [1983] (Würzburg 1985)
Poliakov, L., *Le myth aryen.* Used here: *De arische mythe. Over de bronnen van het racisme en de verschillende vormen van nationalisme* [1971] (Amsterdam 1979).
(Die) Polnischen Greueltaten an den Volksdeutschen in Polen. Im Auftrage des auswärtigen Amtes auf Grund urkundlichen Beweismaterials zusammengestellt, bearbeitet und herausgegeben (Berlin 1940).
Pool, J. and S., *Who financed Hitler? The Secret Funding of Hitler's Rise to Power. 1919-1933* [1978] (New York 1979)
Pomian, K., *Europa en de europese naties.* (Amsterdam 1993)
Prignitz, C., *Vaterlandsliebe und Freiheit. Deutscher Patriotismus von 1750 bis 1850* (Wiesbaden).
Price, M.P., *Hitler's War and Eastern Europe.* (London 1940)
Quinn,M., *The Swastika. Constructing the symbol* (London 1994).
Raddatz, F.J., *Summa iniuria, oder durfte der Papst schweigen? Hochhuts 'Stellvertreter' in der öffentlichen Kritik.* (Reinbek bei Hamburg 1963)
Rahn, R., *Ruheloses Leben. Aufzeichnungen und Erinnerungen.* (Düsseldorf 1949)
Rall, H., *Wilhelm ii. Eine Biogaphie* (Graz/Wien/Köln 1995).
Rathenau, W., *Von kommenden Dingen.* (Berlin 1917)
Rathenau, W., *Der Kaiser, Eine Betrachtung.* (Berlin 1919)
Rauschning, H., *The nihilist revolution. Appearance and reality in the Third Reich* (1939)
Rauschning, H., *Gespräche mit Hitler.* (New York 1940)
Ravenscroft, T., *The Spear of Destiny. The Occult Power behind the Spear which Pierced the Side of Christ.* [1973] (1995).
Reich, W., *Die Massen-psychologie des Faschismus.* [1933] (1977)
Reimann, V., *Goebbels.* (Baarn 1971).
Reinhard, W. (Hg.), *Imperialist Kontinuität und nationale Ungeduld im 19. Jahrhundert.* (Frankfurt am Main 1991).

Reischle, H., *Kann man Deutschland verhungern?* (Berlin 1940).
Recker, K-A., *'Wem wollt iht glauben?' Bischof Berning im Dritten Reich.* (Paderborn 1998)
Ribbentrop, J. von, *Zwischen London und Moskou. Erinnerungen und letzte Aufzeichnungen. Aus dem Nachlass herausgegeben von Annelies von Ribbentrop.* (Leoni am Starnberger See 1953)
Rich, N., *Hitler's War Aims. Ideology, the Nazi State, and the Course of Expansion.* [1973] (New York/London 1993).
Richardi, H-G., *Hitler und seine Hintermänner. Neue Fakten zur Frühgeschichte der NSDAP.* (Munich 1991)
Richardson, W./Freidin, S. (ed.), *The Fatal Decisions.* (London 1956)
Riedel, M., *Bergbau und Eisenhüttenindustrie in der Ukraine unter Deutscher Besatzung (1941-1944). Vierteljahshefte für Zeitgeschichte* (21. Jahrgang 1973 3. Heft/july)
Röhm, E., *Geschichte eines Hochverräters.* (Munich 1934)
Romein, J., *Commodities and politics.* (Amsterdam 1935)
Ros, M., *Jakhalzen van het Derde Rijk. Ondergang van de collabo's 1944-1945.* (Amsterdam 1995)
Rosenberg,A., *Die Protokolle der Weissen von Zion und die jüdische Weltpolitik.* (Munich 1933)
Rosenberg, A., *An die Dunklermänner unserer Zeit. Eine Antwort auf die Angriffe gegen den Mythus des 20. Jahrhunderts.* (Munich 1934)
Rosenberg, A., *Blut und Ehre. Ein Kampf für deutsche Wiedergeburt. Reden und Aufsätze von 1919-1933.* Herausgegeben von Thilo von Trotha (Munich 1935).
Rosenberg, A., *Der Mythos des 20. Jahrhunderts. Eine Wertung der seelischgeistigen Gestaltenkämpfe unserer Zeit.* [1930] (Munich 1936)
Rosenberg, A., *Der Sumpf. Querschnitte durch das 'Geistes'leben der November-Demokratie.* (Munich 1939)
Rosenberg, Arthur, *Entstehung der Weimarer Republik.* (Frankfurt am Main 1961)
Rosinksi, H., *Die Deutsche Armee. Vom Triumph zur Niederlage.* [1966] (1977)
Rössler, M./Schleiermacher, S., *Der 'Generalplan Ost'. Hauptlinien der nationalsozialistischen Planungs- und Vernichtungspolitik.* (Berlin 1993)
Rothfels, H., *Bismarck, der Osten und das Reich.* (Darmstadt 1960)
Rougemont, D. de., *Journal d'Allemagne.* (Used here: *A year in the Third Reich*) (1939)
Rovan, J., *Histoire de l'Allemagne. Des origines a nos jours.* (Used here: *Geschichte der Deutschen. Von ihren Ursprüngen bis Heute*) [1944] (1997)
Royal Institute of International Affairs, South-Eastern Europe. A Political and Economic Survey. (London 1939)
Ruge, W./Schumann, W, *Dokumente zur deutschen Geschichte. 1919-1923.* (Frankfurt am Main 1977)

Ruck, M., *Bibliographie zum Nationalsozialismus*. (1995)
Sabrin, D.B., *Alliance for murder. The Nazi-Ukrainian Nationalist Partnership in Genocide*. (New York 1991)
Sabrow, M., *Die verdrängte Verschwörung. Der Rathenau-Mord und die deutsche Gegenrevolution*. (Frankfurt am Main 1999)
Salemink/Van Dijk, *'Omdat het slechts om politiek gaat.' De machtsovername door de nazi's in 1933 als keerpunt van het politieke christendom*. (Amersfoort/Leuven 1986)
Salewski, M., *Zur deutschen Sicherheitspolitik in der Spätzeit der Weimarer Republik. Schriftenreihe der Vierteljahrshefte für Zeitgeschichte*. (22.Jahrgang 1974. 2. Heft/April)
Samerski, S., *Priest im annektierten Polen. Die Seelsorge deutscher Geistlicher in den an an das Deutsche Reich angeschlossenen polnischen Gebieten1939-1945*.(1997)
Schacht, H., *76 Jahre meines Lebens*. (Bad Wörishofen 1953)
Schirer, W.L., *The Rise and Fall of the Third Reich. A History of Nazi Germany*. [1959] (1973)
Schoeps, J.H./Schloer, J (Hg.), *Antisemitismus, Vorurteile und Mythen*. (Munich 1995)
Schölgen, G., *Die Macht in der Mitte Europas. Stationen deutscher Aussenpolitik. Von Friedrich dem Grossen bis zur Gegenwart.* [1992] (Munich 1994)
Schramm, P.E., *Hitler als militärischer Führer. Erkenntnisse und Erfahrungen aus dem Kriegstagebuch des Oberkommandos der Wehrmacht*. (Frankfurt am Main 1962)
Schubart, W., *Europa und die Seele des Ostens*. [1938] (Lucerne 1946)
Schukow, *Erinnerungen und Gedanken*. (Stuttgart 1969)
Schreiber, G., *Hitler Interpretationen 1923-1983. Ergebnisse, Methoden und Probleme der Forschung*. (Darmstadt 1984)
Schreiner, A., *Hitler treibt zum Krieg. Dokumentarischen Enthüllungen über Hitlers Geheimrüstungen*. [1934] (Frankfurt am Main 1979)
Schwanitz, W. (Hg.), *Jenseits der Legenden. Araber, Juden, Deutsche*. (Berlin 1994).
Schwarzmüller, T., *Zwischen Kaiser und Führer. Generalfeldmarschall August von Mackensen*. (Paderborn 1996)
See, K von, *Barbar, Germane, Arier. Die Suche nach der Identität der Deutschen*. (Heidelberg 1994)
Sektion Philosophie und Geschichte der Friedrich-Schiller-Universität, Prof. Dr. Dieter Fricke (Hg.), *Zur Ukraine-Politik des deutschen Imperialismus. Protokoll einer Arbeitstagung am 23.09.1967*. (Jena 1969)
Seraphim, H.G. (Hg.), *Das politische Tagebuch Alfred Rosenbergs 1934/35 und 1939/40*. [1956] (Munich 1965)
Simonds, F.H., *Can Europe keep the Peace?* (London 1932)
Singer, H.W. (Hg.), *Allgemeines Künstler-Lexicon. Leben und Werke der berühmtesten bildenden Künstler. Dritter band*. (Frankfurt am Main 1898)

Smith, B.F./Peterson,A.F., *Heinrich Himmler. Geheimreden 1933 bis 1945 und other Ansprachen.* (Berlin 1974)

Smith, B.F., *Die Überlieferung der Hossbach-Niederschrift im Lichte neuer Quellen.* in: *Zeitschrift für Geschichtswissenschaft.* (1994)

Smith, M.J.Jr., *The Soviet Army, 1939-1980. A Guide to Sources in English.* (Santa Barbara/Oxford)

Steding, C., *Das Reich und die Krankheit der europäischen Kultur.* (Hamburg 1942).

Soergel, H., *Atlantropa* (Munich 1932)

Sofsky, W., *Die Ordnung des Terrors. Das Konzentrationslager.* (1993)

Speer, A., *Erinnerungen* (Used here: *Memoirs*) (Baarn 1970)

Speidel, H., *Invasion 1944. Der letzte Chef des Generalstabes von Feldmarschall Rommel über die Invasion und das Schicksal seines Oberbefehlhabers.* [1949] (1974)

Steger, B., *Der Hitlerprozess und Bayerns Verhältniss zum Reich 1923/24.* in: *Schriftenreihe der Vierteljahrshefte für Zeitgeschichte* Blz. 441-466 (1977)

Stern, J.P., *Hitler, the Führer and the People.* [1975] (1984)

Sternberg, F., *Hoe lang kan Hitler oorlog voeren? Het lot van Duitsland in de volgende oorlog.*(Amsterdam 1939)

Steinbeck, W., *Johann Gottlieb Fichte, Politik und Weltanschauung. Sein Kampf um die Freiheit in einer Auswahl aus seinen Schriften.* (Stuttgart 1941)

Stein, G.H., *Geschichte der Waffen-SS.* [1966] (1978)

Stein, W.J., *Weltgeschichte im Lichte des heiligen Gral. Band I Das neunte Jahrhundert.* (Stuttgart 1928)

Steiner, F., *Von Clausewitz bis Bulganin. Erkenntnisse und Lehren einer Wehrepoche.* (Bielefeld 1956)

Steiner, J.M., *Über das Glaubensbekenntnis der ss*, in Bracher/Funke/Jacobsen (Hg.), *Nationalsozialistische Dikatur. Eine Bilanz. Schriftenreihe der Bundeszentrale für politische Bildung Band 192* (1983)

Stenbock-Fermor, A., *Der Rote Graf. Baltischer Aristokrat, Weissgardist, Bergarbeiter, Widerstandskämpfer, Schriftsteller.* (Berlin 1973)

Steuer, C., *Theodor Dannecker. Ein Funktionär der 'Endlösung'. Schriften der Bibliothek für Zeitgeschichte-Neue Folge. Band 6.* (Essen 1997)

Stolleis, M., *Gemeinschaft und Volksgemeinschaft. Zur juristischen Terminologie im Nationalsozialismus. Vierteljahshefte für Zeitgeschichte* (21. Jahrgang 1973 3. Heft/july)

Störing, H.J., *Kleine Weltgeschichte der Philosophie* (Used here: *Geschiedenis van de filosofie part 1.*) (Utrecht/Antwerp 1971)

Stoss, A., *Ludendorff der ewige Recke.* (Landsberg an der Warthe 1936)

Strack, H.L., *Jüdische Geheimgesetze?* (Berlin 1925)

Strasser, O., *Kommt es zum Krieg?* (Prag 1937)

Ströle-Bühle, H., *Studentischer Antisemitismus in der Weimarer Republik. Eine Analyse der Burschenschaftlichen Blätter 1918 bis 1933.* in: *Europäische Hoch-*

schulschriften Reihe III Geschichte und ihre Hilfswissenschaften. Band 486. (Frankfurt am Main/Bern/New York 1991)
Suhr, E., *Carl von Ossietzky. Pazifist, Republikaner und Widerstandskämpfer.*
Suworow, V., *Der Eisbrecher. Hitler in Stalin's Kalkül.* (Stuttgart 1989)
Taylor, A.J.P., *Europe: Grandeur and Decline.* (London 1967)
Taylor, A.J.P., *The Origins of the Second World War.* (London 1961)
Taylor, A,J.P., *How Wars Begin.* Used here *Hoe oorlogen beginnen* [1977] (1980).
Taylor, P.J., *Political Geography. World-Economy, Nation-State and Locality.* [1985] (Edinburgh 1995)
Telpuchowski, B.S., *Die sovjetische Geschichte des Grossen Vaterländischen Krieges 1941-1945.* (Frankfurt am Main 1961)
Thamer, H.U., *Verführung und Gewalt, Deutschland 1933-1945. Die deutschen und ihre Nation.* (?)
Theosofische perspectieven. Ronden & Rassen. Onze goddelijke afstamming. Free edited after Getr. W. van Pelt. (Pasadena/Den Haag/Munich 1986)
Theweleit, K., *Männer Phantasien.* Band 1 *Frauen, Fluten, Körper, Geschichte.* [1977] (Reinbek bei Hamburg 1980)
The Third Reich at War. A Historical Bibliography. (Denver 1984)
Thies, J., *Hitler's 'Endziele': Zielloser Aktionismus, Kontinentalimperium oder Weltherrschaft?* in: Bracher/Funke/Jacobsen (Hg.), *Nationalsozialistische Diktatur 1933-1945. Eine Bilanz. Schriftenreihe der Bundeszentrale für politische Bildung. Band 192* (Bonn 1983).
Thijssen, F., *I Paid Hitler* (Used here: *I Paid Hitler. Perplexing revelations by the German Grand Industrialist.* (Amsterdam 1957)
Tieke, W., *Der Kaukasus und das Öl, der Deutsch-Russische Kampf im Kaukasien 1942/43* (Osnabrück 1970)
Toland, J., *Adolf Hitler. The end of a myth.* [1977] (1983)
Tschocke, G., *Der Feldzug im Baltikum 1919 als Ausgang östlicher Siedlung.* 13. Heft der 2.Schriftenreihe Ludendorffs Verlag. (Munich 1935)
Traue, Dr G., *Aryan Gott-Zertrümmerung. Wider falsche Propheten im neuen Deutschland.* (Braunschweig 1934)
Trepper, L., *Die Wahrheit. Autobiographie des 'Grand Chef' der Roten Kapelle. Reihe unerwünschte Bücher zum Faschismus nr.9* [1975] (Freiburg 1995)
Trevor-Roper, H.R. (Ed.), *Hitler's War Directives 1939-1945.* [1964] (London 1966)
Tschuppik, K., *Ludendorff. Die Tragödie des Fachmanns.* (Wien/Leipzig 1931)
Tucholsky, K., *Drei Minuten Gehör. Prosa, Gedichte, Briefe.* (Leipzig 1968)
Turner, J. (Ed), *The Dictionary of Art. Vol.29* (London 1996)
Tyushkevich, S.A., *The Soviet Armed Forces. A History of their Organizational Development. A Soviet View.* (1978)
Überschar, G.R., *Das Unternehmen 'Barbarossa' gegen die Sowjet-Union-ein Präven-*

tivkrieg? Zur Wiederbelebung der alten Rechtfertigungsversuche des deutschen Ueberfalls auf die UdSSR 1941 in: Brigitte Bailer-Galanda/Wolfgang Benz/ Wolfgang Neugebauer (Hg.), Die Auschwitzleugner. (Berlin 1996)
Uhle-Wettler, F., *Erich Ludendorff in seiner Zeit, Soldat-Stratege, Revolutionär. Eine Neubewertung* [1995] (Berg 1996)
Vaksberg, A., *Stalin against the Jews*. (New York 1994)
Váry, A., *A Vörös uralom áldozatai magyarországon* (Victims of the red lord-Hungary) (1993)
Venohr, W., *Ludendorff. Legende und Wirklichkeit*. (Frankfurt am Main 1993)
Vindex, *Die Politik des Ölflecks. Der Sowjetimperialismus im Zweiten Weltkrieg.* (Berlin 1944)
Volovici, L., *Antsemitism in Post-Communist Eastern Europe: A Marginal or Central Issue?* (Jerusalem 1994)
Volkmann, H-E. (Hg.), *Das Russlandbild im Dritten Reich*. (Cologne/Weimar/ Wien (1994)
Volkmann, H-E., *Wirtschaft im Dritten Reich. Bd.1 1933-1939. Schriften der Bibliothek für Zeitgeschichte. Weltkriegbücherei Stuttgart. Neue Folge der Bibliographien der Weltkrieg Bücherei. Band 20*(Munich)/*Wirtschaft im Dritten Reich Bd.2 1939-1945. Band 23* (Koblenz 1984)
Volkov, S., *Kontinuität und Diskontinuität im deutschen Antisemitismus 1878-1945.* in: *Schriftenreihe der Vierteljahrshefte für Zeitgeschichte Heft 2* (1985)
Vonolfen, W./Piel, E.,/Seifert, P., *Der Weg zum Reich*. (Berlin 1944)
Vulfsons, M., *Das lettische Nationalgefühl und die Juden*. (Vorbemerkung Wolfgang Benz) in: *Zeitschrift für Geschichtswissenschaft*. (1995)
Wagner, F./Vosberg, F., *Polenspiegel. Die Aktivitäten der Polen in Deutschland nach ihren eigenen Zeugnissen*. [1908] (1988)
Waite, R.G.L., *Vanguard of Nazism. The Free Corps Movement in Postwar Germany 1918-1923*. [1952] (1969)
Waite, R.G.L., *Adolf Hitler als psychopaat*. [1977] (Amsterdam 1978).
Waite, R.G.L., *Kaiser and Führer, A Comparative Study of Personality and Politics* (1998)
Wegner, B., *Hitler's Politische Soldaten: Die Waffen-SS 1933-1945*. [1982] (Paderborn 1997)
Weinberg,G.L., *Hitlers Zweites Buch. Ein Dokument aus dem Jahr 1928. Quellen und Darstellungen zur Zeitgeschichte Band 7* (Stuttgart 1961)
Weise,E., *Die Amtsgewalt von Papst und Kaiser und die Ostmission*. J.G.Herder Institut (Marburg/Lahn 1971)
Wessel, H., *Münzenbergs Ende 1933-1940. Ein deutscher Kommunist im Widerstand gegen Hitler und Stalin. Die Jahre 1933 bis 1940*. (Berlin 1991)
Wesseling, B.W., *Bayreuth im Dritten Reich. Richards Wagner's politische Erben. Eine Dokumentation*. (Basel 1983)

Wette, W. (Hersg.), *Der Krieg des kleinen Mannes. Eine Militärgeschichte von unten.* (Munich 1992)

Wichtl, F., *Weltfreimaurerei, Weltrevolution, Weltrepublik. Eine Untersuchung über Ursprung und Endziele des Weltkrieges.* (Munich 1923)

Winnig, A., *Das Reich als Republik 1918-1928.* (Stuttgart/Berlin 1928)

Winnig, A., *Vom Proletariat zum Arbeitertum.* [1930] (Hamburg 1940)

Winnig, A., *Europa. Gedanken eines Deutschen.* (Berlin 1938)

Winterbotham, F.W., *The Nazi Connection.* Used here: *De nazi-connectie. Belevenissen van een meesterspion in Hitler-Duitsland.* [1978] (1979)

Wirth Roeper Bosch, H., *Europäische Urreligion und die Externsteine* (Wien 1980).

Wistrich, R., *Wer war wer im Dritten Reich? Ein biographisches Lexikon.* [1982] (Munich 1983)

Wojciechowski, M., *Die Polnisch-Deutschen Beziehungen 1933-1938.* In: *Studien zur Geschichte Osteuropas.* W. Philipp/P. Scheibert (Hg.) Band xii. (Leiden 1971)

Wulf, W.Th.H, *Tierkreis und Hakenkreuz. Als Astrologe an Himmlers Hof.* (1968)

Hall, W., *De verlakkers. Literaire vervalsingen en mystificaties.* (Amsterdam 1991)

Zentner, C., *Adolf Hitler's Mein Kampf. Eine kommentierte Auswahl.* [1974] (Munich 1992)

Zucker, A.E., *Deutschlands vergessene Freiheit. Eine Anthologie freiheitlicher deutscher Schriften von Luther bis zur Gegenwart.* (Berlin 1948)

II. Articles/brochures

Altsächsicher Bardenchor, in: *Odal, Monatschrift für Blut und Boden*, Heft 10 3. Jahrgang Ostermond 1935, p. 779

Augstein, R., *Der Soziologe als Scharfrichter. Augstein über Daniel Jonah Goldhagen's 'Hitler's willing Executioners'.* (Der Spiegel 15/1996)

Augstein, R., *Anschlag auf die 'Ehre' des deutschen Soldaten? Rudolf Augstein zu den Kriegsverbrechen der Wehrmacht im Osten.* (Der Spiegel 11/1997)

Bardeij, G., *Die Eiserne Division 1919-1920.* (two volumes) in DsJB (?)

Beunders, H., *Een volk verleid. Hoe toerekeningsvatbaar is een cultuur van schuld en zorgen?* (NRC-Handelsblad 4-5-1996)

Birnstiel, F., *Generaloberst Hans von Seeckt 1866-1936*

Blokker, B., *Geen Duitsers, geen Endlösung.* (NRC-Handelsblad 4-5-1996)

Brebeck, W.E., *Das Historische Museum des Hochstifts Paderborn. Geschichte, Ausbau, Konzeption. Kreismuseum Wewelsburg.* (1996)

Brumlik, M., *Eine Apologie des Antisemitismus. Ernst Noltes jüngstes Buch* (Neue Zürcher Zeitung 06-10-1998)

Cate, J.H. ten, *Zelfs in volkerenmoord zijn gradaties mogelijk* (de Volkskrant 4-5-1996)

Darré, R.W., *Wir und die Leibesübungen. Odal, Monatschrift für Blut und Boden.* Heft 10. 3.Jahrgang Ostermond (April) 1935. pp. 710-728

Dijkink, G., *Een nieuwe Europese deling? Duitsland en Rusland op zoek naar nationale identiteit. (Internationale Spectator June 1995)*

Dirks, C./Janssen, K.-H., *Plan Otto.* in: Die Zeit no. 38 (September 1997)

Dirks, W., *Fragwürdiges Dokument* (Frankfurter Hefte, Zeitschrift für Kultur und Politik. Heft 6 June 1951) *Driegonaal, extra editie. (Anti)racisme versus anthroposofie.* (1996)

Gritschneder, O., *Das dümmste Gericht. In Namen des bayerischen Volkes: Wie dem Terroristen Hitler 1924 zu Bewährungsfrist verholfen wurde.* (Süddeutschen Zeitung no. 211 13/14 September 1997)

Jansen, E., *Ein genialer 'Feldherr ohne Krieg. Vor 150 jahre wurde Graf Alfred von Schlieffen born*

Janssen, K-H., *Preusse, Nationalist und Hochverräter* (Die Zeit no.15 6-4-1990).

Krüger, N., *Adolf Hitler's Clausewitzkenntnis.* (Wehrwissenschaftliche Rundschau. 18 (1968)

Lewin, L., *Wenen, de wereldhoofdstad van het vergeten, herdenkt Theodor Herzl.* (NRC-Handelsblad 13-4-1996)

Madela, A., *'Volk ohne Raum', Übergangsmomente von Volks- in völkische Literatur* (Wir selbst, Zeitschrift für nationale Identität. Heimat, Identität braucht Raum und Geschichte. Territorialer Imperativ oder Traum vom grenzenlosen Geisterreich. 1/1990)

Molau, A., *Das politische Vermächtnis der Romantik.* (Wir selbst, Zeitschrift für national Identität. Heimat, Identität braucht Raum und Geschichte. Territorialer Imperativ oder Traum vom grenzenlosen Geisterreich. 1/1990)

Neue Männer (Die). (30-6-1933) in *Völkische Beobachter*

Nolte, P., *Das Ende des 19. und Beginn des 20.Jahrhunderts in sozialgeschichtlicher Perspektive.* In: *Geschichte in Wissenschaft und Unterricht.* (5-6-1996)

Pierik, P., *Joden in Rusland slachtoffer en dader.* (Utrechts Nieuwsblad 3-7-1992)

Pierik,P/Reijmerink,M., *Duitsers zijn niet uniek in het kwaad.* (Utrechts Nieuwsblad 25-4-1996)

Reijmerink,M., *Auschwitz is van de joden, niet van de Polen.* (Algemeen Dagblad 26-1-1995)

Schubert, E., *Ein Krieg gegen die Liebenden. Jekyll & Hyde - Sebastian Haffner's Bericht über Deutschland im Jahre 1939.* (Süddeutschen Zeitung no. 280, 4-12-1996)

Silbermann, A., *Erinnern heisst vergessen. Michal Bodemann's Pamphlet gegen die Vergangenheitsbewältigung.* (Frankfurter Allgemeine Zeitung 9-7-1996).

Sommer, T., *Nur Hinsehen macht frei. Münchener Lektionen: Die Rolle der Wehrmacht lässt sich nicht beschönigen.* (Die Zeit 28-2-1997)

Stehle, H., *Endloses Versteckspiel: Erstmals publiziert: die vom Vatikan geheim gehal-*

tene Enzyklika gegen Antisemitismus und Judenverfolgung. (Die Zeit no.39 19-9-1997)

Struckmeier, H-J., *Föderverein Kreismuseum Wewelsburg e.v. Sonderdruck aus 'die Warte'-Summer 1996*

Ullrich, V., *Hitler's willige Mordgesellen.* (Die Zeit 12-4-1996)

Urban, T., *Schreiben und Spitzeln. Die Russische Emigranten in Deutschland, 1918 bis 1941.* (Süddeutsche Zeitung, 3-4-1996)

Volksfront gegen Reaktion, Faschismus und Krieg (Hg.), *Das deutsche Kapital im zweiten Anlauf auf die 'Neuordnung Europas'. Etappen der Entfesselung des Zweiten Weltkrieges: Teil II: Der faschistische Überfall auf Polen und die Sowjetunion/'Europaische Grossraumwirtschaft' als Basis im kampf um Weltherrschaft.* (August 1989)

Zwaap, R., *De keizer van Atlantis. (De Groene Amsterdammer 26-4-1995)*